Arming Against Hitler

Arming Against Hitler

France and the Limits of Military Planning

Eugenia C. Kiesling

 University Press of Kansas

Published by the University Press of Kansas (Lawrence, Kansas 66049),
which was organized by the Kansas Board of Regents and is operated and
funded by Emporia State University, Fort Hays State University, Kansas
State University, Pittsburg State University, the University of Kansas, and
Wichita State University

Library of Congress Cataloging-in-Publication Data

Kiesling, Eugenia C.
  Arming against Hitler : France and the limits of military planning
/ Eugenia C. Kiesling.
     p.   cm. — (Modern war studies)
  Includes bibliographical references and index.
  ISBN 0-7006-0764-1
  1. France.   Armée—History—World War, 1939–1945.   2. World War,
1939–1945—France.   3. France—History, Military—20th century.
4. Military art and science—France.   I. Title.   II. Series.
D761.K54   1996
940.53′44—dc20   95-53924

British Library Cataloguing in Publication Data is available.

Printed in the United States of America

10 9 8 7 6 5 4 3 2 1

The paper used in this publication meets the minimum requirements of the
American National Standard for Permanence of Paper for Printed Library
Materials Z39.48–1984.

Contents

Abbreviations

AHR	*American Historical Review*
AMC	Automitrailleuse de Combat
AMD	Automitrailleuse de Découverte
AMR	Automitrailleuse de Reconnaissance
AN	Archives Nationales (France)
BCC	Bataillon des Chars de Combat
BEF	British Expeditionary Force
BIS	British Intelligence Summary
B1	Renault Medium Battle Tank
CG	Comité de la Guerre
CHEDN	Collège des Hautes Etudes de la Défense Nationale
CHEM	Centre des Hautes Etudes Militaires
CHEN	Centre des Hautes Etudes Navales
CPDN	Comité Permanent de la Défense Nationale
CSDN	Conseil Supérieur de la Défense Nationale
CSG	Conseil Supérieure de la Guerre
DAT	Défense Aérienne du Territoire
DC	Cavalry Division
DCL	Light Cavalry Division
DCR	Armored Division
DGI	Directive Générale sur l'Instruction
DI	Infantry Division
DIC	Colonial Infantry Division
DIM	Motorized Infantry Division
DINA	North African Infantry Division
DLM	Light Mechanized Division

D1	Renault Light Tank
D2	Renault Light Tank
EMA	Etat-Major de l'Armée (Franch General Staff)
	1/EMA—First Bureau of the General Staff
	2/EMA—Second Bureau of the General Staff, etc.
EPOR	Ecole de Perfectionnement des Officiers de Réserve
EPSOR	Ecole de Perfectionnement des Sous-Officiers de Réserve
ESG	Ecole Supérieure de Guerre
FCM 2 Cbis	Forges et Chantiers de la Méditerranée 60-ton tank
FCM-36	Forges et Chantiers de la Méditerranée Light tank
FHS	*French Historical Studies*
GRCA	Corps Reconnaissance Group
HCM	Haute Comité Militaire
H-35	Hotchkiss Model 1935 Light Tank
H-39/40	Hotchkiss Light Tank Model 1939/40 (improved version of H-35)
IGS	Imperial General Staff (Britain)
IGU	*Instruction sur l'emploi tactique des grandes unités*
IHEDN	Institut des Hautes Études de la Défense Nationale
JMH	*Journal of Modern History*
JO, Chambre	*Journal officiel* (published separately for Chamber of Deputies)
JO, Sénat	*Journal officiel* (published separately for Senate)
JRUSI	*Journal of the Royal United Services Institute*
JSS	*Journal of Strategic Studies*
MA	*Military Affairs*
MDN	Ministry of National Defense (France)
PRO	Public Records Office (London, Kew)
PV	Minutes (general)
RA	Artillery Regiment
RAD	Divisional Artillery Regiment
RC	Cavalry Regiment
RCC	Tank Regiment
RDM	*Revue des deux mondes*
RDN	*Revue de défense nationale*
RHA	*Revue historique de l'armée/Revue historique des armées*
RHDGM	*Revue d'histoire de la Deuxième Guerre Mondiale*
RI	Infantry Regiment

RI	*Revue d'infanterie*
RMF	*Revue militaire française*
RMG	*Revue militaire générale*
RP	*Revue de Paris*
R-35	Renault Light Tank (infantry support model 1935)
R-40	Renault Light Tank (improved R-35)
SGCSDN	Secrétariat Générale du Conseil Supérieur de la Défense Nationale
SHAT	Service Historique de l'Armée de Terre
SHM	Service Historique de la Marine
SOMUA	S-35 Cavalry Tank
USNA	National Archives (United States)
WSFH	*Proceedings of the Western Society for French History*

Preface

Among the claims for the study of military history is that peacetime exercises, however strenuous the physical conditions or sophisticated the computer simulation, cannot by themselves prepare soldiers for the ineffable complexity of war. An economical means of sharpening individual judgment, refighting old campaigns spills no new blood and damages reputations mostly among the dead. When historical study is employed to test ideas and concepts for future use, the historian's contribution extends beyond the battlefield to the peacetime activities of military forces. Decisions about force structures, deployment, matériel, training, and doctrine are more difficult to re-create than troop movements on a map, but such decisions offer an equally important means to learn inexpensively from the mistakes and the successes of others.

Because the questions that challenged armed forces in the decades between the twentieth-century's two world wars continue to resonate today, few periods of peacetime military preparation have aroused more intense historical attention. Historians find it a laboratory for the study of how armies behave in the aftermath of recent victory or defeat and investigate both military responses to material limitations imposed by treaty or government parsimony and interservice competition for scarce resources. The period also offers insights into civil-military relations, for it was a time of both greater militarization—as nations strove to adapt to the new notion of "total war"—and the hope that international institutions might end the need for national military organizations. For students of military doctrine, this interwar period provides useful examples of how different armies developed, acquired, and chose to employ the new technologies that had only been introduced during World War I.

As great as the potential value of such studies is the danger that the search for historical validation for today's theories may blind one to more accurate—and perhaps more salutary—interpretations of the past. Evaluations of past decisions in the light of current thinking meet contemporary pedagogical purposes better than they do the canons of the historical profession, and in the process, they often reveal more about modern concepts than about the historical events allegedly under examination. This risk is particularly grave for the student of France between the wars because it is difficult to look at French choices on their own terms, divorcing ourselves from the modern doctrinal assumptions by whose standards those choices were so glaringly wrong.

Tell someone that you are working on a book about French military planning in the 1930s and expect to hear in reply a sniggered version of "I didn't know that there was any." The destruction of the Polish army in September 1939 evokes romantic apocrypha about Polish lancers charging German tanks; few people tactlessly mention that poor Polish preparations condemned brave soldiers to an impossible fight. The British Expeditionary Force is praised for its successful escape from Dunkirk, not excoriated for its ineffectual contribution to the defense of Belgium. That the Soviet Union did badly in 1941 is popularly Stalin's fault or, more broadly, the fault of the communist system, not evidence of national failure. Pearl Harbor is blamed on Japanese treachery or on President Franklin D. Roosevelt's machinations but not the American armed forces.

None of these other catastrophes—Polish, British, Soviet, or American —nor those suffered by China and by other, smaller countries in World War II, has resulted in contempt being added to the injury of defeat. Only the French are dismissed with clichés about "phony war," antiquated generals, national pacifism, and defenses built in the wrong place. Not even the blood of 123,426 dead Frenchmen, 5,213 missing, and more than 200,000 wounded has sufficed to dispel the myth that the French nation simply fell apart in 1940.

I did not set out to crusade against the injustice of judging French actions during the interwar period more harshly than other nations. On the contrary, I initially wanted to understand the inadequacy of French strategic thinking in the 1930s, to search for insight into French mistakes. It was only after having been asked one too many times, How could France have been so stupid? that I came to wonder why that should be considered a fair question. At what cost to the country's political, economic, cultural, psychological, diplomatic, financial, and military institutions and traditions should

France have pursued that optimal relationship between ends and means that we call strategy? I came to see that the proper object of study was, not what France ought, in some abstract sense, to have done, but what determined the choices it made.

It is commonplace to deride France for two kinds of failure—the failure to prepare for war against Germany and the failure to perceive the weaknesses of French national defense policies. What will future historians say about current Western societies that, facing threats to their quality of life at least as grave as that posed by military conquest, understandably prefer, as interwar France understandably preferred, business as usual to unpleasant sacrifice—and therefore assure themselves as their world decays around them that things really are not all that bad?

The process of writing of this book has been so much less depressing than its conclusions because of the support I have received over the years from mentors, colleagues, and friends. First, I finally have the opportunity to thank Williamson Murray for his invitation to join the military history profession and for his encouragement thereafter. That I have obstinately disregarded his subsequent advice alleviates his responsibility but not my lifelong debt.

Without the rigorous and kindly supervision of James J. Sheehan and Herrick E. Chapman, I would have never finished my dissertation, let alone have embarked upon this larger work. Robert A. Doughty put aside more important work to help with a manuscript that a less generous person would have dismissed as unsuccessful and an unnecessary intrusion on to his own turf. My friends Elizabeth Meyer and Elizabeth Chapman focused the strength of character that I admired when we raced boats or bicycles together to the more painful tasks of providing editorial advice and moral support. Hugh Ragsdale and Harold Selesky forced me to meet the University of Alabama's tenure deadline in spite of myself, and in their criticisms of various versions of the manuscript, Paula Thornhill, David Ralston, and Ted Knight offered the insights of a serving officer, a distinguished historian, and a skydiving coach.

I wish also to thank my colleagues in the University of Alabama's History Department who offered aid and comfort and the History Department of the University of Southampton, which made me welcome during a fellowship year. In particular, Martin Alexander both organized my visit to England and allowed me the use of his incomparable library. I am not sure exactly what my husband, Peter Law, contributed to the writing of this book except that it would never have been finished without him.

For financial assistance, I wish to thank the Ford Foundation for a Fellowship in Western Society and International Security at Harvard's Center for International Affairs, the Leverhulme Foundation for a Commonwealth/U.S.A. Research Fellowship, and the University of Alabama for a travel grant to supplement the Leverhulme award.

My research proceeded as smoothly as it did because of the tolerance of many librarians and archivists who put up with impatience, an erratic memory for call numbers, and my vile French. For assisting my research in France, I wish to thank the directors and staffs of the Service Historique de l'Armée de Terre, the Service Historique de la Marine, the Service Historique de l'Armée de l'Air, the Archives Nationale, the Fondation Nationale des Sciences Politiques, the Institut des Hautes Etudes de la Défense Nationale, and the archives of the Senate and the Legislative Assembly. In England, I relied heavily on the the British Museum Newspaper Library, the Public Records Office at Kew, and the library of the Royal Military Academy, Sandhurst. In the United States, I received help from the libraries at the University of Alabama, Stanford University, Harvard University, the United States Military Academy, and the National Defense University as well as from the Hoover Institution and the National Archives.

I would like also to express my thanks to Mike Briggs of the University Press of Kansas for his encouragement during the review process and to the editors who handled the manuscript so professionally.

Before I wrote this book, I deprecated the trite formulas with which authors claim responsibility for the inadequacies of their work. Now, frustrated by the effort to produce a product worthy of the help that I have received, I insist that I alone am responsible for any errors of fact and interpretation that this book contains.

I dedicate this book gratefully to my parents, Nancy H. Kiesling and Roy A. Kiesling; my brothers, Brady, Stephen, and Roy; and to Janet Hutchison—*sine quis nihil.*

Introduction

"This is not a peace but an armistice for twenty years"
—*Marshal Ferdinand Foch (1919)*

Although not all Frenchmen were as prescient as Marshal Foch, many acknowledged the bitter truth that Germany would never accept the verdict of "the war to end all wars." Their dearly bought victory promised not security but the prospect of renewed confrontation with an aggrieved and powerful neighbor. The 1920s saw the brittle joy of the victory parades give way to an apprehension symbolized by the Maginot line. In the 1930s, with the failure of the Geneva disarmament talks, Germany's evasion of the disarmament clauses of the Versailles Treaty, and the rise of Hitler's new Reich, uncertainty hardened into grim awareness of the likelihood of another war. Throughout the twenty-year truce, France hoped to avoid conflict but prepared to defend itself if necessary. Here, in the national effort to address an increasingly grave situation, lies the tragedy of May–June 1940. The defeat of the French Army would be of little interest had it stemmed from blindness to the threat or from the paralysis of terror. The story of the road to 1940 draws its poignancy from the contrast between French confidence in their defenses and the magnitude of the disaster that ensued from the clash of arms.

Much has been written on almost every aspect of French national defense between the two world wars, including excellent and comprehensive studies of French policy-making,[1] finance and rearmament,[2] strategy,[3] military doctrine,[4] and the performance of the French Army in 1940.[5] Instead of reexamining the 1940 debacle at any one of these levels of analysis, this book identifies a set of consistent themes that runs through them all. Although the topic is the French national defense effort as a whole, my approach is not a broad, methodical assault but a blitzkrieg of archival firepower on certain narrow fronts. Specifically, I examine discrete elements of French national security policy, military organization, and military doctrine—in other words, arrangements for organizing military and civilian resources for war, the structure of the French Army, and the set of operating procedures designed to guide French forces in combat. In each of these areas, one finds the same patterns of action and thought—of decisions taken within severe constraints and then justified by calculations serving to prove that relatively unfree choices were also desirable ones.

After conducting an exercise with the First Infantry Division (DI) in August 1933, General Charles Condé concluded that the French Army was in good shape. Improvements remained to be made, but, in the event of war, French soldiers could be confident that "some days we will have victories, some days things will not go quite so well, but we will never have any disasters."[6] Disastrous, of course, is a fair description of the French Army's performance in 1940, and studies of French national defense efforts in the preceding years have naturally focused on how France went wrong. *Strange Defeat, To Lose a Battle, The Collapse of the Third Republic, The Seeds of Disaster, Anatomie d'une défaite, Les problèmes de l'armée de terre, Why France Fell,* and *Assignment to Catastrophe* are only a sampling of the works whose titles promise explanations of failure.[7] Their authors have asked, in essence, how France could have been so intellectually inflexible, so corrupt, so selfish, or so inept as to allow itself to be crushed by an enemy of whose capabilities and intentions it had ample warning.

The title of my book reflects Condé's optimism rather than the historian's hindsight. Instead of beginning with defeat and investigating what went wrong, I describe the efforts of French civilian and military leaders to create the best national defense they could, illuminate some of the reasons why the chosen solutions fell so short of what was necessary, and explain why the French high command nevertheless went to war confident in its ability to win. The results of this inquiry reflect the conundrums of real life. At every level of action, from national security policy to squad-level tactics, French possibilities were severely limited, and the resulting policies, plans, and doctrines ranged from suspect to demonstrably inadequate. Still, neither army nor nation resigned itself to defeat, collapse, disaster, or catastrophe. Instead, French leaders mobilized their defensive resources within the limits of what the polity allowed. The results were less than perfect but were deemed to be good enough. Choosing optimism over cynicism or despair, military and political leaders alike dismissed French weaknesses, exaggerated French strengths, and persuaded themselves of the intrinsic merits of arrangements that they had neither the ability nor the inclination to alter.

From the theme of limitations, the emphasis on the ways in which the structure and day-to-day requirements of the polity and the army constrained French choices, come the book's two philosophical assumptions: military history rests on details, and the study of one nation's failures may prove of only limited utility in guiding others to avoid similar mistakes. The details provide a corrective to abstract notions about how nations and their armies ought to behave. Theoretical assessments of the relative merits of offense and defense, conscript and volunteer armies, or sticks and stones provide fine debating material but are little help in assessing the behavior of real states that may not have the freedom to choose among the items on the menu. Hence the emphasis on particulars, on how French political and military structures circumscribed policy choices.

Behind most explanations for the 1940 defeat—national disunity,[8] flawed civil-military relations,[9] inertia in the high command,[10] poor military doctrine,[11] operational and tactical failure,[12] and strategic mistakes[13]—lies a shared belief that the French nation lost the war because of its own errors and the assumption that identifying French mistakes will help other states to avoid repeating them.[14] Even more difficult to set aside than the tones of condemnation or *Schadenfreude* prevalent in studies of the fall of France is the assumption that it is useful to speak of correct policies and doctrines that France ought to have discerned and followed.

On the first point, that French policy was wrong, one does well to heed Robert Young's query, "without the judgment of 1940, is it genuinely possible to brand the French as foolish for having put everything on a long war, and not the Germans for having put everything on a short war? The fact is that both sides were gambling."[15] With Young's warning in mind, Alistair Horne's claim that "the Germans . . . took the right course in opting for a small *armée de métier*"[16] loses its force. That the professional army turned out well for Germany—and Horne admits that the Versailles Treaty allowed the Germans no alternative—does not mean either that it was necessarily the single right road for any European army or that it was a possible choice for the French Third Republic. There is little to be gained from lamenting the absence of the professional army that France could not have and believed unnecessary.

Anthony Adamthwaite's criticism of French diplomacy leaves us at a similar dead end. Truly, "the most serious failure of the 1930s lay in the lack of a close understanding between statesmen, diplomats and generals. Common sense required that diplomatic and strategic preparations should go hand in hand but no reappraisal of foreign and defense policies took place."[17] But is the identification of an absence of common sense the goal—or even an aspect—of the historian's task? If actions that are now labeled common sense seemed at the time impossible or inconceivable or merely hopelessly difficult, what purpose does the judgment serve? As Tournoux reminds us in dealing with one specific instance, "While it is easy to discuss these questions today, it is appropriate to recall the atmosphere in which the deliberations of the Conseil Supérieur de la Guerre took place in 1933."[18]

If lack of coherent strategy is the charge most commonly lodged against interwar France, second place goes to the accusation that France failed to make the doctrinal innovations necessary to fight a modern, motorized war. Robert Doughty, Douglas Porch, and Barry Posen all assume that there was a correct way to build an army around the armored fighting vehicle and that what needs to be explained is French blindness to the new technology's doctrinal implications. Thus, Porch argues that the French failure to innovate was "the confused response of an army operating in a hostile political environment," Posen describes it as a consequence of, among other things, French alliance policy, and Doughty stresses the high command's increasing rigidity of thought.[19] This book begins with the premise that the French developed their military doctrine in response to their own requirements and circumstances, not to fit an abstract ideal of "modern war." Contemporary technology did not dictate a particular military organization. There was no correct doctrine called blitzkrieg toward which interwar armies ought to have evolved. The doctrine the French created during the 1930s made sense for the army that France had and the war that France planned to fight—and planned to fight, of course, only if the means could not be found to avoid war altogether. It was, as Doughty admits, "the best available thought on what would usually work best on the battlefield."[20] The result, both in form of the long-war strategy and of the doctrine of the methodical battle, was designed to deter war if possible and, if deterrence failed, to maximize the likelihood of eventual victory while minimizing its cost.

Because the decisions that led ultimately to the Wehrmacht's victory procession along the Champs Elysées had natural—perhaps even eradicable—roots in French political and military culture, there was little that French leaders could have chosen to do differently. Furthermore, the lesson to be learned broadens our understanding without, however, offering any prescriptions. It is not that maneuver warfare is good, that defense is bad, or that wars are won through the best hardware or the best understanding of technology. National security policies and military doctrines alike derive not from theoretical judgments but from a confusion of conflicting inputs—political, economic, cultural, technological, psychological, and institutional—within nations and armies. If the French Army lacked the freedom to design an ideal doctrine to meet the military requirements of its day, then we must wonder how free others are to profit from the verdict of 1940. Where the doctrinal bible of the United States Army would have one believe that "tactics, techniques, procedures, organizations, support structure, equipment and training must all derive from [doctrine],"[21] it seems more accurate to say that doctrines usually have to be created to fit existing military organizations. Armies do choose bad doctrines, just as nations develop poor national security policies, but the explanation—and the cure—usually lies in the structures that determine those choices.

But not every study of interwar France has taken as its mission to seek out "the seeds of disaster," to show how France managed "to lose a battle," or to comprehend the "anatomy of a defeat."[22] The revisionist approach advertises itself in the more ambiguous, or even positive, titles of Robert J. Young's *In Command of France: French Foreign Policy and Military Planning, 1933–1940,* Martin S. Alexander's *The Republic in Danger,* and Jeffrey Gunsberg's *Divided and Conquered,* books that emphasize not the fact of French failure but the nature of French efforts to avoid it.[23] This book is in that tradition, inspired by Young's demonstration that French leaders in the 1930s pursued coherent and consistent policies designed to resist the resurrection of German military power, to ensure British support, and to engage in any forthcoming conflict against Germany by using a "long-war" strategy appropriate to the long-term economic advantages enjoyed by the western allies. What is distinctive and important in Young's analysis is the argument that Frenchmen not only created their own policy agenda but attempted with some success to manipulate their allies into accepting it.[24] As his subtitle promises, Young also describes the extent to which political choices were constrained by military realities. Here, however, Young's emphasis on the civilian side of the civil-military balance tends to reduce the argument to a demonstration that in various moments of crisis statesmen were fettered by their awareness of how little they could realistically ask the army to do. What remains to be explored more fully are the reasons why those fetters existed. If France was as energetic in its foreign policy as Young claims, what accounts for its failure to equip itself with an army that would enforce that policy rather than acting as a brake upon it? This book will try to do for the military commanders what Young did for the civilian leadership—to describe how they strove to prepare France for war and what difficulties limited their efforts.

Though it differs both in scope and in purpose, this book models itself directly on Robert Doughty's *The Seeds of Disaster,* the only comprehensive study of interwar French military doctrine. Whereas Doughty's remains the best description of French military doctrine, this analysis uses doctrine as one of several representative examples of the French approach to national defense. I explain French doctrine less as a set of intellectual choices than as an adaptation to the requirements of the French Army's basic organization and training, and thus I find the roots of French difficulties not in doctrine itself but in the structures behind it. Indeed, where Doughty's concern is to explain French failure to develop a modern military doctrine, I am more interested in why they thought themselves to have done exactly that.

In most accounts, France in the late 1930s lacked a coherent national strategy to deal with the German threat. Such a strategy would have linked diplomatic schemes to military strategy, and industrial policy to military doctrine; in principle, it would have orchestrated every national strategic asset from labor power to health policy. Ironically, however, that same unified national strategy whose absence condemns France in the eyes of historians was the object of interwar French planning. Instead of blaming the French for "putting the expedient, that which is *acceptable,* first," it is more fruitful to remind ourselves that nations only do what they find "acceptable."[25] Academics can create rational models for the efficient coordination of national resources for the attainment of defined ends, but nations will stubbornly fail to reorganize themselves to fit strategic requirements. Faced with the likelihood of renewed German aggression, France produced the long-war strategy. Needing a military doctrine appropriate to her military institutions, France developed the methodical battle. What proved more difficult was to translate a strategic idea into a set of specific actions; between theory and practice fell the shadows of political, economic, and social reality. Similarly, a military doctrine had to derive not from theoretical notions of what the tools of modern war could achieve in the abstract but from the existing structure of the French Army.

My approach, then, runs counter to the current historiographical fashion of studying nations as single actors possessed of coherent "grand strategies." Thus, Edward Luttwak's *Grand Strategy of the Roman Empire* recounts a series of Roman frontier policies and concludes that the empire had a grand strategy that endured for two centuries. Following Luttwak's model,

Paul Kennedy's *Grand Strategies in War and Peace* attributes strategic programs to Imperial Rome, seventeenth-century Spain, Britain in three different epochs, and an assortment of twentieth-century states.[26] In *Strategies of Containment*,[27] John L. Gaddis combines a conventional definition of strategy as the rational adaptation of means to ends with a narrative that devotes far more attention to military, political, and economic possibilities and constraints than it does to "strategic" assessments of national requirements. However admirable these works are in their details, they contribute to the current habit of confusing what nations do with conceived strategies. If national successes or failures are attributable to strategies consciously and freely adopted, then the historian can usefully argue that some national strategies have proved better than others and that such verdicts offer lessons for the future. If, however, what we label strategy is simply a set of actions rather than a plan conceived in the ethereal realm of cost-benefit analysis, then the emphasis on strategy per se imposes a misguided rationality on events and distracts attention from their true determinants.

In fact, no matter how much effort governments and military institutions devote to thinking, respectively, about national strategy or military doctrine, they expend enormously more energy in less elevated realms. Just as for civilian leaders the ideals of political philosophy often yield to their constituents' immediate concerns, armies devote more resources to day-to-day matters than to the prospect of future war. One does well to remember the late-nineteenth-century French battleship *Magenta,* whose "three-storied château" of a superstructure made her too unstable to fire her heavy guns. Defending his ship's unmartial accommodations, her captain explained that, whereas the ship might see combat once in her lifetime, the crew would have to live in her for thirty years.[28] So, too, the French Army might fight one war in a generation, but, in the meantime, daily life had to go on. One cannot work for long in the French military archives without noticing an emphasis on matters tangential to fighting. Although this revelation will not surprise anyone who has ever thought about how large organizations, be they armed forces, corporations, governments, or universities, actually operate, the matter deserves more attention than it has received. I argue here that the tyrannical requirements of military organization and housekeeping undermined French "military effectiveness" through both physical obstacles and mental distraction.[29] That French military leaders were overly concerned with bureaucratic details is not new. As Doughty puts it, "Had France's military leaders been less concerned with bureaucratic details and more concerned with the major issues of policy, strategy, and doctrine, she undoubtedly would have fared better in 1940."[30] What is novel is the willingness to delve into the same details that choked French military activities in search of a more complete understanding of French actions. In a sense, therefore, this book is old-fashioned in its insistence that organizational and tactical minutiae matter.

The creators of French strategy and doctrine were aware not only of the constraints on military change but of the dangers of seeking too energetically to overcome them. Military reforms appealing in the abstract could not be sought at the cost of upsetting the fragile domestic balance. The best would prove the enemy of the good if demands for the former revived traditional republican fears of militarism or caused the French people to doubt the army's ability to protect them in the absence of unobtainable reforms. Professional soldiers wanted more men, more materiél, more money, and more favorable diplomatic arrangements, but they would not make their case by arguing that France was not well defended. Responsible military leaders could not afford to use the ratio ultima, for prophecies of impending military defeat could only be self-fulfilling. The revival of German military power that made war more likely also made reevaluation of French readiness more perilous. Thus Doughty points out that French thinking became increasingly rigid over the course of the 1930s.[31] If it was important to remain abreast of modern military developments, self-assurance was an even more vital asset not to be squandered by criticism and by demands for impossible reforms. Indeed, the occasional call for change aroused a backlash of new arguments to reinforce the conventional wisdom. The incentive to accept what could not be remediated adds tragic undertones to the French soldiers' dilemma.

A partial answer to one of the salient questions about interwar French military planning is that confidence itself was a national asset. Why, ask both Robert Young and Patrice Buffotot, was France apparently unable to alter its military plans and organization in response to the excellent information provided by French intelligence about German military capabilities?[32] Buffotot attributes French inertia explicitly to conservatism, Young to a gap between knowledge and understanding engendered by the mechanisms of education and promotion in the French Army—that is, to conservatism by another name. Valid as far as they go, these assessments understate the energy behind conservative choices. French soldiers acted conservatively not from an inability to imagine alternatives but from concern that innovation would undermine faith in the tried and true methods to which contemporary German experiments did not appear to offer an attractive alternative.

The organization of this book stems from its twin purposes of identifying the parallel elements within French national security policy and military doctrine and of explaining why French leaders accepted possible flaws in both rather than attempting comprehensive reform. The six central chapters form three pairs: the first pair treats policy; the last, doctrine.[33] The center pair, which describes the French Army itself, bridges the two apparently distinct topics. Providing the structural details that were the foundations for both policy choices and doctrinal concepts, it also illustrates on the practical level the patterns of thought that French soldiers used to alleviate doubts in less-concrete spheres.

Chapters 1 and 2 describe two little-known peacetime efforts to put France's long-war strategy into practice—the wartime national organization law of 11 July 1938 and the French National Defense College. Conceived in the early 1920s as a radically comprehensive interpretation of the demands of "total war," the limited measure passed in 1938 reveals the difference between the aspirations of the organizers of national defense and what could be achieved through the political process in a peacetime democracy. This largely political story is a detailed narrative of parliamentary debate reflecting the real political world in which national security policy is made. Much of the evidence for this chapter comes from the archives of the French Senate and Chamber of Deputies, but the soldiers assigned to the secretariat of the Conseil Supérieur de la Guerre also left important records in the army archives.[34]

Chapter 2 examines the Collège des Hautes Etudes de la Défense Nationale, an institution created in 1936 to prepare high-ranking administrative and military personnel to implement the long-war strategy. Like the national organization law, the college's story demonstrates the narrow range of possibilities within which French leaders had to operate. The college trained the men destined to execute the nation's grand strategy, but it did not allow them to examine—or attempt to correct—weaknesses and inconsistencies within that strategy. This chapter is based on records of the college found at the Château de Vincennes and in the library of the successor Institut des Hautes Etudes de la Défense Nationale located in the Champs de Mars.

In the second pair of chapters, the arena shifts from national policy to military recruitment, organization, and training. This analysis is partly a response to Martin Alexander's challenge that since "Gamelin and his *cabinet* plainly showed outstanding diligence in their endeavors to improve the preparedness of the French and British armies in France . . . future campaign historians must address questions about the reasons for failures lower down the chain of command—among corps and divisional generals and staffs, and even at the regimental level."[35] Although "even" might be amended to "especially," Alexander's point is well taken—except that one wonders whether failures endemic throughout the units of the French Army can be understood separately rather than as the consequence of structural problems that could only be addressed, if at all, at higher echelons. Thus Chapter 3 describes the impediments to training French conscripts during their period of active service, and Chapter 4 argues that unstable unit organization, inadequate training, and inexperienced leadership undermined the cohesion of reserve formations. These two chapters offer the book's explanation for France's military collapse in 1940. However faulty her war plans, France was defeated less because her strategic decisions played into Germany's plan of attack than because her army's individual units lacked the aggressiveness, determination, and fundamental military skills that come from solid units, thorough training, and experienced leadership. These weaknesses call into question the judgment that the French defeat stemmed from poor doctrine. Had the French Army been better prepared, its doctrine might have proved satisfactory; without improved training and leadership the more aggressive doctrines promoted by historians would have been worse than useless. The material in Chapters 3 and 4 comes not only from official policy documents but from the attaché reports and personal memoirs that describe what the French Army actually was rather than what it was meant to be.

Doctrine is the subject of the third section. Chapter 5 investigates the provenance of French military ideas, and Chapter 6 describes how the resulting doctrine suited the army's objectives and organization. Chapter 5 rejects the charge that French doctrinal rigidity reflected a pernicious adherence to a historical approach to strategy and argues that makers of French doctrine used historical claims largely to justify decisions made for reasons that reflected the concerns of the immediate present. French doctrine was inflexible not because of French intellectual failure but for practical reasons explained in the preceding chapters. Grounding doctrine in organizational realities at once explains the French doctrine in particular and suggests that doctrinal problems may be less amenable to purely intellectual assault than the boffins in the think tanks would have one believe.

The descriptions of the methodical battle and of the development of French armor doctrine found in Chapter 6 owe much to Doughty's exposition but, because the argument rests on the preceding chapter's understanding of French methods of thought, it is less committed to the belief that French doctrine ought to have developed along a particular path. The goal of the chapter is to understand how French doctrine fit the requirements of the French Army and why that army believed itself equal to the challenge from across the Rhine.

The concluding chapter expands on the subject of French sanguinity while, at least in hindsight, disaster loomed. French leaders had reasons to believe in military arrangements that suited their national institutions and were the envy of most of Europe. They also had reasons to conceal any disquiet and did so with notable success; the overall lesson of the French experience between the world wars is not that nations and armies ought to avoid bad choices but that they zealously they adhere to ruinous arrangements in the absence of an attractive alternative.

1
Mobilizing the Nation in Arms

Sometimes, by chance or artifice, a state's military arrangements so suit the warfare of the day that its battlefield dominance appears to flow naturally from its institutions. In the sixth and fifth centuries BC, Sparta's slave-based society fostered a militaristic culture and the best phalanx in Greece. Napoleon's genius had as its tool an army of unprecedented size and flexibility that only the revolutionary principle of universal conscription made possible. By the mid-nineteenth century, the evolution of the Prussian nobility into a professional officer corps and the calculated harnessing of popular energy produced the war machine that built the Kaiserreich. War changed, however, between 1871 and 1914, and Prussian technical proficiency no longer guaranteed success. Victory in the Great War went instead to the side whose greater resources produced the bigger battalions. A war of attrition in the trenches, World War I was something similar on the home front, where the belligerents' productive capacity and social and political cohesion were also tested to their limits.

The advent of "total war," of contests between nations rather armies, restored to France the advantage she had first enjoyed in the revolutionary *levée en masse* of 1793. Although French institutions of the nineteenth century had allowed no scope for exploiting the *nation armée,* it remained an article of faith among Frenchmen, proved yet again in the crucible of World War I, that no other people had the will to make a comparable commitment to their national cause. Less powerful than her eastern neighbor, France could, however, hold her own by more efficient exploitation of her civilian and military resources. Far from resting on their bloody laurels, the French military civilian leaders set out immediately after the war to craft a national strategy suited to their new understanding of twentieth-century war.[1]

Even as French leaders took comfort in their nation's advantages for fighting total war, they recognized the need to redefine the *nation armée* in a new way. The nation in arms of 1793 had been an emergency effort to concentrate the largest number of men on the battlefield with little concern for the national economy, and the 1914–1918 war, while giving greater attention to the industrial requirements of twentieth-century warfare, had seen barely more systematic arrangements for balancing the needs of the home and military fronts.[2] French industry had achieved prodigious levels of production, but the process had distributed the burdens of war inefficiently and inequitably. As Minister of War Paul Painlevé argued later in the Chamber of Deputies:

> But at what price had this industrial miracle been accomplished? . . . at one that still moves us: at the price of murderous delays, bought with the blood of our soldiers, at the price of the waste unavoidable in such prodigious improvisation: at the price, finally, of the scandalous enrichment of some that must never be repeated.[3]

World War I had shown the limits, practical and moral, of the traditional *nation armée*. French leaders after 1918 did not intend to repeat the experiences of the past but to create comprehensive national security arrangements designed to distribute evenly the hardships and the profits of wartime mobilization. Fairness had become a policy concern, lest a patently unjust distribution of war's burdens erode the people's will to fight.

Convinced that a more effective national mobilization was the key to success in a future war against Germany, French leaders began as early as 1920 to formulate a national defense law—a blueprint for total war. Unlike past military laws, which addressed the problem of national defense by regulating the size, composition, and equipment of the army and of the navy, this *Loi sur l'organisation de la nation pour le temps de guerre* (law for the organization of the nation in time of war) would put all of the national resources at the command of the nation. Its particular objectives were to specify the wartime powers of the French government and to codify its relationship with the military commanders, to insure the mobilization of human and material resources, and to allocate responsibility for different elements of the national defense effort among civilian and military agencies. Theoretically a manifestation of the kind of grand strategy that states ought, were they truly rational actors, to formulate, the law instead demonstrates what happens when rational planning collides with political reality. The law's gestation through a legislative process alternately indifferent and disputatious and its subsequent desultory execution demonstrate the limits of France's ability to construct a comprehensive security policy.

The attempt to produce a national defense plan reveals both the seriousness with which French leaders addressed their national defense requirements and the obstacles against which their efforts faltered. Enunciation of the requirements of total war and invocations of the nation in arms were not enough to bring the country to accept the obligations that such a war would bring. The slower pace of peacetime government allowed the luxury of sober reflection and careful calculation, but a peaceful country also demanded more perfect solutions to the practical and moral problems of national defense.

Ignoring Bismarck's stricture that "laws are like sausages; it is better not to see them being made," this chapter uncovers behind the façade of near-universal praise for the principles of the nation-in-arms deep divisions about the form that national organization should take. In particular, the debates in the French Senate and the Chamber of Deputies on four politically charged issues—conscription, the treatment of private property, legislators' obligations to perform military service, and the relationship between the government and the armed forces—reveal the impediments to translating the French vision of her coherent national security policy into practical institutions.

Detailed examination of the actual legislative process brings us from abstract claims about how France ought to have prepared for total war to the concrete realities that influenced its choices. It reveals the French state to have been not a unified rational actor but a conglomeration of competing interests and visions. The story of the national organization law shows not that French political leaders sacrificed the national interest to their political concerns but that the national interest was subject to interpretation. To some, the national mobilization law was a threat to the liberal economic traditions of the Third Republic. To those of a different political persuasion, it was a pernicious reinforcement of the dominant capitalist forces. If both sides could agree on anything, it was that the law promised to turn France into a garrison state, a choice not lightly to be made by individuals who lacked the historian's awareness of the proximity of Hitler's war.

The First Bill

A call for a national mobilization or organization law came from Army Chief of Staff General Edmond Buat as early as 1920, and the government showed itself to be thinking in similar terms by revising the constitution of the old Conseil Superiéur de la Défense Nationale (CSDN) in November 1921 to create an agency competent to deal with the integration of military and civil aspects of national defense planning.[4] In the words of the relevant decree, "the preparation of the nation for war ought to inspire integrated directives on the mechanisms of government in wartime and the distribution of the nation's energies between the strictly military effort and the bodies that maintain the life of the nation."[5] Assisting the council were two new subordinate agencies, a general secretariat, and a study committee. The study committee received the initial charge to draft a bill on the lines sketched by General Buat, and the secretariat, led until 1929 by General Bernard Serrigny, became the legislation's primary champion.

Although war seemed a distant prospect in early 1922, the study committee hastened to draft a national organization bill because members of the Chamber of Deputies wanted to consider the measure alongside a proposal to reduce the period of obligatory military service from three years to eighteen months.[6] Calls to treat the two matters together reflected competing political agendas. Some deputies shared Buat's and Serrigny's vision of coordinating France's industrial capabilities in support of her armed forces and saw comprehensive national mobilization as compensation for reduced military service. For others, including those sensitive to the electorate's distaste for conscription, national mobilization proposals were of rhetorical interest—to be used to justify a lightened military burden and then to be forgotten.[7]

The latter view dominated. When the government finally presented its wartime organization law to the Chamber of Deputies on 10 January 1924, eighteen-month service had been in effect since 1 April 1923, and French deputies revealed no interest in further national defense legislation.[8] In any case, spring 1924 brought the end of the twelfth legislature and new elections; it was not until March 1926 that the bill was again presented by the Chamber of Deputies. French parliamentary practice called for each bill to be approved by one of the Chamber's specialized committees before presentation to the full house by a spokesman (*rapporteur*) assigned by the committee to the particular measure. The Chamber had no national defense committee, so the bill naturally fell into the hands of the army committee, and no one remarked upon the irony of committing a bill designed to correct a spurious equation of national defense with army operations to a body charged solely with military affairs. Appointed rapporteur for the measure was Joseph Paul-Boncour, an independent socialist and the project's strongest political advocate, who presented the bill with the army committee's recommendation to the full Chamber in March 1927.[9]

Paul-Boncour's report identified three requirements for a national organization law: that it prepare France to fight a total war, that it assure a smooth transition from peacetime to wartime organization, and that the legislation be flexible enough to adapt to changing circumstances.[10] He also announced the principle that compensation offered for requisitioned private property was not to exceed its cost (including the interest on capital) to the owner; there would be no *bénéfices* or war profits. The difficulty of transforming these ideas into policy became clear as soon the Chamber began its debate.

The debate on the bill's first article, which dealt with conscription, demonstrates the impact of amendments prompted by political sensibilities. The CSDN's 1922 proposal had proclaimed a "national defense duty" requiring "all French citizens and residents of France" to participate in the work of national defense "according to their capacities" and was accompanied by a detailed exposition of the obligations of "individuals of both sexes, of every age and of every condition."[11] To a casual reader—and to its authors—the wording invoked the sweeping principles of the *levée en masse* of 1793 in coopting men, women, and children alike for national defense. That is how the army committee of the Chamber of Deputies interpreted the article, for its members added the language "without distinction of age or sex," without which the phrase *"tous les français"* could be taken to encompass only males.

The Chamber accepted a slightly amended version of the committee's formula only after a heated debate that revealed powerful opposition from across the political spectrum. Three objections emerged: that the conscription of women was wrong in principle, that conscription might serve the government as a weapon against organized labor, and that, by diluting the distinction between soldiers and civilians, conscription might deprive the latter of the protections granted noncombatants under international law. To clarify the potentially ambiguous status of civilians conscripted for national defense work, Deputy Maurice Marchais successfully proposed adding to Article 1 a clause specifying that Frenchmen could be conscripted either as combatants or as noncombatants "in the maintenance of its material life and morale."[12] Defeated, however, was Communist Party leader Henri Lafont's proposal to restore the ambiguity inherent in "all of the French" by eliminating the qualifying "without distinction of age or sex." Although the article escaped further amendment, many on the Left continued to decry the whole concept of national mobilization as nationalistic and militaristic.

"Nationalist" and "militarist" were far from the strongest pejoratives employed in what was an ugly session even by the standards of parliamentary discourse in the Third Republic. Henri Lafont called the law "the most militaristic that a country has ever known" and attributed to it an "inevitably fascist tone." The fusillade of invective that answered Deputy Cornavin's suggestion that no party in a war is entirely blameless included, "Are you a Frenchman or not?" and "Go say that in the Reichstag!"

If the conscription of women touched French souls, seizure of private property was a scarcely less heartfelt issue, and the debate on the tenth article was marked both by violent rhetoric and by reluctance to discuss unpalatable measures. The question was whether the government should acquire the assets needed for war by negotiation (*accord amiable*) between state and property owner or by requisition through government fiat. The study committee of the CSDN had rejected requisition as likely to require expensive indemnities and to prove harmful to economic efficiency.[13] In the opinion of the commission, "personal interest is one of the important motors of economic activity."[14] Nothing spurred production better than profit, and the trick was to find a level of profit that stimulated production without arousing scandal.[15] In spite of public revulsion against war profiteers, the CSDN's text reflected a belief in the efficacy of financial incentives and asserted that the government would acquire resources "primarily by agreement, with strict limits on the owner's profits (*bénéfices*), and secondarily, in the absence of a satisfactory agreement, by requisition."

The CSDN's invitation to owners to make advance arrangements for the wartime use of their property in exchange for an agreed rate of return angered left-wing deputies on the army committee, who revised Article 10 to read that "the resources necessary for national defense are obtained either by agreement or by requisition without any profit in either case." The dispute was repeated, largely by shouting, in the full Chamber.[16] Where one deputy denounced as "abominable" any defense of factory owners' profits while thousands of workers would be risking their lives, another insisted that victory in a long war would depend on a viable economic organization propelled by well-rewarded entrepreneurs.[17] Paul-Boncour tried to soothe capitalist sensibilities by assuring his colleagues that the government would use the unwieldy mechanism of requisition only as a last resort. The rule, he insisted, would be "negotiation when possible and whenever possible,"[18] but right-wing deputies asked, without success, that the law specify this preference. Suspecting that *accords amiables* would produce favorable bargains for property owners, Deputy Lafont achieved an amendment asserting that the owner of property acquired by negotiation could receive no greater compensation than he would have been offered in the event of wartime requisition, and the article passed in that form.

The third controversy illustrating the difficulty of peacetime national planning for war affected a group much smaller than women or property owners but immensely powerful nonetheless. The question was the wartime role of the elected representatives of the French people, a matter upon which few of those directly concerned wanted to take a public position. The CSDN denied its competence to voice an opinion, and, with a *"délicatesse"* acknowledged by the army committee's president, rapporteur Paul-Boncour preferred to await the committee's verdict rather than to propose his own solution.[19] Even, perhaps especially, under the stresses of war, the legislative assemblies remained responsible for representing the people of France. The challenge was to maintain democratic institutions without arousing popular suspicions that legislators were shirking their military obligations. By going to the front, members of parliament would both abrogate their mandate and undermine the principle of civilian control over the armed forces; the politically unpalatable alternative was to vote their own unique exemption from military service. The solution adopted during World War I, when members of parliament had been mobilized with their units and then furloughed for the duration of each legislative session, had provided fertile ground for charges of hypocrisy. No one favored maintaining a policy that allowed elected officials to exchange at will the dangers of the front for the safety of the Chamber of Deputies and to hide behind parliamentary privilege in criticizing their military superiors.

Deputy Trenchand probably spoke for many of his colleagues in the Chamber's army committee in lamenting that so "delicate" a matter had to be discussed at all—any decision would give rise to "deplorable discussions throughout the country." The issue could not be avoided, however, and the committee produced a text, Article 25bis of the bill, that required members of the government, the Senate, and the Chamber of Deputies to remain in their political offices during mobilization. Any legislator who chose instead to be mobilized into the armed forces would be excluded from politics for the duration of the war.[20]

The committee's proposal appeared to address the major concerns, but the Chamber debate demonstrated that the matter could not be so easily solved. The text acknowledged the supremacy of parliamentary duty, left scope for the exercise of individual conscience, and, by stipulating that mobilized members had to forsake their parliamentary privileges, prevented legislators from merely masquerading as soldiers; however, it still offended those deputies who denied the legitimacy of legislating freedom of action for themselves in a realm in which their constituents had none. Some deputies insisted that legislators ought to fulfill their military duty, others that an elected representative's place was in Paris, not the front. Calling the proffered text of Article 25bis too embarrassing to discuss, Deputy Lafas asked that it be returned forthwith to the army committee—"never to return"—and that a longer and more elaborate formula doing justice to the complexity of the issue be brought before the Chamber. It is hard to doubt that Lafas's motive was to move the sensitive discussion to closed committee session. The army committee declined to reconsider their unanimous decision, and the Chamber accepted the unrevised text with embarrassment.

On the subject of their own wartime employment, members of the Chamber were united in their desire to avoid harmful publicity. Debates on other controversial issues, particularly the mobilization of human and material resources, revealed bitter animosities that boded ill for French efforts to construct a national defense policy. Political tracts opposed the law in terms that admitted no common ground, not even a shared definition of the essence of the nation to be defended. Where communists saw a capitalist conspiracy against labor, the Right decried the "Law Paul-Boncour" as a socialist effort to turn France into a barracks where women would be enslaved and children condemned to the care of strangers.[21] Such invective among parliamentarians deepened political divisions and undermined faith in the institutions of the republic that they purported to defend, and the bill passed by the Chamber on 7 March 1927 and forwarded to the Senate represented anything but a consensus about national preparation for war.

In the Senate, as in the Chamber, the major report on the national mobilization law was the work of the army committee, whose rapporteur, Senator Klotz, unlike the Chamber's Paul-Boncour, was no advocate of the project. Reporting critically to the committee on 25 March 1927, he offered a long list of concerns about the Chamber's text. Noting that the Senate would soon be dealing with two army organization laws, Klotz proposed to table the Chamber's bill until the army laws had been passed and, one suspects, the national organization law forgotten. So far were the senators from the spirit of the government's proposal that Senator Herschauer suggested in committee that, to avoid unnecessarily inconveniencing French commerce and industry, the comprehensive national defense law should be adopted only on the first day of mobilization. Hershauer represented what was probably the majority position among French citizens, who, however willing they were to sacrifice after a conflict began, balked at anticipating events. Instead of letting the bill die, however, the commission chose instead to amend almost every important component.

Most striking were the proposed modifications to the articles dealing with the conscription of French citizens. Senator Voilin proposed to restrict national mobilization to men between the ages of twenty and forty-eight. By admitting the conscription only of those women already employed in public service, another amendment added no one to the labor pool and implied that women already at work were somehow less vulnerable than their unemployed sisters. A third adjustment exempted mothers from conscription, and a fourth took evasive action by leaving the matter to be resolved by administrative decrees.

The centerpiece of the debate, however, was an amendment offered by senators Sari and Merlin that added to Article 6 (which specified measures for executing the principles asserted in Article 1) the blanket statement "these provisions are not applicable to women." Speaking for the Senate's General Committee on Administration, Sari announced that the imposition of involuntary service upon women was morally unacceptable and "would allow every form of abuse." Klotz assured Sari and Merlin that the mobilization of women would not lead to their political enfranchisement, that it would include only some women, and that many of those would be retained in their current employment. The real moral issue in Klotz's view was the prospect of public scandals at the sight of female idleness in a time of national crisis. When senators worried that "young women of good families would have to work side by side with prostitutes," Klotz reassured them that most women (including those under eighteen years of age and mothers with children under five who were married, widowed, or whose husbands had been mobilized) would be exempt.[22] There the matter rested, with the committee having devoted much attention to protecting women from the impact of national service and none to exploring their positive contribution to national defense. The committee had failed to demand either full application of the principles of the nation in arms or equal protection for all female citizens. Agreeing that the mobilization of women was both necessary and distasteful, the members produced a text that hinted that some women, those already in the labor force, for example, would be compelled to make sacrifices not asked of others. The issue would rise again, with a different verdict, in the full Senate.

The committee also tried to dilute the bill by limiting responsibility for mobilizing national resources to the war and navy ministers alone. Nothing could have been further from the wishes of the legislation's authors, whose avowed purpose had been to broaden the concept of national defense to include every department of the government; Serrigny, through the prime minister, persuaded the committee to relent.[23] More cosmetic concessions to political sensitivities were allowed to go through; thus, the army committee achieved the removal of the phrase *"mobilisation nationale"*—evocative of the militarization of the nation and loss of civilian immunities—from the text.

The reports on the bill submitted to the Senate by seven Senate committees and the plethora of proposed amendments reflected a palpable concern that the Chamber had gone too far. Klotz's report asserted that the Chamber's bill granted the government dictatorial powers and warned that national defense did not justify the "abdication of our public and private liberties and the negation of democracy and of the Republic itself."[24]

The Senate debate over conscription repeated in greater detail and with more strident oratory the arguments about the impact on morals and morale of forcing the daughters of mobilized soldiers to work outside of their homes.[25] A tacit understanding existed among the senators that some women ought to be mobilized for war work—but not all women and not under such a broad law that those not intended for inclusion might be swept up in it. If the phrase *"tous les français"* was followed by "without distinction of age of sex," mobilization would fall upon women whom the Senate preferred to protect. Without the elucidating phrase, "all of the French" encompassed all women—grammatically if not legally.[26] Leaving the point vague was not only incompatible with the law's planning function but dishonest. Senator Voilin insisted that the sacrifices to be demanded of the French people should not be hidden behind a "purely grammatical euphemism" and pressed for his amendment limiting the national service obligation to those males between the ages of eighteen and forty-eight.

Senators had no delusions about the essential role to be played by women in the event of national mobilization. The argument over the issue of female conscription was not so much about what would eventually happen but, rather, what would be said about it. Thus in presenting the bill to the Senate, rapporteur Klotz made a point of referring to women being not *"réquisitionné"* but *"requis,"* a gentler word meaning exactly the same thing.[27] Klotz merely minced words. More significant was War Minister Painlevé's announcement that the assertion in Article 1 that "all of the French are . . . required to participate in the defense of the nation" had never imposed any but a moral obligation on the women of France. Painlevé even claimed that the conscription of women would have remained hypothetical had the Senate army committee not given it substance by introducing measures to protect as many women as possible. Painlevé's admission led Klotz to a dramatic turnaround. Repudiating his own proposals to exclude large categories of women from mobilization, Klotz declared his allegiance to Senator Sari's definition of conscription as incumbent upon "all of the French . . . of the male sex." His explanation—preference for Sari's broader conscription over Voilin's limited range of ages—does not explain his abandonment of his own proposition for drafting some women. The national organization law had been in the works since 1922: had Klotz only just realized that its provisions for the employment of women could safely be ignored as rhetorical? Certainly, as soon as he had seen that the government was not pressing for the power to mobilize women, he led the Senate in reinforcing the comfortable illusion that, although their wives and daughters could hardly remain untouched by the demands of a nation engaged in total war, such unpleasantness could be organized at the time and without unseemly measures of coercion.[28]

Similar senatorial reluctance to reify the sacrifices implied in the rhetoric of total war revealed itself in the discussion of industrial mobilization, especially in dismay at the chamber's prohibition of wartime profits. As one senator noted, "one must allow industry and agriculture their customary patterns of work, and those include making money." Agreeing that normal, though not scandalous, levels of profit were a necessary stimulus for economic production, the Senate army committee altered the Chamber's text to discourage the requisition of private property and to reward with "*primes*" those proprietors who negotiated *accords amiables* with the government. *Primes* were exactly the *bénéfices* specifically rejected by the Chamber, but, insisted Klotz, the word seemed less objectionable.[29]

The Senate's decision to give better terms to property owners who negotiated peacetime agreements with the government challenged the chamber's decision that firms were not to be bribed to do their patriotic duty, and an angry Paul-Boncour complained of the "childish delight" taken by senators "in criticizing, ripping, and mutilating my poor law."[30]

The Senate offered no opposition to the Chamber's resolution of the question of parliamentary military service, although, in this instance, silence implied only reluctant consent. Actually, the members of the Senate's army committee believed that the presence of men of military age in a wartime parliament would have "a deplorable effect" on morale and thought it reasonable to require those elected officials still in the first reserve to serve with their military units. It was an awkward point to press, however, since this stricture on men under forty-one years of age had a significant impact on the Chamber of Deputies but little or none on the Senate. On this matter, the Senate, therefore, accepted the Chamber's text.[31]

The Senate passed its version on the bill on 17 February 1928; faced, however, with irreconcilable disagreements between the "socialist" Chamber and the "liberal" Senate on the requisition of property, the government declined to seek a compromise between the two versions, and the whole project was dropped from the legislative agenda for the next six years.[32] However essential to French grand strategy, an efficient national mobilization plan had proved politically unobtainable.

The controversy over the 1927–1928 bill demonstrates the intractability of the political issues at stake rather than the blindness of the antagonists to the needs of the nation. Frenchmen did fear that Germany would eventually attempt to overthrow the Versailles arrangements, but they also believed that they had time to prepare. Committed to fight if need be, they could not face the prospect with anything but grim revulsion. Even as the two houses failed to agree on a national organization law, they passed other measures reorganizing the army and authorizing a very expensive set of fortifications for the northeastern and southeastern frontiers.[33] French politicians would go no further at a time when Germany seemed a distant threat but political and social adversaries an immediate danger. Moreover, whatever their individual political and social agendas, few policymakers saw the proposed national defense law as a harmless insurance policy to protect them in case of a war they hoped never to have to fight. Rather, this blueprint for a garrison state imposed peacetime restrictions upon the political and economic liberties of the French people whose extent could not be predicted. A painful necessity if war were certain, such measures were not to be undertaken if peace could, somehow, be made to prevail.[34]

Legislators saw little political profit in a wartime national law, but the failure of the armed forces to press for the measure demands further analysis. The army had obvious reasons to desire the creation of the economic and social structures necessary to reinforce the long-war strategy. General Buat had been the original author of the national mobilization bill, and General Serrigny, whose "intelligence and activity were behind everything conceived and undertaken," saw to it that the CSDN secretariat drafted the text and followed it through the parliamentary process.[35] The national defense secretariat aside, however, attitudes within the armed forces were, if not subversive of the legislation, no better than indifferent. Representatives of the Ministry of War actually lobbied in the Senate for the bill's defeat. Minister of War Painlevé offered only a lukewarm defense of the bill against right-wing challenges in the Senate, which Paul-Boncour blamed on the conservative politics of the general staff.[36] Serrigny, who saw personal rather than political motives behind the War Ministry's opposition to the bill, claimed that the ministry's secretary general, a man of "immoderate ambition," believed that an expanded concept of national defense would diminish the authority of the War Ministry by placing it under a coordinating Ministry of National Defense.[37] Another soldier, General Maximé Weygand, claimed that the law prescribed an incoherent relationship between the government and the high command.[38] But the armed forces cannot be blamed for the failure of the bill to become law in 1920. They could not have broken the impasse over compensation to property owners. It was this political conflict that doomed the measure, and Paul-Boncour qualified his charges against the military by speaking of the "quasi-hostility, at least the indifference" of the general staff. It was an aloofness he found inexplicable, given the benefits the armed forces should have found in the proposed bill. The army, he decided, simply failed to perceive that the law would have allowed France to organize her production, commerce, transportation, and other necessities of national defense "with the same authority, the same speed of decision, that the army enjoyed in its own domain."[39]

The coolness of the armed forces towards the national mobilization plan is perfectly comprehensible given the history of tension between military and civilian authorities in France and the army's suspicion of the French tradition of the nation in arms. Although the foundation of the Third Republic had occurred in a rare fit of consensus among Frenchmen about the importance of their army, by the end of the nineteenth century the army had come to represent for many a tainted patriotism—militaristic, socially divisive, and politically conservative. The officers corps' desperate defense of the fraudulent conviction of Captain Dreyfus reinforced the Left's suspicions that the army had become a state within a state, a haven for nobles and Catholics in a republican and anticlerical society.[40] Shocked by the army's heavy-handed behavior in the Dreyfus matter, the Left set aside its own divisions to establish civilian mastery over this bastion of conservatism, royalism, and Catholicism. The process of taming the army began with the deliberate transformation of the political and religious composition of the officer corps under the republican general L. J. N. André, who served as minister of war from 1899 to 1904.[41] The second step was the abolition, on 21 March 1905, of exemptions from military service, a move favored by the Left as egalitarian and opposed by the Right because increasing the number of conscripts allowed the period of service to be reduced from three years to two and thereby lessened time available to instill conservative values in recruits. The army had its own objections to universal conscription. It wanted to be a fighting force in its own right, not a training camp for civilians. In these days when the most vocal advocate of the "nation in arms" was socialist leader Jean Jaurès, the phrase hinted at the usurpation of the army's own sacred role by a militia. If the politicians of the Left gloried in the memory of the French Revolution's *levée en masse,* many soldiers saw it as an aberration, militarily inefficient and socially dangerous. Conscription was necessary and desirable as long as the army had time to mold citizens into disciplined imitations of professional soldiers; to give weapons and training but inadequate social indoctrination to young men of every political bent however, was, to unleash the forces of revolution. If the revolutionary *levée en masse* did not appeal to French soldiers, neither did the notion of industrial mobilization, for it too could come to be seen as a substitute for, rather than a reinforcement of, a powerful standing army.[42]

Although the 1914–1918 war only exacerbated civilian suspicions of the soldiers' politics and military loathing of civilian interference, victory produced a perverse kind of reconciliation. Although military leaders never forgot what they viewed as government interference in military concerns and many civilian leaders believed that the generals had squandered French lives in unnecessarily bloody combats, it proved less agonizing afterwards to emphasize the ultimate success of French arms than to analyze the causes, let alone to calculate the price, of either defeat or victory. To inquire into the prosecution of the war was to risk a verdict of unnecessary slaughter too excruciating for the nation to bear. By choosing instead to extol the victory and the generals who were its architects, the civilian leaders who elevated the victors of 1918 to the status of military oracles trapped themselves. Founded on a shared unwillingness to reopen recent wounds, this new relationship between politicians and generals produced not healthy collaboration but a rigid acceptance of defined spheres of influence. When military leaders chose to stand apart from the political effort to achieve a national mobilization law that smacked to them of civilian dictation, étatism, and the disdained nation in arms, there was little the bill's supporters could do about it.

The 1935–1938 Effort

For six years after its initial failure, the national mobilization bill lay forgotten. This was the period of the disarmament talks, and discussion of a national defense bill threatened to undermine French efforts in Geneva. Worldwide depression rendered the economics of peace more pressing than the possibility of war, and the succession of ephemeral governments attempting to steer France through economic and political shoals had no leeway to take up long-term projects. In comparison to such immediate issues as the defense of the franc, social conflict in a depressed economy, France's declining position in an increasingly technological world economy, and the domestic political strife symbolized in the bloody riots of 6 February 1934, a disarmed Germany did not seem terribly important.[43]

Still, the CSDN's responsibility for the wartime mobilization of national resources went beyond drafting the national organization law. Even without the impetus that the law would have provided, the CSDN, its study committee, the national defense secretariat, and individual ministries pursued a range of preparations for mobilization.[44] Although, for example, the Senate and Chamber had been unable to agree on a general mechanism for the requisition of property, the matter was resolved for private automotive vehicles and agricultural tractors by a law of 18 June 1934.[45] Many practical details remained to be settled, but in 1938 an officer wrote optimistically that, although the national organization bill had not yet become law, "its principal technical provisions have been put into place through inter-ministerial instructions or regulations."[46] Some French agencies acted as if the law actually existed, which could be evidence of an underlying commitment to its principles, but it fostered dangerous illusions that necessary preparations had actually been put into action. Thus the army organization law of 13 July 1927 provided for wartime mobilization in accordance with the provisions of the nonexistent *Loi sur l'organisation de l'nation pour le temps de guerre.*

Administrative solutions fell short of a comprehensive plan, and in 1934, when a series of conservative governments followed one another in the wake of the Stavisky scandal and the riots of 6 February 1934, the national organization bill was revived.[47] The renewed effort began on 12 June 1934 when Prime Minister Doumergue instructed the National Defense Secretariat to undertake a new study based on the Senate version of 1928. To avoid the earlier impasse, the CSDN solicited ministerial opinions about the proper treatment of private property in wartime, and President Jean Fabry of the study committee announced that the government had no intention of including women or children in the national mobilization plan.[48]

Delayed by the fall of the Doumergue and Flandin governments, the new draft was finally offered by Prime Minister Pierre Laval to the Chamber of Deputies on 21 June 1935. The German reoccupation of the Rhineland may have lent greater urgency to the matter, and the Chamber's army committee, led by its energetic young Radical Socialist rapporteur Guy La Chambre, gave the measure its support in the spring of 1936, but the fifteenth legislature ended before the bill reached the Chamber floor. After the elections, La Chambre became chairman of the committee, and Réné Richard replaced him as the bill's rapporteur. Moreover, the Popular Front's electoral victory brought to the newly created Ministry of National Defense a new sponsor for the bill in Edouard Daladier.

The first meeting of the new Chamber's army committee to discuss the national organization bill revealed how little commitment remained to the principles voted by the Chamber in 1927. Both the exclusion of women from the national mobilization plan (except as civil defense volunteers) and the payment of *bénéfices* under *accord amiable* were accepted without discussion.[49] Gone too was the freedom of the French people's elected representatives to choose between service as soldiers or as legislators. Those members of parliament who belonged to the *disponibilité* (ready reserve) or to the first reserve, that is, all fit men under forty-one years of age, were required to join their units.[50] This time around, the disputes concerned not personal or property rights but the civil and military structures for command and control in total war. They are less important for their outcomes than for what the process of their resolution reveals French about national defense planning.

The new bill asserted in its second article the government's responsibility to prepare the national defense effort in peacetime with the aid of the CSDN. Article 3 established the roles of the president of the council of ministers, the minister of war, the navy minister, the air minister, and, if applicable, a minister of national defense. Article 5 authorized the president of the council to serve as minister of national defense in coordinating the actions of the army, navy, and air force, establishing and executing armaments programs, mobilizing French industry, and other similar matters. In these efforts, the council president would have the assistance of the Conseil Permanent de la Défense Nationale (CPDN), and he had the option of delegating his authority to a separate minister of national defense.[51] Shifting from peacetime preparation to wartime command, the bill pronounced that the government would direct the war (Article 40), that it would be aided in that task by the CSDN (Article 41), and that the actual policy-making organ would be a wartime Comité de Guerre chaired by the president of the republic (Article 42). Article 42 also instructed the three service commanders-in-chief to direct the military operations authorized by the war committee and provided that "the commander-in-chief of the armed forces organizes the command, establishes missions, and distributes resources."[52] These provisions, whose purpose was to assert the principle of civilian control and to delineate responsibilities, prove on examination to be vague, anachronistic, and ill-matched with actual command arrangements.

Charging the CSDN with peacetime preparation of national defense was a serious defect. In 1929 the council had been expanded to include the entire Council of Ministers and five soldiers as nonvoting advisers (the vice-presidents of the army, navy, and air force councils, the inspector general of anti-aircraft defense, and the vice-president of the CSDN study committee). The only soldier with full voting membership was Marshal Philippe Pétain, who was added by special decree in 1934.[53]

Ironically, the number and importance of its members brought the council a superficial prestige at the cost of effectiveness. A council composed of cabinet ministers was an institutional advertisement of the importance of defense planning, and no ministry wanted to abdicate its formal role in this vital national enterprise, but a council of more than thirty cabinet-level officers could get little done. Ministers had more urgent responsibilities than national defense planning, and the council's membership was as unstable as the cabinets it mirrored. Since the CSDN could not, under the circumstances, be a productive working body, it became a forum for policy proclamations. General Serrigny, head of the council's secretariat, complained that the members changed their opinions with every shift of the political wind; some found advantage in voting one way in the CSDN and then reversing themselves at the cabinet meeting called to consider the council's recommendation. Since no minutes were taken of cabinet meetings, the change of stance could not be proved, and the minister could always cite the minutes of the CSDN as evidence of his, in Serrigny's view, "undeserved" patriotism.[54] To the generals, the council was not a line of communication between soldiers and politicians but merely the cabinet advising itself. It was, in General Serrigny's words, "useless and even dangerous."[55] Useless, the council certainly was; it never met after 1933. Dangerous, too, because it created the comforting illusion that a coordinated national defense effort was being developed at the highest level of government. When Louis Marin proposed to amend the national organization law so as to delegate the CSDN's peacetime planning role to a more streamlined body, Minister of National Defense and War Daladier insisted that "total war" demanded the participation of all of the ministries.[56] The important contradiction in French thinking, of course, was that, if Marin's narrow council failed to meet the theoretical requirements of complete mobilization, Daladier's broader one proved ineffective.

While the CSDN and its study committee slumbered in the mid-1930s, what passed for high-level national defense planning took place in the Haute Comité Militaire (founded in 1932) and the CPDN (established in 1936). These were narrowly constituted gatherings of the service ministers, the designated wartime commanders-in-chief of the three armed forces, and service chiefs of staff; their purview was strictly military.

The article that placed the responsibility for peacetime preparation for war in the hands of a moribund committee was followed by three articles that hedged as to whether military preparations were to be centralized under a ministry of national defense. The bland provisions of the bill, which stressed the authority of the service ministers (Articles 2 and 3) while combining the jobs of prime minister and minister of national defense, were the product of lengthy negotiations in which far more radical notions were proposed and discarded.

The title minister of national defense allowed for a number of possible interpretations. The least radical version was that represented by Prime Minister Leon Blum's appointment of Edouard Daladier in June 1936 as minister of national defense and war rather than simply minister of war. Daladier's primary job was to be the civilian head of the army, but his ministry's coordinating powers encompassed matters of interservice relations, the development of a comprehensive purchasing program, the organization of industrial mobilization, and the management of the national defense budget. The crucial word here is coordination, and Daladier had no control over the internal decisions of the Navy and Air Ministries. His authority was diminished by its extraconstitutional status; the administrative arrangements of the ad hoc national defense ministry would disappear if a future government chose to revert to a simple portfolio for war. The arrangement was, in Paul Reynaud's sarcastic appraisal, "a label stuck on an empty bottle."[57]

Other competing proposals, however, would have made the post of national defense minister not only permanent but far more powerful, the head of a "super-ministry" within which the former army, navy, and air ministries were reduced to mere departments. Against such radical change were a wide range of arguments. On the purely political plane, as Air Minister

Pierre Cot pointed out, any reorganization that reduced the number of cabinet posts by two was unlikely to win parliamentary approval.[58] Nor did history suggest that unification would necessarily produce a more effective organization. The first such experiment, Prime Minister André Tardieu's grouping of the army, navy, and air force under Minister François Piétri from 20 February to 2 June 1932, had achieved nothing beyond "the modification of the headings printed on letters and envelopes."[59] But the strongest objections came from men who feared not a weak national defense minister but a powerful one and who rejected any hint at consolidating the services.

The problem of the national defense minister parallels that of the law as a whole. Just as modern war called for comprehensive and integrated civil-military planning, it no less obviously required tight relationships among the army, navy, and air force, relations so close indeed as to arouse the question whether there need be three distinct services at all or whether, at the very least, they ought to be placed under some form of unified command. As we have seen, when the consequences of full-scale national mobilization of people and property became public, little support materialized for the mechanisms of total war. Similarly, the enthusiasm for drastic reform apparent in early discussions of military command arrangements soon evaporated in the face of interservice tensions.

Possibilities for dramatic change were broached in the Chamber's army and aeronautics committees in early 1936, even before Leon Blum had expanded the war minister's role to include the overall coordination of national defense. Although hesitant to offer a concrete proposal, the army committee instructed its chairman to urge Prime Minister Sarraut "to pursue this task of coordinating the operations of the land and air forces through measures parallel to those . . . facilitating the common action of the three military ministers."[60] The aeronautics committee was bolder, advocating both a new national defense general staff and the appointment of a single commander-in-chief "charged with coordinating the action of the commanders-in-chief of the land, sea, and air forces."[61]

At this point, the exact meaning of words assumed great importance. To coordinate did not necessarily mean to command, but committees' respective intentions were not clear.[62] At its most drastic, the reform proposed by the aeronautics committee would create three powerful new institutions: a ministry of national defense with authority over three service departments, a supreme commander over the armed forces (possibly even appointed in peacetime), and a national defense general staff. More moderate possibilities included a ministry with purely coordinating powers and a peacetime chief of staff of national defense, who could also be the designated wartime commander-in-chief. Understandably, the legislators' sudden interest in using the national organization law to codify relations among the armed forces alarmed the military leadership, who revealed their concerns when the new CPDN met on 2 October 1936 to discuss the notion of giving the head of the national defense secretariat the additional position of chief of staff of national defense. This move was no mere change of nomenclature, as was clear from Marshal Pétain's suggestion that a chief of staff would need a staff supplied from the graduates of the new college of national defense studies[63] and that the natural conclusion of the process would be the appointment of a single commander-in-chief.

The evolution of Pétain's thought from the controversial proposal for a national defense staff to the explosive one of appointing a supreme commander led Navy Minister Gasnier Duparc to suggest closing the discussion, which continued after the Marshal had conceded that the appointment of a commander-in-chief would reflect the unique need for cooperation between army and air force without undermining the independence of the navy. Unsurprisingly, Air Minister Pierre Cot intervened to reject any plan providing for unequal treatment of the three services and proposed the peacetime establishment of a reformed Haute Comité Militaire with a small staff. Daladier then warned of the growing political support for the idea of a unified high command. It would happen someday and, thanks to parliament, perhaps very soon. Presumably to avert reorganization by parliamentary fiat, Daladier suggested that the bill ought to read, "A general officer of the army, the navy, or the air force is appointed to assure the higher coordination of the land, air, and, 'if appropriate,' naval forces." After Cot had achieved the addition of the restrictive "if appropriate" for the air force as well, the council approved this text and called for a peacetime committee of military advisers to ensure that their ministries worked harmoniously as well.[64] The armed forces' representatives, though paying lip service to integrating their efforts, had used the notions of "coordination" and "appropriateness" to defend their autonomy from one another, but the question was to be reconsidered when the CPDN met again on 5 December 1936.

In preparation for that meeting, the four military powers in France—War Minister Daladier, Navy Minister Gasnier Duparc, Air Minister Cot, and Marshal Pétain—each prepared a statement of his position on the question of whether France should have a supreme commander who would command the armed forces in wartime and be aided in peacetime preparation by a national defense staff. The answer of the army, navy, and air force representatives was a firm negative. Their solution to the problem of interservice coop-eration was a Haut Comité Militaire composed of the service ministers and chiefs of staff aided by a small staff and presided over by the minister of na-tional defense. The committee could delegate its authority to a single indi-vidual whenever circumstances dictated, perhaps by establishing a unified command in a specific theatre of operations. Arguing against the three ser-vice chiefs, however, Marshal Pétain demanded a genuine commander-in-chief, dismissing both supreme command by committee and improvised del-egation of authority. He stressed the need for haste—"1937 and the years following" warned the Marshal, "will be still more threatening than 1936."[65]

But the unified command advocated by Marshal Pétain found no support in the CPDN. The navy and air force feared subordination to the army; to civilian leaders, Pétain's suggestion smacked of excessive military power; and the army preferred to avoid reinforcing republican suspicions of mili-tary ambition. A government too nervous about its control over the armed forces to appoint the army's commander until war broke out naturally hesi-tated to establish an even more powerful generalissimo. Even after Pétain conceded that a mere letter of intent, not installation into his functions, would be all that the commander-in-chief needed in peacetime, the commit-tee went no further than to allow the wartime Comité de Guerre to delegate its authority to a "high-ranking person in one of the three services."[66]

Although the CPDN declined to urge the government to accept the depu-ties' invitation to use the national organization bill to create a strong minis-try of national defense, a national defense staff, or a commander-in-chief of the armed services, some members of the Chamber remained dissatisfied with the cautious formula suggested by the national defense committee. Deputy Montigny proposed replacing all of the bill's references to "the com-manders-in-chief of the army, navy, and air force" with "the commander-in-chief of the armed forces" and to establish a minister of national defense with authority over the three services. In spite of Daladier's vigorous defense of the current arrangement as "flexible" (*tellement souple*), the Chamber army committee passed Montigny's amendments, thus insinuating into the measure an unprecedented reorganization of the high command.[67]

When the Chamber met to discuss the new bill in March 1938, the stage was set for a collision between the faction that had pressed the idea of a commander-in-chief upon the Chamber army committee and the adherents of the traditional structure. Rapporteur Pinay of the navy committee led the charge with objections ranging from possibility that a commander-in-chief would make himself dictator to inability of any individual to handle the technical complexities of three distinct kinds of warfare.[68] The Chamber's air committee shared the navy committee's fear of a commander-in-chief, complaining that the appointment would fall to an army general and therefore imply the subjugation of one service to another. The air committee, aware that one possible solution to the high command question was to dissolve the Air Ministry and to divide all aviation units between the army and the navy, was willing to discuss only a weak minister of national defense who did not also hold the army, navy, or air portfolio and whose powers over the services was strictly limited.[69] Instead of defending the merits of the Montigny proposal, the Chamber army committee's president simply offered to replace the offending singular "commander-in-chief" with the plural "commander-in-chiefs," and the controversy—and the prospects for a supreme command—fizzled. The Chamber of Deputies voted unanimously to approve the bill and dispatched it to the Senate.[70]

In the upper house, the issue of unified command was revived by Rapporteur Fabry of the army committee, who believed that the new law ought to make permanent the new positions of minister of national defense and chief of staff of national defense, whose existence rested on the shaky foundation of the decrees of 21 March 1938. Opposing Fabry were his committee's chairman, Senator Daniel-Vincent, who denied that there should be a chief of staff, and, predictably, the Senate navy and air committees.[71] A meeting among representatives of the three military committees ended with the navy committee still implacable. Although Fabry insisted that "it is not a matter of putting the fleets under the command of General Gamelin," the navy's partisans insisted that a national defense staff would either attempt to control fleets directly, with disastrous results, or would interpose itself as a source of friction between the Comité de Guerre and the naval commanders.[72] Since Fabry's own committee manifested a disturbing tendency to defer the issue of reforming the high command, and the three service committees could not agree, Fabry let the matter drop, and the bill went to the Senate with minimal revision.[73]

The Senate acted quickly, taking time only for the rapporteurs of the three military committees to reiterate their concerns. Fabry's speech took the form of a warning of the perils of unpreparedness and a plea for teamwork in national defense. In view of the "suddenness, the rapidity, the brutal character of the opening weeks of a conflict," France had to enter the next war with her defenses fully organized. "System D [the famed notion of wartime improvisation, from the verb *se débrouiller*]," Fabry proclaimed, "no longer exists." The highest officers of the armed forces needed to be imbued with a new "spirit of national defense" rather than the distinct "air force spirit, army spirit, navy spirit." Abandoning futile arguments for the appointment of a generalissimo, Fabry called for a national defense staff, whose chief would work closely with the minister of national defense. Not an operational commander but "half-politician, half-technician," the chief of staff would "orient" the policies determined by the government.[74]

Senator Bergeron, rapporteur of the navy committee, offered all of the navy's usual arguments against both commander-in-chief and national defense staff. Describing present arrangements as "entirely satisfactory" from the naval point of view, Bergeron called for an end to discussions that "disturbed public opinion and impeded the establishment of the indispensable spirit of cooperation among the army, navy, and air force." Strife, in other words, was too high a price for reform. The Senate air committee accepted the principle of a combined national defense staff—as long as it was not headed by a soldier and was not placed under the Ministry of War.[75] The spokesman for the navy committee got his wish; the bill was passed on 17 June 1938 without any element weakening the traditional independence of the separate armed services. Senatorial modifications of the Chamber's text were so trivial that the Chamber army committee waived its right to reconsider the text, and the bill was signed into law on 11 July 1938.[76]

The sixty-eight articles of the new *Loi sur l'organisation de la nation pour le temps de guerre* called upon the government to make peacetime preparations for the mobilization of the population and resources of France to meet the exigencies of war. It delineated the responsibilities of the various civil and military authorities and imposed a national service obligation upon all male residents of France over eighteen years old. The state was empowered to negotiate with private citizens for the wartime use of property, and resources not secured by peacetime negotiation were subject to requisition with the payment of an indemnity. Legislators enrolled in the first reserve would be required to fulfill their military obligations; whether they could also exercise their political mandate was left for the two houses to determine. The government was to be assisted in preparing for wartime mobilization by a chief of staff of national defense, the Conseil Supérieur de la Défense Nationale, and the council's subordinate agencies. The specifically military aspects of national security planning—including the employment of armed forces, the creation and execution of armaments programs, and industrial mobilization—were the responsibility of the Comité Permanent de la Défense National. At the outbreak of hostilities, these military concerns shifted to a new Comité de Guerre chaired by the president of the republic.

The war committee would issue directives to the service commanders-in-chief and could choose to delegate to a single individual the power to coordinate the actions of the army, navy, and air force. The nation's economic mobilization was to be organized by special bureaus within the ministries. Acquisition and distribution of each scarce resource would be the responsibility of a single ministry, and similar centralized control was to be imposed on the national transportation and communications networks. Finally, a substantial portion of the law, eight of the sixty-eight articles, dealt with measures to protect the population of France from aerial bombardment.

This cautious set of arrangements was little to show for almost two decades of work. Many of the provisions either clarified divisions of authority among ineffective agencies or asserted the future role of committees that would not exist until war broke out. Wartime and peacetime authority remained as separate as the three armed services.[77] The law even failed in its aim to keep the higher direction of war in civilian hands. In appointing General Weygand commander-in-chief of the army in May 1940, the government all but abdicated its authority to a general determined to manage his campaign according to his personal political vision.[78] The articles that dealt with such practical matters as the mobilization of persons and property are important mostly as expressions of the political limits on the national defense effort—that is, of French unwillingness to go beyond a "wartime formula for business as usual."[79]

Implementing the National Organization Law

The law of 1 July 1938 was designed only to be a framework, a set of instructions to guide French leaders. As the more cynical critics of the entire project regularly pointed out, references to future administrative decrees and regulations were scattered throughout the national defense law. Announcing that the nation was to mobilize was one thing, transforming the measure from a wish list to a working system would require aggressive leadership. Mobilization planning within each separate ministry would not occur spontaneously, but Edouard Daladier, the man authorized to catalyze the necessary action, lacked a peacetime national defense staff to lighten the load of being both premier and minister of national defense and war.[80] Paul-Boncour complained bitterly that Daladier took notice of the legislation only where it benefited the armed forces and that the General Staff wanted nothing to do with national defense legislation designed to achieve "this total mobilization of all the forces of the nation, this permanent state of requisition of people and property." Though a pale facsimile of its original form, the new law appeared to the army to be "a revolutionary wind."[81] The military had no interest in a Jacobin-style mobilization; its implementation of the all-important measures for distribution of manpower would be described by a later historian as combination of "ill will and negligence."[82] Moreover, in the absence of encouragement from the professional defense experts, civilian agencies naturally shunned the effort of mobilization planning.

Those parts of the *Loi sur l'organisation de la nation pour le temps de guerre* that government agencies did not like were simply ignored. In January 1939, for example, the minister of commerce promulgated a public regulation promising compensation to property owners for the wartime use of their property that was strictly incompatible with the law of 11 July 1938. Noting the problem in a letter to Daladier, the Secrétariat Générald du Conseil Supérieure de la Défense Nationale (SGCSDN) argued that the state could not refuse to offer profit unless it was willing to guarantee against loss. If protected against loss, however, companies would have no incentive to make an effort, and their failures would drain the treasury. Although the secretariat could not repudiate the law of 11 July, it declined to enforce it.[83] Thus a matter that had officially been settled remained open to interpretation and to the kind of improvisation that the law was meant to preclude.

What few efforts were made to put the national defense law into practice began largely with the national defense secretariat. In 1938 General Louis Jamet's men oversaw a number of mobilization exercises, including a large-scale "National Defense Exercise" testing the high-command arrangements detailed in a secret decree of 7 September 1938. At the end of the year, the secretariat reported that, though 1938 had seen the establishment of the law's basic principles, given the necessary resources, the year 1939 "ought to permit a correct execution of national mobilization."

Some improvements occurred. Before 11 July 1938, those ministries that had tried to create mobilization bureaus had fallen afoul of the austerity program that prevented the hiring of additional personnel. Thus, the Ministry of the Post, Telephone, and Telegraph complained in spring 1938 that the finance minister had funded a mobilization staff of 3 instead of the required 111. In accordance with Article 44 of the law, Premier Daladier made the necessary funds available.[84] Among the elements of the twenty-nine major government decrees and regulations promulgated by the end of 1939 in response to the *Loi sur l'organisation de la nation pour le temps de guerre* were the creation of the Institut de la recherche scientifique appliquée à la défense nationale (28 July 1938), requisition of property (28 November 1938, 27 October 1939, and 29 November 1939), censuses (5 January 1939), mobilization bureaus for the prefectures (5 January 1939), regulations on foreign residents in France (12 April 1939), manpower mobilization (12 and 19 April 1938), the insurance of commerce against the hazards of sea trade in wartime (6 May 1939) and in periods of international tension (20 May 1939), and protection against economic espionage (15 May 1939).[85]

The need for mobilization planning did not stop at the national level; department prefects and town mayors had to turn the abstractions of the wartime organization law into concrete action. Concerned that the partial mobilization during the Sudetenland crisis of September 1938 had revealed many of the mayors of France to be utterly ignorant of their national defense responsibilities, the secretariat of the CSDN called for the urgent development of clear and simple plans for use at the local level.[86] To supervise these local arrangements, the Minister of the Interior created a new Inspection Générale des Services Administratives. In 1939 local industrial or agricultural mobilization exercises took place in the departments of the Loire, the Charente, and the Marne; the electrical industries in Paris and Lille tested their mobilization plans; exercises involving ports and transportation were carried out in Dieppe, Nevers, and Oran and Casablanca.[87]

While its proponents urged thorough implementation of the law of 11 July 1938, others argued that the law itself thwarted national defense. For example, some armaments orders had not been placed by the services because of the difficulty of predicting the elusive "just return on capital" allowed by the law. In other cases, the armed services were unable to make contracts attractive enough to get the desired results for fear of offering illegal rates of profit.[88] Paul-Boncour believed, moreover, that the law's strict ban on war profits deterred businessmen from investing in plants likely to be requisitioned. The framers of the law had intended that patriotism and the prospect of government contracts alike would steer industry towards military production, but such stimuli promised results only to a government willing actively to employ them. In the event, small firms proved unwilling to accept government contracts at the rate of profit allowed by law, and the French government proved equally unwilling to exploit its statutory authority to requisition factories.

The weakness of the law of 11 July 1938 can be seen from the fact that many important national defense measures were taken without invoking it. For example, the most serious interwar challenge to private property, the nationalization of defense plants under the law of 11 August 1936, occurred while the national mobilization law was still mired in the legislative process.[89] Rather than taking recourse to the national organization law, Prime Ministers Edouard Daladier and Paul Reynaud instead made extensive use of special decree powers to implement policies ranging from abrogating the forty-hour work week, to improving the national transportation network, to placing aliens under surveillance.[90]

Wartime

The outbreak of war in September 1939 revealed the gaps in the vaunted French national defense organization. Although the organization law had provided for the coordination of transport by a single ministry, rolling stock remained dispersed among competing agencies, and no arrangements existed for efficient loading and unloading.[91] Bottlenecks developed in French ports, and only in February 1940 did domestic factories begin to unload trains on Sundays and holidays. Although balancing wartime industrial and agricultural manpower needs with those of the armed forces was a primary element of national mobilization, the necessary preparations had not been made. In 1939, as in 1914, skilled workmen mobilized for battle had to be recalled from the front. France needed airplanes as fast as her industry could build them, but 20,000 experienced aviation workers were mobilized with their regiments in 1939 and only gradually returned to the labor force.[92] Similarly, armaments factories suffered because the Ministry of Labor failed to prevent the call-up of the many engineers who held commissions as reserve artillery officers.[93] André Maurois described the mobilization fiasco as "fantastic":

> Skilled workmen, who were indispensable for the manufacture of aeroplanes or cannons, were sent to provincial barracks where they swept out courtyards or peeled potatoes. It took weeks or months to locate them again and send them back to their machines. As a result, the Renault Factories, which in peacetime employed more than thirty thousand workers and which should have filled a place of immense importance in the manufacture of tanks and trucks, were reduced, at the outbreak of the war, to a personnel of from six to eight thousand.[94]

Although about 1.2 million men of military age had been granted occupational exemptions military service, 550,000 more were mobilized and then demobilized for factory work in a process that undermined the efficiency of industry and armed forces alike.[95] The recall of skilled workmen from the front stripped formations, especially the already deficient category B reserve divisions, of their technical specialists. Some divisions lost as many as one-half of their reserve officers and noncommissioned officers.[96] Especially hard hit were the motorized combat units that had received large numbers of mechanically trained reservists upon mobilization only to lose them to occupational exemptions.[97]

Compounding the physical consequences of such transfers were psychological ones. The departure of the fortunate angered those left at the front, especially many older men—whose military records did not describe their current occupational skills—and fathers who saw childless men returning home.[98] Some wondered, moreover, how much special training was required for many of the jobs that were a passport to the rear, and suspicions that influence was at work were reinforced by the government's decision to withdraw workmen from combat units one at a time rather than in a single major reorganization. The piecemeal transfers were an effort to avoid drawing attention to the faulty initial mobilization, but the unexplained movements of individual soldiers naturally suggested personal pull rather than public policy, and those left behind hastened to seize whatever strings lay within their reach. Thus, on the individual level, much energy was shifted from preparing for war to seeking ways to be excused from it, and senior officers and government officials were deluged with requests for special treatment.[99] As for the employment of female labor, the decree of 28 February 1940 allowing for an obligatory census as a first step towards later conscription came far too late to have any effect.[100]

French failure to enter World War II with a manpower policy better conceived than that of World War I demonstrates the huge gap between the rhetoric and the reality of the French national mobilization for total war. After the war, Paul-Boncour would insist that the law of 11 July 1938 "had been perverted"[101] by a government reluctant to employ its authority, but it would be more accurate to say that the law itself was less a solution to the problems of national mobilization than a symptom of them. As early as 1924, a critical journalist had denounced the draft bill as only a framework, not a concrete program. He noted that "as soon as one asks a specific question one is referred to another law, to decrees, or to administrative regulations: naturally the laws, decrees, and regulations do not yet exist."[102] He was right, but achieving a sufficiently precise law would have required decisions that were too painful to make in peacetime.

The story of the national organization law illuminates three themes in the history of interwar France: French confidence in the French nation's understanding of their national defense requirements, the practical difficulties of matching their existing political institutions to that vision, and their refusal to acknowledge, let alone to resolve, the tension between theory and reality. Thus French leaders could insist that the prospect of total war required peacetime preparation for the dedication to the national effort of the nation's collective human and material resources but accept a wartime organization law that excluded women, largely protected private property, left unchallenged the particularism of the separate armed forces, and entrusted the necessary preparatory measures to an inadequate national security infrastructure. They made do with a law that was politically acceptable and then told themselves that it would prove to be adequate and that the same agencies that had supported it so grudgingly would take full advantage of its provisions.

The law's evolution from a plan for national transformation into something considerably less substantial shows the reluctance of a democracy to accept in peacetime the degree of national discipline that would be necessary in war; it also helps to explain French confidence in 1939—and the gap between that confidence and French performance. The three pillars of French national security were meant to be manpower, armaments, and the ability, manifested in the national organization law, to harness their national resources efficiently. Given German demographic and industrial strength, only in the third element could France hope to achieve an advantage.[103] By the time it became law, the measure designed to capitalize on the power of the nation in arms had shrunk drastically—as had the time available for its implementation—but Frenchmen were less aware of the defects in their national security infrastructure than they were comforted by the promise that they possessed a blueprint for victory in modern, industrial war.

2
A Staff College for the Nation in Arms

The Origins of the National Defense College

Political difficulties impeded the creation and execution of an effective national organization law in France, but politics alone does not explain the apparent lethargy of those whose job it was to prepare France for the next war. Whereas legislative efforts at national defense organization succumbed to public pressures, the formation of national security policy also took place in other arenas where failures must be explained in different terms. One of these venues, a cornerstone of the interwar French national security edifice, was the Collège des Hautes Etudes de la Défense Nationale (CHEDN), created in 1936 to train military and civilian leaders to mobilize the nation and to lead it in war. In this organization the tensions between French planning and French capabilities could hardly be ignored. Legislators could conceal incoherent policies behind rhetoric and platitudes, but military commanders and civil servants had to create policies capable of execution. Even as Paul Reynaud reminded his colleagues in the Chamber of Deputies on 15 March 1935 that the defensive orientation of the French Army was incompatible with her alliance strategy, diplomats and soldiers had to prepare to carry out their responsibilities within the existing military and diplomatic arrangements. The CHEDN was a place where rhetoric ought to have given way to realism; instead the historian can see there how French leaders tolerated the deficiencies of their national defense.

Like the national organization law, the National War College was a tool to prepare for and to prosecute "total war." It was yet another effort to implement the long-war strategy through an organized, rational, and equitable mobilization of the resources of the *nation armée*. Behind the college lay the premises that the nation needed a comprehensive security policy and that the civilian and military agencies charged with executing that policy in peace and war would have to be staffed by people capable of thinking in terms of the national effort rather than of the interests of separate departments, ministries, or armed services. However obvious the advantages of such a cooperative approach, it was rarely found or encouraged in the rigidly compartmentalized French bureaucracies. Special personnel were required, but proposals to establish an institution to train them met with less than enthusiastic responses from the various interested parties. The debate over the establishment of a national defense college reveals interservice and civil-military tensions; the methods and curriculum of the college provide further evidence both of the constraints within which the men responsible for French national security policy operated and the manner in which they responded to those constraints.

Although the notion of establishing some form of national defense college was broached in 1931 by a certain Major Charles de Gaulle in an unsolicited memorandum to Marshal Philippe Pétain, the first official proposal appeared in a June 1936 paper by Colonel Thiervoz of the national defense secretariat.[1] Thiervoz argued that the secretariat, recently placed under the Conseil Permanent de la Défense Nationale, had the authority to coordinate the national defense effort but lacked a suitable staff familiar with "all of the factors behind the problems that would beset a Great Power at war." Written two weeks after Edouard Daladier's appointment to the new post of minister of national defense and war in the Popular Front government, the proposal certainly reflected the minister's thinking and was probably of his own inspiration.[2] Thiervoz proposed a two-year course in which forty-five military and civilian personnel would study both the national defense effort as a whole and purely military operations. Graduates of the college would be sent in three different directions. Some, civilian and military alike, would be assigned to the Secrétariat Général de la Défense Nationale to form a wartime team to advise the government on economic, financial, and diplomatic matters. The other civilian graduates would create mobilization bureaus in their respective ministries while the remaining officers would join a national defense staff.

The flurry of reactions to Thiervoz's proposal from the three service ministries revealed two sides of the national defense college question. Although the institution promised to foster the efficient national mobilization on which the long-war strategy rested, Thiervoz's passing reference to a national defense staff aroused the kind of alarm about unified command already described in connection with the national organization law. At the least, the college would blur interservice boundaries and threaten to erode traditions of independence. Some even went so far as to suggest, happily or in horror, that the process begun by the creation of a Collège des Hautes Etudes de la Défense Nationale would culminate not merely in the creation of a national defense staff but in the imposition of a single commander over the armed forces. Such future possibilities, if not the college itself, worried representatives of the three armed forces—and not without reason. The CHEDN had hardly graduated its first class when an army officer described it as a step in a process that would not be completed without the appointment of a commander-in-chief.[3]

Of course, had the army, the navy, and the air force shared a common vision of how best to balance service autonomy with interservice cooperation, they could have handled civilian proposals for a national defense college with confidence that no generalissimo would be imposed against their united opposition. It was the absence of such consensus—and the fear that one service or faction might exploit the creation of a national defense college to alter the existing balance of power among the army, navy, and air force—that rendered any proposal for interservice cooperation an object of suspicion to the military chiefs. Of course, all three services acknowledged the principle that strategy ought to be integrated and pointed proudly to existing institutions that furthered that aim. Behind this veneer of agreement, however, lay, a tacit understanding that any public discussion of the issue would reveal how poorly the oft repeated platitudes on the subject described the actual situation.

Because land battle was the centerpiece of French strategy and the supreme commander would naturally be a soldier, many in the army supported the notion of unified command, but even that service was neither uniformly nor vocally in favor of altering existing institutions. The navy vehemently defended its independence, but matters were more complicated within the air force, where attitudes towards interservice cooperation and service autonomy were directly related to doctrinal questions. For reasons that reflected service defensiveness more than an informed acceptance of Giulio Douhet's arguments for employing bombers against cities, official air force doctrine tended towards the strategic bombing doctrine that promised the greatest degree of institutional independence.[4] The minority view that air power should be a tool for the tactical support of the army—and that the latter should exercise some authority over the supporting service—could not, however, be ignored, for it found favor outside of the air force and a ready soapbox in the *Revue Militaire Générale*.[5] The existence within the air force of a fifth column of proponents of interservice cooperation made any discussion of unified command all the more threatening to air force autonomy.

Opposition from all three services sufficed in 1938 to prevent the outright establishment of a supreme commander in the national organization law, but it did not keep proposals for a national defense college off the table. In pushing for the new institution, Daladier offered logical arguments about France's need for personnel trained for total war and the loaded observation that their friends across the Channel had had such an institution since 1926. Once military attachés had called attention to Britain's Imperial Defence College, a French equivalent became necessary to prove that France had a strategic vision worthy of a great power.

Armed with a conviction of the college's importance and with the powerful lever of British competition, Daladier introduced at the CPDN meeting of 29 July 1936 a proposal for a Collège des Hautes Etudes de la Défense Nationale where field-grade officers of recognized potential to achieve the highest rank would join civil servants from all ministries of the French government to study national defense issues. The men selected for the course would be destined to form an élite cadre of leaders, who, ten years or so in the future, would be in place to manage the entire war-making capability of the nation-in-arms. The meeting, however, discussed Daladier's proposal very little, for every service had come with its own counterproposal designed to thwart or at least vitiate that of the defense minister.

Outspokenly opposed to a unified command was the man most likely to be called upon to exercise it—army commander-in-chief designate General Maurice Gamelin. Faced with mounting government pressure for the creation of a national defense college, Gamelin offered an alternate suggestion innocuous to his own service. He proposed an eight-week course in which ten to fourteen military personnel and two token civilians would perform a national defense exercise and attend lectures outlining the general requirements and resources of the French empire and the principal foreign powers. Essentially another level of purely military education, Gamelin's college would be directed by an army general and would share the facilities of the army's Centre des Hautes Etudes Militaires.

General Gamelin was not the only ranking soldier to deprecate the government's proposal, and Marshal Pétain's position on the question is particularly interesting. In May 1936, only one month before Thiervoz offered his proposal, the Marshal had called for the unified direction of the armed forces by a minister of national defense seconded by a chief of staff of national defense. Officers to staff the new ministry would be trained at a new Centre des Hautes Etudes Militaires Interministériel whose subject of study Pétain defined as "problems of strategy and of the higher direction of war."[6] Faced with Daladier's superficially similar proposal for a Collège des Hautes Etudes de la Défense Nationale, the Marshal insisted upon his own plan with a vehemence that implied the defense minister's national defense college was worse than no college at all. It takes, in fact, a careful comparison of the two proposals to reveal the sources of Pétain's concern.

In the Marshal's opinion, all that was required of a new institution was to introduce their graduates to problems of joint operations, since the three existing Centres des Hautes Etudes sufficed to train officers at the highest level of operations within each individual service. The new course, therefore, would simply comprise a number of *"cas concrets"* designed to reflect the current military and diplomatic situation in France and would be directed by General Bineau, the director of the army's own Centre des Hautes Etudes Militaires (CHEM). Pétain's goal was a very limited form of national defense college supplying personnel for a correspondingly narrow ministry of national defense in which civilians would have little role. His chosen label, *"collège interministériel,"* was, if not actually deceptive, at least misleading. In fact, integrated civilian and military planning went no further than participation by a single representative each from the ministries of foreign affairs, finance, public works, and the colonies. Since all current war plans focused on defeating Germany in a land war, the restriction of the course to the study of those plans hinted that Pétain's second purpose was to coordinate the navy and the air force in doing what the army thought best. It was, in short, a proposal leading towards unified command on a pattern unacceptable to the navy and the air force.

Pétain's course was to last for only two months and involve only fifteen officers in addition to the four functionaries. Although two months offered little time for the participants to indulge in unorthodox speculations, the marshal specified a narrow range of subjects—the relationship between government and high command, foreign policy, the military capabilities of potential belligerents, and the economic, financial, and military prospects of France and other nations—and stressed that the focus of the course would be a practical exercise based on the existing plan. Overall, Pétain's national defense college resembled the ministry of national defense he championed in the 1936 discussions of the national organization law—small, doctrinally orthodox, military rather than civilian in emphasis, and designed to reinforce the influence of the army over the other services.[7]

In addition to the competing proposals of Marshal Pétain and General Gamelin, the council received papers on the teaching of national strategy from the air and navy ministries and a joint proposal in the names of the three service ministers. The Air Ministry paper ascribed to a national defense college the same purpose envisioned in the soldiers' proposals—"the exploration of methods common to the high commands of the army, navy, and air force, and the training of personnel to participate in managing the general conduct of war and the employment of combined forces"—but its proposed structure adumbrated a distinct air force agenda.[8] Rather than constituting a distinct level in the hierarchy of military education, the Collège des Hautes Etudes de la Défense Nationale would be attached to the three Centres des Hautes Etudes Militaires and attended by those current students of the centers selected for supplementary national defense studies. This relationship between the Centres des Hautes Etudes and the Collège des Hautes Etudes de la Défense Nationale was meant to preclude redundant discussion of the technical issues being addressed concurrently at each of the service institutions. By preventing the college from introducing officers to the concerns of the other services and by limiting civilian exposure to military matters, the plan maximized parochialism within a nominally triservice enterprise. Threatened with the prospect of becoming an instrument of its sister services, a mere supplier on demand of firepower, transport, and reconnaissance, the air force sought to defend its own autonomy by monopolizing the study of the theory and practice of military aviation.

If maintenance of service independence through specialized knowledge was the hidden agenda in the air force proposal, it was explicit in that of the navy. After paying lip service to the truism that all wartime effort of a nation must be integrated, the navy's analysis stressed the distinctness of naval warfare from the operations of the other services. Although all three services would share common strategic objectives, the navy expected to operate independently and in distant theatres, and its strategy would "necessarily maintain a unique character."[9] The navy's report further claimed that, since combined operations required enormous resources and a very marked naval superiority, they would be infrequent. A Collège des Hautes Etudes de la Défense Nationale, the navy ministry argued, made sense only as long as it emphasized the civilian side of the curriculum. Army, naval, and air strategy were already treated at the existing institutions of higher military education and should be of no concern to a college of national defense except in their relationship to diplomacy, international law, transport, financial resources, industrial resources and requirements, supply and commerce, colonial issues, and relations with neutral and allied powers. The emphasis on the civilian elements of national defense may seem out of place, but its purpose was less to proselytize for the integrated study of national strategy than to preempt any proposals involving joint operations. The navy's surprising deprecation of the role of amphibious warfare suggests a fear that advance planning for such operations would lead to peacetime subordination to a command system dominated by the army. Thus the naval response to Daladier's proposal for a national defense college suggests that, like their air force counterparts, admirals saw themselves as engaged in a struggle against French advocates of a unified command as well as against foreign adversaries.

The navy's attitude towards a national defense college was not entirely negative, however, for sailors had come to see that a concern with French national strategy on the largest scale promised a new emphasis on her role as a world, and by easy extrapolation, a naval power. In documents describing the British Imperial Defence College, the minister of the navy found for contemporary France a reminder that the importance of French overseas lines of communications ought not be obscured by preoccupation with military affairs.[10] If the new national defense college were to concentrate on the large issues of national strategy, then it might prove an ally rather than a threat to the Ministry of the Navy, and the navy, therefore, consistently emphasized the importance of the civilian elements of the course. The higher the level of strategy studied and the greater the civilian role, the further the course would shift from the minutiae of war—and naval subordination to the army—to the safer and more nautical matter of France's position in world politics.

If the individual armed forces were apprehensive that a national defense college would undermine both service autonomy and the balance between civilian and military authority, civilian ministers, led by Air Minister Pierre Cot, expressed equally powerful misgivings about the implications for the government's monopoly on defense policy. Military education and strategic planning were such disparate enterprises, Cot argued, that they could not be handled by a single institution, and the sole purpose of the national defense college should be to prepare officers from the services to solve military problems cooperatively. National Defense Minister Daladier, however, continued to insist that the new college would have to combine military studies with the analysis of national policy on a higher plane; such collaboration was, after all, the essence of the new concept of total war. He believed that the course should indeed teach the higher, or civilian, elements of French policy and that student solutions to practical problems should be made available to the government. Thus the college would assist the government in its policy-making role, not usurp it.

Air Minister Cot's sensitivity to any military forays into the realm of policy reflected the tenuous accommodation achieved between army and government in the late Third Republic and reminds the historian that this apparently technical discussion of military pedagogy had grave political implications. Civilian control over national policy was a republican axiom institutionalized by the refusal to appoint a peacetime commander-in-chief and by the nonvoting status of the military members of the CSDN; French soldiers were supposed to execute policy, not make it. The question raised by Daladier's new proposal for a college of national defense studies was whether the course would tempt the students to assess the policies they studied or even to offer alternatives. In Cot's view, the principle of civilian control denied the college any role beyond training military and civilian functionaries to implement instructions received from above. Daladier, though no less committed to civilian supremacy, believed that the government could profitably use the college as a working group to tackle problems that still lacked official solutions. He did not intend for the students to criticize current conceptions of national security policy nor to speculate about new ones, but the lines remained blurred.

What if, for example, the students were instructed to produce a plan for an invasion of Spain but concluded that the idea was impractical? Cot's interpretation allowed no latitude to question an assignment, but Daladier's implied the freedom at least to append to the scheme a note of warning. Of course, higher authorities had no investment in an invasion of Spain, but the problem would be more immediate if students produced serious reservations about, for example, the current French war plan against Germany. Cot's thesis had the virtue of clarity, but it severely limited the utility of the new institution. Daladier's more flexible approach promised superficial benefits but was likely to prove unworkable whenever the issues involved were important. In any case, the minister of national defense and war eventually dismissed the whole very important topic by reminding the meeting that the task of making French strategy was officially reserved to the CPDN and its secretariat.[11]

After discussing plans proposed by the separate services and skirting the highly charged issue of the college's freedom to criticize existing national security policy, the CPDN meeting of 29 July 1936 finally tackled the official agenda item, a proposal, signed by the three service ministers but primarily representing the views of Edouard Daladier, for a national defense college whose scope exceeded the narrow vision promoted in the military plans.[12] The first goal of the college was to provide an élite group of officers destined for service in the general staff with background in the problems of "combined strategy"; its second was to familiarize these future planners with the impact of economic, political, financial, demographic, and other factors on the conduct of war. The ministerial version was passed after cursory discussion and futile resistance by Marshal Pétain. The new college would be distinct from the existing institutions of higher military education, and its chief would be a general officer named by the minister of national defense from among the three services in rotation. This chief would be seconded by deputies representing the other two services. The participants in the college were to include ten soldiers, five sailors, and five airmen; moreover, each civilian ministry concerned with problems of national defense would send one representative to the ten-month course. The potentially contentious issue of which ministry would run, and therefore finance, the new college, was resolved when Daladier, unsurprisingly, volunteered his own Ministry of National Defense and War. The question of selecting the college's first director, however, reopened the debate about the very nature of a national defense college and revealed that the navy's docile acceptance of Daladier's scheme did not reflect acquiescence to the principles behind it. Minister of the Navy Gasnier Duparc suggested that Admiral Castex's strategic writings made him the man best qualified to head the new college,[13] and Marshal Pétain countered that the navy was less concerned than the army, which ought to select the college's first director. Pétain's argument, riposted Vice-Admiral Durand-Viel, Chef de l'Etat Major de la Marine, demonstrated the incompatibility of the army's and navy's conceptions of what the new college was to do. Whereas the army treated it as a simple extension of its own Centre des Hautes Etudes Militaires, useful for the study of war plans and best headed by a general, the navy thought that an institution so constituted would be redundant. After a lengthy assessment of French strategic needs in a long war, the admiral concluded that problems of national strategy at the highest level, not the technical matters already addressed at the Centre des Hautes Etudes Navales (CHEN), were the proper concern of a national defense college and reaffirmed the role of the civilian participants for whom Pétain and Gamelin had only a cool welcome.[14]

To Daladier's suggestion that the new college would have to fulfill both of the different but equally important roles described by the army and the navy, Pétain retorted that it would be more to the point for the army and the navy to acknowledge the distinctness of their concerns by establishing separate colleges to be attended successively.[15] Pétain's idea, of course, reflected the sort of thinking that the new college was intended to change; conflicts among the services were not to be solved by discussing them in separate venues. As Daladier, no doubt somewhat exasperated, explained, the CHEDN would exist for the very purpose of coordinating the solutions to the military problems studied at the Centres des Hautes Etudes with the larger issues of national policy addressed at the college itself.

In any case, Pétain was swinging after the bell. Daladier's college was a fait accompli, and the committee quickly agreed that it would be funded by the ministry of the army, housed in the air force staff building at 32 boulevard Victor in the southern part of the fifteenth arrondissement and headed by Admiral Raoul Castex. Although the army preferred General Bineau of the Centre des Hautes Etudes Militaires, Castex was France's best-known strategic thinker and a more tolerable choice to the other services.[16] On interservice relations, he held the view—impeccable to the air force and navy—that cooperation was essential but unified command "an imaginary state of affairs, a seductive mental creation unrelated to reality."[17] These arrangements were institutionalized in the presidential decree of 8 August 1936 establishing the Collège des Hautes Etudes de la Défense Nationale.

The College in Operation

The college began its four-month inaugural session on 15 October 1936, and fears that the new college would diminish either the independence of the individual services or civilian control over the armed forces proved unfounded. Castex's institution concerned itself narrowly with the execution, not the assessment, of French national defense plans. Deficiencies in French planning in the 1930s were not to be discussed, let alone remedied, at its highest institution of strategic studies. Certainly the institution would never be the forum for the profound and fruitful controversy among "*gens d'élite*" that Admiral Durand-Viel called for in an article published in the following year.[18]

The atmosphere of the new college may have been less free than Durand-Viel wanted, but the students did represent the cream of the French armed forces. Rushed though they were to come up with appropriate candidates for the first session, all three services produced contingents of officers, mostly lieutenant-colonels, whose remarkable service records pointed them toward the highest command and staff assignments.[19] A distinguished career did not, however, guarantee an ability to concentrate on the purpose of the program. For example, the air force participants in the 1936–1937 class were headed by no less a dignitary than Divisional General Aube. A member of the Conseil Supérieur de l'Air, the inspector general of anti-aircraft defense, and, before he finished the course, chief of the air force general staff, Aube was too busy to attend the sessions. To send such a high-ranking officer proved an empty compliment to the national defense college. The navy appears to have had the greatest shortage of suitable candidates, and several of its five representatives were simultaneously engaged in other duties.

Both the purpose and the tone of the new college were clearly revealed in the inaugural lecture delivered by Director Castex on 15 October 1936. The new academy was to be a utilitarian, not theoretical, institution and would address itself to urgent, practical problems. The course would abstain from speculation, from anything "theoretical and philosophical, divorced from the real."[20] This practical emphasis was consistent with the admiral's pedagogical style as director of the Ecole de Guerre Navale. There, noted an American naval attaché, Castex strove to exclude material that did not offer ready-made conclusions to its officer-students. Castex believed that professional schools should emphasize reality and "extracted truths" and that theoretical knowledge was an "ornament" conducive to doctrinal confusion.[21]

The one theoretical notion that Castex wished to imbue in the students from the very beginning was the "unity of war"; "*la guerre est une*" was to be the college's fundamental axiom.[22] The idea that wars were fought by the consolidated forces of nations rather than by separate armed forces was so little developed, noted Castex, that French policy makers lacked even a term for strategic analysis of actions on the national level and introduced his own label, "*stratégie générale*,"[23] which he defined as "the art of directing, in war and in peace, all of a nation's forces and resources for struggle." General strategy unifies those assets "in the service of a single will."[24]

Castex's purpose was to prepare his students to execute a single plan for the defense of France, and his teaching methods were based on the premise that the necessary plan existed and was to be implemented without further analysis. Although he denied any intention of imposing a specific orthodoxy upon the participants in the course, the pressures for conformity were only thinly concealed behind Castex's assertion that, by stimulating the exchange of ideas, he would serve "like a medicine whose function is to stimulate certain reactions in the body or to induce certain secretions."[25] Just as chemical catalysts generate fixed results, so would the exchange of ideas lead to uniform answers; debate in the course, Castex predicted, "will probably have the result of leading us finally to a great similarity of views."[26] Whether exchanges among the students would have produced heretical ideas is a moot point, however, because the structure of the course left no opportunity for open discussion. The students met not in discussion groups or seminars but for seventy-eight formal lectures by Castex or visiting experts.[27]

One cannot but be struck, moreover, by the contradiction between the constant flux of the strategic situation in Europe and the admiral's deliberate quest to develop a single, definitive curriculum for the course. In order to remain valid from year to year, the lectures had to present an established and uncontroversial body of knowledge about the mechanics of national defense, and so quickly was orthodoxy established that Admiral Castex believed after the third year that the existing syllabus would already stand the test of time. Achievement of a static curriculum meant emphasis on historical and theoretical analysis at the expense of current events. Too many of the lectures resembled one entitled "Conduct of Coalition War" and subtitled "The Lessons of History." Mute on the difficult subject of France's relationship with her Eastern European allies, this lecture focused on the Napoleonic Wars and ignored all events after 1918.

Similarly anachronistic were Castex's pair of lectures covering the effects of foreign policy on strategy and of strategy on foreign policy, potentially the most significant topic studied at the college. An obvious approach would have been to analyze current French military plans within the framework of the nation's diplomacy. The lectures on "The Political Struggle," however, eschewed description of the actual strategic situation in favor of more general arguments. These generalizations were analytical and historical—analytical in their emphasis on definition of words and concepts and historical in their reliance on inferences from the wars of the French Revolution. The "modern" examples included the American Civil War and the Second Balkan War, as well as World War I.[28]

Castex summarized his argument by claiming that the value of having a national consensus on national defense could be seen in the experiences of the Germans after 1806, after 1866, and after 1918, in Italy after the Tunisian and Ethiopian "affairs," in Japan after her eviction from Port Arthur in 1895, and, finally, in France after 1870. By contrast, the absence of such national unity created the flawed policies of Russia before the Russo-Japanese War, Great Britain before 1914, and, "France after 1918, where for a long time many of our compatriots remained deaf and blind in the face of the growing dangers which they perceived only very late."[29] These words could have served to introduce the pressing topic of contemporary French policy but were, instead, the lecture's conclusion, Castex's final word on the vital theme of the impact of national policy on national strategy. The course never mentioned such pressing concerns as relations with Belgium and Great Britain, nor did it examine the implications for French military planning of alliances with Poland and the nations of the Petite Entente. Although each of the director's annual end-of-session reports called for an additional lecture on the strategic situation in contemporary Europe—"to situate the problems of national defense"—Castex never added such a lecture to the curriculum.[30]

Although the admiral's published work revealed strong convictions about French national policy, his lectures avoided subjects that might have led to criticism of the government. The surest way to avoid trespassing into the civilian realm was to eschew practical topics for theoretical ruminations on the relationship of strategy and policy. Thus, instead of analyzing the constituents of French security policy, he argued generally for a balance of military and civilian influence on policy—"a compromise" between contradictory "*nécessités et . . . prétentions.*" Achievement of the necessary liaison between strategy and policy would come through the sharing of information among soldiers and politicians. Political leaders needed to be educated about military strategy, and military men had to learn to appreciate civilian points of view. Cautiously, Castex deprecated the amount of political material to which military men should be introduced. Certainly the soldier was not to "play politician." Nor need he learn very much about the subject, no more in fact than "the man in the street who reads his daily newspaper and who has a good grounding in history, geography, and military studies."[31]

A more practical discussion of the current relationship between French foreign policy and military strategy might reasonably be sought in General Edouard Requin's aforementioned lecture "Conduct of Coalition War: The Lessons of History."[32] Here Requin analyzed the various arrangements tried during World War I and concluded that prosecution of a successful coalition war required a unified command under a single leader. Moreover, fighting a coalition war required more than the appointment of a generalissimo. In conflicts demanding complete national mobilization, the parties to the coalition had to cooperate in the civilian sphere as well. The coordination of industrial and other civilian elements of coalition war was the task of a political council parallel to the Haute Comité Militaire Interalliée that would be composed, for example, of the prime minister and minister of national defense of each state.

Inherent in Requin's discussion was an unasked question. Since the national infrastructure necessary to fight a modern war could not be improvised after the outbreak of hostilities, was it not necessary to make peacetime arrangements to coordinate the efforts of the coalition as a whole? In the absence of an official policy to that effect, Requin said merely that the matter would be resolved at the earliest possible time. This refusal to explore the tension between the actual and the necessary military arrangements was characteristic of the course. The college did not have the mandate to deal with hypothetical policies, and French mechanisms for coalition war were ill-defined; therefore, Requin treated them with the utmost vagueness. Even cooperation with Great Britain, although the basis of all French plans, appeared in the lecture as a contingency, not as a cornerstone of French policy. As for the highly problematic obligations existing between France and her eastern allies, Requin ignored them altogether. The general's approach cannot be explained as lack of foresight, for he concluded with the pessimistic suggestion that his listeners ought to reflect upon what they had heard "so that events, as grave as they are, will not surprise you."

The closest the course came to frank discussion of the contemporary strategic situation was a lecture by General Victor-Henri Schweisguth, the army's representative as deputy director of the college, on "Les données militaires actuelles d'une guerre de coalition européenne," which took the form of a country-by-country survey of the resources and policies of all of the nations likely to be involved in the next war. Unlike Castex or Requin, Schweisguth sought to offer an up-to-date analysis of the current situation, and each year he modified his text, which he delivered at the CHEDN and the CHEM, to meet contemporary conditions.[33]

In many respects, Schweisguth's was an admirably practical and informative lecture, clearly describing the outlines of French foreign policy and the premises about the behavior of other states upon which that policy was based. The method Schweisguth employed was probably as beneficial as the factual material he offered; descriptions of the current state of affairs in Europe were a healthy change from Castex's abstractions. Schweisguth did not, however, allow his examination of contemporary policy to become critical. Although the lecture's subheading "assistance" virtually demanded discussion of French obligations to her allies in Eastern Europe, Schweisguth skirted the question in favor of optimistic predictions of Soviet support for Poland and the Petite Entente.[34] This tacit admission of French inability to intervene in the all-too-likely case of a German attack to the east contrasts with the 1936 version. In the earlier lecture, a concluding encomium to allied loyalty to France described in pious detail the annual ceremony in which recruits in one Czech garrison paraded before a statue of Marshal Foch to be reminded of "what Czechoslovakia is and what France has done for her."[35] If the incongruity between French obligations and French capabilities worried General Schweisguth, he did not mention it; if such questions struck his audience, they had no forum in which to voice them.

In addition to the lectures, the course of study at the national defense college included field trips to factories, training grounds, naval yards, French frontier fortifications, and other points of interest.[36] Castex saw these expeditions as more than merely instructional. Traveling together would give the students something more valuable than the information they learned in lectures—valuable relationships. For Castex saw the college primarily as a means of insinuating within civilian and military agencies a group of men whose professional and personal connections would facilitate the national defense effort. The *esprit d'équipe* (team spirit) of the graduates of the CHEDN would compensate for the absence of a formal civil-military national defense staff.[37]

The centerpiece of the curriculum of the national war college was neither the lectures nor the visits to national defense installations but the annual national defense exercise. Designed to provide practice in executing a national mobilization, these exercises had to reflect actual French intentions and should reveal much about French thinking. It would, however, be unjust to draw too many conclusions, either about the college or about the government policies it exemplified, from the national defense exercise assigned to the participants in the first session. Lacking time to invent a comprehensive exercise, Castex had to settle for a problem, that of sending an expeditionary force to the Balkans, pressed upon him by the army general staff.

Scornfully dismissed by Marshal Pétain as nothing but an exercise for the fourth (logistics) bureau of the general staff, the first year's assignment required nothing of the civilian members of the course members and, indeed, fell largely on the army's eight representatives. Castex complained that it was certainly no different from the exercises done at the three Centres des Hautes Etudes and entirely lacking in the element of thinking "at the national level" that was supposed to be the trademark of the most advanced college. The director reminded the government in his annual report that future exercises ought to treat not only military matters but the concerns of the civilian members of the course. He suggested that the best source of such exercises would be the Secrétariat Général de la Défense Nationale, which could provide the college with pressing national defense questions of the sort appropriate to a national defense study group.

Castex recognized the difficulty of creating an authentic national-level exercise. The "Red" and "Blue" forces in conventional war games were hypothetical constructs assigned arbitrarily to map coordinates, but a nation could not, in Castex's words, be invented. To attempt to do so would be to create a fiction—incomplete, artificial, and irrelevant to the actual situation of France. He saw no point in creating imaginary countries or of studying hypothetical conflicts between Bolivia and Paraguay, Greece and Turkey, or Iraq and Persia. The only contingency worthy of study, a Franco-German war, was a proposition admitting of few and relatively predictable variations. "The range of logical possibilities" was, Castex noted, "very limited."[38] If the premise underlying a national-level defense exercise had to be authentic, so too did the solutions. Castex suggested that analogies between the college's exercises and ordinary war games were misleading. Whereas soldiers at the lesser war colleges could be encouraged to test their imaginations by developing ingenious solutions to military problems, national-level problems sought real answers to real questions.

Another highly revealing Castexian premise was that, although French war games were often done in "double action," with the competing parties reacting to one another's moves, Castex rejected double action as unsuitable for his purposes. Double-action exercises offered the closest simulation of war's dynamic interactions, but students at the CHEDN were being trained to implement highly detailed mobilization plans on a French timetable; responding to German actions was not their concern. The limited time available for the exercises was best used, in Castex's view, not in complicated double-action maneuvers but in more academic analyses of French requirements alone.[39]

The national defense problem set by the SGDN for the 1937–1938 class met some but not all of the director's hopes. Certainly the problem was large-scale, but the element of double action survived in what turned out to be a war game rather than a mobilization exercise, and it only marginally fulfilled Castex's ambition to integrate the activities of military and civilian personnel. The premise of the exercise was that an alliance composed of Germany, Hungary, and Bulgaria had determined to annex Czechoslovakia, Austria, and Yugoslavia while France, the members of the Petite Entente, the Soviet Union, and the republican government of Spain undertook to defend the status quo. Outwardly neutral, but alert to such opportunities for self-aggrandizement as might present themselves, was a third group including

Poland, Italy, the Spanish nationalists, and Japan, whose activities in Manchuria immobilized about a quarter of the Soviet forces. Genuinely neutral were the United Kingdom, Scandinavian and Baltic states, the Netherlands, Belgium, Greece, Turkey, Switzerland, and North and South America.

The exercise assumed a German surprise attack against Czechoslovakia in October 1937, aided by a National Socialist coup in Austria that allowed German troops to enter that country and to attack Czechoslovakia from the south. Pushed back into Bohemia, the Czechs were reinforced by Soviet aviation and, later, by a Soviet army corps transported across Rumania. Loyal to her treaty obligations, France seized a bridgehead on the right bank of the Rhine and advanced eastwards towards Mainz in the hope of distracting Germany from her successful campaign of conquest. French bombers supported the Czechs while the French Navy protected the transfer of colonial troops to the metropole. Poland massed her troops on the Silesian border in anticipation of a partition of Czechoslovakia from which she hoped to gain a common frontier with Hungary.

At the start of the second phase of the exercise, 15 March 1938, the Germans had occupied all of Czechoslovakia save the Tatra and the Ruthenian Carpathians, where Czech and Soviet troops continued to resist. Rumania had been despoiled of Transylvania, and the Yugoslav Army had been pushed southwards. In the west, the French held a continuous front on the rivers Ahr, Rhine, and Necker. Although some Soviet troops brought tardy support to Rumania, most troops defended their own frontiers or continued to fight against the Japanese. Initially taking a wait-and-see attitude towards France, Italy collected bargaining chips in the form of chunks of Croatia, Dalmatia, and Albania. As soon as a western shift of German forces increased the pressure on France, Italy commenced operations against the French forces in the Alps, the Mediterranean, and North Africa while the Spanish nationalists threatened to open yet another front in the Basque country. Teams from the national defense college were assigned to study aspects of this hypothetical scenario beginning thirty days after French mobilization. Their tasks included the whole spectrum of national defense concerns—military movements in the Balkans, recruitment and utilization of female labor, and diplomatic negotiations between France and neutral powers.[40]

Castex and others criticized the 1937–1938 exercise on the grounds that beginning a national mobilization exercise with the situation thirty days after the outbreak of war made little sense. The immediate outbreak of the war not only posed the more interesting problems but could be described in terms of known policies rather than hypothetical contingencies. The director also objected to the insertion into the exercise of the unrealistic assumption that France could act to succor Czechoslovakia or Poland. There is a striking tension here between the director's insistence that the exercise focus on the implementation of actual French policy and that same policy's requirement that the fiction of a possible French offensive to the east be maintained to reassure France's eastern allies. Thus, in spite of ample evidence to the contrary, future managers of the French war effort studied scenarios in which the Rome-Berlin axis did not exist and the Petite Entente acted as a unit in the French interest. However unrealistic the exercises based on such premises, they were in line with established policy—as they had to be. The element of national self-deceit that allowed the French to believe that, somehow, obligations would be met extended all the way to the Collège des Hautes Etudes de la Défense Nationale, whose students studied strategies that realists among them understood could not be carried out.

Criticism of the college's second national defense problem clearly influenced the authors of the next year's assignment, which was more realistic in formulation and less demanding in execution. The case was a European war postulated to begin October 1939 and was clearly meant to represent official analysis of the contemporary situation. The background included increasing threats by Germany to a dismembered Czechoslovakia, Hungarian aspirations to Czech and Rumanian territory, and the virtual disintegration of the Petite Entente. Germany's alliances with Japan and Italy exacerbated French difficulties by drawing the attention of the United States, the Soviet Union, and the British dominions away from Europe and by adding the Italian fleet to French naval problems in the Mediterranean Sea. The German plan, reflecting an unwillingness to re-create the Western Front of World War I, was to attack in Eastern Europe while bombing France to weaken her morale and to interfere with her mobilization efforts. France and Great Britain determined to block German absorption of Czechoslovakia and found themselves joined in their efforts by Egypt, the Soviet Union, and China, all three of whom, however, were distracted by threats from either Italy or Japan.

The distribution of forces for the third exercise acknowledged the drastic deterioration of France's strategic situation. Not only had Italy openly joined the list of likely foes, but the diminished reliability of the Petite Entente revealed itself in the assumption of Rumanian and Yugoslav neutrality. Austria, of course, had ceased to exist, and Czechoslovakia was no longer a viable military power. Spain, whatever her "Blue" sympathies, was constrained to neutrality by internal instability. The only significant improvement for France since the previous exercise was better relations with Great Britain, which allowed the participants in the exercise to assume that the two national general staffs would begin joint planning at the first sign of German action, when they would attempt to rally Poland and the Baltic states to the coalition.

Like the exercise itself, the solutions offered by the 1938-1939 class were noticeably more commensurate with French strength and with the realities of international relations than those of the first two years had been. There were no expeditionary forces to the east, no French incursions into German territory, and no assumptions of aid from beleaguered eastern allies. The students suggested instead an attack against Germany's Italian ally, and that only after considerable delay. Even this plan struck Admiral Castex as too ambitious, and so great was his alarm that he delivered an unscheduled lecture reminding the class of France's long-war strategy and, therefore, of her commitment to maintaining a defensive posture in all theaters of operations.[41]

The incident is revealing both of the admiral's adherence to official policy and of the dilemma faced by those of his students who had more aggressive ideas. The students who replaced the official defensive war plan with an invasion of Italy emulated their superiors in ignoring unpalatable truth. By pretending that a French offensive was a realistic possibility, the soldiers acquiesced in the prevailing refusal to ask the hard strategic questions that might have been the college's focus. Castex's admonishment of the "Red" team is particularly interesting because the war game of the Conseil Supérieur de la Guerre (CSG) that same year included an attack across the Alps towards Turin, whose failure the committee attributed not to a faulty conception but to insufficient French forces. Why did Castex chide his pupils for a similar, albeit larger, offensive?

The disparity in the rules by which the two war games were played highlights the different functions of the CHEDN and the CSG. Behind the latter's exercise lay the intention to persuade the government of France that reinforcements would have to be forthcoming if there was to be even the smallest departure from a rigidly defensive strategy, but the use of war games for experimentation with ideas or to argue points of policy was not within the brief of the national defense college. Its exercises were designed to introduce French leaders to actual plans, and participants were required to produce real, that is official, solutions. By its third year, the CHEDN had made its character clear. Pierre Cot, fearful in 1936 that the study of strategy at the proposed national defense college would usurp government prerogatives, would have been reassured.

Founded only three years before the beginning of World War II, the CHEDN contributed nothing to French performance in that conflict, but it remains an instructive artifact in the history of French national security policy. The debates that preceded the foundation of the college suggest that French commitment to the prosecution of a "total war" could not override the demands of the armed services for autonomy and of the civil government for firm control over national policy. Thus, the students at the national war college, the men being trained to execute the nation's war plan, would receive no opportunity to assess such vital elements of the plan as French alliances, manpower policies, or force structures. At the CHEDN, as in the nation as a whole, the government pretended to have a viable strategy and the armed forces pretended to be able to carry it out. Forgoing intrusion into the sphere of policy analysis, the CHEDN established itself as a high-level staff college, where officers were not trained to create strategy but to write the orders necessary to implement the intentions of their superiors.[42]

Thus, the college proved itself to be not an agency for instilling greater coherence in French defense policy but merely a passive component of the long-war strategy. French assumptions about the next war both justified the new institution and put it in blinders. The desire to integrate all elements of the nation in arms led to the establishment of a national defense college, which could not then offer any alternative strategic analysis. The dangerous assumptions behind the French plans for victory through national mobilization remained unchallenged as that strategy became a straitjacket whose bindings the CHEDN merely tightened.

That the CHEDN did not stimulate a reappraisal of French national security policy was not a failure of the institution itself but a consequence of a narrow mandate to which its director strictly adhered. In its official purpose of providing France with civilian and military organizers of the national defense effort, however, the new college also proved inadequate. The problem was a simple one of numbers, especially on the civilian side. After the first year, in which ten civilian functionaries attended the college, Castex recommended an increase in the civilian contingent to seventeen. For, he argued, at the original rate of one representative per ministry per year, fifty years would be required to establish a national defense cadre within the most important ministries, a calculation that assumed remarkable longevity among bureaucrats. Fifty years was indeed too long to await the appearance of a trained national defense staff, but so, too, was the twenty-five years required if the number of civilian participants were doubled.[43] The failure to address this question from the very beginning suggests that all concerned tacitly accepted that France lacked the manpower for a larger program and that the grand visions of the founders of the CHEDN would remain illusory. The blind eye proponents turned to the college's inability to populate the national administration with defense experts was yet another case of wishful thinking overriding sober analysis.

The national organization law and the CHEDN were two microcosms of French national security planning, products of the belief that the next war would be a contest of mobilized nations for which France was uniquely suited. Both demonstrated the sad truth that an effective national security policy was easier to demand in theory than to hammer out in a democratic political process. Although failed efforts at national mobilization, they were not contemptible ones, and they provide a salutary reminder of the difficulties of translating ideas into action.

3
Training the Peacetime Army

The preceding chapters emphasize the impediments to creating the institutions demanded by French interpretations of total war and the nation in arms. The resulting weaknesses in French national security policy contributed to the disasters of May and June 1940, but they alone do not account for the French defeat. In September 1939, however imperfect its national mobilization arrangements, France fielded a large and well-equipped army against which many German generals thought the Wehrmacht could achieve nothing better than a "costly stalemate."[1] The French collapse the following spring has to be explained in terms of what happened on the battlefield itself: in terms of strategy, of doctrine, or of the fighting quality of the army. Thus, one can argue that the French Army failed because Germany achieved a battlefield advantage by superior strategy, because the French Army's operational doctrine was less effective than the Wehrmacht's, or because poor training and leadership prevented French soldiers from employing their doctrine effectively.[2]

All three of these claims are true, but none of them tells the whole story. Although General Gamelin's Belgian strategy left his army hard-pressed to counter the unexpected German drive through the Ardennes, French forces were not so overmatched in numbers or materiél as to have been unable to recoup their strategic mistake through operational success. Because the French defeat resulted more directly from battlefield failure than from bad strategy, it is tempting is explain the outcome of the campaign by making invidious comparisons between French and German operational doctrine. The remainder of this book will indeed focus on doctrine, but from a somewhat different point of view. Instead of asking why the French Army failed to produce the same answers to the military questions of the interwar period that the Germans did, it will explain why French doctrinal development took its own particular—not peculiar—path.

Just as the national security policies created by real and complicated nations often fail for real and complicated reasons to meet the needs of the situation, military doctrines are produced by individual armies whose unique problems make it pointless to argue that any military doctrine is correct in the abstract and ought therefore to be adopted by contemporary armies. To understand an army's choice of doctrine, one must investigate its range of options, one must understand that army itself. The next two chapters provide the foundation for the analysis of French doctrine in Chapters 5 and 6 by outlining the nature of French military recruitment, organization, and training. Their immediate object is to show how the structure of the French Army both accounts for its doctrine and explains why that army chose to live with doctrinal shortcomings rather than to undertake the reforms that hindsight suggests might have improved French chances in the event of war. Although they serve directly to explain the nature of French doctrine, these chapters also seek to undermine the assumption that poor doctrine was the root cause of French defeat. Having seen the magnitude of French deficiencies in training and leadership, one must wonder whether the French doctrine failed because it was inherently flawed or because it had to be employed by an army unready for war.

The military organization and recruitment laws passed in 1927 and 1928 provided France officially with two different armies—the metropolitan and the colonial—with the metropolitan army divided into active and reserve components.[3] The peacetime active army—composed of professional officers and noncommissioned officers, men who reenlisted after completing their obligatory service, and the conscripts of the semiannual contingents—was responsible for the immediate defense of the national territory and for the training of the conscripts who filled its ranks.[4] The tasks of organizing, training, and mobilizing reserve troops were delegated to a separate system of reserve mobilization centers so that, although it was hardly ready for war, the active army could at least concentrate its energy on training active-duty personnel. In fact, however, the separation of active and reserve forces implied in the army laws was impracticable. Resources for reserve training did not exist outside the active army, and, in any case, separation violated the legislators' intention that soldiers, active and reserve, should train in the units in which they would fight. In any case, the active army lacked the manpower to act independently of its reserve elements.

The most obvious constraint on French military training was the brief duration of the conscript's active service obligation, which was reduced from three years to eighteen months by legislation promulgated on 1 April 1923.

The army organization law of 13 July 1927 further reduced the period of military service to twelve months, beginning with the class of 1930. The twelve- and eighteen-month regimes did not please the army, but more pernicious was the practice of inducting recruits every six months, so that training had to be organized to meet the needs of two or three separate groups of soldiers. One-year service was an imperative political response to the postwar mood; biannual incorporation of recruits ensured that France was always defended by at least half a contingent of trained men. Combined, these two premises were a serious obstacle to military training.[5]

Biannual incorporation allowed the professional cadres only six months to turn recruits into soldiers before the basic training cycle recommenced with a new group of conscripts, even though no one had forgotten that nine or ten months of training had proved necessary during World War I.[6] Moreover, the presence within every unit of men at different levels of training disrupted tactical organization. From 1923 to 1930, the combination of two annual incorporations and an eighteen-month period of active service forced the army to deal at any one time with three different sets of soldiers—recruits, oldsters, and veterans (*récrues, anciens,* and *veterans*)—who had either to be mixed within units or separated from one another.

Each solution had its disadvantages. Mixing the three groups throughout companies and battalions produced larger tactical formations for training but reduced every unit's skill level to that of the raw recruit, thereby trapping the older men into a repetition of basic training. The problem could be reduced by separating the trained soldiers for advanced exercises and specialist studies—or to perform the housekeeping tasks that decimated French formations—only at the cost of dissolving the tactical units. An alternate scheme organized each semester's inductees into homogeneous companies that remained together throughout their active-service period. Although this method spared trained men from an endless loop of basic training, neither tactical training nor unit *esprit* existed above the company, and the cadres had little time to spare for the oldster and veteran companies. Maintaining separate companies of first-, second-, and third-semester soldiers also made for impractical disparities in company size, for the number of recruits varied widely from one incorporation to the next, fall contingents usually being much larger than spring ones.[7]

Upon the instructions of the minister of war, three different organizational patterns were tested in 1923 and 1924 by troops in the twentieth military region. In the first half of 1923, each battalion contained separate companies of recruits, oldsters, and veterans. The second incorporation of 1924 combined the three groups within each company but segregated the battalion's recruits into a temporary training company for basic instruction. The first incorporation of 1924 maintained the mixed companies but left recruit training to be carried out within the company. The first system—that of distinct recruit, oldster, and veteran companies—proved superior for peacetime training but was deemed unacceptable in an army preparing for war. The manifest advantages of retaining men in the same company and under the same leaders during their active-duty period did not outweigh the problem that battalions organized in this manner dissolved at the outbreak of war, when their recruit companies stayed behind for further training and were replaced by reservists. Although the second method retained the necessary three companies, whose untrained members were replaced by reservists upon mobilization, the segregation of the recruits for training undermined the integrity of the companies. Thus, General Penet, commander of the twentieth region, advocated the third arrangement, in which all training took place within the company, on the grounds that it brought the highest return in unit cohesion and morale even though the training never went beyond section level and the cadres, who had to recommence basic training every six months, never profited from the opportunity to instruct troops in higher-level tactics.[8]

Two other organizations were tried in 1925, both based on paired companies within battalions (with the third company to be filled in wartime by reservists).[9] The first system, instituted in the spring, established that one company of each battalion was composed of equal numbers of recruits and veterans while the other company, only half-strength, contained all of the second-semester men. Every six months a new recruit contingent joined the half-strength company, whose original members were now veterans. The other company, reciprocally, shrunk to half-strength as its erstwhile recruits became oldsters and its third-semester contingent returned to civilian life. On the same pattern, machine-gun units alternated sections within a single company and cavalry units alternated platoons within squadrons. Lack of vehicles militated against such a system for tank units, whose recruits were distributed among all units.[10] The defects of the paired system were glaring. Administratively awkward because each company had to double its size and then shrink again during the semiannual transformations, it allowed very little scope for tactical training because the only homogeneous unit at any given time was the half-strength company of second-semester men. For those veterans not enrolled in specialist courses, the third semester of service was largely wasted in fatigue duties and coaching the recruits.

The second contingent inducted in 1925 was also placed in paired companies, but this time the recruits were in one company and the second and third semester contingents combined in another. Because it produced a wartime battalion of one company of trained members of the contingent, one company of reservists, and one untrained company to be left in its depot, this pattern exacerbated the weaknesses General Penet had identified in the twentieth region in spring 1923. Moreover, unit cohesion was not served by a system that shifted men into a company of strangers after their first six months of training.[11] Although the adoption of twelve-month service reduced the number of conscript contingents to two, the problem of simultaneously training recruits and veterans remained and the army proved unable to adopt a uniform policy until 1935, when commanders were instructed to separate recruits and veterans by sections within each company.[12] This organization made the section the largest unit available for tactical exercises during much of the training year.

The sort of practical obstacles that hindered unit training affected the instruction of individuals as well. In principle, each soldier's active-duty experience consisted of four months of basic training within his company, two months of battalion-level exercises in which the newly trained recruits were integrated with the older conscripts, four months of advanced or specialist training, and a second two-month exercise period including maneuvers at a training camp. This ideal, which compares not unfavorably to the training regimen authorized for the Wehrmacht at the end of the 1930s, bore no relation to the reality imposed by biannual incorporation, sparse professional cadres, and a chimerical twelve-month calendar.[13] Only the four-month recruit training period came close to meeting requirements, for it was there that the cadres focused their attention, to the detriment of advanced training for the "veterans." Those veterans not enrolled in specialist courses did housekeeping or clerical tasks or helped to instruct recruits in skills that they themselves had hardly mastered.[14] They were kept busy, but often at tasks with no military value. An American observer noted the large number of men released from training for "special duty and trick jobs."[15] Unless called upon to serve in ad hoc *unités de march* for the instruction of reservists or officers, second-semester men were required to join in training exercises only one or two days a week. Thus, complained the commanding general of the Twenty-third DI, his division consisted not of regiments but of "recruit schools."[16] The problem was worse in the cavalry units, where recruits had priority for the available mounts. On the whole, General Billotte estimated that military skills actually deteriorated during the second semester of service.

Like the specialist training, the two periods of the higher-level exercises were less constructive than advertised. Because training camps large enough for useful maneuvers were usable only in the warmer half of the year, one of the two periods had to be spent in garrison. Units were in a position to make the most effective use of training camps only at the end of the last month of each semester, generally May and September, but they had to take the slots offered to them. The allotment of two months per semester to battalion-level exercises assumed a twelve-month training year. Critics were quick to point out, however, that, thanks to administrative requirements, holidays, leave periods, and other distractions, the six months mandated for recruit training shrank in practice to four or five months.

General Billotte, dispatched by Weygand in 1934 to assess conditions in the interior regions, described initial recruit training as satisfactory but noted that late convocations, excessive leave, and illness reduced the actual number of training days during the nominal four months to an average of between eighty and eighty-four.[17] For many of the individual soldiers, the number of training days was even smaller. Of 250 recruits in the Forty-first Artillery Regiment, 11 participated in fewer than one-fourth of the training sessions, 33 in fewer than one-half, and 75 in fewer than three-fourths.[18] In the Forty-first Artillery Regiment, 34 of 250 recruits missed all of the group instruction and 54 received less than half. Illness was institutionalized in the training calendar of the Fifteenth Chasseur Battalion, whose Christmas leave was always followed by a ten-day quarantine in barracks to stop the spread of scarlet fever, measles, and mumps brought back from home.[19]

So far was French training from meeting its objectives that, on one account, 18 percent of the riflemen in an average infantry regiment had never fired a rifle, 26 percent had never thrown a grenade, 70 percent did not know how to adjust a gas mask, and none had ever fired a pistol.[20] Memoirs by French reservists support the claim that French soldiers were not well-acquainted with their weapons. Jean-Paul Sartre describes the "respectful terror" with which a fellow soldier handled an "unloaded and obsolete" revolver, and Fernand Grenier reports that only two out of twenty men in his unit knew how to use the grenades that his unit received on 20 June 1940.[21] An American observer who spent three months with a tank regiment in 1933 reported that its 365–day calender year was diminished by a 22–day break between contingents, 20 days spent inducting and dismissing each contingent, 49 Sundays, 15 days annual leave, 35 days of agricultural and special leaves and passes, 10 days sickness, 50 days guard duty, and 30 days for national holidays and preparation for material inspections. With only 164 days remaining, the observer reported that "the conscripts while fairly well trained in technique are not well trained for combat."[22]

If recruit training taught little beyond individual skills, unit training was worse. The two months of unit training usually shrank to one, and even companies could not be organized at full strength because soldiers were detached to special duties as soon as they proved proficient at close-order drill.[23] According to an American observer, of eighty-one men in an obviously very short-handed company, the "average maximum" available for training was thirty-nine. The number of men present for company instruction during the months of August and September 1933, the harvest months in which cadres normally took their annual leave, was about eleven.[24] Understandably, the scant training time was not used to practice showmanship, and Billotte complained that the troops' performance on the parade ground contributed less to esprit de corps than to a sense of the ridiculous.

Even before the reduction of active service to twelve months, exercises demonstrated inadequate levels of training. General Weygand's report on maneuvers under his direction in September 1927 observed that the troops moved too slowly and stuck too close to one another. When halted under fire, they only vaguely pretended to dig in. Their efforts to conceal themselves from aircraft were inadequate—"the fog made them confident and their confidence lasted longer than the fog." Unit commanders ensconced in their command posts did not bother to establish contact with neighboring units or to reconnoiter the terrain. Liaison between infantry and artillery consisted of a telephone line between the respective commanders, not an attitude of cooperative effort. Weygand concluded that, because the troops were forgetting everything they had practiced, the expense and effort undertaken to organize the maneuvers were wasted.[25] The 1929 maneuvers were judged by an American observer to have been "hardly satisfactory."[26] He saw some improvement in the following year but reported that "objections to the one-year service laws were pretty general and the tendency was to excuse the failures on the grounds of an insufficient period of service."

Some observers, however, were impressed with the amount that French conscripts assimilated during their brief recruit training. Describing an exercise done largely by men with only five months of service, the military attaché from the United States noted that "the troops were careful in all matters of camouflage discipline, particularly against airplanes. . . . The physical condition of the troops seemed excellent. . . . In advancing, the troops used covered approaches or advanced by thin lines, rushing from cover to cover in which the soldiers used good judgment."[27]

In some units, at least, training was carried out with great attention to realism.

> The men in exercises really dig, and the camouflage of defensive works is excellent for the most part. . . . In approach march exercises small bridges and exposed places are crossed by individuals at a run, even when no enemy is known to be near. Signal communications men, carrying their equipment, advance and string wire in their daily exercise as if under fire, rushing and occasionally crawling. Blank ammunition is used in huge quantities to give an impression of war situations to the men. "Enemy" troops fired blank rounds at recruits to underscore mistakes.[28]

Noting that "the training for war is practical and few bad habits are inculcated in their soldiers which must be unlearned under fire," the American concluded that "in this respect we are far behind them."

Another American was so impressed by French maneuvers in July 1930 as to admit to feeling "grouchy" for days thereafter.

> Nothing was left to the imagination. Trenches, dug-outs, machine gun emplacements were *actually dug* and it was good hard rocky soil. . . . Their defense was so perfect, all their personnel from the battalion commander down functioned with such smoothness—knew their business so well and were so intensely interested—that I could not help contrasting them with us and this contrast didn't raise my spirit to say the least.

Afterward, the battalion marched back to camp actually singing: "The spirit displayed by these troops was difficult for me to understand. In war—yes, but on a peacetime maneuver—no!"[29]

Good will and hard work could, however, only mitigate, not cure, the consequences of a flawed organization. Even if the short period of service and rapid turnover of recruits had not encouraged an exclusive emphasis on individual skills, the tactical training in combat units was severely hindered by the absence of full-strength formations. The need to spread active units throughout France to provide training for the reservists organized by the reserve mobilization centers meant that the number of such units exceeded what France could man, and most formations were reduced to one-third of their personnel. Thus, regiments had to consolidate into battalions for field training while a nominal division could turn out for exercises only as a full-strength regiment. Even if such amalgamations could be achieved, they had their cost; in the acerbic words of one critic, "to create artificial units, one destroyed actual units."[30] The dispersal of units among the mobilization centers usually precluded such consolidation, however, and few soldiers ever served in a garrison containing more than a nominal battalion or ever trained in a unit above company size.[31] Reservists could fill some of the gaps, but only in those years when they were due for training and the legislature provided the necessary funds.[32] On the whole, the organization of the French Army allowed very little opportunity for exercises with large units, and it was the conclusion of the United States military attaché that "the training of units above the battalion in two-thirds of the 1st echelon divisions and in all of the 2nd echelon divisions will not be satisfactory. The entire 1st line army cannot be counted on at once to secure results commensurate with its numerical strength and equipment."[33]

The problems created by skeletonizing active formations in order to link them with mobilization centers underscore a failure to achieve the separation of recruit training from mobilization that was intended by the framers of the 1927 and 1928 army laws. In fact, it proved impossible to sustain a useful distinction between the two missions. The distribution of labor between active formations and mobilization centers made sense when it was a matter of, on the one hand, conscript training and, on the other, stockpiling equipment and preparing mobilization orders; it dissolved, however, when the matter at hand was reserve training. For training, although organized by the mobilization centers, had to be executed, at whatever inconvenience, by the active units. In the Seventeenth region, for example, a single understrength infantry regiment was responsible during 1938 for the convocation of 200 reserve officers and 4,500 men as well as for supervising *écoles de perfectionnement* for reserve officers and noncommissioned officers.[34] Reserve convocations were a heavy drain for several reasons: because they were so frequent, with reservists called up in driblets so as not to overload garrison accommodation; because they required instructors from the active contingent; and because they diverted the conscripts from their own training to fatigue duties on behalf of the reservists.[35]

Retaining the April 1935 contingent for eighteen months and the subsequent contingents for two years brought no immediate improvement in training and threatened to increase the number of separate contingents in the army to three and then to four, each at a different level of proficiency. To avoid chaos, Gamelin decreed that soldiers in the first semester of their second year were to assist the cadres with the instruction of recruits while the second-semester men of both years would be combined in training units. The scheme brought no substantive changes to the training program.[36] As it happened, however, although there were three different contingents in service from April to October 1936, the comparatively moderate chaos of a system with men in only two distinct states of readiness was restored in the spring of 1936 through the establishment of a single annual induction. If two-year service did not complicate training, however, neither did it ameliorate training deficiencies. The pattern of training remained unchanged, except that almost twice as much time was available to do the same amount of work.[37] Formations remained below strength because the extended service merely brought the half-size contingents of the "hollow years" to their normal inadequate level. Recruits and trained soldiers still could not be integrated into cohesive units, and the care and feeding of reservists continued to divert the attention of the cadres. Moreover, the opportunity for professional officers and noncommissioned officers to devote greater attention to training coincided with the reduction of their meager pay to such a level that financial hardship undermined their concentration on their instructional duties.[38]

The organizational problems that undermined French military training stemmed from political decisions about army size, duration of military service, and the relationship between active and reserve forces, matters upon which the soldiers of the Third Republic had to defer to the will of the French people. If longer service and annual incorporation were unobtainable, the army could only look for methods to improve the ability of conscripts to profit from their brief period of active service. One step, taken in 1929, was to raise the age of induction to twenty-one years on the theory that mature recruits would learn better and prove more resistant to the physical demands and health hazards of military life. This move, however, was only a palliative; what the army proposed was a comprehensive program of premilitary education to prepare recruits physically and emotionally for induction. Thus, the general staff qualified its acceptance of the one-year active service law with the stipulation that the change be accompanied by the creation of "the complete organization of military preparation."[39] Like other details left unfinished in the army reorganization laws, pre–military education remained unachieved, but it remained a perennial subject of discussion in the legislative army commissions. Advocates of pre–military training regularly reminded the government that the reintroduction of conscription in Germany had been conjoined with programs in schools, the Hitler Youth, the Labor Service, and various military-sport camps to insure the Wehrmacht a supply of physically and mentally hardened recruits.[40] Compulsory physical education programs in French schools remained, however, at the inadequate standard set by the physical education law of 1880, and all other pre-military training was voluntary. Only about one-tenth of young Frenchmen earned the *brevet de préparation militaire*. Some youngsters, especially in rural communes, lacked access to the necessary instruction and facilities, and others did not find the reward, the privilege of choosing one's regiment, worth the effort.[41] University students were eligible for the more intense two-year course for the *brevet de préparation militaire supérieure*, which qualified them upon induction for noncommissioned or commissioned officer training, but this program did nothing to improve the deficient fitness of the rank and file.[42]

The idea of universal and compulsory pre-military education found no more than a scattering of adherents in the political and financial climate of the 1930s. The cost of such a program repelled legislators of every stamp, most representatives of the Left opposed military infiltration into the school system, and the Right saw no value in a military education course handled by the proverbial socialist schoolmaster of the Third Republic.[43] There was, moreover, a disingenuousness in the army's demands, or rather mutterings, on the subject. When criticized, the army pointed to the short period of active service and hinted that, if extended service were impossible, pre-military education would be better than nothing. It never pressed the unpopular proposal, possibly for lack of resources, possibly for fear that pre–military training could become, in General Billotte's words, "the road to a militia."[44] The subject was brought up from time to time to excuse the failings of the short-service army and to remind the government both that it had reneged on the bargain behind the twelve-month service law and that some things might be harder to sell than an eighteen-month service law, not because the army had any desire to go into the business of physical education at boys' high schools.

The fundamental weaknesses of French military training came from the army's structure. For organizational reasons, the army could not simultaneously provide basic training for recruits and advanced work for the trained portion of the conscript contingent. Moreover, it could not train full-strength formations or provide much in the way of realistic tactical exercises for the skeleton units that served in their place. These were glaring flaws in an army that saw as its own strength the esprit de corps instilled in French conscripts during their period of active service.

Physical constraints on the effective training of conscripts exacerbated these organizational flaws. Garrisons often had neither proper firing ranges nor sufficient maneuver space; the former was a particularly serious problem for cavalry, artillery, and tank formations.[45] Under such circumstances, troops could accomplish realistic training only at the ten large and twenty-three small regional training camps, and even these could prove too small for realistic cavalry actions or for simultaneous infantry and artillery fire training.[46] For example, to ensure that shells landed within the boundaries of the Coetquidan Camp, even 75mm guns had to fire from outside the perimeter.[47] Before 1937, when a portion of Suippes camp was set aside for the purpose, France had no exercise ground suitable for fire training by armored vehicles. Plans to build a major armor camp at Lunéville had not yet been executed when World War II began.[48] Travel to exercises was time consuming, especially for units whose native region had no training camp. Because active formations, reserve convocations, large-scale maneuvers, and small-scale experimental exercises all competed for precious space at overused facilities, the regulation calling for all active troops to spend forty days in camp per year (and alpine units seventy-five days) was unrealistic.[49] The camps themselves, although deemed barely adequate in 1914, had received little money in the interwar years. Many of the living arrangements were unpleasant, and some were deplorable.

Along with inadequate training grounds came insufficient matériel. Although foreigners were impressed by the lavish expenditure of blank ammunition to add realism to training exercises, French commanders complained constantly of insufficient ammunition for training.[50] Allocations of both live and blank munitions were reduced after the budget cuts of 1932, and, at the September–October 1935 exercises at Mourmelon, two important new weapons, the new 25mm antitank gun and Hotchkiss 13.2mm machine gun, could not be fired at all.[51] Of the matériel that should have been delivered by 1 August 1938, the French Army had received only 35 percent of the 8mm cartridges, 56 percent of the 7.5mm rounds, 65 percent of the 25mm rounds, 66 percent of the 60mm rounds, and 55 percent of the grenades. At that time, the French Army had no 47mm antiaircraft shells, 50mm mortar rounds, and no shells for its 220mm, 240mm, and 280mm guns.[52]

Supplies available for training declined in the second half of the decade. Infantry ammunition allotments for 1937, 1938, and 1939 were only one-third, and artillery allotments only two-thirds, of those for 1936; moreover, safety standards were relaxed to allow the use of marginal ammunition.[53] Even in the comparatively happy days of 1936, however, riflemen in one regiment fired only ten rounds a week.[54] Presumably, shortages of ammunition spurred the French Army's pioneering use of motion pictures to simulate small arms training.[55]

The best weapons in the world, and some French models were exactly that, were wasted on troops who in 1940 had never used them before and whose commanders remained uncertain about their proper employment.[56] Most of the soldiers mobilized in 1939 had done their active service in units lacking modern tanks, 25mm or 47mm antitank guns, or the new 1934 model automatic rifle. Men assigned at the last minute to units newly equipped with the highly complicated B-1bis tank might have trained only with the ancient Renault FT Model 1917 Tank. For example, the Forty-seventh Tank Battalion joined General de Gaulle's new Fourth Armored Division in May 1940 without having practiced with its 47mm tank guns or having done any company-level tactical exercises.[57] The Laffly 75mm self-propelled antitank gun, which appeared only in late May 1940, was served by crews experienced, at best, with horse-drawn antitank guns.[58] The Lafflys proved remarkably effective, but not all untested equipment worked so well. The First Light Mechanized Division went into battle in May 1940 with SOMUA (Society d'Outillage Mécanique et d'Usinage d'Artillerie) tanks whose newly installed radio sets lasted only until the first firing of the 47mm gun, when they were pulverized by the ejected shell casings.[59] Radios were also a problem for the First Armored Division, which received sets for company commanders' tanks in spring 1940 only to discover the turret of the H-39 to be too small to hold both the radio and the 37mm gun.[60] As one consequence of using unfamiliar equipment, crews ignorant of the B tanks' emergency fuel reservoirs prematurely abandoned machines that appeared to be out of fuel.[61]

Historians have paid too little attention to the special problems of distributing new material to an army composed largely of reservists, but, more remarkably, contemporaries also largely ignored them. As a lecturer at the CHEDN pointed out, the division of labor among the various bureaus allowed the problem to remain unresolved.[62] Of course, the active-reserve split created problems in both directions, and men who graduated from the *disponibilité* to ill-equipped reserve regiments were expected to use older equipment as unfamiliar to them as the newer models were to the reservists.[63]

If the tank crews did not know their own tanks, it is hardly surprising that armor training proved very deficient both at the tactical level and at that of combined arms.[64] Even the tank school at Saint-Maxient lacked machines for training.[65] A maneuver ground for mechanized exercises, albeit a poor one, did become available in February 1939,[66] but even the elements of France's future armored divisions had never exercised under a divisional organization when the war began. Only one B tank battalion had trained as a unit, two others had done company-level exercises, and the fourth received its tanks only at the start of mobilization. As for the infantry units that might be called upon to coordinate actions with tank units in the framework of the methodical battle, they never saw a tank more advanced than the ponderous Renault FT, unless, as was the case for the Seventy-first Infantry Regiment (RI), a generous local tank battalion commander agreed to participate in an infantry formation's exercise.[67] Mourmelon Camp received a tank battalion on 28 March 1940 to provide week-long familiarization courses for infantry divisions,[68] but this was "familiarization" only in a general sense because the unit chosen, the Seventh Tank Battalion (BCC), was one of only two in the entire French Army equipped with FCM tanks.[69]

Although Colonel de Lattre complained that regimental training in 1936 was hindered by the need to use one armored car to represent two or four and by the lack of radio communication with supporting aircraft, his 151st RI was probably better off than most units.[70] So many units lacked motorcycles for the instruction of their reconnaissance units that, in 1937, groups of ten machines were rotated among the regional camps.[71] Such palliatives notwithstanding, 45 of the 125 men in one squadron of a corps reconnaissance group had never ridden a motorcycle when the unit mobilized for war in 1939.[72]

Training grounds, tanks, guns, and ammunition are obvious military necessities, but other shortages also impeded training.[73] Lack of gasoline was a perpetual hindrance to maneuvers, as was the dearth of vehicles.[74] Possessing only about 30,000 trucks, the French Army would in the event of war demand 300,000 more—as well as cars, tractors, and motorcycles—from civilian sources. Although necessary for an army that could neither purchase nor maintain the huge number of vehicles required for war, this system based on wartime requisition was unsuitable for peacetime activities. The lack of horses often reduced the amount of artillery that could be employed in exercises,[75] and the Renault FT tanks could not be employed properly without the trucks required to move them.[76] In the absence of mobile field kitchens, French troops on some maneuvers had to subsist on the cold rations from their haversacks while others had their congealing meals trucked out to the field. The most solicitous commanders authorized long lunch breaks for a return to camp, while the least compassionate let their soldiers go hungry. Tolerable during brief maneuvers, none of these expedients met the requirements of a drawn-out campaign. In a worse manifestation of French logistical weaknesses, horses went without fodder for the duration of exercises, and lack of prevision in this area may explain why so many requisitioned horses died of starvation during the war.[77]

The reliance on requisitioned vehicles created problems that went beyond their unavailability for peacetime training, for the civilian economy provided few reasonable facsimiles of specialized military vehicles like communications trucks.[78] Moreover, civilian firms sometimes protected their more valuable transportation assets by purchasing second-hand vehicles solely to be foisted off on the army, a practice that may help to explain why 40,000 vehicles required repair within a few months of requisition.[79] One French officer complained that his unit received vehicles so old that "it would have been cruel to demand further effort from them."[80] Ten of the thirty-five vehicles requisitioned by another unit had been driven more than 100,000 km., but the officer offering this observation, who describes the entire requisition process as scandalous, admits that soldiers could be blamed for choosing the worst vehicles in order to appease civilians.[81] Maintenance, repair, and training were complicated by the baffling variety of vehicle types with which units had to contend. One unit received forty-two models of vehicle from twenty-four different manufacturers.[82] Supply trains that resembled gypsy camps and circus parades of trucks emblazoned with commercial advertisements produced a decidedly unmartial atmosphere.[83] Some 30,000 vehicles designated for wartime requisition never materialized.[84]

The most mundane material wants interfered with peacetime training. Some units could not provide soldiers with a second pair of shoes or trousers and cancelled exercises in inclement weather because their men would not have dry clothes to wear afterward.[85] Conscripts were offered reimbursement for supplying their own boots, belts, shirts, wool socks, spoons and forks, and blankets.[86] Reservists were encouraged to wear their own shoes for training periods, but most chose to suffer with ill-fitting army issue as the reimbursement would not replace a decent pair of civilian shoes.[87] An armor battalion inspected in December 1939 proved not only to be without its allotment of tanks and vehicles but also poorly housed and inadequately fed. Items in short supply included beds, uniforms, boots, leather jackets, helmets, water bottles, and the goggles essential for motorcyclists. Rations were inadequate even in the officers' mess, and the men ate cold meals because of the distance between the kitchen and the barracks.[88] For an economical evaluation of the material defects of the French army, one need only note that even after the 14-million-franc procurement program of 1937–1940 had been supplemented in 1938 with an additional 12 million francs, the allocation deemed necessary after Germany's annexation of Czechoslovakia was more than 64 million francs. This "eloquent sum," remarks Pierre Hoff, reveals "how much the French army fell short of being a truly modern army."[89]

Whatever other necessities were in short supply, the French army appears never to have suffered from a shortage of paper—or at least of paperwork. French battalions were "enmeshed in a web of administration": a movement order at regimental level filled more than thirty pages.[90] Worries about the ability of reserve officers to carry out their assignments led to "long and voluminous orders dotting the i's and crossing the t's" and to regulation books that approached the size of the *Larousse* dictionary.[91] Every training operation involved the production of multiple copies of long orders, and typewriters were rare.[92] Such distractions did not vanish with the outbreak of war, and Captain Barlone complained of being "deluged with paper work." Receiving "20 to 40 papers a day" dealing with "changes of one or two centimes in the scale of charges for coal, firewood, soap, candles, rations in kind or allowance" convinced him that "behind the lines everyone is expending his energy upon absurd and insignificant details."[93] Alistair Horne points out that "Gamelin's G.Q.G. would issue instructions nineteen pages long on the conduct of patrol actions, while officers at the front wondered why on earth it was not holding exercises to simulate dive-bomber attacks."[94] Every patrol, Goutard insists, "necessitated such a cascade of meticulous orders, and involved, after the operation, the making out of such a multiplicity of reports, vindications, and explanation of the least casualty or loss, as to set the whole military hierarchy buzzing from top to bottom."[95] Among the writing assignments that diverted Lieutenant Felsenhardt from more profitable labors were reports persuading higher authorities that missing weapons had not been stolen but rather incinerated in barns inadvertently set on fire by freezing soldiers. The amount of paperwork required was, he asserts, "difficult to imagine," but "the general staff was an accounting school and, like our entire bureaucratic corps, the best in the world."[96]

Bureaucrats could be forgiven if their efforts aimed at alleviating the conditions that led French soldiers to build open fires in barns or at streamlining operations in the field, but "the bureaucratic mentality that ruled in the army" reflected a diversion of energy from training.[97] One observer reported that "lack of attention to details in preparing exercises was the rule, not the exception," and treated as characteristic an "interesting but not instructive" debacle involving simultaneous attempts by three different platoons to attack the same ground.[98]

More pernicious to the standard of training than administrative distractions, however, were the shortcuts taken in training exercises either to dodge questions about the efficacy of current matériel or tactical doctrine, to avoid inconvenience, or to produce satisfactory performances for watching notables. Major maneuvers, after all, were not only training exercises but performances designed to impress foreign armies, domestic politicians, and the French population as a whole, and the press cooperated in disseminating accounts of military maneuvers intended to foster confidence rather than introspection. Military correspondents emphasized the spectacular: thus *Action Française*'s purple description of an early mechanized operation— "mastodons spitting fire, machine guns sweeping the earth, bombardments by 75mm cannon, fighter and reconnaissance squadrons, aerial combat, the tableau lacked nothing"; and *Le Temps*'s observation that the Mailly exercises of 1935 ended, in the presence of the president of the republic, with an attack by a light mechanized division (DLM) and counterattack by assault tanks—"an impressive spectacle which replaced for those present the cavalry charges of before the war."[99] In maneuvers at the Valdehon Camp in 1938 the final attack would have been judged a failure had the authorities not wanted to end with a dramatic, rather than credible, spectacle and to reward the efforts of the attacking troops. The scenario may have been dubious, admitted a correspondent, but the attack by the Eighth Regiment of Tirailleurs Moroccans gave "great satisfaction to the cameramen present."[100] To ensure that public exercises gave the right impression, units were instructed that, "in the presence of strangers," they were to avoid "overly complex problems or those not yet completely understood," in other words, serious efforts at training.[101] Similarly, Minister of National Defense Daladier warned the organizer of an armored exercise at Metz in 1939 that the operations should be kept as simple and as spectacular as possible in view of the attendance of a military attaché from the United States.[102]

The French were sensitive to charges that maneuvers were exercises in public relations rather than training. General Héring, who directed the September 1937 "grand maneuvers" attended by British Secretary of State for War Leslie Hore-Belisha, Chief of the Imperial General Staff Cyril Deverell, and a host of other foreign dignitaries, insisted in what *Le Temps* described as "expressive" language that "I don't want a show for the black king."[103]

Deverell's report, however, stressed French efforts to make a good impression, efforts vindicated in Hore-Belisha's enthusiastic assessments of his host's army as "invincible,"[104] "an army that cannot be beaten,"[105] and manifesting "the highest degree of perfection which human genius can attain."[106] Shortly thereafter, Deverell's experience as a guest at similar German exercises led him to reassess the French hospitality that he had recently praised with such enthusiasm. Now Deverell saw French war games as "subservient to an ulterior aim—the dominant desire to impress in every way possible the need for those present to cooperate with France." For the Germans, by contrast, "business came first: the military operations were paramount in importance."[107]

Public relations concerns are one explanation for the lack of realism in French military training, but concerns of comfort and convenience played a role as well. For example, when a dawn attack featured in an exercise posed "the difficult problem of producing twelve tanks from the edge of a thick wood,"[108] the armor unit was spared the ordeal of groping through the trees in the dark by a command decision that dawn on that summer morning would take place at 0930. The infantry involved in the exercise also eschewed the highly educational discomfort of nocturnal operations, choosing to bed down for the night instead of reconnoitering the obstacles before it. The British delegation present was unimpressed with an exercise that was "little more than a parade movement, all the difficulties of initial deployment being evaded" and reported that "in actual fact [the attack] would almost certainly have resulted in complete failure."[109] Things were no different four years later, when, in a war game observed by an American officer, "the Blue forces were adjudged to have reached all objectives by noon of the ninth, more probably because it was desired to execute the second phase of the maneuvers on the 10th than because the attack had been really successful."[110]

Distant problems could be ignored, but, in accordance with Samuel Johnson's well-known observation about the behavioral consequences of the expectation of hanging, one would expect to see a powerful concentration of French military minds during the respite granted them between September 1939 and May 1940. Yet although production of matériel took on a noticeable urgency, training did not. Even when the abominable weather of winter 1939–1940 permitted soldiers to exercise, priority was given to building whatever fortifications could be constructed in frozen ground. Such was the emphasis on the building of defensive works that only half a day per week was set aside for training in the First and Second Armies, so little time that General Ruby of the Second Army reported that, as late as March 1940, "many infantry units had still not fired a rifle and have never used their anti-tank and anti-aircraft weapons."[111] With snow falling on the northeast frontier until late March 1940, planned training and lecture programs were abandoned and soldiers spent their days huddled around barracks' stoves; one soldier summed up the winter with the observation that "militarily speaking, we did literally nothing."[112] On another front, the official week of the Seventy-first Infantry Regiment (Nineteenth DI) in spring 1940 contained five days of work, one day of training, and one day of rest.[113] Things were no different on the Belgian frontiers, where a soldier in the Second DI disdainfully compared his sections's morning routine of stationary stretching exercises to the "little" fitness routine broadcast on peacetime morning radio. Except for requiring attendance at formation at 1100, noncommissioned officers left soldiers alone in the interest of avoiding "incidents" (*histoires*).[114]

Orders substituting make-work projects and recreation for training mystified their recipients as much as they have historians who can describe but not satisfactorily explain the "prolonged inactivity" that "fostered a state of mind akin to that of peacetime."[115] A contemporary critic is probably right to emphasize the high command's anxiety about low spirits among the troops, but not everyone agreed that the best remedy was, "give them theater, give them cinema, improve the mess and you will see morale go up."[116] Captain Barlone, who had been pleased with the effects of training done in September, complained in his diary of the army's later inertia: "We are doing all we can to keep up the spirits of the troops, in spite of the inaction. Cinema, once a week in billets, football teams everywhere, etc. Fine, but the best thing would be to carry on with training and work the men hard instead of letting them rust. These are, however, the orders from G.H.Q., so they must be obeyed."[117] Another junior officer, who explicitly blamed left-wing political leaders for the army's inaction, complained afterwards that "our soldiers might have been asked during those eight months to work relentlessly night and day on the building of huge antitank ditches between the North Sea and Switzerland." Private Sadoul, a radio operator in the Thirteenth DI, noted that radio courses were begun but ceased to meet within a week, even though the adjutant continued regularly to relay to division headquarters not only the program of instruction but lists of men who had allegedly qualified as radio operators. In fact, however, the men lost their skills for lack of practice. From mobilization until the end of April, Sadoul's radio company obeyed the convention of establishing daily frequencies, call signs, and communications schedules, but "these bureaucratic exercises did not correspond to any reality. The command posts existed only on paper, the radio sets were deployed in the barns of Hirsingue, and the men were playing cards in their billets." From the end of April, moreover, when the lieutenant who had performed this task moved to other duties, the radio posts no longer received frequencies or call signs and the commencement of active hostilities found the units incapable of establishing communications.[118] The soldiers of the Second Regiment of Engineers spent months of the phony war building beds and tables for their barracks, taking time for military drill only once in anticipation of a general's visit.[119] In the meantime, obvious tasks remained undone. For example, only in May 1940 did the commander of the Seventy-first Alpine Battalion decide that French engineers ought to do something about the fact that his unit's water supply came from across the Italian border.[120]

Soldiers who might have been training or building fortifications received regular leave, or, if leave was not granted them, took it anyway.[121] The generous leave policies proved particularly costly whenever one man's absence impeded the training of a whole unit, but General Bruneau's decision that the tank crews of his First Armored Division (DCR) would take leave together was revoked by higher authorities.[122] According to Captain de Vibraye, the percentage of his company away on leave at any given time rose over the course of the winter from seven to ten and eventually to twelve.[123] Leave not only disorganized combat units and distracted young soldiers with thoughts of home but tied up transport in ferrying men to and from railway stations.[124]

Men not on leave wasted their time playing cards, drinking, and writing letters. As the army's sense of purpose evaporated, soldiers bathed less frequently, stopped shaving, and ceased to clean their barracks. A lieutenant at the front describes the pervasive lassitude—"an ennui which slowly sapped the morale of the most resolute"—among men who found nothing to do but play belotte, drink, trap animals, or fish with grenades in the Meuse.[125] The commander of the 140th Régiment d'infanterie alpine (RIA) wrote on 2 January 1940 that his troops lived in "an ambiance of peace" and "had the preoccupations of peacetime."[126] The meaninglessness of frontline activities sapped the troops' spirits. As one officer describes it, "in September, 1939, the French farmer or peasant was ready and willing to fight and give his life for his country. He was not so ready, however, to remain inactive in trenches or billets for eight long months with the feeling that his fields were abandoned and being neglected."[127] On the whole, after eight months of "phony war," General Menu thought that "the units were scarcely better in May

1940 than in September 1939," and "some would even say, with sadness in their hearts, that they were worse."[128]

Training considerations add a crucial element to the long-standing argument over whether or not the French Army was materially prepared for the May 1940 campaign. Afterward, military apologists for French failure joined with right-wing politicians and critics of the Third Republic to denounce the government's failure to provide the army with the tools of war. In their own defense, the politicians responsible insisted that they had granted, even exceeded, the War Ministry's every request, indeed that military budgets had been higher under the Popular Front than the army itself had proposed and that the Ministry of War had failed to take advantage of the credits available.[129] "No production was delayed or interrupted by lack of money," insisted Contrôleur Général Jacomet.[130] Historians, bolstered by statistics, have tended to take the side of the politicians because, in May 1940, the army possessed virtually all of the tanks, artillery, mortars, and antitank guns it had ordered during the 1930s and its matériel was not inferior, either in quantity or in quality, to that of the Wehrmacht.[131] As a French officer wrote in 1939, "the French infantry is, at the present day, the one equipped with the most modern and most efficient armament . . . it has all the material means to retain the rank conquered in 1918: the first."[132]

Although the French had the military hardware they needed when the Germans attacked, much of the equipment available in 1940 did not exist for training purposes before the war. Of the 9,980 60mm mortars on hand in May 1940, only 1,050 had been produced by 1 January 1937 and 4,170 by 1 September 1939. Only 1,800 of 6,000 25mm antitank guns and none of the 1,280 47mm antitank guns were in service at the beginning of 1937.[133] What new equipment did exist before the war was too precious to be worn out in an endless series of training exercises, and, in the interest of preserving the top-of-the-line matériel, most training camps were allocated only a single company of light tanks.[134]

The connection between inadequate training and battlefield failure would be revealed in the 1940 campaign. For example, by May 1490, the French Army had developed a doctrine for the employment of medium tank divisions with infantry, but the new armored divisions organized in the winter and spring of 1940 had had little opportunity to learn to employ the newly authorized methods.[135] Such, at least, was the verdict of Twenty-first Corps commander Flavigny, who had to decide on 14 May 1940 how to combine General Brocard's Third Armored Division with the Third Motorized Infantry Division (DIM) in a coordinated attack towards Sedan. Skeptical of the armored division's ability to fight as a unit, Flavigny ordered Brocard to disperse his tanks among the local infantry forces so as to cover a broad expanse of territory.[136] As Doughty points out, Flavigny was influenced in his decision not only by his own impressions of the Third DCR's tardy approach that day but by his observations of an exercise by the Second DCR on 8 May 1940.

None of these hindrances to preparing French troops for combat—not the skeletal units, the brevity of the effective training year, the army's material deficiencies, the burdens of administration, or the shortcuts taken in training exercises—was unknown to French officers, whose own reports provide much of the evidence for these very problems. But the complaints were fewer than the situation warranted and were increasingly offset by analyses that softened specific technical criticisms with vague but comforting claims about the high morale of French troops. As war became more likely, the temptation to seek encouragement from the exercises grew. Thus, General Héring derived "strong moral reinforcement" from his assessment of the high morale of the troops he commanded in the 1937 "grand maneuvers."[137]

The tension in the minds of French soldiers between the desire to remedy weaknesses and to deny their existence stands out in a memoir from the Thirty-sixth DI.[138] Even as the officers who took part in the division's last prewar cadre exercise of September 1938 took pride in their unit's record of accomplishment, they agonized over the question "Are we ready?" At La Courtine in 1936, they remembered, General Dufieux had called their division "one of the finest units in the French Army," and the director of infantry, General François, had denied that he had ever seen a more impressive spectacle than a special performance by its bands. In the same year, Gamelin had rated the Thirty-sixth DI as "exceptional" in the southwest maneuvers. They did not forget, however, that the general's praise had been directed to the division's music, and their pride did not efface uneasiness about missing antitank guns, radios, and vehicles, the uncertain morale of the reservists, the uneven quality of requisitioned material, and the unit's lack of training with aircraft and tanks. The officers of the division also recognized that the maneuvers in which they had scored such high marks had involved routine problems and unreal conditions, that the umpires had prevented any exercise of initiative, and that the Blue force only poorly simulated the behavior of the Wehrmacht.

Examination of the organization and training of the French active army between the wars not only goes a long way to explain why that army collapsed so completely before an adversary that had no overwhelming material advantage but suggests why visible defects remained unmended. The point is not that French soldiers ought to have been better trained but that a close look at the circumstances in which training took place reveals a "tyranny of the mundane"—the sheer organizational and physical impediments to doing what the army acknowledged it had to do. Undoubtedly the French Army, like every such organization, had some men for whom the slavery imposed by skeleton units, material deficiencies, and administrative burdens seemed a liberation from the demands of real soldiering. For those men, however, who chafed at the physical frictions that blocked efforts to train for war, there were no good choices. To complain that the job required more men, time, and material than the existing institutions provided could both evoke queries about one's own competence and undermine the morale upon which French leaders put so much faith. The alternative was to suppress well-founded worries, to employ the quality of "determination" that Clausewitz describes as an antidote to the frictions of war. Morale may have been slim compensation for physical deficiencies of the French Army, but it was the kind of "faint light" that a determined commander would have to use "to limit the agonies of doubt and the perils of hesitations when the motives for action are inadequate."[139]

4
The Unready Reserve

"Loose the *Reichswehr* into the middle of the French militia as it is in the process of concentrating on the first day of the war, and you will have loosed a bulldog in a china shop."[1] Behind General Von Seeckt's disparaging reference to the French "militia" lies the crucial fact that the French Army's strength lay in its vast reserve organization. Even the so-called active units filled almost half of their wartime slots with reservists. The type A divisions of the first reserve had only a small professional cadre, and the type B reserve divisions consisted almost entirely of older reservists.[2] The proficiency of the ensemble depended, therefore, upon the quality of the reservists and their efficient integration with the active troops.

If it was difficult to train French conscripts during their period of active duty, the reservists faced even greater obstacles. Although the French sought to create a reserve organization of solid units prepared by peacetime exercises for immediate service, practical difficulties undermined their efforts, and the army that mobilized for war in September 1939 lacked cohesion, training, and leadership. The weaknesses of the reserve army explain the French performance in May and June 1940 directly, by accounting for reduced combat effectiveness, and indirectly, by explaining why the French Army adopted the military doctrines described in the succeeding chapters. France fell, not because its troops were outnumbered by the Germans, but because they were outfought—and outfought because of a failure to create the cohesive, well-trained, and well-officered reserve units upon which combat power relied.[3]

Reinforcing a small active army with large numbers of trained reserves was a French tradition, dating effectively to 1872 and tested in World War I;[4] what changed with the 1927 army organization law was the relationship between the two components. Reducing the period of active service from eighteen months to a mere twelve left the active army little enough time for its own training and none to cater to the needs of the reserve formations upon which the active army now more than ever depended.[5] In acknowledgement of the new pressures placed on the active troops, the 1927 law called for reserves to have their own separate organization, training, and cadres, in short, an existence independent of the conscript army.[6] Or, as General Brindel described it, with the conscripts of the "peacetime army" engaged solely in their own training, the reserves had become the real "wartime army." As the younger half of the annual contingent had to continue training in the event of mobilization, truly "the reserve has become the active force and the active force provides the reserve."[7]

Under the provisions of the army organization laws of 1927 and 1928, healthy French males were liable to military service for twenty-eight years, of which only the first year was intended to be spent on active service, or, more precisely, in training to become a combat-ready reservist.[8] By the time a soldier was fully trained, his active duty obligation was finished and he graduated to a ready reserve called the *disponibilité*.[9] For the next three years, he remained attached to his active-duty regiment, was liable for a three-week training period, and could be recalled to the colors by the minister of war.[10] In the event of war, each active infantry regiment absorbed about 2,000 men from the *disponibilité* and left behind for further training its 700–1,000 first-semester recruits.[11] After the *disponibilité* came sixteen years in the first-line reserve, during which the reservist could be called up twice for three-week training periods.[12] Military obligations concluded with eight years in the second-line reserve, theoretically including a seven-day exercise.

The reserve-training obligation totaled nine or ten weeks, but its actual incidence depended on funding by parsimonious and antimilitarist parliamentarians. At seven francs a day per man, reserve exercises were an expense that the French government chose to avoid from 1919 to 1927.[13] In spite of the provisions of the 1927 law, no class of the *disponibilité* was called up for reserve training until 1933, and the next two years saw convocations from the *disponibilité* but not from the first-line reserve.[14]

The general staff accepted the twelve-month service law with the stipulation that, as compensation for the abbreviated period of active duty, the reserve system would be strengthened by bonding soldiers together into permanent units. Reservists were to be assigned to units derived from their active-service regiments and to perform their training exercises within their complete wartime organizations.[15] Thus, from the beginning of recruit training until their final retirement from the reserves, groups of men were to serve together continuously in units that drew their cohesion from long acquaintance both in the barracks and in civilian life. As the General Staff explained, "Men who will fight together in wartime must already have had the opportunity to get to know one another in time of peace. They must already know their leaders and their leaders must know them."[16] Such was the theory behind the organization of 1927–1928, a plausible enough idea when understood in conjunction with the army's traditional geographically based organization.

For the smooth incorporation of conscripts for active service and the convocation of reservists for further training, France was organized in twenty military regions, each, in principle, containing a corps headquarters, one active infantry division, and two reserve divisions. The subdivisions in each region had recruiting bureaus whose job it was to keep track of the local supply of military manpower—assigning recruits to active units for training and trained soldiers to mobilization centers for service with active or reserve formations.[17] Thus, regiments drew their recruits from their designated subregions, and soldiers, whether active or reserve, served in local units.[18] Stationing conscripts in their home regions built esprit de corps and protected vulnerable young men from contact with unfamiliar germs lurking in distant regions.[19] Regional organization simplified reserve convocations, and, even in the absence of organized training, reservists from the same area would remain in contact with one another, if not through contacts in daily life, then at veterans' meetings and in reserve officer and noncommissioned training courses.[20]

Such, at least, was the comforting theory that allowed French leaders to assume that their army's fundamental structure was conducive both to morale and to efficiency. Even people who knew better acted as if French military units were genuinely regional. As late as 1938, General Duval informed the French reading public that all of the elements of each division came from that division's home region.[21] In fact, because the twelve-month service law left the army too small to fill twenty three-regiment divisions, four divisions had been eliminated. Also, since military needs were not equally distributed around the country, in the smaller army of the 1930s, frontier regions like the sixth and twentieth contained as many as six active infantry regiments, while the interior regions, the fourth, ninth, and seventeenth, each had only one thinned-down regiment of two companies per battalion.

Actual recruiting patterns contradicted the neat regional picture in ways that went far beyond these two acknowledged concessions to demography. Even when the necessary recruits were available locally, French regiments and divisions did not, whatever theory demanded, recruit from single home regions. For example, the first military region, which called up 3,183 future infantrymen in the half-class of March 1935, needed 1,932 recruits to fill slots in the 1st, 43rd, and 110th regiments of the 1st DI.[22] The region kept, however, only 1,478 men, sending the remaining 1,705 to regiments stationed in the second, sixth, and twentieth regions and receiving in return 445 men from the 2nd region and from Paris for the First DI. The first and second regions exchanged recruits (and France and North Africa exchanged 15,000 men annually), which demonstrates that exceptions to the regional pattern were not dictated by manpower shortages in one region.[23] In March 1935 only two of France's fifty-five active infantry regiments recruited from a single region, and fully a third drew from four or more different regions.[24]

Though undesirable for reserve call-ups, such a system would have proved tolerably efficient if geographical patterns had been repeated from year to year so that units always recruited, if not from the same single region, at least from the same set of regions. But consistent catchment areas from year to year were the exception. Only two infantry regiments, the Fifty-first RI and the Ninety-ninth RI, recruited in 1938 from the same regions as in 1935, and these cases were not necessarily simple. The Ninety-ninth RI may have inducted men on a consistent regional pattern, but there were five different regions involved.[25] More typical was Twenty-fourth RI, which recruited largely from fifth and twelfth regions in 1935 but from the tenth region three years later. The instability of the recruitment system is more striking at the level of the subregion. Of the twelve local mobilization centers that dispatched troops to the Twenty-fourth RI in 1935, only Chartres in the fourth region, which had provided twenty-five men two years previously, sent recruits (but only ten) in 1938.

The clash between the theory of regional recruitment and the actual method of manning French units is even clearer in the smaller armored units, whose regional nature was advertised in a system of nomenclature that gave the same number to a regiment and a mobilization center. Armored units had a greater tendency towards geographical homogeneity. Although most regiments recruited from at least two different regions, contingents from a given bureau usually served together in a single unit.[26] The ideal of consistent recruitment from the same region is represented by the 509th Tank Regiment (RCC), whose depot was Tank Mobilization Center No. 509 at Mauberge in the first region and which received additional recruits only from Center No. 513 at Rouen, whose third region had no indigenous regiment. More typical, however, was the confusing situation in which Tank Mobilization Center No. 503 sent men to the 507th, 508th, and 510th RCC while the eponymous 503th RCC drew instead from bureaus located in the third, fifth, ninth, and twelfth regions.[27]

To some extent, such dispersal reflected a deliberate, if unpublicized, effort to reduce the impact of a costly engagement on any single community. A broad geographical spread within a unit made for a similar distribution of letters of condolence.[28] Moreover, even had it been seen as desirable, purely regional recruiting would have been an impracticable throwback to days when the army had contained a far narrower range of occupational specialities than it did in the 1930s. For example, the Lille recruiting center from the first military region supplied men for metropolitan infantry regiments, chasseurs *à pied,* North African units (Zouaves, *tirailleurs algeriens, tirailleurs tunisiens*), armored units, mechanical support units for armor, horsed cavalry units (dragoons, chasseurs *à cheval,* and chasseurs *d'Afrique*), motorized cavalry units (cuirassiers, dragoons, and motorized machine-gun units), and for horse-drawn, motorized, and railroad artillery units. It also found men for fortified regions, antiaircraft units, a chemical weapons company, training establishments, engineer units (including sappers, mechanics, electromechanical engineers, and telegraphists), supply companies (horse-drawn and automotive), clerical and other administrative units, medical units, balloon detachments, the navy, and the air force. Most units other than the infantry recruited from many bureaus, with engineering, mechanical, supply, medical, and administrative units usually taking no more than five or ten men from each. For the engineers and mechanical units, recruiting by driblets reflected the lack of skilled manpower, and the army preferred not to concentrate the less onerous or dangerous jobs in any single locality. A rigidly geographical pattern, however convenient administratively, would not have combined the need to make the best use of the skills possessed by recruits with a reasonably fair distribution of risk.

Other explicit requirements modified the principle of regional recruiting. Since all troops serving in the mountainous fourteenth, fifteenth, and sixteenth regions were expected to meet the physical standards of Alpine troops, fitness took precedence over place of origin. The army also had to take into account regional variations in education and language. Thus, for example, Breton units received drafts from major cities to increase their supply of literate noncommissioned officer material, and illiterates were excluded from the small European contingents assigned to North African and racially mixed units.[29] Recruits from Alsace-Lorraine could volunteer to serve in an interior region, while those who did not speak French were posted to areas where they would learn the national language.

The manpower jigsaw puzzle was rendered more complicated by certain units' voracious appetites for skilled men. Armored battalions demanded that 15 percent of their inductees be trained metalworkers, 10 percent be woodworkers, and 20 percent have driving licenses; the remainder were to be either skilled workers like radio operators, painters, bootmakers, and saddlemakers or suitable candidates for instruction as drivers. Cavalry remount units accepted only accountants, blacksmiths, tailors, bootmakers, saddlemakers, and woodworkers. Engineering and air force units also demanded men with technical skills. Another group for whom regional provenance was ignored were former criminals, who went automatically to the light infantry battalion in Tunisia. Other units stationed in North Africa were filled by volunteers, or, if necessary, by a lottery among metropolitan conscripts.

Some individual factors overrode the regional model, and others, like family circumstances, reinforced it. The process of assigning conscripts to units began by placing holders of the *brevet de préparation militaire* in the regiment of their choice, regardless of its recruitment district. Second preference went to fathers, who received assignment to the units closest to their homes,[30] and men who had no children but had been married for at least one month were assigned as close to home as possible. The next task was to assign holders of aptitude certificates for any of a wide range of skills including riding, driving, music, mechanics, nursing, piloting, and navigation to units requiring their skills and without geographical limitations.[31] Also handled at this stage were volunteers for service in the navy or in North Africa and sons of large families, who had priority for local units. Men whose employers vouched for their competence as accountants, typists, bakers, butchers, cooks, tailors, masons, painters, and so forth were apportioned according to established tables of organization. After these special cases had been dealt with, the remainder of the contingent were distributed, the fittest men going to the infantry, engineers, and artillery. In principle, illiterates were barred from some units altogether, limited to a maximum of 5 percent of drafts for cavalry, telegraph, and carrier pigeon units, and distributed among other units in proportion to their numbers in the contingent as a whole, but the sheer numbers of such men in some regions apparently defied efforts to minimize their impact on individual units. General Billotte described one regimental intake at Limoges as composed of 22.5 percent illiterate and 55 percent semiliterate recruits, and, in defiance of the official standards for recruits, some mounted units in western France had rates of illiteracy or semiliteracy of up to 50 percent.[32]

Although most distortions of the regional pattern were a matter of public record, it was not meant to be widely known that recruits branded by local authorities with the code letters PR for "*propaganda révolutionaire*" were subject to special restrictions. Barred from certain kinds of formations (motorized units, the garrisons of the fortified regions, and African or mixed contingents), they were also not sent to units near their homes or accepted for reserve noncommissioned officer or officer training. Should one of these undesirables threaten to pass the examination for admission to an officer-candidate platoon, his patriotic and moral inadequacies could be used to justify an unsatisfactory "general aptitude" mark.[33] These were the only conscripts who could be sent to North Africa other than by choice, by lot, or as members of the light infantry battalion. They were not permitted to extend their engagements beyond their ordinary obligation and were barred from the reserve unit nearest their homes.

Although meant to be secret, the PR system came to public attention in 1928 when certain local commanders, embarrassed to explain the arbitrary rejection of apparently qualified officer applicants, admitted the existence of the blacklist and were rebuked for this "serious indiscretion."[34] Because politically unsuitable men continued to slip into the reserve officer course, security checks were intensified in 1937. In the same year, however, Minister of National Defense Daladier cautioned the general staff to limit the PR list to those guilty of actual acts of propaganda against the country, the army, or republican institutions, and warned against discrimination on the basis of a man's political opinions or choice of companions.[35] Finally, although the 1928 recruitment law prohibited special concessions to individuals, there was a widespread perception that the system was subjected to manipulation. The comrade to whom Jean-Paul Sartre confessed having "made the mistake of wangling myself a safe spot in the Met corps" replied with a bitter reference to the "five hundred thousand individuals who've pulled strings just like me."[36]

But how much does it matter that in March 1935 the Fourth RI recruited from Auxerre (eighth region), Châteauroux, Niort, Poitiers, Tours, Angers (ninth region), Algiers and Oran (nineteenth), whereas three years later its personnel came from Auxerre (eighth), Nevers, Bourges (fifth), Dijon (eighth), Angoulême (twelfth), Toulon, Marseilles (fifteenth), Montpellier (sixteenth) and Algiers (nineteenth)? Is it truly important that a shoemaker, a telegraph operator, or a potential tank driver might find himself assigned to a distant specialist unit rather than to the infantry regiment in which his less-skilled neighbors were called upon to serve? Dispatching recruits to distant regions for their year of active duty disappointed families (and a disappointed pater familias was a disgruntled voter), increased the health risks associated with military service, and complicated leave arrangements, but did not compromise military training. What makes nongeographical elements in the organization of the French Army anything other than a nuisance for the officers of the recruiting bureaus and a minor footnote in the history of military administration was the relationship between the active and reserve forces. The active army, which gained from the flexibility to organize soldiers in accordance with its needs rather than their place of residence, had little reason for allegiance to the regional organization other than the possibility that regional loyalty—and antipathy to foreigners—could strengthen unit morale.[37] But for the reserve units, the subversion of the regional organization had severe consequences.[38]

Because the efficiency of reserve units rested less on extended military experience than on the soldiers' personal bonds, the makers of the 1927–1928 laws assumed that the shift from active to reserve assignments would preserve the integrity of primary units. Thus each soldier's reserve regiment would be a "spin-off" (*derivé*) unit of his active regiment, and he would, therefore, remain during his reserve service with his comrades of the previous four years.[39] But the neat relationship between active and reserve units demanded by the army and by the authors of the 1927–1928 army laws rested on the spurious premise that conscripts were inducted into units on a geographical basis. When a soldier left the *disponibilité,* he exchanged the authority of his regiment for that of the mobilization center of his particular arm closest to his home. If his active duty assignment had not been in his home region, the shift cut him off from his original regiment because mobilization centers concerned to fill local reserve formations did not dispatch reservists to serve with their erstwhile active-service comrades. Only the minority of soldiers who were conscripted into the active units based in their home region remained with their primary groups as they joined locally based reserve units.[40]

The example of the Fourth RI of the Fifteenth DI from the eighth military region, stationed at Auxerre, illustrates the situation. Thirty of the men drafted into the regiment in 1937 came from Auxerre itself. Of the remaining 790, only the 140 from Dijon came from the 8th region. If Nevers (169 men) and Bourges (55) were close by in the fifth region, Angoulême (256) was 320 kilometers away and Toulon (55), Marseilles (25), and Montpellier

(50) were about 500 kilometers distant. Forty other members of the regiment came from Algeria. There was no logic in assigning these men to a reserve regiment based in the eighth region or indeed to any single regiment, since their files would be administered by nine different regional mobilization bureaus. The case for trying to keep cohorts together as men moved from active to reserve assignments was also undermined by the shifting of regimental catchment areas. As long as each active unit lacked a consistent geographical base, little was to be gained from the effort to construct reserve units out of the graduates of a single active unit. Nine weeks of reserve training over the course of nineteen years would inculcate little sense of fraternity in strangers whose only shared experience was that of having each at some time spent twelve months in a particular barracks.

Graduation from the *disponibilité* to the first reserve often not only separated a soldier from his comrades in arms but forced him to acquire a new military specialty. Trained chasseurs *à pied* or Zouaves residing in regions that did not recruit for those units were assigned to reserve infantry formations while chasseur units that could not fill their ranks from local chasseur reservists had to accept infantrymen instead.[41] The neophyte gunners in one artillery battery first fired the famous French 75mm gun in April 1940.[42] Changes in methods of warfare also brought new personnel assignments. With the introduction of the motorcycle, for example, some men were assigned to divisional reconnaissance squadrons simply because they possessed a driving license, and the resulting mixture of cavalry reservists and infantry untrained for reconnaissance work was of disputable value.[43]

Reserve organization was not local for specialist units. Marcel Pétain, who was from Saint-Pol, described his section as having a Parisian sergeant, a corporal from Hem-Lenglet, and men from Frévent, Calais, Saint-André-lez-Lille, Dainville, Valenciennes, Camblain-l'Abbé, an ex-sailor, and three others.[44] Private Fernard Grenier, a communist member of the Chamber of Deputies, mentions that the hundred men of the third company of the Fourth Regiment of Engineers came from the north, east, Alps, and the Midi, whereas he himself resided in Paris. He gives more precise information for a detachment of six men—one Savoyard whose active service had taken place in Syria, a man from Eperney, a Marseillais, himself, and "two drunkards."[45]

The passage from active to reserve assignments was further complicated because some elements of the French war machine, notably armored and air force units, required large numbers of active duty personnel but relatively few reservists.[46] Thus, one French objection to the acquisition of armored fighting vehicles was that training their crews diminished the supply of infantry reservists. In theory, twenty armored regiments that trained 1,000 personnel every year would encumber the army after ten years with 200,000 reservists unprepared for infantry service.[47] In fact, in September 1939, a regimental commander discovered that a sentry who did not know how to present arms had done his conscript year as an officer's batman and that fully 150 of the men in his regiment were products of the navy, the air force, the cavalry, or the tank arm. These men, who had never undergone the basic "school of the soldier," had to be removed from their companies to be trained as infantrymen. Supply units experienced the opposite problem, receiving only small numbers of conscripts in peacetime and forced to draw upon reservists trained in other arms. Thus Captain Barlone, whose previous service had always been in infantry and mechanized units, found himself commanding a horse-drawn transport company in the Second North African Infantry Division, whose members were as unfamiliar to one another as they were to their commander.[48]

However pernicious, such differences between active and reserve postings are at least explicable, but one wonders why peacetime command of the D tank battalion of the 508th RCC went to a man, one Commandant Devaux, whose wartime assignment was in the railway service.[49] Far from being thoroughly prepared for their wartime positions, many men received their assignments only upon mobilization. Reporting to the new colonel of the Fifty-seventh RI in September 1939, Lieutenant Felsenhardt, for example, found himself appointed division liaison officer not because he had trained for the job but because his well-tailored uniform set him apart from his shabbier fellows.[50]

For all these reasons, the units that mobilized for war were often composed of men who were strangers both to one another and to their new responsibilities. Moreover, whatever cohesion existed upon mobilization of a unit tended to dissolve thereafter. Although commanders had reasons to strive for durable units, large- and small-scale shifts of personnel seem to have been the order of the day.[51] Many individual assignments had to be modified as the men proved to be incapable of accomplishing their duties for reasons of age, skill, or health.[52] Sometimes the instability of personnel suggests low-level confusion, at other times it is indicative of major conceptual failure. Exemplifying the first are the peregrinations of Private Grenier, a communist member of the Chamber of Deputies who was mobilized in September 1939 at Bergerac and then transferred successively to units at Metz, Grenoble, and Gex (on the Swiss border). Grenier's trajectory was relatively smooth compared to that of fellow communist Georges Sadoul, whose assignments took him to two different divisions and required him to serve at various times as typist, medical orderly, food storeman, and radio operator and who suspected that he and sixteen other men had received one transfer because a garbled telephoned request for recruits (*"des bleus"*) had resulted in orders being issued to "the old men" (*"des vieux"*).[53]

It is less surprising that mobilizing authorities dealt inconsistently with a few individual communists than that they failed to calculate that some hundreds of thousands of mobilized workers would have to be released from their reserve assignments for work in industry. Had these men been assigned to factories from the outset, the army would not have had to recall them from active service at great cost to cohesion and morale.[54] Another major upheaval in unit organization stemmed from a belated recognition that the young soldiers stationed on the Maginot Line would be better used in mobile divisions while older reservists manned the forts. Thus, on 24 December 1939, General Georges ordered the first-line reservists to be replaced with category B troops. The shift, begun only in April, broke up the highly trained fortress "crews" for the dubious advantage of adding some younger, but unfamiliar, soldiers to the category B regiments.[55] On a smaller scale is a colonel's complaint about the exchange of two battalions between the Thirty-sixth and Twenty-second DI that "did not at all facilitate the exercise of command."[56]

Other upheavals came from the need to recreate new regiments from established ones. Thus, the 6th RI, disbanded after World War I, was ceremonially reconstituted on 18 October 1939 from instructional battalions of the 151st RI (sixth region), 94th RI (sixth region), 26th RI (twentieth region), and 170th RI (twentieth region). Men were in short supply, however, and the new regiment found itself with companies of 130 men, sections of 18 instead of 40, and groups of 5 instead of 12. These men had not trained together in peacetime, for individual companies contained men from Lyon, the east, the north, and Paris.[57]

The solidarity of reserve units was supposed to derive from a stable nucleus of reserve officers trained together in peacetime, but mobilization saw a considerable reshuffling of officer assignments. The Seventy-first RI lost its second in command and two of its three battalion commanders to unexpected transfers and had to provide officer cadres for the newly remobilized 93d and 102d Infantry Regiments. Three reserve captains were removed from the regiment because they were over forty-five years old, other officers were given instructional jobs in training camps, and some noncommissioned officers were sent to strengthen a reserve regiment. In return for these losses, the regiment received 2 officers, 4 noncommissioned officers, and 140 men, mostly over thirty years old who were entitled to "safe" assignments because they were fathers of large families or had lost a brother or father in World War I.[58] Captain Tony de Vibraye, commander of the machine gun and anti-tank squadron of the Third Corps Reconnaisance Group (GRCA), had met three of his four subalterns briefly at a reserve exercise two years before the war; Captain Lami knew both of his lieutenants well from reserve training, but the men of his battery of 75mm guns came from all over France and were complete strangers to him.[59]

As the phony war dragged on, bored officers tried to transfer from their regiments to more interesting or more comfortable duties—air observation, liaison with British units, and administration being favorites. A colonel who tried to block those applications as "harmful to the solidarity of the regiment" could not always withstand political influence, although Lieutenant Felsenhardt managed to prevent his father from securing him transfer to the British staff at Dunkirk. Marc Bloch admitted that "wire-pulling with the object of landing a better job is not an activity in which one naturally takes much pride, but it was scarcely my fault that only thus could I find any outlet for my enthusiasm."[60] Captain Lami of the Thirty-eighth Divisional Artillery Regiment (RAD) struggled without success to save for his battery a skilled soldier whom the colonel wanted available at headquarters to contribute to regimental theatricals.[61] Georges Sadoul surely exaggerates in claiming that the sections in his unit were reorganized—"randomly"—for the tenth time on 17 October 1939, but the general picture of improvisation is entirely credible.[62] If these experiences are typical, there is every reason to believe that the French Army failed to create the solid units that were intended to compensate for the limited training of conscripts.

The contrast between the vision of the authors of the 1927–1928 army laws and the haphazard units sent to the front in 1940 reflects the dichotomy between active and reserve forces created by the army law of 28 March 1928. The active army's mission was now limited to organizing and training the conscript contingent, and responsibility for reserve training and mobilization fell upon the 495 reserve mobilization centers, each responsible for one active unit and its associated reserve units.[63] Distinct from both active army and mobilization centers were the recruiting bureaus. These kept the personnel files necessary to assign conscripts to active units and reservists to mobilization centers, which were responsible in turn for distributing the reservists among active and reserve formations.[64] The separation between active and reserve units was intended, in the words of the general staff to permit the optimal use of the twelve-month active-service period by relieving active formations of the "parasitical fatigues" (*besognes parasites*) associated with organizing and training reserve formations.[65]

Because mobilization centers and combat formations existed in parallel chains of command that merged only at the regional headquarters, a regimental commander had no authority over mobilization procedures. He did not know which soldiers of his own regiment would actually be his in combat until he received the personnel list from the mobilization center along with a request for a copy of his proposed wartime table of organization. Using the framework proposed by the colonel, the mobilization center then produced a plan to fill the regiment's remaining slots—and those of the spin-off regiments—with reserve officers, noncommissioned officers, and men. The entire organization had to be revised semiannually as recruits became trained soldiers, trained soldiers graduated to the *disponibilité, disponibles* passed to the first-line reserve, and first-line reservists moved to the second line; it also had to reflect less predictable changes as individual soldiers were promoted, acquired new specialties, changed their place of residence to another military region, became physically incapacitated, had children, or otherwise changed their mobilization status.[66]

For each reserve regiment, the mobilization centers also created an elaborate *"journal de mobilisation,"* a day-by-day manual detailing the process of convoking, organizing, and equipping the unit for war.[67] To compile these books, the centers calculated wartime requirements for the animals, vehicles, and other supplies, determining what could be requisitioned in time of need and what had to be stored in advance. The mobilization centers were also the sites of "cadre convocations" of the active and reserve officers of each division, which were meant to take place every second or third year. For senior officers, these gatherings provided six-and-a-half days to rehearse the division's wartime role. Junior officers attended for three days, during which they studied the *journaux de mobilisation,* verified personnel assignments, inspected stored supplies and equipment, attended demonstrations of new weapons, participated in terrain reconnaissances, and, in theory, became voluntary publicists for the thoroughness of their nation's military organization.[68]

In spite of their heavy responsibilities, mobilization centers were minimally staffed, mostly with retired soldiers called *agents militaires* who worked as clerks, accountants, and storekeepers. A center responsible for 18,000 men might have only a commanding officer, two subalterns, three noncommissioned officers, and one private in addition to twenty-one *agents militaires* of varying ranks.[69] The civilians, described by one region's commander as virtual illiterates and useless former prison guards, were often of dubious value, but the centers' military personnel returned to their original units on mobilization, leaving a vacuum "at the moment when the center had to function at its maximum."[70] Assignment of soldiers to the centers, however frugally done, proved a drain on the army's overstretched professional cadres, and reports following the partial mobilization of 1938 suggest that many men at the centers were not up to their jobs.[71] A commander desirous of improving his unit's readiness for war complained that the mobilization centers had no incentive "to move heaven and earth" and that their requests to inspect the center met with demurrers that "now wasn't the time."[72]

It would have taken cleverer personnel than the mobilization centers enjoyed to keep the groups formed during active service intact and to make the best use of the specialists' skills while still placing every soldier in the reserve unit closest to his home. Geography, rather than integrity of the primary group, was the first determinant of reserve assignments, but reserve units could not achieve the geographical homogeneity that eluded even the more flexible active army. Large cities produced more than their share of officers and noncommissioned officers. Tank drivers, engineers, and typists had to be assigned according to military specialty rather than place of residence. Every light mechanized division required 1,356 motorcyclists, whencesoever they came.[73] Riflemen, who had the best chance of serving in a locally based regiment, comprised only 39 percent of the French Army.[74]

Nowhere were the consequences of the bifurcated active-reserve army more glaring than in the obstacles that it imposed for the training of reservists in their combat units. If theory called for an army of cohesive formations whose soldiers would be mobilized into familiar jobs among known comrades, the reality was constant improvisation. Reservists did not necessarily serve in familiar units, nor did reserve units normally do their training as whole formations under the command of their wartime officers. As for the notion that reserve regiments profited from drawing cadres from their parent regiments, it was arguable, as a contemporary critic complained, whether the sudden displacement of a few dozen men upon mobilization was likely to produce two cohesive units or two disorganized ones.[75]

Reserve training was inherently difficult for cavalry, armor, and other specialist branches that recruited from across France but had limited numbers of active garrisons. The law required such reservists to be sent to active units for the necessary training, but such movements were expensive, and there is no evidence that mobilization centers, whose primary responsibility was to fill slots in locally based regiments, actually arranged them. In the absence of appropriate local units, specialists were more likely to spend their reserve periods marking time in rifle companies.

More surprising than the failure of the reserve-training system to handle specialists effectively was the inability of ordinary reserve infantry regiments to fulfill the law's mandate for regular unit training under authentic wartime organization. Before the 1927–1928 army organization laws, unit training was not even attempted, and reservists were called up not by unit affiliation but by year class. The authors of the army reorganization insisted, however, on replacing the traditional "horizontal" or class convocations by a new system of unit or "vertical" convocations so that training could create cohesion—"confidence of the soldiers in themselves and among themselves, reciprocal confidence of commanders and soldiers."[76] Vertical convocations also promised to improve the French Army's ability to introduce new matériel or doctrine to entire units. When units were called up in fragments according to year class, it took years for instruction in the use of a new radio or antitank gun to filter through the entire formation.[77]

Though desirable in theory and required by law, attempts to train whole reserve units at one time provoked numerous practical objections. The first of these, applying only to the period of transition from horizontal to vertical convocations, was that some of the men called up with their regiments would have already undergone a period of reserve training with their class. Although legally possible, a second period of training was deemed unfair and, more to the point, required begging extra funds from an unenthusiastic legislature. More important in the long term was that vertical convocations violated the time-honored practice of allowing reservists to choose from among a number of training periods in their assigned year.[78] Furthermore, the postponements normally granted to farmers meant that the units would be far from complete.[79] In any case, lack of facilities made convocations of whole regiments, let alone divisions, virtually impossible, and the Ministry of War acknowledged that the number of reservists called up at a given time could be no larger than the number of spare beds that could be borrowed from the host unit or training camp.[80]

Whole reserve formations could not be called up in any case, and debate therefore ensued over whether the packets of reservists ought to train by themselves in ad hoc *unités de march* or be amalgamated with active soldiers. The first system better approximated wartime organization and pleased those politicians who feared abuse of citizen-soldiers by the professional cadres, but it required the detachment of active troops to perform the military housekeeping chores for which the reservists did not have time, and it assumed that the reserve officers were capable of training their own men.[81] Isolating reservists from active troops minimized the distraction of the active contingent from its own training and, less laudably, concealed the difficulties of amalgamating active and reserve troops. Thus, a chasseur officer reported that reservists could not participate in regimental maneuvers because they were untrained in current doctrine and had insufficient stamina on horseback.[82]

Given the inconvenience of mixing reservists with conscripts and the inadequacy of reserve officers as instructors, the army generally sacrificed the principle that troops should train under their wartime leaders by putting regular officers in charge of temporary reservist units. As an observer pointed out, the resulting unfamiliarity of officers and men "did and will in the future promote disorganization on the first days of mobilization."[83] Some military regions were so sparsely endowed with infantry garrisons in the 1930s that they had to adopt the expedient, wholly at odds with official policy, of importing cadres from elsewhere for reserve training.[84]

The alternative arrangement, placing reservists in active units, brought simplicity at the cost of all efforts to simulate wartime organization. Reserve training under such circumstances refreshed military skills, interfered with the activities of the contingent, and utterly ignored the primary purpose of reserve training, the creation of cohesive units. It was, however, necessary in the case of men assigned to armored units, who otherwise had no machines for training, and it was established as the norm whenever active and reserve troops found themselves sharing an instructional camp.[85]

The organizational limitations on the verisimilitude of training can be seen in the Twenty-third DI's 1937 session at La Courtine camp. What was called a division was in fact only three battalions, consolidated into two for the duration of the exercises. Of these, one received its wartime complement of reservists, and the other, with only forty reservists, remained below-strength. The first twelve days of the maneuvers focused on infantry, with the artillery represented only by liaison detachments; the bulk of the artillery showed up only to participate in the final two-day exercise before beginning a separate ten-day training period.[86] The Twenty-third DI did not achieve its wartime organization or offer more than minimal infantry-artillery combined arms training. In any case, by the time the division's reservists trained again, they would belong not to the Twenty-third DI but to a reserve division that might or might not have any affinity with their original unit. Such arrangements did not fulfill the objective of training soldiers with the men alongside whom or under whose command they would go into battle.

The discrepancy between the solid reserve organization adumbrated in the army laws and the ethereal reality did not escape critical attention, and in 1934 the army determined to test its battle-readiness through a vertical convocation of a representative reserve division. Chosen for the exercise was the Forty-first DI, a largely Parisian formation, 8,000 of whose 17,000 men were summoned for training in September 1934.[87] Expectations for the exercise were high. Older, physically more developed, and mentally sharper than young conscripts, the reservists were expected to show greater endurance than active troops and, if well commanded, to prove equal in performance.[88] Thus, General Barrard's orders of the day exhorted his division to make the maneuvers not a test but a demonstration: "Let us show to those who are observing us that the French, though generous, are still determined to defend the peace, the peace of the 1,500,000 dead of the World War. . . . This experiment must prove that France can count on her army."[89]

The results of the experiment, which took place from 16 to 28 September at the Mourmelon Camp and ended with a two-day wargame against the active army's Second Cavalry Division (DC), proved, in the tactful words of the British attaché, "an unexpected surprise." The good news was that only thirty hours were required to equip and organize the division, the bad news was that supplying the necessary material so strained the active contingents of the Paris region that training was impeded for six weeks. Nor did the training received by the reserve troops compensate for that lost by the active ones. Rather, General Prételat observed that the division's reserve officers and noncommissioned officers were so unprepared to act as instructors for their men as to call into question the whole concept of the vertical call-up.[90]

The performance of the reserve officers proved a special concern. Not up to their jobs mentally, physically, or in professional knowledge, their mistakes imposed unnecessary burdens on their troops. Unsurprisingly, therefore, they appeared hesitant, even embarrassed, to exert their authority, and the soldiers took advantage of their officers' obvious desire to avoid "*des histoires*" ("incidents"). Noncommissioned officers trained under the one-year service law proved equally unsatisfactory.[91] Given poor leadership, other deficiencies were only to be expected. Use of camouflage was inadequate, fire plans were defective, reconnaissances were improperly executed, and coordination between infantry, artillery, and armor was erratic. Though betraying no outright ill will, the soldiers generally managed to do as little as possible. Lieutenant Colonel Charles de Gaulle of the arbitration staff reported that delays were frequent and, that, as the troops were dispersed, signs of activity correspondingly diminished, to the point that isolated units were virtually inert. Although planned maneuvers were performed satisfactorily, any improvisation produced general confusion.[92] Another, particularly scathing, report branded the divisional artillery as *"médiocre à tous régards"* ("second-rate in every respect"). It was *"médiocrement instruit,"* ("poorly trained"), had *"médiocre moral"* (low morale"), and manifested *"mauvais esprit"* ("a bad attitude"). If the reserve subalterns were *"gauches"* ("clumsy") from inexperience, the noncommissioned officiers were *"inexistants"* ("useless").[93]

Division Commander Barrard judged the men cooperative but far from enthusiastic. Their failure to salute in towns reflected a lack of military élan, but they understood the importance of the exercise and cooperated. The only major source of complaint was army food, and the general deemed meals to be the likely focus of incidents of indiscipline. Discriminating Parisian palates went with tender Parisian feet, quickly crippled by cheap army shoes. Although the soldiers carried no packs and good weather meant easy marching, the men of the Forty-first DI proved discouragingly unfit. The exercise critique concluded that it would take seven or eight weeks to prepare such a division to meet the physical demands of war and that the quarter of the troops incapable of long marches would have to be replaced with fitter men.[94] Barrard concluded his report with the hope that things might be better in wartime, with mobilization providing a salutary *"coup de fouet,"* but warned against false optimism: "The complex and inexorable realities of tomorrow's war do not lend themselves to improvisation," he said. On the whole, he judged the situation "disquieting."

The various critiques of the exercise emphasized three points: the willingness of the reservists if properly led, the importance of morale, and the implications of the low level of physical fitness demonstrated by the Forty-first DI. Particularly striking are the reassuring comments about the overall quality of the French reservist.[95] General Prételat insisted that, in spite of reports suggesting low morale and physical conditioning, the infantry looked satisfactory in their final review. Colonel de Gaulle's otherwise discouraging report admitted that the Forty-first was "a good-enough dough" lacking only "leavening" and a minimum moral and physical "adaptability." The yeast metaphor appears also in Chief Arbitrator Pigeaud's assessment that the troops were malleable and could probably have been transformed if leavened by spirited cadres. Although noting the need for improved training, Pigeaud saw improved morale as the more urgent objective. Both of these arguments, the fundamental soundness of the men and the potential of morale to compensate for deficiencies in training, reflected the most optimistic readings of the situation and, correspondingly, implied that inexpensive remedies would suffice.

To complain about the overall quality of the reservists was to challenge the army's basic structure, and calls for efforts to raise morale—largely through improved leadership—reaffirmed commitment to the reserve army and the one-year regime. Such suggestions bore lighter political and financial price tags than would proposals to increase the length of military service or the intensity of reserve training. The contrast between the army's obvious dissatisfaction with the performance of the Forty-first DI and the anodyne prescriptions it offered suggests that soldiers were carefully avoiding taboo subjects. Only General Prételat argued explicitly that the exercise proved eighteen months of service to be insufficient to produce soldiers capable of filling A units. Pigeaud and Barrard contented themselves with pointing out—without explicitly drawing damning conclusions—that the reservists of the Forty-first, who had done eighteen months of active service, were as good as the French Army had.

Military leaders were less reticent about the implications of the alarmingly poor physical condition of the reservists. Most of men of the Forty-first DI were in their mid-twenties and the oldest only thirty-two; that they were not fit to march boded ill for reserve units containing even older men and posed a problem that could not entirely be ignored. If the Forty-first were representative of the reserve divisions as a whole, then France would have to give up any hope of an early shift to offensive operations. Pigeaud's report went as far as to insist that reserve troops wasted their time on offensive exercises and that training periods ought to be devoted to defense. The only remedial action proposed (only tentatively, because it fell in the political sphere) was the establishment of physical training programs to condition young men before their year of military service. But, as we have seen, the army's devotion to pre–military training did not go beyond lip service. Rather than pressing the point, the army merely reduced the soldier's marching kit to ten kilos and expressed the pious hope that war would see things go better than worse.[96] They did not. One French reservist noted that an eight kilometer march in September 1939 found his section in "complete disorder," with men stopping to rest every ten to twenty meters.[97] In September 1939 a captain recorded his relief that a planned attack was delayed long enough to allow his fat, winded reservists to catch their breath.[98]

What could not be cured had to be not only endured but concealed. Thus, when Deputy Forcinal argued in the Army Commission of the Chamber of Deputies that the performance of the Forty-first DI demonstrated the inadequacy of one-year service, War Minister General Maurin warned him against spreading gloom: "Should one say this out loud? Should we denigrate the value of our army in legislative reports? The reserves will do better in war than in maneuvers, and, if eighteen-month service would be an improvement, now is not a good time to say so. If I am guarded in public judgments about the value of our army, it is because I have found it inopportune to admit abroad to any weakness whatsoever." A similar exchange took place in the Senate, where Senator Dalbiz reassured Senator Messimy that the Forty-first DI's disappointing performance did not fairly reflect its wartime potential. "The conditions of such a call-up," he argued, are entirely different from those of wartime mobilization. It lacks conviction and passion. When French officers expressed concern about the results of the Mourmelon exercise, they tended to do so privately.[99]

The performance of the Forty-first DI revealed vertical convocations to be an unsatisfactory solution to the reserve army's poor state of training and that the legislators who had imposed them upon the army "appeared not to have seen all of the repercussions."[100] Reserve training by unit meant calling up seven or eight divisions a year, thus depriving an equal number of active units of the training camp space, vehicles, and personnel. Vertical convocations assumed reserve divisions to be capable of training themselves, a task for which the officers and noncommissioned of the Forty-first DI had proved unready. Vertical convocations remained, therefore, a theoretical ideal, but the army determined that they would in future have to be small enough to take place without excessive demands on active units.[101] Thus, what was officially a "divisional" call-up of the Fifty-second DI at Sissone Camp in 1935 occurred on a much-reduced scale, involving only one battalion from each of three regiments, the divisional reconnaissance unit, and some artillery and communications formations.[102] The 1935 scheme revealed expectations much lowered from the previous year, with the division receiving a fortnight's training before tackling the straightforward problem of establishing a defensive position along the Meuse River. The silence of the press about this exercise contrasts with the attention given the Forty-first Division in the previous year and suggests that the army did not publicly advertize it as a divisional convocation. In 1936, divisional convocations were abandoned altogether as unduly expensive and too large to be executed at a mobilization center, but the high command made a virtue of necessity by arguing that smaller exercises could be spread among a greater number of units.[103] Thereafter, unit call-ups tended to be nominally regimental but to involve only the regimental headquarters and a single battalion. As the number of command elements rose in proportion to the number of soldiers participating, the emphasis of the exercises shifted from tactical testing and training to practicing command arrangements. Still, the number of participants in vertical convocations increased from 8,000 men in 1934 to 22,000 in 1935, 23,000 in 1936, 50,000 in 1937, and 40,000 in 1938 with plans to convoke 50,000 in 1939.[104]

Divisional training usually took the form of a cadre convocation (also called the *convocation profonde*) of the unit's full complement of active and reserve officers. Sometimes such convocations were combined with a partial call-up of reservists so as to provide soldiers for the officers' field training, but most exercises were for officers alone. Getting acquainted was a primary objective, and units were encouraged to provide opportunities for *"la vie en popote"*—the comradeship of the officer's mess.[105] Of course, the utility of these gatherings depended on the degree of participation, and reserve officers could be less than diligent. Fifty-nine officers out of 230 summoned for the Twenty-second DI's exercise of 20–26 September 1936 failed to appear, most of them without having been excused. Because of poor attendance, the convocations proved an unreliable mechanism for higher commanders to meet their officers and to relieve the unsuitable ones. The price was paid upon mobilization in September 1939, when a typical division discovered that its reserve officers "came from the four corners of France and did not know one another. Those who possessed some practical notion of their role on campaign could be counted on one's fingers."[106]

Divisional convocations tended to reveal deficiencies that a few personnel changes could not remedy. As General Lafont reported after a 1935 cadre convocation of reserve units from the seventeenth region, the results of such exercises "are unhappily not at all reassuring."[107] The overall level of military competence among soldiers, noncommissioned officers, and officers alike was "clearly insufficient." Even in the Thirty-third Colonial Infantry Regiment (RIC), an A unit, a substantial percentage of the reservists proved unfamiliar with the current automatic weapon. In another cadre convocation, the Sixty-seventh DI received such low marks in its exercise that its combat capability upon mobilization was deemed to be "very weak, if not non-existent."[108]

Cadre convocations had more to do with assessing unit competence than increasing it. Three days offered time enough to insure that junior officers

knew their assignments but little for extra instruction. Half a day was allocated to a demonstration of new equipment, not much in an army where active officers lacked experience with new weapons like the 25mm cannon and
60mm mortar.[109] Weapons familiarization was difficult because mobilization
centers often lacked the required matériel.[110] Centers sharing facilities with
active garrisons might borrow what they needed for demonstrations, but
otherwise the director of artillery authorized the movement of one gun to an
exercise if and only if the personnel involved were not displaced for more
than forty-eight hours.[111]

Virtually no report on a reserve convocation of the 1930s failed to express
concern about the inadequate standard of reserve officers and noncommissioned officers. The reduction of active service to twelve months, which im-
paired the training of private soldiers, posed far more serious difficulties in
recruiting its leaders, 60 to 70 percent of whom were reservists.[112]

There were a number of routes to a reserve commission.[113] One relatively
small group consisted of officers and noncommissioned officers retired
from the active army. The law required that at least 10 percent of reserve
sublieutenants be promoted from reserve noncommissioned officers who
had qualified as section leaders during their active service or during a later
training period.[114] Another path to a commission lay through education
rather than military service. Graduates of the *grandes écoles,* the elite institutions at the pinnacle of the French university hierarchy, who took the appropriate courses entered the army as "aspirant" reserve sublieutenants and
then spent six months in an officer training company at an *école d'application* (Saint-Maxient for infantry, Versailles for tanks, Metz or Poitiers for artillery, and Saumur for cavalry, supply, and veterinary service) before completing their obligatory service in active units. The most common route to a
reserve commission, however, accounting for about three-quarters of the total, was achievement of the *brevet de préparation militaire supérieure*
through a two-year course at an ordinary university. Holders of the brevet
received five months of preliminary training as privates in a preparatory platoon, remained at the rank of private during a further five months in a student officer battalion at the appropriate *école d'application,* and then completed their conscript service as "aspirant" sublieutenants in an active
unit.[115] Conscripts without the certificate of military preparation could attain their colonel's permission to take an examination for admission to the
preparatory platoon.[116]

However they achieved their commissions, the vast majority of reserve officers had in common inexperience both of troop service and of command.

Even the *grandes écoles* route, the most demanding of the officer-training programs, was all too brief in principle and could be farcical in practice. Robert Felsenhardt, a university graduate who applied for entry into a student officer platoon in 1922, received eighteen marks out of a possible twenty on the entrance examination simply for applauding his examiner's demonstration of bayonet drill. He claimed to have learned during his four months at Saint-Maixent only to install barbed wire, handle wire cutters, and slither through mud. As a sublieutenant in the 107th Infantry Regiment, Felsenhardt's manifest inability to lead troops on parade or to instruct them in weapons handling led to his relegation to the task of preparing the regiment's Bastille Day fête.[117]

Given that the twelve-month training year was an administrative fiction depleted in reality by a wide range of distractions, even the products of the *grandes écoles* acquired only a few months of unrealistic active-duty experience. Most found themselves supernumeraries in active units, a role that provided little guidance for future reserve section leaders. The large percentage of new reserve officers who went through both the preparatory platoon and the student officer battalion had virtually no opportunity to serve as officers before the end of their active-duty year.[118] The extension of military service in 1935 could have provided reserve officers with needed experience, but the Ministry of War saw two-year service as bringing not a blessed opportunity to improve the proficiency of subalterns but a regrettable obligation to pay them for the extra time in grade. Thus, a cost-conscious legislature determined, over the objections of the general staff, that potential reserve sublieutenants incorporated after October 1935 were to spend six months at the new, and less munificently rewarded rank of *aspirant de réserve,* part of the time away from the troops at a new "Training Center for Aspirants." The system produced some competent leaders, but all too many others proved noteworthy for their "apathy, their lack of initiative, and their unconcern for their men."[119] Criticized for failing to exercise their authority, reserve officers responded resentfully, "Command? . . . But we aren't used to it!"[120]

For that matter, any time spent with the troops by the new sublieutenant was under difficult circumstances. Segregated from the very beginning from his conscript class, the new subaltern found himself isolated both from his fellow conscripts, who treated him as an officer, and from the active officers, who did not. As an American observer described it: "They are officers, and as such, are entitled to all the moral and material privileges of the rank; but they are also soldiers of the contingent who are performing their compulsory military service." A British visitor to a French officers' mess noted that relations between regular and reserve subalterns "were not quite as cordial as might have been expected."[121] The officers had difficulty establishing their authority over the men under their command. Even the most ignorant soldiers were contemptuous of green officers who knew nothing about their jobs except that they were entitled to command others.[122]

Anecdote offers a generally unfavorable verdict on the relationship between French officers and their men. Sartre's observations, characteristically, emphasize alienation: "Wherever I've gone, I've found the same hatred of officers . . . which . . . is entirely concrete and empirical, and which is always accompanied by an 'I don't say there aren't any good ones, but I haven't come across one.' "[123] Describing a lunch during which members of a chasseur regiment spoke casually "about bumping off their officers," Sartre concluded that the soldiers felt less anger towards their officers than contempt—justifiable contempt if an anecdote told by the owner of a small hotel in southwestern France is representative.[124] One day in late September 1939, Madame Carles's restaurant was filled with older reservists seeking refuge from army cooking. When their colonel insisted that the dining room be cleared for his own lunch and Madame Carles refused to eject the soldiers from their meal, he attempted to requisition the hotel dining room as a stable. Later, he succeeded in having Carles posted to a teaching job distant from her husband, family, and hotel.[125] One much-loathed captain in a Maginot Line fortress learned better manners when soldiers cut off the electricity to an elevator in which he was riding. After a claustrophobic hour and a half, "he understood."[126] The existentialist philosopher, the pacifist innkeeper, and the communist soldier may not offer representative assessments of the French officer corps, but historian Alistair Horne agrees that French officers had "deplorably little contact with their men."[127]

After finishing his active service, a reserve officer was obliged to participate in a total of four months of reserve training and had the option of serving an additional fifteen days a year—without pay.[128] Although reserve sublieutenants automatically became lieutenants after two years in grade, further promotions depended upon reserve training and the recommendation of regimental commanders.[129] Reservists could only fulfill their obligations when the legislature saw fit to fund training; cancellation of reserve exercises so blocked the promotion ladder that in 1934 the Ministry of War took extraordinary measures to provide training opportunities for the 5,000 men who had not had a single period of reserve duty during their five years as reserve lieutenants.[130]

The impediments to training reserve officers were not solely financial. More than 17,000 reserve officers were called up in 1933, 18,000 in 1934, and 20,000 in 1935, but summoning these men to the colors proved easier than finding appropriate duties for them to perform.[131] Because of the small number of troops available, 300 reserve officers called up for the Haute Marne maneuvers of 1936 merely watched as the Fifteenth DIM practiced an attack against the Twenty-first RI and 107th RA.[132] Observing the cadre exercises at Valenciennes at the end of May 1937 were 500 otherwise unemployed reserve officers.[133] When a reserve officer was called up for training, it was more often than not in the form of cadre convocation: three days of checking mobilization arrangements with nary an enlisted man in sight.

Reserve officers who found themselves in training camps simultaneously with the men of their wartime units had to compete for the opportunity to command them, for professional officers were equally in need of practice with full-strength units.[134] Moreover, while the reserve officers needed command time, their troops needed experienced instructors, and big maneuvers, attended as they were by flocks of superior officers, journalists, parliamentary observers, and foreign attachés, were perhaps not the safest arena for exercising green junior officers. From 1927, when legislators who attended maneuvers complained that reserve officers were incompetent to train their own men, the army normally relied on regular officers during exercises, leaving the reserve officers little opportunity either to establish their authority or to reinforce their own shaky military skills.[135] Under the circumstances, it is not surprising to hear of a reserve machine gun officer who assured a British observer that he would learn after mobilization how to lay out a fire plan, of a brigade of Spahis receiving reserve officers in September 1939 who had never before served with African troops, and of a Parisian lieutenant who found himself mobilized into an unfamiliar unit stationed in the alien environment of a Maginot line fort.[136]

The machine gunner's claim that he would learn his trade after the war started was evidence less of procrastination than of the multitude of other responsibilities that occupied a reserve officer in training camp. Arriving two days in advance of his men, he was expected to use the time to familiarize himself with new weapons, doctrine, and regulations, but it was also his job to inspect the barracks, kitchens, and latrines that his men would use during their training and to learn the myriad administrative tasks involved in keeping soldiers fed, clothed, housed, and healthy in wartime. Since he had probably never met the members of his unit, he had to study the personnel records and memorize the place of birth, profession, military experience, state of training, and family situation of each reservist.[137]

The dearth of command opportunities for reserve officers sparked a special study in the winter of 1935–1936 and the inauguration of special training programs for reserve captains and lieutenants being considered for promotion. Thereafter, eighty captains each year spent twenty days at the Campe de Ruchard working with two battalions of infantry and a company of tanks, while two groups of a hundred lieutenants received a similar period of special training. Another program ignored the usual barrier between officers and noncommissioned officers by attaching reserve artillery officers to courses on new mortars and antitanks at the Ecole de Perfectionnement de Sous-Officiers de Carrière.[138] By 1938 about 800 of the army's 120,000 reserve officers participated each year in the three programs.

The French Army knew well a brief period of active service and occasional reserve exercises were hardly sufficient preparation for an officer. It attempted to maintain enthusiasm and professional standards by organizing a Union Nationale des Officiers de Réserve, disseminating the journal *L'officier de réserve,* and, above all, encouraging regular participation in courses offered at regional Ecoles de Perfectionnement des Officiers de Réserve.[139] As the only means of keeping reserve officers abreast of changes in military hardware and doctrine, the twelve half-day sessions a year in the reserve schools were fundamental to the reserve system, but they were also voluntary, the only rewards for participation being a railway pass allowing the bearer first-class travel on a third-class ticket and promises of future promotion in the Légion d'honneur. The one-year validity of the rail pass reflected the presumption that officers would repeat the course regularly, but the army waged a constant struggle for both enrollment and attendance. Of 34,000 officers enrolled in the inaugural course of 1926, only 3,500 attended with sufficient regularity to earn the rail pass, numbers that improved in 1927 to 42,000 and 12,000 respectively. In 1928, 22,000 were deemed to have been "assiduous," 26,700 in 1929, and 33,000 in 1930, or still only a quarter of the eligible officers.[140]

These numbers were considered far from satisfactory, especially since the younger and least-experienced officers were most conspicuously absent from the courses.[141] In an effort to increase participation, one regional commander wrote letters to the unenrolled officers of his region asking for explanations of their nonparticipation. He wrote again to announce that his letter had produced about 1,350 replies and 75 new enrollments and to castigate the many who admitted to abstaining because they saw rewards as insufficient.[142] Another regional questionnaire elicited complaints that the instructors, all regular officers, volunteered only reluctantly for the extra duty while their nonparticipating colleagues treated the course with little respect.[143] Marc Bloch, a notably energetic officer in wartime, probably spoke for many others in admitting his failure to attend the reserve courses while asserting that he could not have spared the time from his work, that he would not have learned anything useful, and that he paid for his failure by remaining the oldest captain in the French Army.[144]

Reservists had reason to disparage what General Baratier too sanguinely described as the "substantial advantages" awarded for attending reserve courses.[145] The first-class rail pass might be worth three or four thousand francs a year to a traveling salesman, and at holiday time it saved money for affluent families who traveled first class in any case. But most reserve officers were small proprietors who rarely had occasion to travel alone and could not afford to buy first-class tickets for their families.[146]

When these inducements proved ineffectual, reserve-training enthusiasts tried other measures to improve participation in the *écoles de perfectionnement*. In 1931 and again in 1933, the annual congresses of reserve officers (congeries of the keener representatives of the species) proposed that attendance become a prerequisite for further promotion, but the minister denied his authority to alter the promotion requirements established by the law of 8 January 1925.[147] In 1934 the army determined to hold an extra training session for truant sublieutenants.[148] The following year, members of the Chamber of Deputies proposed offering family rail passes and free uniforms every five years to officers in the reserve course, but the general staff objected that the national railroad company would not provide the former, and that the latter would be expensive and would discriminate against officers with valid reasons for skipping the course.[149] Arguing that many officers were completely ignorant of contemporary weapons, tanks, and communications equipment, Minister of National Defense Edouard Daladier ordered a six-day training period in 1938 for all officers who had not attended the reserve schools. In the following year he sponsored a law that made participation compulsory on pain of extra reserve training.[150] Whether or not in response to Daladier's efforts, attendance reached 50,012 in 1938.[151]

If the lecture given by French armor expert Lieutenant Colonel Jean Perré on the "the modern tank" is a fair sample of the course, poor attendance was not the only defect of French reserve-officer education.[152] Perré spent fourteen pages on definitions (What is a tank? What are its essential elements—armor, armament, speed, strategic mobility, weight?) before offering a six-page discussion, including further definitions of maneuver and accompaniment tanks, of the employment of tanks in the attack. The point of the lecture appears to have been to convince the audience that French armor doctrine could be irrefutably deduced from the essential nature of the tank, that, given the definitions, "the deductions are obvious."[153] Little in Perre's rationalist discourse would likely be useful in the field to an inexperienced reserve officer.

Bad as the situation was for reserve officers, the 300,000 reserve noncommissioned officers were even less well prepared for their responsibilities.[154] Arguably, it was impossible to produce adequate noncommissioned officers under the twelve-month service.[155] Immediately upon induction into the army, each regiment separated potential non-commissioned officers—holders of the *brevet de préparation militaire,* for example—into three special training platoons that lived and messed together as a company and were spared all fatigues. After five months of training, the successful candidates were promoted to reserve corporal or, for those who had taken the military preparation course, *corporal chef* (senior corporal).[156] At the end of the active year, some of the corporals became category B reserve sergeants and, therefore, section leaders without having exercised either rank or function during training, and it is hardly surprising that many proved inadequate for their jobs.[157] Those who missed immediate promotion could qualify as section leaders later by doing an extra eight-day reserve exercise.[158] This dizzy passage from green recruit to sergeant contrasted strikingly with the period of three-year service, which allowed two years of training before promotion to noncommissioned rank and a further year of leadership experience. With the institution of two-year service in 1935, the reserve noncommissioned officer training course was lengthened to six months, a step designed simultaneously to improve training and to economize (by one month) on noncommissioned officer pay.[159] Two-year service also produced the anomaly that, during their second year, the hastily trained category B reserve sergeants outranked future professional soldiers following a slower career pattern. The army tolerated the unfairness because the reserve sergeants were so desperately needed and defended it with the excuse that the regulars would enjoy greater opportunities in the long run.[160]

Recruitment of noncommissioned officers from within each conscript contingent served the cause of unit cohesion and administrative efficiency, but the reciprocal of common age and, theoretically, shared local loyalty was diffidence. Placed in charge of neighbors whose military service had been exactly as long as their own, reserve noncommissioned officers exercised their authority reluctantly.[161] As a French newspaper reported after the 1934 Mourmelon maneuvers, "Noncommissioned officers do not order, they request. They do not consequently obtain results, or else they are obtained in an unsatisfactory manner."[162] Upon arrival in training camp, reserve noncommissioned officers found it difficult to assert authority over men who had been their equals until the train reached the station and the reservists donned uniforms and insignia.[163] Marcel Pétain says that his boss preferred cooking to command (a true "corporal chef"?) and repeatedly announced, "I never asked to be a corporal—fend for yourselves."[164] Captain de Vibraye struggled unsuccessfully to eradicate from reserve noncommissioned officers "a deplorable tendency towards familiarity with the men—in particular an unacceptable *tutoiement.*"[165] Jean-Paul Sartre sums up his relationship with his corporal—"He's ashamed of being a leader, but nevertheless wants to make me obey him; and I'm an undisciplined soldier, who doesn't want to obey him and appeals to the socialist in him against the military superior"— and gloats that his refusal to cooperate reminds the corporal "that by his own free choice he regrets being a leader, so consequently he should be my accomplice when I resist him."[166]

Leadership defects in which Sartre took a certain obvious pleasure aroused very different emotions in the high command, and reports on the performance of reserve noncommissioned officers resound with variations on the adjective "incapable."[167] If noncommissioned officers are the backbone of an army, that of the French Army was desperately in need of stiffening. One proposed remedial measure, the inclusion of noncommissioned officers in reserve division cadre exercises, was rejected by the general staff. A three-and-a-half day cadre convocation would have replaced a fifteen or twenty-one day reserve convocation, but the legal obstacle was removed by a law redefining the reserve-training obligation as seventy days rather than four convocations. Still, the staff doubted whether the experience would be worth its cost in pay, inconvenience, and distraction from the officers' study of mobilization arrangements.[168] Moreover, noncommissioned officers needed to teach and lead soldiers, not to study the divisional mobilization schedules.

On 6 October 1930, the French Army opened its first Ecole de Perfectionnement des Sous-officiers de Réserve at Turcoing to a class of 400. The course of twenty-four lectures a year was a poor substitute for practical experience; it shared many of the weaknesses of the officers' schools and had some of its own. Instructors, themselves reserve officers, were difficult to find, for the only compensation was the prospect of promotion in the Légion d'honneur.[169] That the forementioned Lieutenant Felsenhardt taught in the program gives one further pause.[170] The students could not be expected to travel, and great numbers of schools, each too small to cater to the necessary range of specialties, had to be dispersed across the country. Noncommissioned reservists were frequently unaware of the programs offered and had no incentive to attend other than the offer of reduced-price rail tickets. The 980 schools established in the first year (1930–1931) enrolled 18,283 students of whom 3,097 attended twelve sessions, 930 attended 15, and 856 attended 18 or more, totals compared favorably by General Niessel, the head of the noncommissioned officers association, with officer participation when railway cards were offered but far short of the desired 100,000 participants a year.[171] As of September 1934, however, only 9 percent of the noncommissioned officers (in comparison to 35 percent of the officers) of the Forty-first DI had attended an école de perfectionnement, and only 56,700 of all French noncommissioned officers, 19 percent of the total, attended courses in 1938.[172]

The noncommissioned officer situation remained a cause for concern in December 1939, when General Gamelin observed to General Georges that "the noncommissioned officers of our units are often of inadequate quality, as demonstrated by, among other things, the torpor and lack of initiative that reigns in certain units as well as the frequent manifestations of indiscipline (looting, etc.)."[173] Grenier reports that his sergeant, known to his subordinates as that *"petit merdeux"* ("little shit"), had been promoted from private to sergeant over the course of a few weeks "without ever having shown any particular ability" and made himself hated by attempting to steal the men's pay.[174]

The French Army's shortage of proficient reserve officers and noncommissioned officers was symptomatic of the consistent disparity between theory and practice in the organization of the reserve *armée de guerre*. Local organization and leadership recruitment from the conscript classes promised stable, cohesive, and well-trained regiments ready at need to "spring spontaneously from the nation's soil."[175] It is hard to see, however, how the system, when implemented in the real world rather than in the fantasies of the lawmakers and the first bureau of the general staff, could have produced anything other than an army of makeshift units—constantly shifting their personnel, never testing their wartime organization, and resigned to training in ad hoc units and with borrowed equipment—led by inexperienced junior officers and noncommissioned officers. Here the French Army compares unfavorably with the Wehrmacht, whose strengths included a firmly regional organization and thoroughly trained cadres.

If there is a single explanation for the French Army's poor performance in combat, it lies in the fragility of the reserve units, a fragility engendered by poor unit cohesion, inexperienced leadership, and inadequate training, and manifested in poor morale. The nature of the dual active-reserve army also shaped the military doctrine that contributed to French defeat. Behind every doctrinal decision made by French military leaders was the knowledge that France had an army of interchangeable parts in which reservists trained as visitors in one unit and fought as members of another and whose recent conscripts had to work with men whose military training had occurred years in the past. Thus, doctrine had to be designed for soldiers who rarely had the opportunity to refresh their military skills, and new ideas could be instilled in the active units only at the cost of creating a rift with the reserves. Historians use these glaring structural defects in the interwar French Army as a evidence of the imperative of military reform. Contemporary soldiers recognized the same shortcomings, but they were more likely to emphasize the implacable obstacles to change and the cost, both in morale and in civil-military harmony, of challenging the immutable. Their mission was to devise military doctrines to make the best use they could of the organization ordained by their polity.

5
The Sources of French Military Doctrine

Central to the French Army's interwar mission was the creation of doctrine—a body of uniform concepts and procedures—to guide its operations.[1] Because French doctrine so manifestly failed the test in 1940, it has been the target of careful analysis and severe criticism. Thanks especially to work by Robert Doughty and Ladislas Mysyrowicz, the substance of French doctrine is well understood, and dismissive remarks about generals who learned the lessons of the last war have been replaced by more sophisticated explanations that recognize that the French Army of 1940 was hardly a carbon copy of the one that marched victorious down the Champs Elysées in 1919.[2] What remains to be done is to address the subject with greater attention to contemporary concerns and less conviction that French soldiers ought to have followed a particular path. Whereas Mysyrowicz's intellectual approach pays too little attention to the practical world in which French military leaders had to work, Doughty grounds his argument in solid detail but never resolves the tension between his acknowledgment of the reasons for French doctrine and his conviction that interwar France ought to have done something different in order to develop "a viable doctrine."[3]

The notion of "modernity" is at the core of Doughty's final assessment of French doctrine. Variations of the words "modern" and "modernize" appear eight times in the first six pages[4] of his concluding chapter, which argues that "French doctrine was not so modern as it might have been," "that mechanization got firmly off track," and that because "most officers failed to ask hard questions," they failed to produce the answers necessary for modern war.[5] Doughty insists that the French Army should have seen the correct, the modern, way to fight and that, by failing in the 1930s to embrace the potentials of new military technology, "French doctrine in a relative sense had regressed rather than progressed."[6] Although he laments the road taken by the French Army—"if only French doctrine had been more modern"—Doughty goes further than any previous historian in describing the barriers that impeded the necessary degree of progress.[7] Although noting the unwillingness of French officers to challenge their doctrinal assumptions Doughty insists that these men were, nonetheless, intelligent and dedicated officers. His astute description of French doctrine as a "masterpiece of Cartesian logic and bureaucratic compromise"[8] invites further investigation of what these competent officers thought they were doing and why they put so much faith in the construct they created. Doughty admits that the "ultimately . . . inadequate French doctrine . . . possessed a logic and coherency rarely found in modern armies' thinking," and the contradiction begs exploration.[9] This chapter and the next will look at the sources and elements of French doctrine in an effort to understand not why French soldiers failed to meet our standards of modernity but why they believed their army to be modern in contemporary terms.

The story of French doctrinal development is a demonstration that doctrine is not made in a vacuum, that military leaders cannot devise methods of fighting and then expect their nations to organize army and foreign policies to match. The relationship goes the other way. A defensive strategy and an army composed largely of poorly trained reservists were two immutable facts to which interwar French doctrine had to conform. To reject them, to demand a different kind of army in the pursuit of doctrinal innovation, would have been to violate the principle of military subordination to political leaders. It also meant abandoning an apparently reliable set of military ideas for an uncertain future. Fortunately for the piece of mind of French military leaders, the doctrine that suited their army and their strategy also seemed to satisfy the military conditions of their day.

Often criticized for being too conservative, the French Army was less conservative—that is, less committed to protecting an existing set of institutions and values—than it was careful and cautious.[10] World War I had given French soldiers a glimpse into the abyss of defeat while making them all too agonizingly conscious of the toll of survival. Their pride in victory was brittle, marred by awareness of its staggering cost, by remembered reliance on a coalition of allies, and by the knowledge that France remained weaker than Germany demographically and industrially. In planning for the next war, their challenge was to protect a population with scant enthusiasm for further sacrifices and with little faith in the leaders who would demand them. The army had to create the safest possible doctrine, one designed to win defensive war using the short-service conscript army that French citizens were willing to provide. Only in the sense that doctrine challenged neither the army's organization nor the goals of national policy did it stem explicitly from conservative sentiments. True, the actual elements of doctrine easily bear the conservative label, but only because the doctrines that seemed best for military reasons had visible roots in traditional French military institutions.

French doctrine had to be safe, and, to engender confidence among the soldiers and the citizens of France, it had to appear to be safe. The impression of safety came both from the inherent plausibility of the doctrine's constituent elements—firepower, the defensive, and the methodical battle—and from its relative stability. This need for confidence, even more than the practical impediments to communicating new doctrine to reserve troops, discouraged the army from offering novel or experimental ideas.[11] Far from trying to impress the country with repeated innovation, the high command took the position that regulations bearing the imprimateur of the general staff were gospel. Change required discussion and discussion hinted of uncertainty; therefore, "the price of infallibility was prudence."[12] Debate could be, and was, publicly discouraged, but the preferred approach was to present doctrine in a form so authoritative that it rendered challenge inconceivable.

Authority came from multiple sources, most obviously from the French victory in World War I. It had been under French command that armies of the Allied and Associated Powers had launched the final successful offensives of 1918. The Grand Quartier Général, not the famous German General Staff, had earned the laurel wreath, and the Ecole Supérieure de Guerre (ESG) had replaced the Kriegsakademie as the world's premier institution of higher military study. Five-hundred foreign officers from thirty-eight countries attended the ESG during the interwar period, almost ten times the total for the thirty years before 1914.[13] As Winston Churchill reminds us, "No one can understand the decisions of that period without realizing the immense authority wielded by the French military leaders and the belief of every French officer that France had the primacy in the military art."[14] After World War I, the *auctoritas* of men like General Debeney, the victor at the Battle of Montdidier of 8 August 1918 and a major influence on the fundamental *Provisional Instructions on the Tactical Employment of Large Units* of 1921, compelled belief.[15] But French regulations of the interwar period rested their claims not on the reputations of their authors but on the validity of the methods employed in their formulation. The French Army, in Doughty's words, "organized a complex and sophisticated system for considering new ideas and new technologies"[16] in order to ensure that the doctrines produced would be respected for their explicit and unimpeachable intellectual foundations.

How the French went about the process of identifying the correct principles of military action has been the subject of some historical study. Superficially, French military circles were divided between the historical and the material, or "positive," schools of analysis. Whereas the adherents of the historical argued that the study of history revealed universally applicable truths, the materialists or positivists denied the existence of such principles in a world of changing technology and insisted that ideas had constantly to be reexamined in the light of new material conditions.[17] On this analysis, the struggle over doctrine in interwar France was waged between those who claimed that history ratified firepower, defensive warfare, and the methodical battle and proponents of the thesis that contemporary technology would usher in an age of mobile, offensive war.[18]

To describe a doctrinal conflict as a struggle over epistemology may appear to be the imposition of a historian's—or a philosopher's—perspective upon practical soldiers, but the French armed forces thought in these very terms. Teaching the 1884–1885 tactics course at the ESG, Colonel A. G. Maillard distinguished the historical method, in which one "takes a fact of which the result is known and studies its causes, development, and effects in order to draw conclusions from them," from the positive method of "studying a priori one's forces and their sphere of action in order to draw a conclusion."[19] The late-nineteenth-century debate over French naval strategy and doctrine between the "*guerre d'escadron*" school and the "*jeune école*" had been explicitly no less methodological than substantive. The historically minded advocates of a "blue water" navy defended Admiral Alfred Thayer Mahan's thesis that history demonstrated the centrality of command of the sea exercised by the battleship fleet. The materialists of the *jeune école* countered that new devices like the torpedo boat and, later, the submarine offered an economical means of putting paid both to the capital ship and to the strategic pretensions of its advocates.[20] The historians won the struggle over French navy policy, but they did so only with help from members of another materialist faction, men who shared the *jeune école*'s enthusiasm for technology but insisted that the big gun, not the torpedo, ought to be the basis of naval strategy and doctrine. Although the capital ship reified the Mahanian ideal of struggle for command of the sea for its historically oriented champions, the materialist group merely judged it the best platform for naval artillery.[21] After World War I, practical debates continued to be couched in methodological terms. Thus, Captain Charles de Gaulle's first challenge to orthodoxy took the form of an article in the *Revue militaire française* warning against a national inclination to deduce doctrine from abstract principles rather than responding flexibly to the conditions of the moment.[22] The official line, however, was that taken by the anonymous contributor to the *Revue d'artillerie* who concluded an article on the use of tanks with the observation that "technology serves tactics, but it does not determine them. It does not transform general principles."[23]

Certainly, the historical and materialist categories were actively used by French military thinkers, but one cannot explain French doctrinal disputes in terms of a clear dichotomy between material and historical methods. Just as, in the argument over the *jeune école,* the identification of the battleship school with the historical method ignores its important materialist component, so, too, the French Army's use of historical examples to justify its doctrine can be shown to conceal a more complex process of thought than simple reliance on the lessons of history.[24]

The historical school has borne the brunt of the blame for French doctrinal failings in the interwar period. Mysyrowicz describes how the army responded to World War I by enlarging the historical section of the army general staff and founding new military journals whose articles evidenced a pronounced historical bent.[25] He then shows how the "history" produced by these institutions focused virtually without exception on the recent conflict, whose events became the sole source for French doctrine, and how, as the veterans of that war retired from service, history had to be harnessed as a substitute for lost personal experience and as an antidote to the seductive arguments of the materialists. For Mysyrowicz, history and doctrine were inextricably connected: "History therefore serves as the foundation of doctrine and, in return, doctrine controls history at the source."[26]

If Mysyrowicz attributes the failure of interwar French doctrine to an obsession with the lessons of history, Doughty argues that soldiers of the period simultaneously deemphasized and misused historical argument. Smarting at the accusation that the study of history had led the army to the holocaust of 1914, the ESG used its new postwar military history course not to deduce immutable historical truths but to demonstrate the fluidity of military conditions over time. Historical lessons were designed to reinforce the essential message of the practical and material part of the course—"*le feu tue*" ("fire kills")—and to reassure students that the interwar army had learned the "correct" lessons from an immediate past that shared the material conditions of the present. Having offered a more nuanced and persuasive description of what the French actually did, Doughty concludes his analysis, however, with a condemnation of the historical method that might have come from Mysyrowicz: "By overreliance on the historical example as the correct model for the conduct of operations, the French doctrine for the methodical battle was molded more by past experiences than by technological or conceptual advances, or by careful analysis of more recent wars."[27]

Neither Mysyrowicz nor Doughty demonstrates that the manner in which the French Army used historical evidence to justify its doctrine corresponds to the "historical method" that they condemn. In fact, their own arguments for the centrality of World War I in French historical analysis actually undermine the thesis of the dominance of the historical approach. Instead of studying history writ large, interwar military reviews focused uniquely on the years from 1914 to 1918.[28] The ESG, which had formerly taught military history as a component of the general course on tactics, established in 1919 a separate history course "whose essential mission was to present the lessons of the last war,"[29] allowing, as Doughty points out, the tactical course to teach by the positive method lessons that would be reinforced by the history syllabus. French military historians did not peer into the dimmer corners of historical experience but looked only under the dazzling flare of World War I. The lessons they found there—the superiority of the defensive and the primacy of fire over maneuver—stemmed directly from the weapons with which the war had been fought, that is, they derived from the contingent material circumstances of a specific historical epoch, not from universalizable principles. "*Le feu tue*" was not shorthand for a historical truth—"the killing power of fire has always favored the defense"—but, rather, for a material fact that "today's fire kills because the weapons are like those of 1914–1918 when fire demonstrably did kill."

That the French high command asserted a historical basis for its doctrine does not make it so. A man better qualified than most to judge such claims, medieval historian and reserve officer Marc Bloch, insists that the instruction at the ESG "never, really, had anything to do with history. It was, if I may say so, at the very opposite pole from the science it was supposed to be inculcating. History is, in its essentials, the science of change. It knows and it teaches that it is impossible to find two events that are ever exactly alike, because the conditions from which they spring are never identical."[30] In another context, Bloch observes: "But just because our teachers of history are inclined to focus their attention *only* on the present, or at most on the very recent past, they find the present more and more difficult to explain. They are like oceanographers who refuse to look at the stars because they are too remote from the sea, and consequently are unable to discover the causes of the tides."[31]

An army frequently accused of having paid too much attention to past events paid them, in fact, too little. General Camon pointed out in 1929 that history was taught neither at the staff college, which focused on the practical aspects of handling an infantry division, nor at the Centre des Hautes Etudes Militaires, where the course on operations at the army and army group levels emphasized logistical concerns.[32] Even the Service Historique de l'Armée, created after the Franco-Prussian War in belated response to Napoleon's suggestion that only the study of history could substitute for personal experience in teaching the art of war, did not meet the need. The officers of the historical service pursued matters of personal interest, and the tomes that resulted had no impact, Camon argued, upon the general staff. Reorganized after World War I, the historical service took upon itself the huge task of classifying the archives from that conflict, a project that spawned further large and costly volumes but undertook no systematic study of the war's history.[33]

The rare soldier-historians had little influence in the French Army, and the works that were most often cited for their historical lessons were not truly historical at all. The French Army sought not to understand the past but to use it to illustrate the present, a purpose for which only recent history was suitable. The resulting myopic approach to history is exemplified in that favorite interwar staff college text, Marius Daille's account of the battle of Montdidier.[34] Daille offered less a historical study than an exegesis of lessons deemed appropriate for the present. His conclusions—the importance of centralized command and the superiority of the homogeneous French Army over a German force divided into "shock" and "occupation" components—cannot be said to be justified by the historical method, but they did serve the purpose of validating contemporary doctrine. The methodology authorized for the journal *Revue Militaire Générale*, established in 1937, also fails to support the thesis that French soldiers actively studied history in the search for universally applicable principles. Articles submitted to the new journal were not to be historical in content; instead the authors were instructed to "limit themselves to exploiting history . . . without detailed recital of events."[35] General Debeney, the hero of Daille's demonstration of the pedagogical value of historical study, went so far as to deny that French soldiers were capable of writing history at all. The true historian had to employ the "strictest critical methods," wrote Debeney, but, "when one begins historical studies at the age of thirty or forty without having been previously imbued with the methods of historical work, one can only ask one thing of the document, that is to illustrate in one way or another an opinion already formed in other ways."[36]

Debeney was right. Although they referred to historical events, studies like Daille's *Montdidier* and the articles in the *Revue Militaire Générale* actually represented a materialist approach. That is, they did not seek to deduce from history general principles about war but rather to make an argument, using historical examples but not depending upon them, about how best to use the weapons of the current day. A more recent head of the French Army's historical service, Colonel Jean Delmas, argues that "after 1914–1918, the method in force could only be the positive [i.e., the material] method."[37] An army commanded entirely by veterans of World War I had no need to look beyond their own experience and the nature of the weapons with which they had personal experience. Delmas's suggestion that, since 1918 remained the point of reference even as the years passed, "the so-called positive method quickly became historical,"[38] misses the point. Makers of French doctrine did not actually shift from a material to a historical approach but merely allowed the passage of time to justify attaching the historical label to an essentially materialist analysis.

The French high command had two reasons to advertise as the product of historical analysis a set of doctrines actually derived from material analysis. On the one hand, the Great War was a historical event with undeniable pedagogical value: every component of doctrine illustrated, the stakes painfully clear, and the outcome a vindication of French military thought. On the other hand, the makers of official doctrine could use its historical pedigree to seize from potential challengers the methodological high ground and thereby avoid a potentially harmful debate. The heretics in the French Army, the advocates of offensive doctrines based on the new technology of motorized transport and mechanized firepower, were necessarily materialists. Fought on their own materialist terms, a struggle between the rival claims of defensive firepower and offensive mobility could go either way—so the promulgators of doctrines of the defensive and the methodical battle avoided the materialist arena altogether and relied on alleged historical principles to bring to their arguments intellectual stature as well as supporting evidence.[39]

It is, therefore, misleading to claim that belief in the lessons of history led the French Army to catastrophe in 1940. Sometimes accused of methodological rigidity, of blind faith in historical precedent, and of Cartesian rationalism, makers of French doctrine actually defended their positions with an eclectic range of arguments. Although they understood the differences between the historical and material methods of argument, makers of French doctrine conflated the two to serve their purposes. Thus, Marshal Pétain's effusive introduction to General Chauvineau's *Une invasion, est-elle encore possible?* praises the general for demonstrating that the material as well as the positive method could be used to justify the doctrine of the continuous front.[40] Similarly, General Vauthier of the air force informed students at the Ecole Libre des Sciences Politiques that the study of war must be both historical and positive.[41] The most important work of contemporary strategic analysis, Admiral Castex's *Théories stratégiques,* is, among other things, a five-volume methodological argument for the proper integration of material considerations into a strategic vision derived fundamentally from historical principles. His is, in fact, a rare effort to present an intellectually rigorous distinction between historical and material arguments. In general, military writers borrowed promiscuously from both kinds of analysis while giving intellectual precedence to the historical evidence. For example, a 1937 essay on the offensive uses historical examples from antiquity to 1918 to establish general principles about the offensive, but it concludes by implying that, because changes in technology tend to impede attack and to strengthen defense, material factors can be decisive. Thus, the historically based conclusion that "the best method of defense is to attack" appears alongside the materialist thesis that "armament rules doctrine."[42]

Careful consideration of the intellectual underpinnings of French doctrine calls into question the validity of two common criticisms of interwar French military thought: that the general staff had a mistaken faith in the "lessons of history" and that it was preparing to fight the last war instead of the next. Neither charge acknowledges the extent to which French soldiers used history to justify prescriptions derived from contemporary material conditions. In fact, in an interesting twist on a commonplace charge, both Mysyrowicz and Doughty imply that if the French erred in trying to fight the next war with the lessons of the last, their mistake lay in not looking far enough into the past. Their sin was to adopt a "historical" approach that included yesterday's events but not those of the day before.

French soldiers talked about the origin of their doctrine in order to render their conclusions unimpeachable, but method did not determine doctrine. Nothing in the nature of historical argument precluded a doctrinal verdict favoring strategic offensives by armored forces. Nor did materialist arguments necessarily have to focus, as the (secretly materialist) orthodoxy focused, on the weaknesses of the tank rather than on its strengths. But the men who developed French doctrine were free neither to scour history for insights nor to investigate all possible ways of exploiting new developments in military technology. Their range of exploration—and the kinds of doctrine that could result from it—was rigidly circumscribed by strategy, military organization, and politics.

The excellence of the French high command's performance in World War I was a component of that climate as fundamental as the idea of total war and as inviolable as French territory. The question of whether other methods might have won the war at a smaller cost could not be asked without also asking how many of the 1,300,000 Frenchmen killed or missing from 1914 to 1918 had died unnecessarily. The battle of Montdidier became the model because French generalship had to have been exemplary. But unwillingness to challenge the price paid for the recent victory did not imply a willingness to repeat the experience. On the contrary, the army feared that time would cloud memory and that the safe doctrines inspired by the hecatombs of World War I would be ignored in favor of rash theoretical ideas. Fear of forgetting led to constant reiteration of Pétain's maxim *"le feu tue,"* while the editors of the 1938 infantry regulations took it upon themselves to preserve the memory of "certain lessons of the Great War that were so vivid in the hearts and minds of veterans."[43]

Surely it was a concern for safety, a fear that innovation might lead to bloody errors, rather than conservatism for its own sake that guided doctrinal development by the French high command. The remark, attributed to "une haute personalité militaire" ("a high-ranking member of the military") in 1919, that the main imperative was "not to make any mistakes" (*de ne pas faire de bêtises*)[44] actually referred to postwar army reorganization but could well have been an explanation of the high command's rigid control over doctrine. And rigid it was. Labeling an element of doctrine "experimental" was not an invitation to test it in the field but a stricture against unsupervised experiments that might contaminate the army with unorthodox ideas. Thus, General Gamelin forbade maneuvers by medium tank units except in the presence of a member of the Conseil Supérieur de la Guerre until an official doctrine on the subject had been developed.[45] Fear of unsupervised operations drove the decision to form the experimental armored division authorized for exercises from 30 August to 3 September 1937 immediately before the test period.[46] According to then Captain André Beaufre of the general staff, Gamelin silenced the prevailing "widespread discussion of motorization and mechanization" with a stiff admonition that "the sole authority for the establishment of doctrine is the General Headquarters of the Army," and he warned that no articles or lectures on doctrine were to be published or delivered without official authorization.[47] Indeed, certain matters, especially the employment of battle tanks, were so highly sensitive that, when an official doctrine for the employment of the armored divisions was created in 1939, it remained restricted to the high command—with the happy result, Jeffrey Gunsberg notes, that German intelligence remained ignorant of the French intentions for the use of armored vehicles.[48] In other cases, however, tactical tests were permissible. Officers of the 131st RI admitted to an American observer that in using their new armored cars "they are merely experimenting," and the shift from horses to armored cars provoked doctrinal controversy within a cavalry squadron.[49]

Doctrines imposed from above were not meant to be dissected below: "The junior officers refrained from discussing the fundamental problems because such discussion might have entailed criticism of their superiors, and that might have been interpreted as a violation of discipline."[50] As noted previously, the high-ranking officers attending the Collège des Hautes Etudes de Défense Nationale may have been selected for their potential to achieve positions in which they would influence policy and strategy, but they were kept on a tight rein in the meantime.[51]

Even France's most senior soldiers were not free to spread their opinions indiscriminately. Generals Gamelin, Georges, and Dufieux all agreed on the sensitivity of General Condé's report on cadre exercises he had conducted for mechanized units in the Cambrai region in 1937. Denied permission to create an armored division even on paper, Condé had nevertheless postulated the use of rapid tank attacks using direct radio communication between the tanks and their supporting artillery—ideas susceptible to dangerous misinterpretations. To protect the army from risky experiments and doctrinal confusion in the absence of an officially sanctioned "safe, simple, and precise way of employing modern tanks," Condé's paper was dismissed as "more theoretical than practical," and its circulation beyond the Conseil Supérieur de Guerre was forbidden.[52]

It is easy, however, to exaggerate the French high command's intent and ability to block the flow of all ideas incompatible with official doctrine, and perhaps too much has been made of Beaufre's bitter memoirs and of such unsubstantiated assertions as sociologist Stefan Possony's claim that "in peacetime only those officers were selected for the higher ranks whose conformance to the doctrine was brilliantly convincing."[53] Colonel Mainié's staff college lecture on motorization, for example, was published in the *Revue d'infanterie,* a heresy that cannot be attributed, as one historian would have it, to editorial carelessness.[54] Some articles in the *Revue militaire française* and the *Revue de cavalerie* were accompanied by the disclaimer that they did not represent official policy; even more heretical views emerged, often pseudonymously, in newspapers.[55] Indeed, so many unorthodox books appeared that in 1939 the government stiffened the regulations, requiring officers on active duty to obtain the permission of the Ministry of War before publishing about war since 1914, foreign powers or armies, current military policy, or "questions pertaining to contemporary personalities, or whose nature is such as to give rise to political or religious controversies."[56] Military journals were published under the eye, but not in the iron grip, of the general staff, a situation that led General Colson to complain in 1935 that many of the historical pieces in the recent issues of the official *Revue militaire française* provided a forum for academically inclined authors but failed to reinforce doctrine. Colson called for the journal to entrust "constructive studies" to selected officers, guiding them in their choice of subjects and "towards the ideas and lessons to be emphasized."[57] When Colson argued that the journal ought systematically to disseminate lessons chosen by the high command, the staff replied, that the review was already too much an official instrument and should, indeed, be replaced by a free-thinking journal independent of the military hierarchy—a response startling to those imbued with notions of French commitment to doctrinal uniformity.[58]

The general staff's call for greater doctrinal discussion was met in the following year by the creation of the *Revue militaire générale*.[59] In introducing the new publication, Marshal Franchet d'Esperey heralded the end of "the era of intellectual dictatorship."[60] The new journal did indeed provide a forum for debate. The 1937 and 1938 issues saw many contributions on the contentious matter of unified command, and pieces like Captain H. Grimaux's essay on armored warfare certainly did not reflect the general staff's view on the matter. Not even the officially sanctioned historical method was sacrosanct in a journal that published an article by Colonel Amédée Bernard denying the relevance of past lessons to contemporary problems.[61]

Claims that a pernicious uniformity of thought stifled the French Army rest in part on the notion that the Ecole Supérieure de Guerre was captive to the elder Moltke's idea that, faced with the same problem, any number of staff officers should produce a single, identical solution.[62] Ironically, the German general staff attributed its success in 1940 partially to a pernicious conformity sown by the French staff college throughout the French Army.[63] Indeed, before World War I, the staff college was renowned both for its demanding entrance requirements and for its efforts to instill in future staff of-

ficers uniform responses to any set of circumstances. Speaking to the class
of 1901, General Bonnel argued that "frequently repeated exercises reinforce reflexes" and insisted that, with practice, officers would be able to respond spontaneously, without reflection, to any situation.[64]

After World War I, however, the ESG took on a new look. As run by
General Debeney from 1919, it defined its mission as the development of
each officer's personality and spirit of decision.[65] Instead of imposing
"school solutions" to specific problems, the college taught an approved
method of reasoning, whose principal elements were the mission, the available resources and time, the terrain, and the forces and possibilities available
to the enemy.[66] "Continually dinned into the students," reported American
graduate Major Ralph K. Smith, was "the phrase '*Pas de schema,*' 'No
fixed formulas,' no set-ups to apply blindly to different situations."[67] For all
that Smith insisted on the instructors' receptivity to individual styles of command, however, the approved method tended to guide the students towards
identical solutions, especially since the students worked under notorious
time pressure. Afternoon map exercises compressed five hours' worth of order writing into three hours, and the weekly homework problems each demanded twenty to fifty hours of work. The purpose of these daunting assignments appeared to an English participant "not to be so much to attain
the impossible as to train officers to think and work quickly and in a somewhat rattled state of mind," and the mandatory early-morning riding sessions served to add an element of physical tiredness as well.[68]

The staff college pursued flexibility of thought by challenging the students with scenarios too bizarre for textbook answers. "This method," observed Maj. R. K. Sutherland of the United States Army, "teaches mental
agility and inculcates the ability to adapt oneself to extreme situations, but I
believe a student should have as a base of departure the ability to solve rapidly and accurately an ordinary problem, acquired through considerable
practice, before being given the extremely unusual situations calling for
equally unusual solutions."[69] Although designed to prevent officers from depending on rote solutions, these problems were not intended to encourage
rashness. On the contrary, Sutherland emphasized that "this idea of caution
is apparent throughout and to one trained in American methods, appears at
times excessive." In particular, he saw the preponderant role given to artillery fire in French planning as reflecting "a combination of great trust in the
75s and the idea of caution."[70] It seems likely that the unconventional problems offered to the staff-college students taught not creative thought but the

mental gymnastics necessary to render even the most awkward situation amenable to an orthodox solution.

The staff college, of course, was not a source but a disseminator of military doctrine—or so one is constantly reminded by repeated, almost shrill, official declarations of the high command's monopoly. When General Rageneau, director of the Centre des Hautes Etudes Militaires, spoke to participants in the 1931 staff tour at the Ecole Supérieure de Guerre, he chose as his theme the dangers of a growing tendency to depart from the doctrines prescribed in the official manuals.[71] Debeney, who insisted on the ESG's role in developing the personalities of staff officers, denied any greater ambition: "The role of the Ecole de Guerre is not to produce a doctrine . . . Doctrine must come from the responsible commanders." Remembering that the prewar ESG had been accused of pressing Colonel Grandmaison's *l'offensive à l'outrance* ("to the limit") against the wishes of the General Staff, Debeney strove to calm "old suspicions" that the college's instructors might exercise an influence over the students disproportionate to their rank and authority.[72]

Officially, the high command's responsibility was to make doctrine, and the military schools' mission was to teach it. This distinction was blurred, however, because the Ecole Supérieure de Guerre and the Collège des Hautes Etudes Militaires were the only institutions equipped to carry out detailed analyses of doctrinal questions. The officers of the general staff, meanwhile, were "distinct from the troops, absorbed by bureaucratic occupations . . . insufficiently informed to be good judges of the weighty questions inherent in a doctrine for war."[73] Equally constrained as a potential source of doctrine was the CSG, a committee of senior generals lacking any working group to which it could delegate projects. One reason for the unchanging nature of interwar French doctrine was that the agencies empowered to revise it lacked the tools, and those organizations that had (or could have developed) the tools were restricted solely to teaching doctrine. For the high command was less worried that its doctrine would become moribund than concerned that control over doctrine might slip from the CSG and the general staff to mere war college professors. Debeney's defensiveness and Rageneau's alarm suggest, moreover, that the ESG was not unwilling to enter the realm of doctrinal development. As a 1921 study of French military education suggests, the ESG's quiescence on doctrinal matters reflected the reigning consensus in the immediate aftermath of World War I, but "it is not to be doubted that one will in the future once again see doctrine emanating from the ESG."[74]

French institutions of higher military education handled military doctrine in much the same way the army as a whole did. Even though the high command invoked the importance of creative thinking, its own regulations, textbooks, and exercises hammered home the importance of adhering to approved concepts. Unorthodox notions were not completely squashed, but they made no headway in an army that lacked institutional methods for reevaluating its own ideas. Because it was the product of rigorous analysis resting on a firm methodological base, official doctrine could be presented as evidence not of hide-bound conservatism but of up-to-date military thought. Thus, the "complex and sophisticated system for considering new ideas and new technologies" identified by Doughty produced not only the substance of French doctrine but reasons to have faith in it as well.[75]

Before examining specific elements of French doctrine, I address two of its more commonly misunderstood components: the continuous front and maneuver. Though no recent academic analysis repeats the old shibboleth that French belief in the impenetrability of prepared defenses imbued them with a fatal contempt for maneuver, such oversimplifications remain common in the military and popular studies that reach a large audience. Whatever the contemporary press and the French public claimed about the "inviolability of fronts," their army knew better. Intrinsic to the long-war strategy was the intention of fighting the Germans on French terms—and not on French territory—and, therefore, as Pétain reminded the Conseil Supérieur de la Défense Nationale in June 1928, "assuring the inviolability of the national soil is thus one of the major lessons of the war."[76] But the demand that the land of France be sacrosanct did not imply that fortifications would necessarily make it so, and French leaders argued about whether to build a single, unbroken line of frontier fortifications or to fortify selected points in an effort to achieve defense in depth and a base for counterattack. In either case, what was to be "inviolable" was French soil, not French defensive works.[77] The Conseil Supérieur de la Guerre recommended the creation of fortified regions rather than a continuous front, but money and troops were available to sustain only a poor compromise, a perimeter neither continuous nor deep. Even as the French were building frontier defenses that fell far short of the desired defense in depth, the magic adjective "inviolable" shifted, however, from France as a whole to the new fortifications named for André Maginot.

When completed in 1935, the Maginot line was in fact impenetrable to the existing German Army. After Germany began to rearm, the line continued to be treated as unbreachable by French governments that needed to assure taxpayers they had gotten their money's worth and by French soldiers who had no additional resources to devote to the country's northeastern flank. Still, General Gamelin knew that, "from 1915, . . . whenever the necessary means were judiciously employed, ONE ALWAYS BROKE A FRONT."[78]

Gamelin was himself a member of the defense-in-depth school who described prepared defenses as the "framework of maneuver" and insisted that "no more in strategy than in tactics is there defense without counterattack." Faced with the task of defending a thinly held frontier, he grumbled that "an initial LINEAR DEPLOYMENT of forces remains always AN ERROR and an ABDICATION OF COMMAND. THERE IS NO MORE DEFENSIVE MANEUVER THAN OFFENSIVE MANEUVER WITHOUT THE NOTION OF 'CENTERS OF FORCE' that is to say of 'THE PRINCIPLE EFFORT.' "[79] The commander-in-chief's rejection of linear organization in favor of defensive maneuver will come as a surprise to believers in the "Maginot line mentality."

Although the 1921 infantry regulations had given no space whatsoever to maneuver, the word had been reinstated in the French military lexicon by the end of the decade. In fact, General Maurin insisted, on maneuver's centrality in his report on the 1928 Mailly exercises: "Every maneuver can be criticized, but what is unpardonable is not to have a maneuver idea or, if one possesses one, not to make it penetrate into the brains of one's subordinates."[80] Nor were fixed defenses a panacea for General Weygand, who asserted that "even on the defensive, especially on the defensive, an army having neither the will nor the ability to maneuver is doomed to defeat."[81] Maneuver was officially restored to favor in the following article in the 1936 regulations: "However powerful are the fortified fronts, the decision, tomorrow as yesterday, will only be attained through maneuver, whose essential elements are speed and mobility."[82]

But what exactly did the French mean by maneuver? Omitted from the list of twenty-some key terms defined for use at the Centre des Hautes Etudes Militaire and the Ecole Supérieure de Guerre, the word had no authorized definition, very possibly because the high command did not want to commit itself.[83] Soldiers used the word in two different ways: first, to refer generally to any plan that employed resources to achieve a specific objective, and, second and more specifically, to denote a particular type of plan that uses such elements as rapid movement and surprise to compensate for lack of mass. The latter is represented by Winston Churchill's observation that "battles are won by slaughter and manoeuvre. The greater the general, the more he contributes in manoeuvre, the less he demands in slaughter,"[84] has virtually displaced the former since World War II. Maneuver has become the exploitation of mobility and, often, surprise to achieve an advantage in position.[85] Both usages appeared in the 1936 regulations, where maneuver was "a combination of efforts to attain a precise goal,"[86] and sample maneuvers included attack against a flank or a gap in a front and maneuver by using fire from one unit to support another's advance.[87] Although the regulations further described "speed" and "mobility" as the "essential elements of maneuver," they were not meant to replace material force. The passage equating maneuver and mobility, moreover, was balanced by uses of the word maneuver that lacked the notion of mobility. By defining the army as the *"fundamental unit of maneuver,* equipped with all of the means necessary to accomplish it *in the tactical realm,"* the chapter on the army in battle implied that a maneuver was any plan executed by an army.[88]

Frenchmen did not share the Anglo-American assumption that maneuver implied the substitution of movement for direct physical force of the subject, as Admiral Castex's discussion of the subject demonstrates. Having defined "strategic maneuver" as "to move intelligently in order to create a favorable situation," Castex offers examples of "maneuvers" that have nothing to do with movement. Even something as static as the development of warship specifications is actually a form of maneuver: "Given a set displacement, one also maneuvers—this time with tonnage. One obviously seeks the greatest offensive power, armament and speed, which, the first above all, constitute the principal objective. Other things, protection especially, generally play the role of secondary objectives."[89] Even more peculiar from the Anglo-American point of view is a French colonel's typology of three types of maneuver: strategic maneuver, industrial maneuver, and *"maneuver des études et recherches"* ("maneuver of research").[90] When General Gamelin observed that a front too broad for the forces available could be defended only by maneuver—for example, by concentrating forces on a portion of the threatened front—he clearly saw movement to be the essence of maneuver.[91] In the Mailly report, however, General Maurin's "maneuver idea" was a plan of action, and his advice was common sense rather than an invitation to mobile warfare.

Movement was not central to maneuver, for French soldiers did not see maneuver as a substitute for fire but as its employment. "Maneuver by fire," a concept dismissed by the notoriously heretical General Héring as "insubstantial as a cream puff" (*"fameuse tarte à la crème"*), was not a contradiction in terms but a fundamental concept.[92] Furthermore, French soldiers did not treat movement as a means of achieving surprise, an element of war that they feared in the hands of others but made little effort to exploit for themselves.[93] As Doughty points out:

They perceived maneuver predominantly in the sense of moving units to have them deliver fire or of moving fire without moving units. They rarely emphasized the advantages of moving units to gain something other than an advantage in firepower over an enemy. That is, the doctrine stressed the physical destruction of the enemy's soldiers and equipment to destroy his will to fight, not the movement of a unit so it could have a decided advantage over the enemy and weaken the morale and cohesion of his units.[94]

Thus, of the two distinct senses in which the soldiers of interwar France used the word "maneuver"—a plan or a plan based on mobility—the former was clearly primary. The purpose of maneuver was to focus firepower on a target. If that objective could be achieved without moving, so much the better. As General Gamelin declared in a lecture at the Centre des Hautes Etudes Militaires, at the decisive moment, questions of terrain and maneuver yield to mass, and "it is too late for finesse."[95] The gradual mechanization of the French Army in the second half of the 1930s, however fostered an interpretation of maneuver that acknowledged the suitability of the new armored fighting vehicles for a war of movement. As Dutailly observes, the general training directive issued to the army in 1935 "manifested a new will in calling for the study of large and rapid maneuvers. They were evidence of a degree of boldness because the French Army did not possess the material necessary to conduct a war of movement."[96] Dutailly argues that Gamelin's efforts to replace the rigid doctrine of centralized command in favor of mobile operations and local initiative failed for lack of equipment and because the general staff ignored the instructions of its chief, thereby so embarrassing the frustrated Gamelin that he omitted his initiatives from his memoirs. Blaming the French Army for failing to carry out its commander's wishes understates the extent to which Gamelin's cautious formulas undermined his own invitation to innovate. He juxtaposed references to mobility with reminders that the new war of movement brought new risks. Although "the boldest conceptions bring the greatest results," Gamelin also warned that, for an army of young soldiers, the execution of daring plans demanded "rigorous method."[97] Gamelin's suggestions for maneuver make no reference to the notion of surprise and insist above all on *firepower.* The 1935 training direction, like the 1936 regulations, reiterates the need to emphasize the awesome power of artillery for troops trained since 1918. What stands out in the document, for all its adumbrations of a more mobile style of warfare, are the warnings that encourage strict adherence to the doctrine of the methodical battle.[98]

Mobility received even less emphasis in the updated training instruction published two years later, which treated a maneuver simply as a plan. If modern war would be war of movement and would demand initiative at every level, all the more reason, implied the new directive, to avoid complexity. Underscored in the text is the admonition that *"the operations that succeed are the simplest ones."*[99] This document forbade unsupervised experiments with independent armored units. A year later, the 1938 training order defined maneuver as "concentrating through combined fire and movement the effort of a certain number of units upon a given part of the enemy line" for the purpose of achieving fire superiority.[100] Thus the French Army had returned to the position of the 1927 Ecole Supérieure de Guerre lecture that "maneuver really begins only with the army corps: the infantry division only produces an effort, or a series of efforts, in a single direction."[101]

These arguments about definitions have a twofold importance. How the French Army defined maneuver determined how—or whether—it maneuvered on the battlefield. How historians understand the process of French military thought determines how useful the lessons drawn from the French experience will be. The study of the sources of French doctrine reveals a tension within the process of making doctrine. Doctrine had to be demonstrably valid and, therefore, had to have survived rigorous analysis of a kind possible only in an institution that encourages freedom of thought. Open discussion threatened, however, to do more harm than good. At best, it would produce useful new ideas that could be inculcated in the active-reserve army gradually, piecemeal, and at a great cost to cohesion. At worst, it would sow doubt about existing doctrine while offering no viable remedies. The answer to this tension between the need for visibly sound doctrine and uniformity of views was to "solve" doctrinal dilemmas quickly at the highest level and to structure the subsequent debate so that the official verdict suffered no dangerous challenges.

Because the doctrinal lessons of World War I were so clear and the structure of the French Army sacrosanct, the first project—the creation of the doctrine of firepower in defense and method in attack—proved straightforward. It was the second project, the intellectual reinforcement of official doctrine, that challenged the high command between the wars. The trick was not to prevent debates altogether but to win them by setting their rules and defining their terms. Thus, the defenders of orthodoxy preempted any challenge by advocates of mobile maneuver warfare by claiming the term maneuver for themselves. They deprecated the value of material arguments while insisting on the epistemological primacy of those allegedly derived from history. Although heretics found it difficult under such circumstances to present their arguments, the general staff could claim that, because the institutions and periodicals devoted to higher military education tolerated debate, their conclusions constituted a powerful ratification of existing doctrine.

French soldiers clearly put more effort into reinforcing the intellectual pillars of their conceptual edifice than into constructing it in the first place. It seems, therefore, futile to insist that they should have sought a different style of architecture. French doctrinal choices were determined by the nature of the French Army, and French doctrinal analysis was devoted not to a search for alternatives but to strengthening the case for defensive firepower and the methodical battle. If French methods were, in General Touchon's words, "rigid and constrained, especially in comparison the rapid German attacks," that was what was wanted for "an army composed primarily of reservists, very impressionable."[102] Theoreticians could have developed doctrines to take better advantage of modern technological possibilities, but the active-reserve split within the French Army would have prevented their uniform adoption and left France with an army unready to employ the new methods and shaken in its faith in the old.

6
A Very Careful Doctrine

Firepower and the Defensive[1]

The methods used by the French Army to evaluate its doctrine served better to reinforce the validity of existing conceptions than to discover new ones, a fact that reflected the high command's assessment of the relative merits of orthodoxy and innovation and acknowledged the political and social barriers to significant institutional change. This picture of an army working within inflexible constraints becomes even sharper when one shifts from studying the principles behind the development of doctrine to its component elements. Investigation of the elements of the doctrine so often blamed for the French defeat in 1940 suggests that, however bad the result in 1940, the French Army would have found it very difficult to fight differently.

The roots of French military doctrine lay neither in an obsession with the events of World War I nor in a blind determination to repress any form of novelty but in the nature of the conscript-reserve army. The constituent principles of that doctrine—the importance of firepower, the primacy of the defensive, and the methodical battle—made sense individually and formed a coherent package designed to defend France at a tolerable price.[2]

The indisputable key to interwar French military doctrine was respect for the murderous efficacy of artillery and automatic weapons. In the oft-quoted words of the first postwar version of the French "Instruction for the Tactical Employment of Large Units": "The power of fire has proved itself to be overwhelming. Fire is the dominant factor in combat. Attack is the advance of fire, defense is immobilizing the enemy by fire."[3] Pétain's dictum was simpler—"fire kills" (*le feu tue*). Makers of French doctrine agreed that fire would dominate the battlefield and would favor the defender over the attacker. The warnings in French regulations about the power of defensive fire had two purposes—to promote confidence in the army's defensive capabilities and to discourage less than perfectly prepared attacks—but these same regulations also reminded the troops that wars were not won by defense.

The tension between the two themes—the imperative of attack to achieve significant results and the inherent superiority of the defense—stood out in the 1936 edition of the regulations. On the one hand, the description of the attack as "the essential mode of action," missing from the 1921 version, was restored to the text; on the other hand, however, and counterbalancing this expression of renewed offensive-mindedness, was the new presentation of the chapter describing the importance of artillery.[4] Previously printed in normal type, the following article was now printed in boldface:

> The effects of fire are both physical and psychological. They create zones of death where the troops undergo massive and shattering losses which render them incapable of action. Either the matériel is destroyed or the units are fragmented.[5]

The change of font communicated to the historian as well as to the contemporary soldier that claims made about artillery in 1936 were not rote repetition of received wisdom but the considered conclusion of postwar analysis. The editors of the new edition were strongly motivated by the fear that time would dull institutional memory and French soldiers would have to relearn the bloody lessons of 1914–1918.[6] It was, therefore, the explicit purpose of the 1936 regulations to assume the role of the vanishing veterans of World War I and to preserve from oblivion "certain lessons that the war had impressed so vividly on their hearts and spirits.[7]

The warnings printed in the regulations were vividly reinforced by giving the artillery center stage in French military maneuvers. "The immense trouble taken to give reality to the imaginary artillery fire emphasizes the outstanding importance that the French ascribe to the artillery arm."[8] Fire demonstrations were meant to impress, to teach on the training ground a lesson in the destructiveness of artillery that would then not have to be repeated more expensively on the battlefield. Thus, General Maurin described the purpose of maneuvers: "The farther one gets from the war, the vaguer the realities of battle. The terrible effects of fire are therefore unknown to young officers, sometimes even forgotten by those who have suffered them."[9]

Fire exercises designed to "provide striking demonstrations of the effects of artillery" were also intended to demonstrate how much firepower would be required to support a successful attack,[10] and the two themes reinforced one another in discouraging offensive action. An American officer watching a battalion-level infantry attack at La Courtine on 17 September 1932 deduced that the purpose of the exercise was to illustrate, principally for the fifty or so reserve officers in attendance, "the careful arrangements necessary for such an operation."[11] The emphasis was not on a well-prepared attack's potential for success but on the hurdles to be overcome in achieving a sufficient degree of preparation. Demonstrations of the efficacy of their own defensive firepower also made clear what attacking French infantry would suffer from German guns. Meanwhile, the catalog of difficulties to be overcome by an attacking French Army—stockpiling ammunition, control of a rolling barrage, and avoidance of friendly fire casualties—served to discourage offensive ideas.[12] From such training methods, French infantry thoroughly absorbed the lesson of the fearsomeness of defensive artillery. The reciprocal thesis, that attacks supported by sufficient firepower would succeed, stood out as the cautioning qualifier. Attack was possible if and only if the attacker possessed a vast defensive advantage; under any other circumstances, it was foolish.

The use of offensive wargames to instill caution is clearly demonstrated by an exercise against simulated German fortifications at La Courtine camp from 18 to 29 August 1938.[13] Before its successful assault on the Siegfried line, the Twenty-third DI spent six days reconnoitering the terrain, placing its artillery, and bringing up the necessary munitions. There followed two days of artillery bombardment by four groups of large-caliber mortars in preparation for a two-day attack in which an infantry regiment was supported by artillery, a section of medium B tanks, a company of D1 light tanks, and prototypes of a new self-propelled gun. In proving that German fortifications could be broken with enough tanks, artillery, smoke shells, and time, such exercises also established minimum requirements for success and could, therefore, be advanced either to bolster French confidence or to justify French inaction during the Polish campaign. Thus, although General Gamelin claimed before the war that the exercises at La Courtine proved the French Army capable of breaking the Siegfried line,[14] General Georges testified at Riom that experimental attacks on the model Siegfried line in 1939 and 1940 had proved that the French Army could not have brought her ally any useful aid. No French attack was possible before seventeen days after mobilization, and "no one ever thought it was."[15]

The French emphasis on fire extended from the artillery all the way down to infantry squad tactics, in which the light automatic weapon received pride of place to the exclusion of aimed rifle fire.[16] Squads were taught to advance against the enemy not in a skirmish line but in a column behind the man carrying the Chatellerault fusil-mitrailleur. "In a word, the Infantry attack of small units consists in advancing the automatic rifle to assault distance and then hopping to it with the bayonet so that the individual rifle fire is hardly used until after the assault is on its objective."[17] The emphasis on automatic weapons was intended to give the troops confidence in the squad's firepower, but in fact it undermined respect for the undervalued rifle. Because rifle sections "can best be described as a maneuvering, ammunition carrying, protective force for the automatic rifleman,"[18] riflemen had little reason to believe in their ability to influence a battle and no incentive to attempt to do so.

It is no surprise, therefore, that efforts to induce offensive thinking in French soldiers made little headway against the defensive habits ingrained in them by the emphasis on artillery. The Lorraine maneuvers of September 1930 directed by General Brécard, were designed to reintroduce aggressive maneuvers as an alternative to "the dilatory methods that are the direct results of the long static periods of trench warfare," but most noticeable in infantry attacks were lack of energy and insistence on artillery cover for even the smallest attack. "The one thing universally understood and adhered to," reported a British observer, "was the fireplan."[19] An American attaché observed that the division's advances were methodical and slow, preceded by a careful marshaling of resources and executed through concentrated artillery fire rather than maneuvers by troops. Tactical difficulties were less often resolved on the spot than referred to higher command. Even small units finding themselves under enemy automatic weapons fire tended to "sit tight," "call for artillery support," and "pass the buck" to the regimental commander.[20] Things were no different a year later, when observers noted that the slow preparation of attacks permitted the enemy to withdraw from threatened positions and that attacking troops attempted to achieve their objectives through artillery fire alone.[21] British reports on maneuvers by the First Cavalry Division noted that defense was emphasized over attack and that offensive operations were so slow as to invoke severe criticism from the French observer.[22] Attending these maneuvers as inspector general, Gamelin was chagrined at the "sporadic and feeble actions" and embarrassed to hear that a German attaché had wondered whether "infantry did not know how to attack." Gamelin dismissed the operation as "not an attack but a funeral procession . . . the infantry following the tanks like hearses."[23] An otherwise positive report the following year said that, although the soldiers of an infantry regiment performed well in defensive exercises, the "idea of assaulting seemed repugnant."[24] Things were no different during the 1936 maneuvers in southeastern France, where attacks were executed "with undue deliberation."[25]

The Methodical Battle

The caution with which French soldiers flexed their offensive muscles in interwar exercises does not mean that the French Army did not see the need for an offensive capability. Though trained to emphasize the advantages of defense, French soldiers recognized that war would call upon them to undertake various forms of attack: tactical counterattack to seal off a breach, strategic counterattack as the culmination of the long-war strategy, or a thrust into Germany in aid of France's central European allies. The companion of French defensive confidence was the belief that attacking was inherently dangerous, and thus for French soldiers to think offensively required either cognitive dissonance—believing simultaneously that French defenses would stop German attacks and that French attacks would penetrate German defenses—or a plan to overcome the defender's acknowledged advantages. A certain measure of the former, the presumption that one's own army is capable of deeds of which the enemy's forces are not, may be intrinsic to fighting spirit, but the French, seared by the memory of what dependence on élan had cost in 1914, also sought and found a solution to the problem of defensive firepower in the doctrine of what they called the methodical battle (*bataille conduite*).

As General Debeney had proved against Ludendorff at Montdidier on 8 August 1918, successful attack was possible—but only under specific conditions of material superiority and tactical organization. The Montdidier victory demonstrated what became the three central tenets of offensive thinking in the French Army after 1918. The first, rigidly centralized control over the battle, facilitated the other two—supporting every infantry attack with large amounts of artillery ("attack is the advance of fire") and the division of any offensive operation into a series of subordinate efforts, each with a clearly delineated objective. Offensives in the first half of World War I had been launched with unlimited goals, offering the attacking forces no respite short of victory or death; after Nivelle's bloody effort of April 1917, and the mutinies it inspired, French commanders replaced the single all-out thrust with a series of carefully modulated attacks designed to keep the enemy under constant pressure. Supported by artillery, infantry units would advance in bounds of no more than 1,500 meters before halting for a half-hour to reorganize and to allow the artillery to shift its targets and to reposition its forward observers.[26] After several such bounds, a total advance of four or five kilometers, the infantry would have reached the end of its artillery support, and a longer halt would be necessary to move the guns.[27]

Topography determined the framework of the methodical battle; ridges and hollows divided the battlefield into a "mosaic" of "compartments" naturally shielded from the direct fire of adjoining sections.[28] Out of rifle fire meant out of sight, a definition with important implications, since the defining characteristics of the methodical battle were coordination and communication. Terrain features enhanced coordination by clarifying unit boundaries and providing unambiguous phase lines for the attack, but, by emphasizing the physical separation of units, they created a psychological isolation that was easily exacerbated by the physical difficulties of communication.

Throughout the 1930s, wargames revealed that French commanders took to heart the strictures of the methodical battle against acting upon less than perfect information about both opposing and supporting forces. In one typical case, an observer reported:

> The attacking force impressed one as over cautious in the extreme as they invariably spent much time in reconnoitering all elements of any resistance encountered. Until a commander had assured himself of the exact position occupied by the opposing forces, the flanks of the position held, and the strength of the enemy by a thorough reconnaissance, no forward movement was entertained. As a consequence, small detachments of the defending forces were often able to hold up the advance of many times their own strength for long periods of time.

Such caution was in stark contrast to the regulations of 1913, which insisted that "an energetic commander-in-chief, having confidence in himself, his subordinates, and his troops, never allows his adversary priority of action under the pretext of waiting for more precise intelligence.[29]

Though critical of exaggerated caution, American military attaché Sumner Waite appreciated certain merits of the methodical approach. Shortly after viewing the "overcautious" September grand maneuvers at Aix-en-

Provence, Waite praised an exercise in coordinated attack by the infantry and D tanks of the 508th Tank Regiment. "The advance was beautifully employed." Thanks to radio, "the liaison within the tank units and the coordination between elements engaged in the attack were practically flawless. . . . The entire advance was a logical progression bringing into play the correct use of ground and cover and employing at the proper time and place the characteristics of the various weapons."[30]

Waite's condemnation of the glacial caution of the French movement in the September maneuvers and his contrasting praise for the businesslike advance of the 508th Tank Regiment suggest that methodical battle could be either the surest, safest exploitation of the varied tools of modern war or a recipe for inertia and that the difference between the two outcomes depended largely on the efficiency of communications. The methodical battle dictated that units move only when in possession of clear information about conditions to its front and in conjunction with the units on both flanks. Therefore, the whole machine would grind to a halt after loss of contact with reconnaissance troops or neighboring formations. Thus, communications held a central place in French doctrine. Within a single division could be found flags, motorcyclists, automobiles, airplanes, telephones, three types of radio, radio telephones, carrier pigeons, and searchlights.[31] The presence of carrier pigeons alongside radio sets reminds us that the latter were in their infancy—complicated, fragile, difficult to use, and easily blocked by terrain.[32] Although the army adopted some thirty-two different models of radio telephone, radio telegraph, and receiver between 1928 and 1939, many units depended on older methods.[33]

If communications failure could halt the methodical battle, good communications were its lubrication, for French doctrine had redefined the notion of speed of movement. The rate at which soldiers could move was deemed to be virtually fixed, with few dividends to be gained by pushing the pace. What could be hastened, what made the difference between a slow advance and a rapid one, was the period between forward bounds. The methodical battle could be rapid if the necessary reorganization and preparation were accomplished quickly—if, that is, the commanders on the spot could communicate easily with their own units, with those to their flanks, with supporting artillery and armor, and with higher echelons. Thus, as General Paquettte reminded a class of high-ranking officers, "speed is to be sought in methodical preparation and not in impetuous boldness."[34]

If communications were the center of the methodical battle, they had to be the focus of training as well. And indeed they were "the one point in the instruction that took up more time, produced more errors, and occasioned more delay than any other point."[35] Maneuvers conducted by General Condé in August 1933 demonstrated the difficulty of maintaining the most necessary communication link—that between advancing infantry and supporting artillery—as troops advanced beyond their first objective and under the fire of their own guns. In the same exercise, orders delaying an attack reached the troops too late.[36] The lessons drawn from the exercise were that commanders must exercise control on the battlefield and avoid independent action when communications could not be assured.

Good communications were crucial not only to conducting the methodical battle but to preventing "encounter battles" or "meeting engagements" arising out of unexpected contacts with the enemy,[37] but the available means of communications left much to be desired. Radios, with their short range and vulnerability to eavesdropping, were unsatisfactory for transmitting information from forward elements to headquarters. Regulations called for messages to be carried by motorcycle, but the method was slow, especially if a moving recipient had to be located, and the messenger was vulnerable. An armored car was deemed a more reliable choice, if one could be spared by the forward contingents.[38] In the absence of surer means of command and control, local commanders were forbidden to commit to action any troops that could not be disengaged, and they were expected to keep a short leash on the mechanized reconnaissance forces that might otherwise draw their parent units into combat. Advanced guards were kept small to discourage them from "premature engagement" and generals exercised "extreme caution" in keeping divisional reconnaissance groups "tied down."[39]

The methodical battle was the centerpiece of French doctrine. It resolved the tension between the manifest tactical superiority of defensive firepower and the imperative that, whether for operational reasons or strategic ones, the French Army had to be ready to undertake offensive operations. The methodical battle explained how attacks could be carried out but also established daunting prerequisites for their success. It was a doctrine appropriate not only to French strategic requirements but to the abilities of an inexperienced army, and it instilled confidence in generals who believed themselves to have learned the lessons of one war and to be preparing appropriately for the next. The whole elaborate edifice was threatened from the beginning, however, by the development of a new weapon, the armored fighting vehicle, that had either to be integrated into the methodical battle or to be used as the basis of a new doctrine.

Motorization

No component of the French Army's doctrine has received more criticism than its treatment of the possibilities offered by the internal combustion engine. The performance of French Armored units in 1940 was so unimpressive compared to the stunning successes of the German Panzer divisions that it took years to discredit the assumption that such a result could only have reflected a French rejection of mechanized war.[40] In fact, France actually possessed more tanks than Germany in 1940, and French machines were as good as, and in many cases better than, the German ones. This discovery has led historians to conclude that if the French had tanks, they did not know how to use them and that French military leaders must have accepted mechanization slowly, reluctantly, and in a manner calculated not to subvert the premises of their defensive doctrine. Obsessively cautious, they preferred to distribute light tanks by battalion, company, or even section to support individual infantry units and shied away from creating independent formations of medium (battle) tanks. When the need for armored divisions became apparent, there was no time to construct vehicles suited for the pace of armored war.

None of these observations is wholly false, but like other aspects of doctrinal development in interwar France, the story of armor doctrine is not one of blind conservatism, or sloth, or stupidity, or national poverty either physical or intellectual. It is a story of intractable problems, irreconcilable requirements, and a particular, reasoned set of strategic and doctrinal judgments.[41] Charges that the French Army was laggard in embracing the internal combustion engine not only ignore the extent to which that organization was responding to its own particular needs and was hindered by political and economic constraints but, worse, assume the existence of a single true road to modern warfare that the French Army should have seen.

France finished World War I with the world's largest supply of tanks (Renault FTs) and no doubt at all that tanks, and the trucks that had served as Verdun's lifeline, would play a role in any future war. In the 1921 *Revue de cavalerie,* General Weygand made a case for the motorization of French cavalry divisions, and motorization was a common theme in the *Revue militaire française* throughout the 1920s.[42] The Rhône maneuvers of September 1923 featured the use of motorized machine guns,[43] and major cavalry exercises in September 1927 had as their object "to study the combination of mounted and automobile elements in a cavalry division in an operation" and were noteworthy for the use of aircraft to support ground forces.[44] In the same year, tactical experiments took place at Brittany's Coëtquidan camp to determine whether tanks were best employed in sections of three or five machines.[45] As early as the summer of 1927, enough field exercises had been done with tanks that Colonel Pol-Maurice Velpry felt ready to publish a doctrinal study in the *Revue militaire française*.[46]

In August 1928, experiments at Mailly Camp under the direction of General Maurin studied the organization of a tank regiment, supply of an infantry regiment by truck, and the employment of a mechanized divisional reconnaissance group.[47] Maurin's report, full of ideas for the future, belies the notion that Frenchmen were incapable of seeing beyond the last war. He notes that, because tanks were invented during the static phase of World War I, they had been confined to set-piece battles against established enemy positions and had never been tested in what promised to be their most useful roles—making initial contact and engaging the enemy. Maurin argued that tanks ought to be employed en masse and that the worthy goal of cooperation between infantry and armor ought not to be interpreted to mean that penny packets of infantry would follow single tanks forced to slow their pace to that of the foot soldiers. Rather, "the two arms ought to support and not impede one another." In particular, tanks had to be free to retain their own pace. Predicting further improvements in tanks' weapons, vision, and speed, Maurin concluded with a call for further study.[48] The 1929 maneuvers featured experiments with motorized supply, the use of mechanized infantry (*dragons portées*), and the motorization of light artillery.[49] In the 1930 maneuvers of the 8th Military Region an entire infantry division was resupplied by small trucks and automobiles.[50]

Initial motorization efforts were by no means uniformly encouraging. The British military attaché who attended maneuvers of the Twentieth Corps in the Vosges in September 1928 reported that "with the existing bad material and the reservist or [Vietnamese] drivers it is very doubtful if the French General Staff will be able to carry out successfully large-scale maneuvers of troops by lorry at the outset of a campaign."[51] Inspector General of Cavalry Brécard insisted in a May 1929 lecture at Saumur (where the audience was likely to share the British cavalryman's view that motorized units "smelled like a garage and looked like a circus") that:

> automobiles, particularly for troop transportation, are very often undependable and dangerous playthings, the nearer they approach the front in war time. Our experiences in the Rhineland last year proved to me that one may order a truck troop move-

ment, but that one should next begin to pray. One may not insure execution of those orders, no matter what precautions are taken. If true in peace time, how much truer will it be in war time.[52]

The discouraging results of contemporary British experiments gave the French further reason for caution.[53]

Some cavalrymen may have felt an emotional antipathy to "motorization mania,"[54] but they were not short of substantive arguments. Why spend scarce funds to purchase matériel that would increase both operational supply problems and the nation's strategic dependence on imported petroleum? An American observer took the same line when he argued that difficulties involving fuel supplies in French maneuvers were an argument in favor of retaining the horse: "It is certain that these maneuvers have shown up the limitations of motorized units as compared to mounted units in an unexpected manner. While the [dragoons] are a necessary and valuable addition to the cavalry division, the only real cross country unit without limitations is the mounted unit."[55] Horses and fodder were natural French resources, and the supply would rapidly dry up if military purchases were interrupted by an expensive flirtation with the internal combustion engine.[56] Moreover, the Chamber's practice of voting military budgets one year at a time discouraged long-term projects.[57] Motorization promised other problems—a cacophony of motorized, mechanized, horsed, bicycle-mounted, and foot-slogging components moving at different speeds, requiring different roads, and powered by different fuels.[58] By increasing the number of specialists required by the army, motorization complicated the induction and training of recruits and the distribution of reservists among regiments.[59] If General Chauvineau was correct in predicting that motorization would merely increase the amount of matériel massed at the front, its consequence would be not mobile warfare but increasing stagnation.[60]

In return for all these inconveniences, motorization promised relatively small gains as long as the French Army stuck to a defensive plan of operations. After all, a motorized unit was simply one possessed of a certain number of trucks, many of them requisitioned from civilians and others temporarily borrowed from corps headquarters, to be used solely for the transportation of men and material by road. Motorization enhanced strategic mobility, the ability to move to the battlefield, but it reduced the division's organic artillery and increased its vulnerability in transit. Indeed, French commanders entertained nightmares about German aircraft making target practice of road-bound columns.[61] Their fears were reinforced by observations gleaned from the Civil War in Spain, whose events "highlighted the fearsome efficacy of attacks on columns by low-flying aircraft."[62] Motorized infantry could not fight from its thin-skinned trucks; while on the march and while unloading it had to be protected by forces that could. Thus, if trucks were to be used to advance into contested areas, not merely to shift forces behind the front at a rate of 150 kilometers per day, security would have to be provided by equally mobile but combat-ready units designed for cavalry's traditional scouting and screening duties—in other words, by armored divisions.[63] Only with such protection could motorized units advance without fear of the encounter battle that French doctrine discouraged for ordinary infantry and emphatically rejected for the more vulnerable motorized troops.[64] With these considerations in mind, it is easy to understand the French command's reply to a 1937 offer of funds to motorize one additional division from each of the first, second, and twentieth military regions that, while the division from the first region might prove useful in Belgium, there was no value in motorizing units stationed only 25–30 kilometers from their battle positions.[65]

The French did not reject motorization altogether, but their anxiety about the demerits of motorized forces led them to experiment thoughtfully with the proper composition and use of motorized units.[66] In spite of the mixed results of such experiments, a decree of 4 July 1930 expanded the French motorization effort to encompass five infantry divisions and made the French Army the world's most mobile.[67]

Mechanization

But the July 1930 decree went beyond motorization to authorize the transformation of a cavalry division into an experimental light mechanized division (Division Légère Mécanique or DLM) and to "mechanize" one brigade from each of the other five cavalry divisions. The words "motorized" and "mechanized" were at first used unsystematically, but, by the end of the decade, "motorization" came to refer to the use of wheeled vehicles for rapid road movement by troops that fought like ordinary infantry, whereas "mechanized" units moved and fought in armored all-terrain vehicles.[68] The DLM authorized in 1930 first manifested itself in 1933 as an assortment of Citroen-Kergresse wheeled armored cars (*automitrailleuses de combat*), trucks, motorcycles, and horses. Its soldiers, like the horse cavalry they replaced, dismounted from their unarmored trucks as soon as they came into contact with the enemy.[69] Mobile and lightly armed, the light mechanized division was intended to bring modern mobility and firepower to the cavalry's traditional missions of strategic reconnaissance, screening, and delaying actions.[70] If the nomenclature promised more at the beginning than the DLM could deliver, by the end of the decade it understated the power of what had become a full-fledged armored division. Ironically, the DLM acquired the qualifying "light," a label no more precise for military formations than for food products today, only because the more impressive title, Division Mécanique, would have created a confusion of acronyms with the Division Morocain.[71] Even its original *automitrailleuses de combat* (AMC) and *automitrailleuses de reconnaissance* (AMR) equalled the earliest German "tanks" and the H-35 and SOMUA were a match for the Panzerkampfwagen III and IV, respectively, but the DLM never shed the image of being too "light" to handle the ostensibly "heavy" Panzer divisions.[72]

But the SOMUA and the H-35 are ahead of the story. In its first incarnation, more *légère* than *mécanique*, the DLM was a cavalry unit in a new guise. It was also not an unqualified success. In particular, the Renault AMC adopted in 1934 may have been a tank by another name, but it was not a very good tank.[73] Armored cars and motorcycles proved an ill-matched reconnaissance team, unable to handle the same terrain and each too vulnerable to offer effective support to the other.[74] Also, the DLM would not live up to expectations as a fighting force until its divisional artillery, two groups of 75mm guns and one of 105mm howitzers, were tracked.[75]

Historians have tended to emphasize French hesitation to create armored divisions, but for some contemporary military analysts, the DLM represented excessive haste to adopt an untried form of warfare. In response to an optimistic appraisal of the tank in the *Revue de Paris* of 7 July 1934, an anonymous contributor to *Action française* insisted not only that tanks were unwieldy and likely to be destroyed by hidden guns but that organizers of recent French maneuvers had deliberately concealed the machines' deficiencies. Was it not true, he asked, that tanks and armored cars had proven incapable of operating in broken country or of crossing rivers once the bridges had been destroyed? Had not a mechanized division in one exercise been trapped by infantry in a wood and escaped only because the arbitrator intervened? Did attacking tanks not usually pass over entrenched and camouflaged enemy soldiers—who then emerged from concealment to massacre the following infantry? However shrill the author's tone, these were fair questions, and they offer a salutary reminder that the French high command had to worry at least as much about being too quick to embrace the armored fighting vehicle as it did about being left behind by technological developments.[76]

The difficulties of the first light mechanized division stemmed largely from its primitive equipment and were rapidly addressed because the unit's importance for providing intelligence and protection for motorized infantry formations was indisputable.[77] When it came to other potential applications of armor—close support of infantry and independent armored operations— there were fewer compelling reasons to adopt a new technology that threatened the very nature of the French military doctrine and organization.

Nonetheless, there was never any prospect of French infantry's abjuring the tank, and, throughout the decade after the end of World War I, France maintained a large arsenal of 1918 vintage machines and began planning for their future replacement. As Weygand pointed out, "We had won the war thanks to the tanks, whose use had transformed the tactics of our attacks in 1918, and we were not stupid enough to forget it."[78] The pace of armor development was glacial during the 1920s, however, for the perfectly sensible reason that the 3,500 existing Renault FTs were, though obsolete by the 1930s, perfectly adequate against an enemy who, thanks to the Treaty of Versailles, lacked anything better.[79] Moreover, the FTs represented a large financial investment and served as a reminder that any replacement tank would be an expensive and ephemeral asset.[80] The cost of the next generation of armored fighting vehicle was unpredictable but would certainly be high; their vulnerability to future antitank guns was uncertain, but, given the cost, not a matter to be miscalculated. Investing vast sums to build machines that were obsolescent at the moment mass production began was a dismaying prospect for an underfunded French Army. Equally depressing were the difficulties of producing tank crews from one-year conscripts and the possible contradictions between the logic of the methodical battle and the most efficient employment of armored fighting vehicles. The French knew that whatever tanks cost, however awkwardly they meshed with the methodical battle, and however problematic their survival on battlefields dominated by artillery and antitank guns, the machines were indisputably necessary. For French infantry had become accustomed to close tank support in 1918, and attacking infantry could not, or at least would not, advance without it.[81] For this task, what was wanted was large numbers of comparatively small and inexpensive tanks, a psychological asset that could be spread as widely as possible.

But alongside the thesis that the tank's proper roles bound it to serve in small tactical units tied closely to the infantry was a rival theory. The originator and driving spirit behind the original French tank program, General Jean-Baptiste Estienne, had from the very beginning conceived of massive "land battleships" armed with heavy ordnance and designed to operate independently of traditional arms. His vision can be seen in the first French tanks ever built, the 14.6 ton Schneider and the heavier 23-ton Saint-Chamond, which were for all practical purposes massive 75mm self-propelled guns.[82] Although the poor battlefield performance of these undependable and vulnerable machines led the disappointed Estienne to shift his support temporarily to the Renault company's light, mass-producible FT infantry tank, he continued to believe that the forty-ton 2C breakthrough tank under development by Forges et Chantiers de la Méditerranée (FCM) would prove the eventual war-winner.[83] The end of the war left Estienne unshaken in his commitment to the liberation of the tank from the infantry.[84] Almost alone in an army that treasured the Renault FT light tank as the key to victory (*"l'enfant cheri de la victoire"*), he urged that "the idea and the label 'accompaniment tank' should be abandoned . . . Motorization consists solely and essentially of putting at the disposition of the commander the largest and most powerful reserve of battle tanks possible."[85] When the army's official tank program of the summer of 1921, as established by the artillery branch's Section Technique des Chars de Combat, stipulated that the mission of the tank was to accompany infantry and called for the development only of a thirteen-ton infantry tank and a heavy "rupture tank," Estienne, though his new position as inspector general of tanks was merely advisory, refused to let the artillery have the last word. Making up in energy what he lacked in authority and in spite of his inability to promise that the French Army would purchase enough machines to make up for research and development costs, Estienne persuaded five leading armaments firms to offer designs for a twenty-ton "battle tank" meant to have sufficient protection, armament, and range for independent action.[86] In 1924 Estienne's dream took shape in the form of four experimental machines; the one chosen for further development was the ancestor of what would be the best tank in the world in 1940, the Char B1bis.[87]

It was one thing for Estienne to outflank the Infantry Department by appealing directly to French industry; two greater challenges were to gain the support of the Conseil Supérieure de la Guerre for the tank's further development and to persuade the infantry branch to employ it appropriately.[88] The first problem was solved easily enough, and a 1925 study group led by Tank Inspector General Giraud was sufficiently impressed by Estienne's project to recommend to a study session of the CSG that a twenty-ton medium-tank program be added to the infantry accompaniment and heavy-tank programs established in 1921.[89] Deciding to build the machines proved easier than determining their proper use. The War Council reached no consensus on whether to deploy the battle tanks with the cavalry or to harness them to the infantry, and no one advocated their independent use. After further declarations of the partnership between infantry and armor, the council reiterated the 1921 decision to build a light tank to replace the FT and voted to build three prototype medium or battle tanks for testing.

Interestingly, the council voted at the same meeting to discontinue development of the 2-C heavy tank, thus abandoning a machine that had a relatively firm place in the brief French tank tradition, while introducing another that had no place in French armor theory.[90] In short, doctrine played a smaller role than institutional influence in determining the course of French tank development. The battle tank survived because it had the Tank Inspectorate's sponsorship, and, thanks to that sponsor's energy, the momentum of being an ongoing project. Although assigned by French doctrine the tasks of assisting infantry in penetrating solid defenses and fighting off enemy tanks, the heavy tank was abandoned because the infantry branch had no desire to pay for an expensive project of unknown technical feasibility.[91] Actually, the story of the heavy tank's demise took an amusing twist when Prime Minister Doumergue interrogated the CSG in 1934 about the status of the heavy-tank project. Speaking for the council, Marshal Pétain replied that the machine had not been abandoned but already existed. Thus, although the 2-C had no place in French visions of the next war, it reassured politicians and allowed generals to decline further offers with "no thank you, we already have a breakthrough tank."[92]

The origins of the medium tank demonstrate the disjunction between the men who designed tanks and those who determined how they were to be used. The Tank Inspectorate determined to build a medium tank, but it would be up to the Infantry Directorate to incorporate the result into its doctrine. Lack of coordination between Tank Inspectorate and Infantry Directorate, between tank designers and the devisers of doctrine, was even more striking in the case of the light tank, the machine most coveted by the infantry and despised by Estienne's tankers. When called upon to create an infantry support tank, the Tank Inspectorate ignored the specifications established by the infantry branch and quietly pursued its own ideas. Abetting the battle-tank advocates' pursuit of their separate agenda were the artillery branch's lack of interest in this section of its nominal bailiwick and the relaxed attitude of the infantry branch.[93] Content that the Renault FTs were both adequate and paid for, the infantry neither pressed for their rapid replacement nor kept a watchful eye on the progress of the matériel with which the Tank Inspectorate would eventually propose to replace them.

Commissioned in 1926 to design an infantry support tank that would weigh no more than thirteen tons and would be too slow to escape from the infantry and "act independently," the Tank Inspectorate offered the Renault D1. Weighing the full thirteen tons, the D1 had 30mm of armor plate and a top speed of 18 kph. It carried a 47mm gun, two 7.5mm machine guns, and a radio set designed for communication with other tanks but not with troops on foot.[94] In proportion to its weight, the D1's engine was even less powerful than that of the FT.[95] Although, as the infantry branch objected, the machine was too fast to be an infantry tank, it was neither fast enough nor sufficiently well armored for independent operation as a "maneuver tank." The turret was so badly designed that the tank commander could not see outside without standing on a box, and he could not operate the gun without bending himself double.[96] The first ten D1s were ordered in 1929, but the machine's thin armor and weak engine aroused such concern that the tank technical section was already working in 1930 to increase the machine's protection and speed, two improvements of no interest to the infantry branch.[97] Tactical exercises with the new D1 and B1 (the medium tank) tanks scheduled for October 1931 could not be carried out because the machines had not yet been delivered, but studies on paper suggested that both machines would tend to outrun the infantry they were expected to support.[98] This conclusion would hardly have surprised the men of the Tank Inspectorate, who knew exactly what they were doing, but the infantry perceived itself not to have gained a battle tank but to have lost an infantry one; its doctrine offered no role to the B1, and the D1 was unsuitable for its intended accompaniment mission.

The delivery of the new machines enabled tactical tests to take place at Mailly Camp in September 1932. General Gamelin directed "combined exercises" involving the Second North African and Fifteenth Motorized Infantry Divisions, the nascent Light Mechanized Division, and, most strikingly, a mechanized detachment including forty-five D1 tanks and France's entire arsenal of three new B1s. Assigned to reinforce an attack by the motorized infantry division against the North African troops, the mechanized detachment failed, in Weygand's words, "to produce the result expected."[99] Sent out far ahead of the infantry and lacking sufficient artillery support, the D tanks suffered heavy losses. The experiment convinced both Inspector of Tanks Dufieux and Chief of Staff Weygand of the futility of independent tank action and the importance of keeping the armored forces within the general reserve.[100] Gamelin claimed later to regret that any conclusions had been drawn from an exercise in which tanks had been so mishandled.[101]

If the 1932 exercises convinced many that the D1 could not function as a maneuver tank, tests carried out the following summer by General Dufieux at Coëtquidan Camp proved the machine's 18kph top speed to be unacceptably high for an infantry support role. Although General Delestraint of the 505th Tank Regiment argued that D1s could operate like FTs, the general opinion was reflected on 16 January 1935 in the decision of the Comité Consultatif de l'Armement to reclassify the D1 as a medium rather than a light tank.[102] Unfazed by the reception of its first "infantry" tank, the tank designers offered a new prototype, the 18.2-ton, 23kph D2. At this point, however, the infantry branch reminded the tank technical section of the light-tank specifications defined back in 1926 and demanded a replacement for the FT rather than another unwanted medium tank. On 2 August 1933 the government authorized construction of a new series of infantry tanks.[103] These were to weigh six tons, to carry a machine gun or a 37mm cannon, and to be simple and reliable enough to be manned by conscripts. Resulting from this program were the R-35 Light Tank, the FCM-36 Infantry Tank, and the H-35 and H-39 Hotchkiss Light Tanks. The two Hotchkiss models were later rejected by the infantry for their high speed and complex engine, but they found a home in those cavalry units not yet equipped with the SOMUA cavalry tanks.[104] The diesel FCM was so expensive that only one hundred were built. The Renault became the infantry's standard accompaniment tank, although discouraging trials in 1937 aroused complaints that the infantry might as well have stuck with the manifestly unsuitable D2.[105] Meanwhile, fifty D2s were produced in 1936 and 1937, when production ceased because the D2 required special steel needed for the more important SOMUA. Manufacture of the D2 was resumed in 1940 as a substitute for the ever-so-slowly produced B1bis. The 150 existing D1s were eventually shipped across the Mediterranean because the R-35 and H-35 infantry tanks could not handle North African terrain.[106]

Historians have generally found the details of the D tank imbroglio uninteresting and have treated the whole effort to develop an infantry tank as a pernicious distraction from the development of real tanks—fast, powerful machines designed to serve in armored divisions. Given France's defensive strategy, its belief in the efficacy of the methodical battle, and the slow pace of German armor development, the "failure" to develop the battle tanks and armored divisions that France did not want is less interesting than the bumpy history of the crucial infantry accompaniment machine. Medium-tank advocates insinuated the B1 into an official program that called only for light and heavy tanks and, when called upon to create an infantry tank, they shamelessly unveiled the D series. They may in fact have had a better theory about tanks than their contemporaries, but their disregard for the infantry tank program shows how out of touch they were with their own army. The French Army did not seek a machina ex deo to liberate it from the methodical battle; tanks were wanted to reinforce the methodical recipe for victory (and were not, therefore, as Harvey suggests, "machina non grata").[107] "Tanks," the 1929 armor regulations asserted, "are only supplementary means of action placed temporarily at the disposition of the infantry. They considerably reinforce the action of the infantry, but they do not replace it."[108]

Integrating even the infantry accompaniment tanks into the methodical battle was no simple matter. When Major General Sir Edmund Ironside declared that attending a high-level French training course in 1927 had left him with "no clear idea of how a combined infantry and tank attack, as we understand it, should be mounted," he doubtless attributed to French sloth or carelessness the failure to solve what was actually a daunting problem.[109] Obviously, tanks and infantry had some natural affinity. Advancing together, the tanks could provide immediate fire support against enemy strongpoints; in return, the infantry would provide assistance by locating and destroying antitank weapons. During the halt at the end of each phase of the methodical battle, however, the large machines would act as magnets, drawing artillery fire upon themselves and the foot soldiers nearby. Able to take ground but not to hold it, happier in motion than stationary, even the ponderous FT fit badly into the methodical battle.[110] If stationary machines would prove vulnerable between bounds, those that failed to halt would outrun the infantry upon whom they relied to detect the enemy positions they were themselves too blind to see. The result would be everything the methodical battle was designed to avoid. While the overextended armored vehicles were picked off by antitank guns, the infantry following would be held up by concealed strongpoints overlooked during the tanks' headlong advance. Once upon a time, eliminating such strongpoints would have been the task of the artillery, whose job became much more difficult with the introduction of the mobile combat vehicles. Foot soldiers moved at a predictably slow pace, but tanks had to be prevented from advancing under the fire of their own artillery. Thus, in the absence of reliable communications, tanks did not promise to open the battlefield to fluid, independent operations but intensified the need for disciplined adherence to prearranged plans. If tanks were going to introduce a new element of surprise into battle, artillery preparation would have to be shortened—and more guns would have to be massed to achieve the required impact. Thus, tank attacks required not less artillery support but "as many guns as possible" and increased the material requirements of the methodical battle. On one calculation, an attack with tank support needed between 80 and 144 cannon per kilometer where only 22–40 would have been authorized under the conditions of the previous war.[111] So grave were these problems and so uncertain the answers that fifteen years after the first French experiments with infantry-armor cooperation, the world's most intensively mechanized army was still improvising on the battlefield.[112]

That tanks could reduce method to chaos was amply demonstrated in a 1933 armor-infantry cooperation exercise. Because only one of two D1 tank companies received a radioed order to advance in support of an infantry regiment, half of the regiment made progress while the other half, and its FT infantry tanks, were held up by the obstacles meant to have been cleared by the D1s.[113] Such a disjointed advance brought on all of the ills the methodical battle was meant to avoid: irregular fronts, vulnerable flanks, and unpredictable rates of advance confounding the artillery fire plan. General Delestraint also complained that the noisy D tanks, audible at a distance of three kilometers, had to creep to their start line to avoid revealing their positions, a problem to which no better remedy could be proposed than having aircraft fly overhead to mask the noise of tank motors.[114] On the whole, the exercise could be seen as evidence of the dangers, not the imperative, of adding tanks to the established infantry-artillery team. The problems of armor-infantry cooperation looked equally daunting during similar trials four years later at Sissone. The exercise saw the tanks reach the first objective, a distance of 1,500–2,000m, in five or ten minutes, only to have to wait, performing "more or less bizarre maneuvers" during the one-half to three-quarters of an hour required by infantry moving at two kilometers an hour to cover the same distance.[115] In maneuvers in 1936, a battalion of B tanks raced ahead of the infantry to seize the enemy command post, only to be chided by Dufieux for its precipitous advance.[116]

Although tanks threatened to dislocate the methodical battle and to sabotage the French Army's formula for victory, they could not be rejected outright by an army that credited the FT tank with the victories of 1918 and by a government that vocally refused to defend French soil again with the bodies ("*avec les poitrines*") of her citizens. There would have to be tanks, and those tanks would have to become part of the methodical battle, which would have to become even more methodical in consequence. To compensate for poor communications between infantry and armor, the two would have to be glued together during each advance by a careful timetable.[117] By staying close to the infantry, accompaniment tanks could keep it apprised of the situation immediately ahead, return easily to deal with overlooked pockets of enemy resistance, and avoid infringing on the artillery's sphere of operations. This vision of tank-infantry cooperation naturally led to the organization of the infantry tanks in battalions capable of being distributed where needed in the methodical battle.

Concern for the tank's vulnerability in the face of increasingly effective antitank measures reinforced the widespread conviction that the tank could not be employed in any context other than that of the methodical battle.[118] It was hard to know whether tanks produced at the expense of infantry weapons and defensive material would survive to make their impact on the battlefield. Calculations of armor efficacy versus projectile penetration had to be made before the matériel existed to perform concrete experiments, and no one could be certain of the future utility of tests done with current models. In any case, tanks had to be designed to meet future, not present, antitank capabilities. That both the D1 and B1 tanks had to be replaced immediately with more heavily protected models illustrated the difficulty of keeping abreast of antitank developments.

Claims about the relative effectiveness of tanks and antitank guns reflected the premises, the biases, and the wishful thinking of their proponents. We cannot know what was in the mind of the umpire at Mailly exercises in July 1929 who determined that a single antitank gun had knocked five or six tanks out of action at a range of about six-hundred yards, but tank enthusiasts were quick to point out that the worst enemy of the tank was the umpire's pencil.[119] Nor is it always easy to distinguish doctrines adopted after careful assessment of the alternatives from those chosen thoughtlessly or in desperation. How does one interpret the views of the lieutenant who informed British inquirers that, if attacking light tanks were not stopped by divisional artillery, his own 37mm guns, and the (as yet undeveloped) infantry antitank weapons, he would order his men to lie flat until the attacking vehicles went away?[120] Was this confidence in artillery, refusal to take tanks seriously, or the studied insouciance of a recent St. Cyr graduate?[121]

The more charitable interpretation, that the subaltern had faith in the ability of artillery to stop tanks, was in line with most French thinking on the subject and helps to explain the course of French armor development. Tanks were calculated to be able to neutralize enemy guns at a range of no more than 300m—less if the guns were well camouflaged—but were vulnerable to antitank guns placed up to 1,000m away.[122] Thus each attacking tank would have to traverse 700m of shooting gallery before it could return fire. Tank opponents cited such events from the Spanish Civil War as a battle outside of Madrid in which nationalist antitank weapons were alleged to have destroyed forty-seven of the sixty Russian tanks engaged, and claimed that a single tank cost the price of fifty antitank guns.[123] If artillery was less expensive than tanks, antitank mines were very cheap indeed. To mine a 4-km divisional front required 6,000 mines, 30 tons of material that could be carried by 15 2-ton trucks and could be laid by 250 men in eight hours. By comparison, a division's artillery totaled 160 tons and required 80 3-ton trucks.[124] The official verdict on the tank-antitank controversy favored the latter. As General Martin informed the students at the CHEM, most armies underestimated the effectiveness of the antitank gun and exaggerated the tank's usefulness both for infantry support and for independent action.[125] France, it was argued, needed not more tanks but more antitank guns and a proper understanding of their tactical employment.[126]

Until 1935 the French could be sanguine about their antitank capability because the thin-skinned, machine-gun carrying vehicles under production across the Rhine were vulnerable even to the model 1918 Puteaux 37mm gun that, along with the versatile 75mm field gun, constituted France's current antitank defense.[127] Even in the absence of a proper antitank gun, however, the French were confident that improvised means could stop tanks. In a more sophisticated version of the young lieutenant's assertion that tanks would overlook men lying on the ground, the French later experimented with digging antitank pits three yards long, five-and-a-half feet deep, and two-and-a-half feet wide. The three or four men concealed in each pit would be invulnerable to machines rolling over them and not even much hurt should their officers call down artillery fire on the enemy tanks, an attribute of the antitank trench that was not advertised to the troops.[128]

In the second half of the decade, the perceived balance between the vulnerable tank and the antitank gun tipped further towards the latter with the acquisition of two modern antitank guns—the 25mm Hotchkiss model 1934 and the 47mm gun Puteaux model 1937. Both of these horse-drawn guns would be effective even against Germany's PzKpfw III's and IV's (at 1,600m and 800m, respectively), and projectiles from the Puteaux could pass through both sides of any German tank available in 1940.[129] The new weapons reinforced the thesis of the vulnerability of the tank: since 1918, "nothing has developed . . . to change the situation except considerable improvement in antitank weapons and training in antitank defense."[130] When it suited his purposes, Gamelin was capable of insisting that, "just as bullets did not kill all of the infantrymen, the antitank gun will not destroy all of the tanks," but the message of the 1936 armor instructions remained that of 1929: "In the offensive, it cannot be emphasized too strongly that today the antitank weapon is to the tank what the machine gun was to the infantry during the World War."[131]

Belief in the superiority of the antitank gun over the tank was not a uniquely Gallic aberration. General Gamelin's announcement of 24 May 1937 that events in Spain had demonstrated the efficacy of even 25mm antitank guns spurred an British officer to suggest that Germany had erred in following Britain's lead in building fast light tanks and "was now equipped with many hundreds of tanks that would prove to be useless in an attack against an organized position."[132] The Soviet Army's response to events in Spain was to break up existing armored formations and redistribute the tanks among infantry units.[133] When a French officer wrote in favor of the construction of fast light tanks, it was an American observer who criticized the proposal for failure to take sufficiently into account the tanks' vulnerability to antitank guns.[134] The American officer who reported in 1937 that "the French Army feels that, at the present time, the antitank weapon is superior to the tank" had nothing but praise for French antitank training.[135] Although the American army would create sixteen armored divisions in World War II, the majority of its tanks would be organized into more than one hundred independent tank battalions.[136]

Even in the German Army, the interwar period saw a "healthy debate" over whether the tank would actually open the battlefield to mobile warfare.[137] Members of the "if only the French had listened to de Gaulle" school should note that even tank advocates in the Wehrmacht dismissed de Gaulle's book as "fantastical." As General Rommel complained, "there was a particular clique that still fought bitterly against any drastic modernization of methods and clung fast to the axiom that the infantry must be regarded as the most important constituent of any army." Although the first three Panzer divisions were authorized on 15 October 1935, as late as September 1939 only 1,251 of Germany's 3,195 tanks and 9 of her 33 tank battalions were in armored divisions rather than in infantry-support roles.[138]

The orthodox verdict on the antitank gun found confirmation in exercises umpired by men whose job was to protect the soldiers from the bloody consequences of doctrinal error. In the Normandy maneuvers, motorized and mechanized forces were often deemed to have been immobilized by natural or artificial obstacles. For example, umpires determined that a force composed of one battalion each of motorized infantry, motorized artillery, and tanks aided by an armored car reconnaissance group was blocked at a stream by a single infantry company, two antitank guns, and demolitions. The conclusion of the exercises as a whole was that defense was now more powerful than ever before and that attacks would require massive concentration of resources against one objective at a time.[139]

In prewar exercises, the army sought to prove the value of its defensive system against the most effective attacks it could imagine. In June 1937, for example, General Billotte evaluated the effectiveness of a section of the Maginot line by postulating an innovative German attack that interdicted French reinforcements, sealed off the individual forts with gas, and screened the tanks' progress with smoke shells. Although Billotte acknowledged such defensive shortcomings as the inadequate number of antitank guns, the lack of antitank mines, and the French divisions' inexperience in operating within a fortified zone, he concluded that, even in a wargame game rigged in favor of the attackers, the local successes achieved would have fallen short of penetration.[140]

Achieving the desired results from such exercises required appropriate premises, and it is interesting to compare French assumptions about the efficacy of antitank guns with those of their neighbors across the Rhine. In 1937, while General Billotte was reporting that even incomplete French defenses would serve their purpose, a German analysis reprinted in the *Revue d'infanterie* produced dramatically different conclusions.[141] Major von Schell assumed that a regiment assigned to cover 3,000 meters had nine antitank guns at its disposal, that is, one gun for every 330 meters of front, and that an attacker could mass 100 tanks per kilometer—a ratio of 30 tanks for every antitank gun. The guns would be effective at 800 meters, which a tank moving at twelve kilometers per hour would traverse in four minutes. At six shots per minute, four minutes allowed time for twenty-four shots, of which one-quarter would be on target. Thus, according to von Schell's arithmetic, only 6 tanks out of 30 would be destroyed, and the defending regiment would be unable to hold its position.

A similar analysis was repeated for the division, whose entire antitank complement of fifty-four guns was deemed sufficient to cover only two or three kilometers of the unit's prescribed ten-kilometer front.[142] In contrast to the French Army, which counted a division's organic 75mm guns as additional antitank defense, von Schell argued that conventional artillery would be useful only in rare cases when large numbers of tanks were grouped together. He also denied the usefulness of aircraft against tanks and noted the infantry's lack of an effective antitank weapon.[143] The *Revue d'infanterie* dismissed the German's gloomy assessment of the effectiveness of the antitank gun on the grounds that 100 tanks per kilometer constituted an exceptionally powerful attack and 12 kilometers per hour was an unrealistically rapid rate of movement.[144] Taking an approach all too characteristic of French doctrinal analysis, the French officer's conclusion abandoned argument for eloquence: "We would not like to end this exposé on the same pessimistic note as the author of *Fighting Against Tanks*. Let us hope, at least, that our antitank defense, taken as the sum of all of our efforts, will be efficacious enough to defend all of the objectives that are threatened by armored attack."[145]

The word hope (*espérer*) appears with disconcerting frequency in French discussions of antitank warfare, but hope was bolstered by statistics. A contemporary French study reported by one Captain Brouillard asserted that the nine French 25mm antitank guns assigned to each regiment could fire fifteen rounds per minute and would be effective against current German tank models at ranges of up to 1,000m.[146] On this calculation—and Brouillard's was not even the most optimistic evaluation of the 25mm gun—a single antitank gun could destroy nineteen out of thirty attacking tanks even if only one shot in four were on target. Furthermore, Brouillard noted that "one can hope" that the defender's positions would be hidden by terrain features.[147]

This combination of analysis, hope, and exhortation left French soldiers with little reason to fear enemy tanks. They could dismiss the German emphasis on armored warfare as misguided and believe themselves to be better prepared than their neighbors for the realities of modern war. In the French analysis, thanks to proper understanding of the balance of forces, "the tanks will no longer terrify the infantryman, for only surprise is fearful. . . . Now that the means of defense against the tanks are known, and the technique of their utilization has been worked out, this obsession with tanks must cease." General Touchon believed that French soldiers had absorbed this lesson all too well and complained of his inability to persuade his troops to take German tanks seriously.[148] They could also take comfort in not being alone in believing in the gun's superiority to the tank. As an American pointed out, "tanks can fulfill their mission only when the hostile artillery has been practically knocked out prior to the entry of the tanks into the line."[149]

Heavy Armored Divisions

Until the middle of the 1930s, the French Army studied motorized and mechanized warfare under conditions of comfortable military superiority over its likely adversary. As the balance with Germany changed for the worse, French choices became more crucial, and the best solutions were not obvious. If the French command would not defend France *avec les poitrines* of French manhood, neither would it stake the nation's survival on untested machines and untried methods. Thus, as they moved towards an ever more costly investment in armor, French leaders redoubled their efforts not to blunder. By producing tanks designed to support the mechanical battle and arming themselves with effective antitank weapons, they hoped to profit from what the new technology had to offer while avoiding the traps into which unsystematic thinking could lead the unwary. Committed to a fundamentally defensive strategy, the French Army preferred to disperse its armored fighting vehicles in dozens of independent battalions rather than to concentrate them into a few powerful armored divisions. Moreover, given their own convictions about the defensive power of artillery and the poor capabilities of contemporary German "tanks"—most of which were suitable only for training—French confidence in their own doctrine is readily explained.[150]

In 1936, however, Germany's decision to create whole divisions of tanks led the French to ask whether their current force structure could handle an attack by the new Panzer divisions. Against a highly mobile army, the horse-drawn artillery upon which French antitank doctrine depended would be too slow and the independent tank battalions too weak. To shift adequate forces to the threatened point would require, Gamelin argued, an new instrument, the armored division based on the medium tank.[151]

An even more ambitious assessment appears in a general staff paper of June 1936 that insisted that tanks would have to be massed in armored divisions because the existing independent tank battalions were too vulnerable to the fifty-four antitank guns now allocated to every German infantry division.[152] The paper advocated the creation of four armored divisions, two to participate in the advance to a defensive position on the Escaut River in Belgium and two for the general reserve. Consistent throughout the paper is the emphasis on offensive action as the armored division's natural role: "When the French army has rediscovered the vigor of 1918, the High Command, in order to end the war victoriously, will have to pass to offensive operations; perhaps it will also have to do so to relieve the pressure upon our central or eastern European allies."[153]

Gamelin's new interest in the acquisition of armored divisions to match those of the Germans placed him, a man who prided himself on orchestrating consensus rather than imposing his views, in an uncomfortable minority position within the Conseil Supérieur de la Guerre, where only General Pierre Héring was a determined advocate of armored divisions.[154] Although "undoubtedly one of the French generals most favorably disposed to the offensive organization of the army through the use of mechanical power,"[155] Gamelin was a man whose ability to act upon his convictions was sapped by his all-too-clear awareness of the obstacles—political suspicion, inadequate material, and tactical uncertainty.[156] Although he instructed the council to study the armored division in October 1936, there is no reason to believe that he had utterly forgotten his past reservations. As recently as 29 April 1936 he had told the CSG that "the development of the antitank weapon has caused the renunciation of [large tank units]," and he would insist in 1939 that "just because the Germans have committed an enormous error does not mean we must do likewise. Understand that there will never be a battlefield large enough for several armored divisions. They can handle local operations, like reducing a pocket, but not an offensive action."[157] His proposal for the creation of three armored divisions was couched in language calculated to soothe members of the CSG or the government who thought differently. He reassured the council that what they were being asked to approve were experiments; France, moreover, had her own requirements and no need to copy the Panzer division. French armor would not operate independently; it could not *faire cavalier seul* because it relied on other units to provide it with infantry, artillery, and reconnaissance units.[158] Two days of discussion within the council produced evidence of the wide range of views to be found within the CSG and the conclusion that the matter warranted further study.[159] The largest combat formation of French tanks remained the battalion and the largest administrative organization the brigade, with exercises testing a divisional organization ordered for the following summer.[160]

But 1937 proved a mixed year for armor's advocates. Supporting their cause was a February 1937 general staff study reiterating their strongest argument: Although rupture and exploitation forces could be created by temporarily attaching reserve tank battalions to infantry or cavalry divisions, only an organized armored division combined the speed and power to counter an enemy breakthrough. The same study concluded that the new division ought to be reduced from six battalions to two brigades of four battalions each. Furthermore, a report the next summer, following combined armor-infantry cadre exercises at Sissonne camp, insisted that an armor division had to be permanently organized rather than cobbled together as needed from available reserve battalions. Coordinating the operations of infantry and tanks proved to be a tricky business requiring much practice, and improvised units were at "risk of failure or of excessive losses."[161] The report, by General Georges, also supported the medium-tank enthusiasts by asserting that an armored division should contain machines of roughly similar capabilities and that only the B and D2 tanks were suitable. It was Georges's view that B and D2 brigades ought to be established as soon as the necessary machines became available and without waiting until a full division was feasible.[162] The large-scale armored exercises scheduled for the summer were canceled, however, because the necessary medium tanks had not yet arrived from the factories and the general staff believed that substituting light tanks would vitiate the whole experiment.[163]

Incidentally, it is commonplace to point out that France's tiny arsenal of medium tanks—27 B1 tanks and 40 D2s at the end of 1936, 62 B1s and 50 D2s a year later[164]—made the question of creating an armored division academic; what is more remarkable than this shortage, however, is that the French Army had any medium tanks at all in the absence of a doctrine for their use. If General Estienne and his colleagues had not pushed the B tank project in spite of the official plans, if the tank section had not designed the D tank in accordance with its own doctrinal vision rather than in obedience to the requirements of the infantry branch, then the material objections to Gamelin's 1936 judgment that France needed armored divisions would have been not merely daunting but insurmountable.[165] Even so, it would be a long time before enough matériel existed for the unit Gamelin had in mind, a powerful force of six B-tank battalions.

The experiments of 1937 generated a set of tentative armor regulations, whose opening paragraphs cautiously reiterated the limitations of the new weapon.[166] Although their ability to bring fire to bear at close range promised to increase the speed of operations while reducing ammunition consumption, tanks could neither hold terrain nor clear it completely of enemy positions. Except against a disorganized adversary, tanks could operate "only in close collaboration with other arms, especially infantry." The machines had a limited range of action and required six hours of daily maintenance and an additional full day of attention after three or four days of operation. Tank mobility was not what it might have been; to minimize wear on treads, the machines were to be transported by train whenever possible. The instruction went on to describe tanks, within these limitations, as offensive weapons best used for surprise attacks in large numbers on broad fronts. Although operating in conjunction with infantry and artillery, tanks would impart their own tempo to the battle, allowing for the inclusion of more distant objectives and for a more rapid pace of advance than otherwise possible. Tank missions were divided into two types, accompaniment and maneuver.[167] Tanks assigned to accompany infantry would keep in close proximity to their charges and would concentrate on the task of neutralizing enemy automatic weapons. Maneuver tanks, always D or B machines, would be organized in companies or battalions to advance independently of the mixed groups of infantrymen and accompaniment tanks, while maintaining the closest possible contact with them. Like infantry attacks, advances by maneuver tanks were to be directed at a specific objective or a series of objectives, and the advances required artillery support. This was the methodical battle with the maneuver tank as an added element, an effort to exploit the tank's tactical possibilities without releasing it from rigidly centralized command.

A meeting of the CSG on 15 December 1937 concerning the hypothetical *division cuirassée* produced similar conclusions. As defined in a general staff briefing paper prepared for the session, the primary purpose of the new unit was to be *"powerful action within the framework of the general battle* and in close liaison with other divisions." The sledgehammer of massed medium tanks was to be wielded only in conjunction with the other components of the methodical battle. Its missions were aggressive ones—counterattack, flank attack, exploitation, and rupture of organized fronts—but it would not attempt to advance until other French forces had silenced the enemy antitank defenses.[168] This type of division could not, therefore, be treated as an independent unit but only as one cog in a machine composed of infantry, artillery, cavalry, and armor. In response to the suggestion that an armored division ought to be organized so that it could operate on its own, there was General Debeney's 1935 assessment of the likely outcome of the sort of armored offensive recommended by the maverick Lieutenant Colonel de Gaulle: "We will have a brilliant communiqué at the outset and, a few days later, a useless S.O.S."[169] The council concluded by authorizing General Martin, the inspector of cavalry, to organize a comprehensive training program for an experimental armored brigade.

But 1938 proved to be yet another year of frustration. The experimental armored brigade—three battalions of tanks (B1, B1bis, D2), two chasseur battalions, and two artillery groups under the command of Colonel Marie Bruneau—was dissolved during the Sudetenland crisis lest its constituent units be away from their stations in the event of mobilization. Nonetheless, paper exercises brought some useful results. For example, General Martin reported difficulties in handling even a four-battalion division and recommended a structure of two brigades, each composed of two tank and one infantry battalion. He also called for additional divisional elements: a reconnaissance group, air support, and an antiaircraft unit.[170]

With Martin's report in hand, the CSG met on 2 December 1938 to determine the composition of two new reserve armor divisions (Divisions Cuirassée de Réserve). The original six-battalion organization was trimmed to four, though not necessarily because of Martin's arguments about command and control. Rather, such was the desperate slowness of B-tank production that only sixty machines were available at the end of 1938, too few even for two battalions of thirty-three tanks each. The proposed divisions would have to contain two battalions of D2s, which thereby escaped from their uncongenial infantry-support role.[171] The council authorized further experiments with a division composed of tanks, mechanized infantry, and artillery, which was designed to function in conjunction with other forces. Héring, meanwhile, submitted a minority report calling for adding an organic reconnaissance element of fast tanks, a battery of self-propelled antitank guns, an antiaircraft battery, and maintenance and supply elements so that the division would operate independently of other forces.[172] The very name of the new division is instructive. What would logically have been called the Division Cuirassée received the modifier "de Réserve" in other to distinguish its acronym from that of the Division de Cavalerie, but the word "reserve" also reassured skeptics that armored divisions would operate only under corps or army control.

Héring's belief that an armored division ought to be a self-contained organization capable of independent action found no place in the official statement on armor doctrine issued by General Gamelin on 18 December 1938.[173] The note specified that the "large armored units" were to launch their swift powerful blows only against enemy forces that were materially inferior, not yet organized for defense, or already undermined by French actions. Always part of a corps or of a mechanized group, the armored unit would not protect its own movements or provide its own reconnaissance. The note sketched four tactical situations in which an armored division might be employed. In the first situation, an attack on a well-organized position, the initial advance would normally involve infantry and light tanks heavily supported by artillery. Only after the infantry had advanced to the limit of its artillery support would the armored division enter the battle and accelerate the tempo of operations. Second, an armored division could be employed as part of a corps in the exploitation of a successful offensive. In the third case, it would join with a DLM to form a mechanized group for operations on an enemy flank. The group would be followed by motorized infantry divisions and could include cavalry divisions as well. The fourth scenario, counterattack, involved two distinct variations. In the case of a coordinated attack to retake lost terrain, the doctrine was the same as that for an attack on a well-organized position; in a *coup d'arrêt* to disrupt an enemy in motion, the armored unit would join either with a DLM (producing a mechanized group) or with an infantry corps.

The Gamelin note gives one a sense of the limited place of armored divisions in French thinking. However useful when their special attributes—speed, power, and mass—allowed them to contribute to operations, armor divisions were not central players and were not to be unshackled from the confines of the methodical battle. Never does this note, or any other statement on French doctrine, imply armored divisions to be essential rather than merely desirable. Never does it suggest that any conceivable operational problem would exceed the combined defensive resources of France's infantry, cavalry, mechanized cavalry, and independent tank battalions. The thesis that tank attacks required more supporting guns than did infantry alone meant that armored divisions could not distance themselves from the units capable of lending them additional firepower. But what of Gamelin's 1936 argument that France needed armored divisions as the specific antidote to German developments, that only such a unit had the speed and firepower to block a German Panzer penetration? And if the special virtue of the armored division was not defensive power (arguably less than that of an infantry division) but the speed with which it could parry and riposte against German thrusts, surely it could not be tied by its lack of reconnaissance elements to the pace of slower formations. Nor could armored divisions move across blocked terrain or unbridged rivers if they had no combat engineers.[174] There were doctrinal problems that would not be solved within the framework of the methodical battle and, therefore, remained unresolved.

The years 1937 and 1938 were uncertain ones in the history of French armor. On the one hand, mechanized cavalry began to come into its own with the arrival of SOMUA tanks, improved armored cars, and the transformation of the Fifth Cavalry Division into the Second Light Mechanized Division.[175] The newly equipped formations were deemed capable of limited offensive operations in addition to scouting and screening missions, and exercises in 1937 pitting a DLM against a notional German Panzer division produced such a satisfactory result that General Gamelin later described the DLM as "a fortunate solution, more fortunate than the Panzer division."[176] During the same period the French Army determined to establish the first Division Cuirassée de Réserve—matériel and other circumstances permitting. On the other hand, however, 1939 began with France no nearer to the actual creation of the two planned armored divisions than she had been two years earlier. Apparent complacency about armored capabilities reflected French confidence that they were on the right track and that, mutandis mutandi, they were following the same lines of thought as the German Army. It took the Panzer divisions' shocking contribution to the Polish campaign to instill any urgency into Gamelin's cautious advocacy for an armored division, and the final decision to create the first Division Cuirassée de Réserve was taken only on 16 December 1939.[177]

The purpose of the new division, reinforcement of the methodical battle, remained as specified in Gamelin's November 1938 note on the armored warfare. The battle would begin with an attack by infantry supported by artillery and accompaniment tanks. After the infantry had advanced far enough to require the artillery to shift forward, the medium tanks would advance to deprive the defender of any respite and with a particular eye to destroying enemy antitank guns. The medium tanks would then fall back and regroup while a third wave composed of the reserve armored division's light tanks and mechanized infantry mopped up any remaining opposition. With the position secured, the third wave would regroup and the whole sequence of infantry, medium-tank, and light-tank and mechanized-infantry attack would be repeated.[178]

Sources of Satisfaction

As they pursued their own investigations of armored warfare, some Frenchmen kept an interested eye on German developments, aware of what was happening across the Rhine and not particularly alarmed by it.[179] German use of armored vehicles did not, in fact, seem so very different from their own. As Minister of National Defense Daladier informed the Senate's Army Commission in 1936: "No one has even seen the famous German armor division maneuver in open country. . . . Germany will employ the tank exactly as we do, as an instrument of counter-attack and in close liaison with infantry, in short, with the tank tactics demonstrated in the last war."[180] Daladier's remark might be dismissed as premature, Gallocentric, or simply civilian, but indeed the two armies continued to manifest similar views on the use of armor even at the end of the decade.

In confidential lecture comparing French and German armor doctrine, an officer of the 511th Tank Regiment asserted that the two armies saw speed, power, and mass as the essential qualities of the tank and both regarded the machine as a tool for rapid movement to achieve local fire superiority.[181] The only substantive difference between the two conceptions was that the French intended to employ armored divisions within the framework of a normal corps, relying on the larger formations to provide screening, reconnaissance, and other supporting forces, whereas German tank theorists proposed to create independent armored corps.[182] In sum, "the German tank unit breaks the enemy front and exploits the success to the limit. The French tank unit breaks the enemy front, begins the exploitation and prepares for its completion by other arms."[183] Otherwise, the two armies thought so similarly that the American attaché present at the lecture abbreviated his synopsis by describing French doctrine as corresponding in its "basic principles" to the German.[184] Presenting even Heinz Guderian, an advocate on independent armored action, as a kindred spirit, the French lecturer spoke approvingly of other German armor theorists, Colonel Nehring and Captain Keilmansec, who insisted upon the need for close cooperation between tanks and infantry. For them, deep penetrations by independent armored units smacked of the futile cavalry raids of 1914, and Colonel Nehring's scheme for coordinating infantry, artillery, armor, aircraft, and paratroopers in the breakthrough phase of a modern battle would have passed muster at the Ecole Supérieure de Guerre.

Nehring's presentation of a doctrine so similar to that of the methodical battle must have given the French analyst pause. The German's ideas were too similar to French doctrine to be dismissed, but they could not be endorsed as offering an antidote to French defenses. The French lecturer's reminder that "naturally only the Germans know of the difficulties which were experienced during the march on Vienna" offered no theoretical objection to the offensive use of armor under controlled conditions but hinted at practical obstacles. Nehring's presentation was thus used to reinforce the French notion of incorporating the tank into the methodical battle but was not allowed to undermine the assumption that French defensive doctrine was fundamentally sound.

The French officer found further evidence of the kinship of French and German doctrine—and of the German Army's preference for Nehring's version of the methodical battle over Guderian's independent armor approach—in a German wargame of September 1938 against hypothetical Czech frontier fortifications. Infantry, engineer, and antitank units made the initial assault with a battalion of heavy tanks joining the operation only after some of the enemy antitank weapons had been eliminated. "At this point," noted the French lecturer, "it should be remarked that the employment of the accompanying tanks . . . is contrary to the principles of Guderian." The tanks moved ahead of the infantry only during the third, exploitation, phase of the movement, as if in obedience to Gamelin's instruction that "the tanks of the armored division will be engaged only after the first resistance has been overcome, for the attack will then progress over ground with fewer obstacles and a dislocated and more shallow anti-tank defense." Only at the end of the lecture did the Frenchman concede that there might be major differences between French and German attitudes towards armor, and these, he argued, stemmed naturally from differences in the kinds of fortifications against which each army was preparing to fight. The strong but thin Maginot line invited the Germans to attempt a penetrating thrust, whereas the deeper Siegfried line demanded "more concentrated maneuver" designed to chip away at successive lines of resistance.[185] The French believed that the Germans intended to use Panzer divisions not for frontal assaults on strongly defended positions but instead for mobile action against weak adversaries in open terrain.[186]

In matters of armor doctrine, and of military doctrine as a whole, the French recognized certain differences between their own and German practice. French intelligence contrasted German emphasis on decentralized action with their own insistence on central command and control; German units were more widely dispersed than the French system allowed and were expected to act independently without tying their rate of movement to the progress of other units. French observers could see the advantages of the German approach: "The cult of the initiative, the principle of decentralization, speed of execution, and the active search for intelligence are the methods which ought to allow the exploitation of every advantageous situation."[187] But to see those advantages was not to yield to the temptation to copy a system that did not fit the needs of an army of reservists preparing to fight a defensive war. For that matter, the success of the similar Russian T26 and T28 tanks in Spain suggested the superiority of French tank ideas over German and offered "new confirmation of the solidity of the foundations upon which French doctrine is constructed."[188] French soldiers saw the Wehrmacht as being of uneven quality and deemed the Luftwaffe "incapable of effecting a military decision."[189]

On the whole, studying German doctrine reinforced French confidence in their own methods. Similarities were stressed, perhaps even wishfully invented. When possible, discrepancies like those arising from conflicting judgments of the relative effectiveness of the tank and of the antitank gun were ascribed to German miscalculation. Others were attributed to the differences in the two armies' composition and mission. French leaders might have felt even more confident in their own judgment had they known of the German officer who suggested in 1937 that Germany could learn from the French because of their greater experience with the tanks during and after the war.[190]

Even after the Polish campaign, the French had no doubts that their understanding of contemporary warfare was, if not abstractly superior to that of the Germans, appropriate to their army's abilities and to their nation's requirements. The valiant Polish effort failed because the Poles chose poor strategy and put their faith in inadequate defensive fortifications. But France did not offer a countryside as hospitable to the Panzers as the flat plains of eastern Europe, and French and British were pleased to note that, even employed in inadequate numbers on unfavorable terrain, Polish antitank guns took a high toll on German tanks and blocked a German assault on Warsaw.[191] For Tank Inspector General Dufieux, Poland only confirmed the French thesis that tanks could succeed only in partnership with artillery and infantry.[192] Such lessons from the Polish campaign were studied by the high command and disseminated throughout the army. After reading a detailed analysis of the German tactics in Poland, Lieutenant Felsenhardt, although no uncritical admirer of French doctrine, doubted that the methods used by the Germans in Poland would work as well against France: "We have the Maginot Line, our troops are deployed in depth, our aviation is more powerful and has the benefit of experience in another war."[193]

It is easy to condemn French leaders for refusing to see the light after the German victory in Poland, but the true path remained uncertain. A change in doctrine in 1939 would have challenged not only the French Army's theoretical edifice but views held in other contemporary armies. In December 1939 an American attaché noted that the French armored division was more powerful than a Panzer division, had reached "very good balance between speed and armor," and had been "vindicated in the fighting to date."[194] The most important confrontation between French and German armored units, between General Jules Prioux's Cavalry Corps (Second and Third DLM) and General Eric Hoepner's Sixteenth Army Corps (Third and Fourth Panzer Divisions) on the Belgium plain, did not produce a clear theoretical verdict in favor of either organization. Prioux's corps accomplished, admittedly at heavy cost, its mission of delaying Hoepner's Panzers while General Billotte's First Army deployed in the vital Gembloux gap.[195] Given the number of variables involved—matériel, leadership, strategy, doctrine, training, and courage—the battle was hardly a decisive test; "Neither side," Gunsberg argues, "was equipped properly by the standards of the day to carry out its mechanized doctrine."[196] Even after the fall of France, General Leslie Mac-Nair of the offensively minded American army used the Louisiana maneuvers of September 1941 to demonstrate to his satisfaction that, whatever German armor had achieved against Polish, French, and Soviet forces, it would be stopped by the antitank guns of the United States Army.[197]

After spending two years in France, future American general Ralph K. Smith offered a balanced assessment of the French Army. Although concluding that French "doctrine is not suited in its entirety for American purposes," he insisted that the French "have a good army, trained by a system that is adapted to their needs."[198] If French doctrine was not what Smith would have chosen for the United States Army or Guderian for the Wehrmacht, it suited the Third Republic. It was not a doctrine created for an ideal army but for the army France had. That army was composed of overworked professionals, short-service conscripts, and badly prepared reservists. Unstable personnel assignments and the practice of training reservists in temporary units did little for unit cohesion, and the reservists who provided most of the army's leadership in combat would be asked to make up in courage what they lacked in military skills. More ambitious doctrine would have required a different army, but the mission of the French high command was to heed the nation's political, economic, and psychological limitations and to develop simple, stable, and credible methods appropriate for a nation in arms.

French generals could have balked at the task put before them, but unsuccessfully challenging immutable structures would only have worsened the situation. To the British attaché who wondered why "a nation as quick-witted and individualistic as the French" would adopt military doctrines of such a "considerable degree of rigidity,"[199] one can answer that, self-confidence being the foundation of morale, French soldiers had every reason to advertise their faith in existing methods and little incentive to experiment with novel ones.[200] In any case, who could infallibly recognize the right way to employ untested tools of war? The doctrine of the methodical battle lacked the panache of blitzkrieg, but dash had cost France dearly in 1914, and the methodical battle looked to be, if not the fastest road to victory, the safest and the surest.

Conclusion:
Cognitive Dissonance and the
Tyranny of the Mundane

In spite of French efforts to prepare a national defense formidable enough to win any war that Germany was not deterred from starting, the six-week campaign of 10 May through 25 June 1940 produced the very catastrophe against which French national defense organization, defensive preparations, and military doctrine had meant to guarantee. In a very obvious way, the disaster resulted from a strategic mistake. Racing northward towards Breda, the powerful left wing of the French Army ultimately contributed nothing to the decisive battle far to the south and east. There, in the Ardennes sector, Prételat's outnumbered Second Army Group collapsed before the main German effort, allowing German forces to swing west and envelop the Allied forces in Belgium. The ill-conceived Dyle-Breda maneuver, though it undeniably placed the armies of France at a disadvantage, did not, however, in itself doom the French Army to defeat.[1] Nowhere were French ground forces so outnumbered or ill-placed that they could not have remedied the consequences of their strategic mistake through operational or tactical success. The campaign took the turn it did, at such enormous cost, because, in spite of two decades of effort, neither the French Army nor the nation it defended was ready for war.[2]

The roots of that unreadiness have been described. The French Army went to battle in 1939 with a strategy designed to fight a long defensive war in which its superior national mobilization would compensate for Germany's economic and demographic advantages. The plan was to fight deep in Belgium, maximizing the Belgian contribution and shielding France's industrial north.[3] To reach defensible lines in Belgium in advance of the German Army, French leaders prepared a highly mobile army for a reflexive northern deployment in response to any German initiative. A German thrust anywhere else than into Belgium would undermine the premises of the French plan, but behind the whole scheme lay a defensive doctrine promising success even should the bulk of the Wehrmacht strike the lightly manned regions shielded by the Maginot line and the Ardennes forest. The program was designed to guarantee France the greatest chance of surviving an unwanted war from which it had nothing to gain. Not a formula for decisive victory, it was meant to be proof against catastrophic failure.

Such was the theory whose requirements French preparations for war failed to meet. Because the national organization plan, the cornerstone of French security policy, was an empty shell, the mobilization in 1939 repeated many of the blunders of 1914. Costly in productivity and efficiency, continued reliance on the notorious System D also reinforced popular suspicions that, once again, the burdens of war would fall hardest on ordinary Frenchmen while the profits accrued to a selfish elite. The national defense college produced some national security specialists, but its curriculum was too narrow and its graduates were too few for the course to affect French policy, even had the war not intervened so early. In any case, it was not designed to do so, for fear of military intrusion into the sphere of policy restricted the college's role to uncritical reaffirmation of existing plans.

The French Army had conspicuous virtues, but numbers and an increasingly large arsenal of modern equipment were inadequate compensation for the deficiencies in unit cohesion, training, and leadership that impelled French generals towards the safest possible doctrines. The limited options prompted little concern within a high command that could not imagine how doctrines based on defensive firepower could be dangerously wrong. We will never know whether the doctrines of firepower and the methodical battle would have met the case if supported by the kind of training and leadership to which the high command paid rhetorical homage, for the same constraints that reduced doctrinal options undermined the army's combat effectiveness as a whole.

To treat the 1940 campaign as a simple contest between a good German offensive doctrine and a bad French defensive one is to ignore the reasons why French soldiers were unprepared to execute the former and to forget that the Wehrmacht, though better trained and led, did not go to war with a clear set of solutions to the problems of modern war. Both sides had to adapt to unexpected circumstances, but improvisation was encouraged among German soldiers and anathema among French ones. The disastrous magnitude of France's final defeat tends to obscure the initial clashes, the hard-fought local engagements in which the consistent German victories reflected German initiative and command style rather than an inherently superior doctrine.[4] Employed by a better-prepared army, French doctrine might have proved effective, but the history of the army that France had is the story of mundane but unyielding obstacles to the reforms necessary to achieve military efficiency.

The physical state of the French Army has been discussed; what remains to be examined is its state of mind, that mixture of faith, hope, resignation, and—among those who denied that the Third Republic represented the true France (*le pays réel*) as opposed to a pernicious set of constitutional arrangements (*le pays légal*)[5]—even disinterest with which it prepared for war during the 1930s and mobilized in September 1939. Critics have asked how French soldiers could have believed themselves ready to fight the Germans, but the tone of the question is wrong. Given that French soldiers faced a choice between belief and resignation to defeat, the more interesting task is to discover the mechanisms that reinforced faith in French military preparations.

For many French soldiers, confidence came easily. General Véron, who as a colonel had been deputy chief of staff of the Ninth Army, insisted after the war that the army's morale had been excellent and the cadres' confidence "absolute." For him, the oft-derided official battlecry of 1939—"we will win because we are the stronger"—was the simple truth. Even the initial disquiet that Véron felt on realizing how little the army's arms, material, and doctrine had changed since 1918 was transmuted into confidence in the familiar.[6]

For officers who lacked Véron's simple faith, there were a range of possible psychological mechanisms—some of them politically charged—for handling intimations of French weakness. Right-wing opponents of the Third Republic had perhaps the easiest time, for they did not have to persuade themselves that France would necessarily triumph. If it did, the victory would be a tribute to the constancy of the army against Germans and unpatriotic Frenchmen alike. Defeat, on the other hand, could be blamed by the Right on the decadence of the republic and endured as part of the painful process of purifying France and restoring its honor. In his astute study of General Weygand, Philip Bankwitz argues that the general's pessimistic writings suggest that he was "intellectually and emotionally conditioned for disaster during this period, just as he was accepting the idea of regeneration through suffering." In Paul-Boncour's bitter postwar assessment, the "military chiefs did not commit treason, but they accepted defeat with a light heart."[7] Soldiers in the opposite camp, the *poilus* who preferred the "Internationale" to the "Marseillaise," dismissed French military deficiencies as irrelevant because conflict between French and German capitalists would not go beyond bluster. They saw French military activities as a sham and feared that any genuine national mobilization would be directed not against Germany but against the Soviet Union and domestic Communism.[8]

The majority of Frenchmen, those who believed both in the legitimacy of the republic and the reality of the struggle with Germany, faced a more difficult challenge in reconciling their uncertainties about the military situation with confidence in victory. They did not deny that war would bring some serious problems, especially in the area of defense against the aircraft with which the Germany were believed to be so lavishly equipped. Well-informed about German military capabilities, such men took refuge in optimistic assessments of those of France.[9] Hence, for example, Lieutenant Felsenhardt's fatuous observation that "our aviation is more powerful and has the benefit of experience in another war."[10]

A typical French answer to queries about their readiness to match doctrinal developments across the Rhine was to claim German doctrine as their own. For example, warnings about German plans to use aircraft to support ground troops in combat were met with French claims to have been thinking along the same lines. Thinking about it they were; their mistake was to equate reflection with useful results. As early as 1923, General Buat had suggested the creation of an "intervention force" composed principally of bombers and tank-based light divisions.[11] By 1927 French regulations called for airplanes to spot enemy antitank guns and to direct artillery fire against them but did not describe how this feat was to be accomplished.[12] The following year the chief of the tank school claimed that "naturally" aircraft and tanks would work together but admitted that the idea remained purely theoretical.[13] In 1934, a cavalry colonel published a study of the use of bombers to support troops.[14]

Although the 1934 regulations for the use of D tanks asserted that "the air force will intervene, if necessary, to complete the system of fire," nothing was done to prepare it for the role.[15] When asked to demonstrate an air strike against motorized columns during maneuvers in 1935, the air force grudgingly produced an attack by Bloch 200 bombers at treetop level that cost all of the attacking planes. The airmen appear not to have learned the lesson, and their performance in maneuvers two years later evoked from the British air attaché the understated observation that "if it is really the intention of the French Air Staff to use flights of ponderous heavy bombers flying slowly in formation at 200 feet to machine gun batteries of artillery on the ground, I fear that in war the French Air Force will not get the best results from what aircraft they have."[16]

That the role of aircraft in providing a form of extended artillery support for infantry and tanks in the methodical battle was clearly set out in the 1936 regulations meant little.[17] Air-ground cooperation exercises at Sissonne in 1936 and Nancy in 1938 were carried out half-heartedly, not only for lack of proper equipment but because of the air force's lack of interest in the whole business.[18] German operations in Poland in September 1939 stimulated reflection on such matters as the *"possible* addition of dive bombing squadrons to the organic aviation of the armored *groupment."*[19] In 1939 the French Air Force tested the use of radio-equipped aircraft to spot targets with for friendly tanks, and the armored division formed that winter had a squadron of reconnaissance planes.[20] But the gap between theory and practice remained huge. The assault bomber groups organized in the spring of 1940 were unprepared for their mission and played an unimportant—albeit occasionally sacrificial—role in the campaign.

Just as the French Army acted as if the equipment, training, and doctrine necessary for air-ground cooperation would materialize at need, it believed itself already to possess the constituents of an effective defense against German tactical aviation. Admitting during the September 1937 maneuvers that their air force would be unable to defeat the Luftwaffe in the air, French leaders remained sanguine because "they could make the antiaircraft ground defenses very strong by a veritable forest of guns."[21] This confident assessment was not matched, however, by an effort to plant the required "forest." Similarly, a French captain argued in the 1939 *Revue d'infanterie* that low-flying aircraft could be heard when they were twenty to twenty-five seconds away and that defenders possessing a "very seriously organized" alert system could react in ten seconds. His conclusion that columns of troops were in little danger from low-flying aircraft rested on such calculations rather than on a demonstration that the alert system existed and that the troops were ready to respond within the allotted time.[22] Moreover, the officer admonished skeptics not to challenge his reassuring conclusion; infantry can fight successfully against aircraft only "if it believes in the efficacy" of its antiaircraft defense.[23]

Similar mental tricks helped to "solve" apparent weaknesses in French frontier defenses, most notoriously the problem that Maginot line did not cover the Ardennes region. In 1934 Marshal Pétain told the Senate Army Committee that its wooded and hilly terrain rendered the Ardennes "impenetrable" if such "special dispositions" as roadblocks and defensive works were provided.[24] No such constructions were undertaken, but the region continued to be treated as a safe one that could be held largely by category B divisions. The phantom obstacles in the Ardennes were like the hundreds of thousands of antitank mines that French doctrine evoked to stop the Panzer divisions. These worked excellently in paper exercises, but far too few actually existed.[25] Of course, the French Army did not have a monopoly on grasping at such straws, and one is reminded of the memorandum to President Roosevelt on 24 April 1941 in which General George Marshall asserted that enemy ships approaching Oahu would come under attack at a range of 750 miles but ignored the absence of long-range reconnaissance aircraft in Hawaii.[26]

No episode is more revealing of the French Army's ability to think away disconcerting evidence than a map exercise conducted by General Prételat in May and June 1938. Perhaps because he thought it possible, undoubtedly because consideration of the scenario was incumbent upon him as commander of the Sedan-Montmedy region—and could be used to argue for additional resources—Prételat set his Second Army the task of responding to a German surprise attack through the "inpenetrable" Ardennes. Prételat concluded from the exercise that sixty hours after crossing the Rhine the enemy could reach the Meuse with a force of three corps, seven infantry divisions (three of them motorized), an armored division, and sixteen artillery regiments. His report to higher authorities suggested that, since the Luftwaffe would prevent the arrival of French reinforcements after the attack began, the Second Army required another division.[27]

If Prételat's argument that the Wehrmacht was capable of a rapid and powerful thrust through the lightly held Sedan-Montmedy sector was valid, however, then finding a supplementary division for the Second Army was less urgent than reexamining the plan to commit the bulk of French resources to Belgium. Because it was easier to reject Prételat's report than to rethink plans that took full advantage of French motorized forces, added the Belgian army to the French side of the scale, and promised to fight the war away from French national soil, higher authorities ignored the unwanted information. Even, noted General Georges, in the unlikely event that the Germans could gather the vast quantity of motorized transport and air support necessary for Prételat's operation and were able to move at the speed required, their advance would probably be one day slower than Prételat calculated, thereby giving French troops time enough to reach their defensive positions.[28] One day's grace was deemed a sufficient margin, because one day was all that there was. By 1938 French military commanders had no place for wargames that threatened to undermine confidence in the plans to which they were committed.

Another problem the French Army could not readily solve was organizing the army's planned move into Belgium in the absence of Belgian cooperation. An exercise done by the Conseil Supérieur de la Guerre in 1934–1935 concluded that French troops in Belgium would have to be deployed on a line chosen, reconnoitered, and prepared before the offensive began, but it then acknowledged diplomatic constraints by adding parenthetically, "at least intellectually."[29] An "intellectually prepared" defensive system offered a thin substitute for the organized battlefield that the CSG had envisioned when it adopted war plans involving an advance into Belgium, but, in the absence of an alternative, it had to suffice, even if the gap between conception and execution could prove to be fatal.

On too many occasions and on too many subjects, a French soldier found himself in a genuine dilemma. Whereas the desirability of more men, money, and material tempted him to offer strident warnings about German strength, the requirements of national morale fostered insistence on the army's overall excellence. If he could not perform the difficult feat of believing simultaneously that the army was ready and unready for war, confidence—whether resting on doctrinal analysis or pride—must have seemed the more soldierly choice.

Concerns about French inadequacies lost their urgent tone in a process exemplified in the penciled corrections of Inspector General of Cavalry Robert Altmeyer to a report on a map exercise he had executed in the Ardennes in 1935.[30] The original text painted a grim picture of the logistical problems facing the Ardennes forces: "The exercise demonstrates that the Ardennes detachment cannot under present circumstances accomplish its mission, which is fixed to the east of the Meuse." As motorized formations halted for lack of fuel, only mounted units would be able to fight. The revised version—"the exercises demonstrated that the detachment has insufficient transport to accomplish its mission east of the Meuse"—could be read to imply that the detachment could, however, usefully operate west of the river. The new version also omitted both the invidious comparison between horsed and motorized cavalry and the pointed prediction that the existing allotment of roads would create "veritable paralysis." Perhaps Altmeyer had a healthy dislike for wordy prose, but the elimination of *"fort"* (from *"il serait fort utile"*) and *"très"* (from *"à très grande distance"* and *"très malaisées"*) suggests an effort to tone down bad news. Other amendments, like replacing *"totalement insolubles"* with *"parfois insolubles,"* dulled the letter's critical tone and left the reader with a deceptively positive view of the situation.

The defense of French confidence led Altmeyer to hedge his assessments and Gamelin to outright prevarication. During French discussions of its Eastern European engagements, according to Martin Alexander, Gamelin "understood both the scale of French military unpreparedness and the risk of politico-strategic collapse if it were admitted. The result was a policy towards the east during 1937–9 that posterity has not considered honest."[31] In the staff talks of 16 and 17 May 1939, Gamelin and Air Force Chief of Staff Vuillemin deliberately misled the Poles about French intentions, and, as Alexander notes, "on the French side, these conversations were marked by a lack of candor, no little cynicism and a measure of deception that did no credit to the general staff, the air staff or the foreign minister."[32]

Hard truths were blurred both by optimistic language and by refusal to ask questions whose answers might have proved unsettling. Thus, a general staff document describing French assistance to Poland in the event of a German attack speaks of "sure and effective indirect support and direct help if a Central European front can be constituted thanks to Italian support."[33] Since the nature of the "indirect" aid to be offered is unspecified, there is no reason to believe claims of certainty and effectiveness. The predication of direct support on Italian cooperation led the army not to urge the government to seek the necessary accommodation with the Italians but to pigeonhole the Polish question with other problems too intractable to address.

In spring 1939 German pressure on Poland and the hardening of the Berlin-Rome axis stimulated French initiatives towards Poland, but, because it was to come into force only upon the ratification of a political agreement, the military convention negotiated by the two general staffs in the month of May was an empty gesture.[34] So far were French political and military leaders from a candid weighing of their national intentions and capabilities that foreign minister Georges Bonnet could testify at Riom that he had expected the French Army to offer Poland "prompt and effective support, that is to say a real and immediate offensive by our armies, the only sort of offensive that could have spared Poland from complete occupation and from submission for an indeterminate period of time to German domination"—and this unconvincing and self-serving denial was not laughed out of court.[35] Not that French policy was conducive to public discussion. Gamelin hardly wanted to advertise to Poland that her forces were to be sacrificed in order to gain time for the mobilization of French and British forces.[36]

Cognitive dissonance can be seen in the dog that did nothing in the night, the questions that were not asked, and the arguments that were not offered. What would France do if Germany were to attack its eastern allies? What if Belgium refused to allow French troops to make their fight on Belgian soil?

What if the B reserve divisions, suspect for their superannuated soldiers, inadequate equipment, and poor cadres, had to take the brunt of a German attack? When General Gouraud suggested on 14 December 1927 that the Conseil Supérieur de la Guerre ought to express its concern about the inadequacy of the initial mobilization to protect France's frontiers, Minister of War Painlévé and Marshal Pétain admitted the existence of the problem but rejected warnings to that effect as useless and dangerous. At the council meeting of 28 May 1932, Minister of War Piétri schemed to avoid parliamentary debate about the fortifications of the northern frontier lest disquieting things be said about Belgium's uncertain attitude or about the military situation as a whole.[37] Forced to consider the repercussions on French strategy of new German frontier fortifications, General Gamelin was grasping at straws when he suggested to the CSG that, because the German works were not built to French specifications, they "will be perhaps more easily attacked, considering modern weapons."[38] At every level, from small unit tactics to grand strategy, French soldiers "solved" their less tractable problems through mental gymnastics. They assumed the existence of material resources that were not available, made unrealistic but comforting diplomatic assessments, and calculated the efficacy of their doctrine on the basis of what had to work.

The self-confidence of the French Army may have been bolstered by intellectual efforts, but it did not lack a physical basis, not least of which was its record in World War I. Long before allied production and American troops had brought the material resources for the final victory, it had been French soldiers who, undaunted by heavy losses and a harrowing retreat, had turned in victorious counterattack on the Marne.[39] The *poilus* had fought tenaciously thereafter, until broken in 1917 less by German effort than by the callousness of their own commanders. The French Army recovered in 1918 and returned to the offensive with a modern force based on artillery, tanks, and aircraft. Twenty years later, France could still claim to have "the most modern and most efficient armament" in the world.[40] French regulations offered a comprehensive offensive doctrine—the methodical battle—when the German Army still lacked a single coherent theory for the integration of infantry and armor.[41] The reserve army had its weaknesses, but many French units were of high quality. Thus, André Maurois tempered his scathing criticism of French unpreparedness for war with a passionate description of a motorized dragoon regiment's 1939 Christmas Day review: "What fine soldiers! Their step was vigorous, their heads snapped to the left an instant before they came abreast of the general, their eyes, fixed on his, were young and ardent; their heels thudded on the ground at the salute. In truth, the Grenadier Guards could not have done better."[42]

Arguments about how well French soldiers responded to the major problems they faced distract one from the more significant truth that day-to-day concerns preempted larger questions about the army's overall readiness for war. In a note assessing the French strategic situation in early 1933, General Weygand warned that decisions tended to be made "from day to day, under the pressure of budgetary requirements, political influences, and international blackmail" and reflected "detail" rather than overall policy.[43] Weygand was right, and French national defense arrangements were not so much guided by a broad strategic vision as enslaved to organizational detail. The mechanisms for inducting and training recruits, preparing junior leaders, and organizing its reserve forces exercised tyrannical constraints on French choices while leaving French soldiers little time to wonder whether their time and energy could be better spent.

There is little reason, however, to believe such emphasis on quotidian matters over long-term policy to have been a French vice rather than a general characteristic of military and other organizations. If, as John Lennon has it, "life is what happens when you're busy doing other things," an army can allow war to become an afterthought, only to discover itself to be unprepared to fulfill its raison d'être. In other words, war can be an army's reason for being without being the center of its peacetime existence. The matters that absorbed most of the French Army's energy—the recruitment, organization, and training of active and reserve soldiers—were carried out in a world in which the practical present outweighed a hypothetical future. The myopic concentration on small details that prevented the French Army from addressing larger-scale problems had the merit of preventing those insoluable problems from undermining French belief in their nation's strength. Peacetime habit proved hard to break, however, and wartime demands for "military effectiveness" failed to override the "tyranny of the mundane."

If French national defense arrangements had a single purpose, it was to instill in the nation the confidence necessary for success. At the highest levels, they succeeded. Whatever mental methods Gamelin used to reconcile contradictory information, he remained sanguine in the face of an increasingly gloomy strategic situation. In September 1938, his *chef de cabinet* Colonel Petibon, a man whose "intuitive rapport with Gamelin was uncanny,"[44] offered the British military attaché a most positive assessment of French possibilities. In a report of 26 February 1940, Gamelin himself asserted that, although the Germans would have a military advantage until the spring of 1941, that point would see "a reversal of the situation in favor of the Allies, if not with regard to manpower, at least from the point of view of armaments."[45] Of course, he did not expect Hitler to delay his attack until the balance shifted in France's favor. Germany could be expected to attack in 1940, the offensive would come through Holland and Belgium, the German Army would have, in de la Gorce's words, "a transitory but undeniable superiority." But Gamelin believed his army capable of holding off even a superior German force.[46]

Nothing better demonstrates Gamelin's confidence in the defensive quality of the French Army than the amendments to Plan E of 15 and 23 November 1939 that shifted the Seventh Army to the far left wing in anticipation of an advance all the way to Breda. Raising the number of French divisions committed to the northward movement from ten to thirty and deepening their penetration into Belgium reduced the flexibility of French arrangements and left General Georges's Army Group North without a strategic reserve.[47] These were not decisions that the notoriously cautious Gamelin would have made had he not been convinced of the ability of outnumbered French troops to hold their ground in other sectors.[48] Gamelin personified an army that not only bowed to the obligation to conceal its concerns from the French government and its weaknesses from France's allies but that believed in itself. "We will win because we are the stronger" reflected the attitude of an army that suffered, in Doughty's words, from "what proved to be an unwarranted confidence in their doctrine."[49]

If the French high command's manifest self-confidence was the product of delusion, it was a delusion widely shared by foreign observers. An American at the front in 1939 described French Army morale as "splendid everywhere." Rather than hoping for peace, "from the private soldier up, the French want to do away with the threat of German domination for good and all."[50] A visit by Lieutenant Colonel Sumner Waite two months later to the First Armored Division elicited an even more positive verdict. Reservists gave "the impression that they had been soldiering for years. Though the wine be frozen and the potatoes ditto, the expression of the day is, 'La vie est belle,' and they mean it."[51] Waite praised the "keenness and enthusiasm of reserve officers as well as regulars" and noted that "a gallant and pugnacious spirit was met at every turn. They're ready to meet the best the enemy has." Describing the behavior of the men during a decoration ceremony in freezing rain, he concluded, "They're tough." Nothing contradicted Waite's report of the previous year in which he noted that the German Army had suffered many mechanical problems during its entry in Austria and that its rapid expansion had left it with inadequate cadres. The French Army, he had concluded, "is second to none in leadership, staff, cadres and trained men."[52]

Though they tended to disparage the appearance of French troops, foreigners indicated a high regard for their practical skills. Another American concluded that the United States Army could learn from French realism and methods of teaching small-unit combat: "The French infantry does not waste much time on theoretical training. They get out on the terrain and do things. They do not look impressive and for this reason I believe there is a tendency on the part of foreign observers to underestimate them."[53] To Lord Ironside, French disdain for spit and polish betokened an admirable practicality from which the British army could learn a lesson.[54]

The British army's annual intelligence reports spoke positively of their future allies. The 1935 version noted that the French Army had ameliorated its fortifications, mobility, numbers, length of service, rear echelon organization, and arms procurement. Improvement needed only to continue at the current rate for the French Army to "become a more powerful and more quickly mobilizable fighting machine than at any period since the return to peace conditions after the war."[55] In 1936 British military attaché Colonel F. Beaumont-Nesbitt stressed the high quality of the French commanders and argued that the French people as a whole supported their army. Even reservists from hotbeds of communism like Marseilles demonstrated "good *morale* and sound discipline." Communism was hardly a problem in the French Army. A reserve battalion might march into training camp singing "The Red Flag" and "The Internationale," but would obey orders to confine itself thereafter to the "Marseillaise." Communists before and after their reserve periods, reservists were patriots when they had to be.[56] Another British report called the French Army "a well trained, efficient, and powerful weapon, primarily designed for a defensive rôle, but possessing adequate facilities to pass to the offensive whenever the strategical or tactical situation should call for such action." If there were "shortcomings in material and instructions" these were "gradually being made good." Whatever dissensions existed in French public life had not affected the morale of the army.[57]

Beaumont-Nesbitt's 1937 study is especially interesting for its explicit comparison of French and German armored units.[58] If the French light mechanized divisions "have as yet scarcely emerged from the experimental state," the Panzer divisions "were still a subject of discussion in Germany, since agreement had not yet been reached as to how they might best be organized and employed." Beaumont-Nesbett also reported an encouraging conversation with General Billotte, who said that his troops' morale "had never been better and was improving daily." Although Billotte stressed the need for further hard work, he was optimistic and pleased with the result of a five-division map exercise in which the Blue forces failed to break the Maginot line in spite of every advantage. To be sure, Billotte paid more attention to the positive outcome of the exercise than to the deficiencies it demonstrated, a response characteristic of French attitudes, but the British too had their own strategies for reassuring themselves. Wanting to believe in the French Army, Beaumont-Nesbitt emphasized that General Billotte was "broad shouldered," nearly six feet tall, and gave "the impression of great physical strength."[59] Although the report expressed concern about the nature of political and economic life under Leon Blum's Popular Front government, the army was judged to be "unaffected by the conditions prevailing throughout the country." "The French are . . . not pacifist. A military nation, without being militarist, they are prepared to defend their country at all times." Though "the expenditure of enormous sums on unproductive objects, is directly contrary to their way of thinking . . . the army as the historical symbol of France is widely popular." The Char B1bis appeared to be the best tank in the world and the French officer demonstrated "amazing industry and devotion to duty."

Almost apologetic references in the Englishman's report to the inflexibility of French military ideas are mitigated by the suggestion that "rigidity doubtless does not extend to high command" and that "the personality of junior leaders will assert itself, but tempered by the rigid training which they have undergone." Given a choice, a country's decision to fight against rather than alongside France "would be engendered more from dislike, or fear, of French politics, than from any lack of respect for the French Army." In conclusion, the report pronounced the French Army "a highly efficient machine, undergoing constant revision and improvement, to fit it to meet the problems with which it is confronted. There is no doubt whatever that General Gamelin has at his disposal a force which no potential enemy could afford to treat lightly."[60]

I have already described the enthusiastic approval of the French Army evinced by British Secretary of State for War Sir Leslie Hore-Belisha after the September 1937 Alençon maneuvers.[61] Interestingly, Hore-Belisha's note to the cabinet about his trip remarks not only on morale but on French tendencies to deprecate their own achievements; Sir Orme Sargent of the Foreign Office appended to Hore-Belisha's report a sobering minute wishing that "we could feel equally confident about the French air force as we do about the French Army."[62] Even Chief of the Imperial General Staff Cyril

Deverell's invidious comparisons with the German exercises that he attended immediately thereafter had little effect on British confidence in their allies. Though admitting that Deverell's assessment "goes a long way towards removing the pleasant feeling" left by Hore-Belisha's exuberant report, a Foreign Office official tried to tone down the impact of Deverell's bleak assessment. Deverell, he suggested, "has underestimated the French capacity for pulling themselves together and achieving marvels with small resources, possibly, too, he underrated Germany's raw-material and financial weakness and the real if imponderable value to France of her free institutions."[63]

Such arguments were a common answer to concerns about French weaknesses, and the British desire to believe in the French Army was as logical as the latter's need to believe in itself. Thus, Anthony Eden added a reassuring annotation to a note in which Air Attaché Colyer called the French Air Force "a broken reed upon which it would be unwise to place too much reliance."

> While it is no doubt true that there is much that is unsatisfactory about the state of the French Air Force and that of the French Navy, we should, I think, be careful not to exaggerate their weakness, while at the same time over-estimating the strength of the dictator states. We know of the short-comings of the democracies; those of the totalitarian States are withheld from us.[64]

In this context, Winston Churchill's notorious description of the French Army on 14 April 1938 as "the most perfectly trained and faithful mobile force in Europe" was neither rhetoric nor wishful thinking.[65]

Admiration for the French Army was not limited to potential allies susceptible to charges of wishful thinking. Italian ambassador Vittorio Cerruti advised his foreign minister, Count Galeazzo Ciano, that "the French Army was the finest in the world." Italian and German diplomats shared the belief that their own objective assessments of French strength were contradicted in Rome and Berlin by the self-serving ones of politicians. Thus German Count Johannes von Welczeck complained of the difficulties created by "the absurd reports sent to the Nazi big-wigs such as Goering, Goebbels, and Rosenberg by their agents in France, who tell their masters what they wish to hear and not what they ought to know," and he insisted that his own concerns about French strength were shared by the German military attachés in Paris.[66] The Italian military attaché in Bucharest told Sir Reginald Hoare, British Minister in Bucharest, that "the great majority of Italian officers in positions of responsibility and with access to the abundant sources of information available, were quite convinced of the excellence of the French Army." The attaché deemed the French general staff the most efficient in the world, far superior in its flexibility to the German. Though French politics were "unsound," the army remained unaffected. If only, the attaché lamented, the Italian politicians would listen to the experts.[67]

Those who bet on France in a Franco-German confrontation were wrong in 1940, when Germany proved indisputably to have the better army, but the shift of power had been a gradual one. Hindsight encourages the historian to stress every indication of French stagnation or of German innovation; many contemporaries, however, did not discern Germany's emerging military superiority over France, perhaps because they chose not to do so, perhaps because it was not obvious, perhaps because it was only partially there.

The lessons to be learned from this story are as complex and frustrating as were the challenges that France tried unsuccessfully to meet. Friction, Clausewitz's "great chasms between *planning and execution*," exists not only at the tactical and operational levels but in the incomparably greater impediments to action on the level of national strategy.[68] The battlefield friction that comes from commanders' uncertainties and lack of information and that makes "action in war like movement in a resistant element" is more easily remedied than the political and institutional frictions that choke the efforts of whole nations.[69] Although the complexities of any military organization will challenge a commander's efforts to manipulate it, even a joint-theater command is simple compared to leading a nation-state. The latter is not an entity united to compete in an uncooperative environment but a collection of discordant elements whose internal contradictions militate against consistent effort. Rarely capable of concentrating their energies on a single objective, states devise plans to secure their national security only with great difficulty and rarely approach the "total war" that is alleged to be the characteristic conflict of the twentieth century.

In the tactical realm, the antidotes to friction are strength of character, determination, and what Clausewitz calls "coup d'oeil"—"the quick recognition of a truth that the mind would ordinarily miss or would perceive only after long study and reflection."[70] Armed with the ability to visualize the situation and the courage to act upon his judgment, the battlefield commander presses on through the resistant medium. In the making of national security policy, however, accurate perception and willpower must be combined with favorable political circumstances. Adolph Hitler's uncanny vision and demonic will were well matched by the nation he came to lead. In the second century BC, Gaius Marius led Romans to victory against Jugurtha and the German invasions only by revolutionizing Roman military organization and political practices.

Interwar France had no such leader. Daladier and Gamelin worked within the institutions of the Republic they served. The absence of what might be called revolutionary leadership is not an explanation for what happened to France in the 1930s but another symptom of the contemporary climate. Roman institutions, though ostensibly designed to punish undue accretions of power, were susceptible to manipulation by a man who combined political and military skill with insatiable ambition. Interwar France, aptly labeled by Stanley Hoffmann the "stalemate society," was far more resistant to change.[71] Her successful politicians, even the leaders of parties dedicated to overthrowing the capitalist republic, were men whose personal aspirations did not exceed what the republic offered. Many soldiers were less committed to republican institutions, but their rebellion took the form of increasing aloofness from the corrupting influences of civilian politics.[72] However despicable they found the "partisan and demagogic" democracy,[73] they could not have maintained their claims to be the true defenders of French moral values while denying their ability to protect its equally sacred soil.

General Gamelin has been derided for announcing to the Conseil Permanent de la Défense Nationale on 23 August 1939 that "the French Army is ready." His explanation after the fact was that the meeting had been an informal one and that he meant only that the army was ready for mobilization and concentration.[74] He should have stuck to his guns. His army was as ready as he believed he could have made it given the circumstances. As for Paul Reynaud's warnings that France needed to have either "the army of her policy or the policy of her army," one could have replied that France had, if not an army geared to support her diplomatic engagements, one that reflected her politics in the largest possible sense.[75] It was an army unready for war against the Wehrmacht in 1940, but it could not have been different and remained the army of the Third Republic.

Notes

Introduction

1. Robert J. Young, *In Command of France: French Foreign Policy and Military Planning, 1933–1940* (Cambridge, MA, and London, 1978); Martin S. Alexander, *The Republic in Danger: General Maurice Gamelin and the Politics of French Defence, 1933–1940* (Cambridge, 1992).

2. Robert Frankenstein, *Le prix du réarmament français* (Paris, 1982); Pierre Hoff, *Les programmes d'armement de 1919 à 1939* (Vincennes, 1972).

3. Jeffrey A. Gunsberg, *Divided and Conquered: The French High Command and the Defeat of the West, 1940* (Westport, CT, 1979).

4. Robert A. Doughty, *The Seeds of Disaster: The Development of French Army Doctrine 1919–1939* (Hamden, CT, 1985); Ladislas Mysyrowicz, *Anatomie d'une défaite: Origines de l'effondrement militaire français de 1940* (Lausanne, 1973); Faris Russell Kirkland, "The French Officer Corps and the Fall of France—1920–1940" (Ph.D. dissertation, University of Pennsylvania, 1982).

5. Robert A. Doughty, *The Breaking Point: Sedan and the Fall of France, 1940* (Hamden, CT, 1990); Marc Bloch, *Strange Defeat: A Statement of Evidence Written in 1940,* trans. Gerard Hopkins (New York, 1968); Adolphe Goutard, *1940: La guerre des occasions perdues* (Paris, 1956), trans. A. R. P. Burgess as *The Battle of France, 1940* (London, 1958).

6. Quoted in Richard G. Tindall, "Period of Duty with the French Army," 12 October 1933, 24 (G-2 19,791-W), United States National Archives, Record Group 165, 2015-1161/1. All material from the United States National Archives (hereafter USNA) is from Record Group 165 (Military Intelligence Division); G-2 19,791-W indicates the original document number, and 2015-1161/1 stands for carton 2015-file 1161/document 1.

7. Bloch, *Strange Defeat;* Alistair Horne, *To Lose a Battle: France 1940* (Harmondsworth, Eng., 1969); William L. Shirer, *The Collapse of the Third Republic* (New York, 1969); Henry Dutailly, *Les problèmes de l'armée de terre française (1935–1939)* (Paris, 1980); Guy Chapman, *Why France Fell* (New York, 1968);

Edward Spears, *Assignment to Catastrophe,* 2 vols. (New York, 1954-1955); Doughty, *Seeds of Disaster;* Mysyrowicz, *Anatomie d'une défaite.*

8. Bloch, *Strange Defeat.*

9. Philip Bankwitz, *Maximé Weygand and Civil-Military Relations in Modern France* (Cambridge, MA, 1967); Richard Challener, *The French Theory of the Nation in Arms 1866-1939* (New York, 1955).

10. André Beaufre, *1940: The Fall of France,* trans. D. Flower (New York, 1968).

11. Doughty, *Seeds of Disaster,* and Mysyrowicz, *Anatomie d'une défaite.*

12. Goutard, *1940;* Doughty, *Breaking Point.*

13. Young, *In Command of France.*

14. Few recent studies of the interwar period are as openly didactic as Williamson Murray's *The Change in the European Balance of Power 1938-1939: The Path to Ruin* (Princeton, 1984), which explicitly undertakes to "judge the effectiveness of national policies, strategies, and decision-making processes on the basis of their overall response to the challenges of the late 1930s" (355).

15. Robert J. Young, "La Guerre de Longue Durée: Some Reflections on French Strategy and Diplomacy in the 1930s," in Adrian Preston, ed., *General Staffs and Diplomacy Before the Second World War* (London, 1978), 45.

16. Alistair Horne, *The French Army and Politics, 1870-1970* (London, 1984), 56.

17. Anthony Adamthwaite, *France and the Coming of the Second World War, 1936-1939* (London, 1977), 172.

18. Paul Emile Tournoux, *Haut Commandement: Gouvernement et défense des frontières du nord et de l'est, 1919-1939* (Paris, 1960), 212.

19. Douglas Porch, "Arms and Alliances: French Grand Strategy and Policy in 1914 and 1940," in Paul Kennedy, ed., *Grand Strategies in War and Peace* (New Haven and London, 1991), 141; Barry A. Posen, *The Sources of Military Doctrine: France, Britain, and Germany Between the World Wars* (Ithaca, NY, 1984); Doughty, *Seeds of Disaster,* 11.

20. Doughty, *Seeds of Disaster,* 6.

21. U.S. FM 100-5, *Operations,* 1986.

22. Thus Doughty, *Seeds of Disaster;* Horne, *To Lose a Battle;* Mysyrowicz, *Anatomie d'une défaite;* Shirer, *Collapse of the Third Republic.*

23. For a parallel reassessment of interwar German military thinking tending to modify assumptions about the alacrity and conviction with which the German army seized upon the doctrine now called "Blitzkrieg," see Matthew Cooper, *The German Army 1933-1945: Its Political and Military Failure* (London, 1978); Doughty, *Breaking Point* is a very useful description of how the Wehrmacht actually fought in 1940.

24. Young, *In Command of France,* 1, 6-7.

25. Horne, *French Army,* 54.

26. Edward N. Luttwak, *The Grand Strategy of the Roman Empire From the First Century A.D. to the Third* (Baltimore and London, 1976); Paul Kennedy, *Grand Strategies in War and Peace* (New Haven and London, 1991).

27. John Lewis Gaddis, *Strategies of Containment* (Oxford, 1982).

28. Theodore Ropp, *The Development of a Modern Navy: French Naval Policy 1871-1904* (Annapolis, 1987), 220.

29. I borrow here the useful definition of "military effectiveness" offered in Allan R. Millett and Williamson Murray, *Military Effectiveness,* Vol. 1; *The First World War* (London, Sydney, Wellington, 1988), 1–30.

30. Doughty, *Seeds of Disaster,* 183.

31. *Ibid.,* 11.

32. Robert J. Young, "French Military Intelligence and Nazi Germany, 1938–1939," in Ernst R. May, *Knowing One's Enemies: Intelligence Assessment Before the Two World Wars* (Princeton, 1984), 271–309; Patrice Buffotot, "La perception du réarmament allemand par les organismes de renseignement français de 1936 à 1939," *Revue historique des armées* 6 (1979): 173–184. See also Steven Ross, "French Net Assessment," in Williamson Murray and Allen R. Millet, eds. *Calculations: Net Assessment and the Coming of World War II* (New York, 1992), 136–174. For the claim that "none of the international crises provoked by Germany from January 1935 to September 1939 surprised the high command," see Dutailly, *Problèmes de l'armée,* 72.

33. "Military" is used here in a strict sense dealing exclusively with armies. There will be, regrettably, only passing references here to naval or air force matters. The latter, in particular, is a fertile area of investigation for scholars qualified to build on the pioneering work of Robert J. Young, "The Strategic Dream: French Air Doctrine in the Inter-War Period, 1919–1939," *Journal of Contemporary History* 9 (1974): 57–76, and Faris R. Kirkland, "The French Air Force in 1940: Was it Defeated by the Luftwaffe or by Politics?" *Air University Review* 36 (1985): 101–17.

34. All material for the *Service historique de l'armée de terre* is identified as SHAT plus carton number.

35. Alexander, *Republic in Danger,* 343.

Chapter 1. Mobilizing the Nation in Arms

1. The seminal study is Richard D. Challener, *The French Theory of the Nation in Arms 1866–1939* (New York, 1955), 184–214.

2. J. Monteilhet, *Les institutions militaires de la France (1814–1932)* (Paris, 1932), 411.

3. France, Assemblée Nationale, *Journal officiel de la république française 1870–1940, Chambre des députés, Débats parlementaires et documents parlementaires* (Paris, 1st sess., 4 March 1927, 485 (hereafter *JO, Chambre*). Except where noted, all translations are mine.

4. As created in 1906, the CSDN was chaired by the president of the republic and contained the ministers of foreign affairs, finance, war, the navy, the colonies, and, from 1913, the interior. The reform of 17 November 1921 added the minister of public works, allowed the vice-presidents of the Conseil Supérieur de la Guerre and the Conseil Supérieur de la Marine to participate in an advisory capacity, and gave the chair either to the president of the Republic or the president of the Council of Ministers, See François-André Paoli, ed., *L'Armée française de 1919 à 1939,* 4 vols. (Paris, 1969–1971, 2:74).

5. Decree of 17 November 1921, quoted in Paoli, *L'Armée française,* 2:134.

6. *Procès Verbaux* (hereafter *PV*), CSDN study commission (second section), 31 March 1922, 7 April 1922, SHAT 2N20.

7. Deputy Picot proposed that official statistics about the state of national mobilization should be used to calculate further reductions of military service; see summaries of the Chamber debates of 28 February; 2, 10, 16, 22, 29 March; 20, 27 June 1922 in SHAT 2N201/1.

8. Among the factors contributing to the delay were interdepartmental arguments documented in SHAT 2N201 and 2N203.

9. For Paul-Boncour's efforts on behalf of the law, see Serrigny's letter to the president of the Council of Ministers of 5 November 1924, SHAT 2N203/1; *Annales de la Chambre des Députés, Documents Parlementaires. 13ère legislature, session extraordinaire de 1925,* annexe 1879, session of 7 July 1925, 114–128; Paul-Boncour's statement, *PV,* Cham. Army Comm., 2 February 1927.

10. Though undefined, the phrase "total war" appears repeatedly both in the sense of the war fought without restraint, as threatened by the writings of Douhet, Ludendorff, and (as read by the French) Clausewitz (*JO, Chambre,* 22 March 1938, 870–871) and in the sense of a war for which a nation mobilizes its civilian as well as its military resources (Monteilhet, *Institutions militaires,* 411).

11. The crucial phrase is "*toutes les personnes de nationalité française, et les ressortissants français,*" SGCSDN, "Projet de loi sur l'organisation générale de la nation pour le temps de guerre," 20 April 1923; CSDN (study commission), "Exposé des motifs," 31 March 1922, 33, SHAT 2N5/10.

12. *JO, Chambre,* 1st sess., 4 March 1927, 491.

13. Why the council thought the indemnities would cost more than negotiated settlements—or could not be avoided altogether—is unclear.

14. Quoted in *Annales, 13ème legislature, session extraordinaire de 1925,* annexe 1879, 7 July 1925, 119–120.

15. *PV,* CSDN study commission (2d section), 7 April 1922, SHAT 2N2/1.

16. *JO, Chambre,* 2d sess., 4 March 1927, 502.

17. Ibid., 503.

18. Ibid., 507.

19. Ibid., 7 March 1927, 546.

20. *PV,* Cham. Army Comm., 8 February 1927, Paul-Boncour report, 264.

21. For a widely disseminated piece of propaganda against the law, see Paoli, *L'Armée française,* 3:48, 83.

22. *PV,* Sen. Army Comm., 13 February 1928.

23. Serrigny to minister of war, 18 May 1927, *PV,* Sen. Army Comm., 20 May 1927; Serrigny to President Painlevé, 1 June 1927, *PV,* Sen. Army Comm., 10 June 1927.

24. Quoted by Lucien Voilin, *PV,* Sen. Army Comm., 7 February 1928, 106.

25. *JO, Sénat,* 17 February 1928, 200.

26. Voilin, *JO, Sénat,* 7 February 1928, 106.

27. Klotz, *JO, Sénat,* 10 February 1928, 142.

28. In a lecture at the CHEDN, Lt. Col. Charles de Gaulle attributed women's exclusion from mobilization to the need for child care and the requirements of international law (de Gaulle, "Le projet de loi d'organisation de la nation pour le temps

de guerre," 22 October 1936, 17 SHAT 2N279). A lecture to the 1937–1938 class, however, stressed the probable "moral . . . abuses."

29. *PV,* Sen. Army Comm., 18 May 1927.

30. Joseph Paul-Boncour, *Entre deux guerres: Souvenirs de la IIIe République,* 3 vols. (Paris, 1946), 2:260.

31. *PV,* Sen. Army Comm., 20 May 1927.

32. The "liberal" and "socialist" labels come from Paoli, *L'Armée française,* 3:50. Nine substantive differences between the texts are outlined in Réné Richard, "Rapport fait au nom de la Commission de l'Armée . . . sur le projet de Loi sur l'organisation de la nation pour le temps de guerre," 2d sess., 23 March 1937, SHAT 5N581/1.

33. The significant laws are the Army General Organization Law of 13 July 1927 (*JO, Lois et Décrets,* 14 July 1927, 7266–7270; Paoli, *L'Armée française,* 3:51–62), the "Cadres and Effectifs" Law of 28 March 1928 (*JO, Lois et Décrets,* 3 April 1928, 3792–3797; Paoli, *L'Armée française,* 3:62–72), the Recruitment Law of 31 March 1928 (*JO, Lois et Décrets,* 3 April 1928, 3808–3855; Paoli, *L'Armée française,* 3:72–76), and the Frontier Defense law of 14 January 1930 (*JO, Lois et Décrets,* January 1930, 446–447).

34. Thus, the report by the Aeronautical Commission of the Chamber in 1936 attributed the bill's failure in 1928 to a fatal collision between the demands of national discipline and individual interest ("Avis présenté au nom de la Commission de l'Aéronautique sur le projet du loi sur l'organisation de la nation pour le temps de guerre par M. Andraud, Député," *Annales, 16th legislature, session ordinaire,* annexe 6820, 517).

35. For this description of Serrigny's role by a member of the secretariat see de Gaulle, "Le projet de loi," 15, SHAT 2N279. For another soldier's argument for the importance of national organization, though without mentioning the law in question, see Marie-Eugène Debeney, *La guerre et les hommes: Reflexions d'après-guerre* (Paris, 1937), 49–58.

36. Paul-Boncour, *Entre deux guerres,* 2:257, 260.

37. Bernard Serrigny, "L'organisation de notre défense nationale," *RDM* 7:59 (September–October 1930): 35.

38. Maxime Weygand, *La France, est-elle defendue?* (Berlin, 1983), 87.

39. Paul-Boncour, *Entre deux guerres,* 2:254.

40. For the composition of the officer corps see Raoul Girardet, *La société militaire dans la France contemporaine, 1815–1939* (Paris, 1953), 200. The navy was at least as conservative: see R. Chalmers Hood, *Royal Republicans* (Baton Rouge and London, 1983).

41. Alistair Horne, *The French Army and Politics* (London, 1984), 25–26; Jan K. Tannenbaum, *General Maurice Sarrail, 1856–1929* (Chapel Hill, 1974), 16–17; Paul Marie de la Gorce, *The French Army: A Military-Political History,* trans. Kenneth Douglas (New York, 1963), 51–54.

42. Challener, *French Theory,* 210–211.

43. For the absence of a visible military threat, see Jean Senac, "L'organisation de la nation pour le temps de guerre," *La Concorde,* 3 December 1935, quoted in

Richard, "Rapport," 7, and Robert J. Young, "L'Attaque Brusquée and Its Use as a Myth in Interwar France," *Historical Reflections* 81 (1981): 93–113.

44. For an example of mobilization planning in the absence of a comprehensive law, see the SGCSDN's 133-page "Guide pratique pour l'établissement des plans de mobilisation nationale," 1 July 1931, SHAT 2N213/1 and Paoli, *L'Armée française,* 3:49, 102–104. These preparations, however, "lacked the executive impetus that only a law could give them," La Chambre, *PV,* Cham. Army Comm, 29 January 1936, 4.

45. James A. Lester, "Census, Classification and Requisition of Automobile Vehicles," (G-2 20,603-W), USNA RG165 2281-C-155/1.

46. Amédée Bernard, "Théorèmes de défense nationale," *RMG* 2 (1938): 28.

47. A tawdry affair in which Radical Socialist politicians were accused of protecting and government police then of "suiciding" a small-time confidence man.

48. *PV,* CSDN Study Committee, 9 November 1934, SHAT 2N206/1, 7.

49. *PV,* Cham. Army Comm., 23 December 1936. Men conscripted for defense work were entitled to normal wages and, if authorized, for bonuses as well (de Gaulle, "Le projet de loi," 21).

50. *PV,* Cham. Army Comm., 19 February 1936. For French reserve organization, see Chapter 4.

51. Ibid., 22 March 1938, 887–892. The CPDN was established on 6 June 1936. Although similar in membership to the HCM, it had the use of the CSDN's secretariat. For information about the various civil-military consultative bodies, see the untitled study prepared by the SGCSDN, 16 September 1936, SHAT 2N223/1, and Eugenia C. Kiesling, "A Staff College for the Nation in Arms: The Collège des Hautes Etudes de la Défense Nationale" (Ph.D. dissertation, Stanford University, 1988), 30–40.

52. *JO, Chambre* (2d session), 24 March 1938, 948.

53. Decree of 13 November 1934, *JO, Lois et Décrets,* 14 November 1934, 11298.

54. Serrigny, "L'Organisation de notre défense," 30.

55. See Weygand's complaints in France, Assemblée Nationale, Session de 1947, No. 2344, *Rapport fait au nom de la commission chargée d'enquêter sur les événements survenus en France de 1933 à 1945. Annexes. Témoignages et documents recueillis par la commission d'enquête parlementaire,* 9 vols. (Paris, 1951) (hereafter *Evénements*), Annex 1, 242, and Serrigny, "L'organisation de notre défense," 32. Deputy Louis Marin called the council "nothing other than the government advising itself," *JO, Chambre,* 22 March 1938, 889.

56. *JO, Chambre,* 2d sess., 24 March 1938, 946.

57. Quoted in Martin S. Alexander, *The Republic in Danger* (Cambridge, 1992), 91.

58. *PV,* CPDN, 5 December 1936, 20–21. *"Super-Ministre"* is Daladier's phrase.

59. The evaluation comes from the untitled SGSCDN document of 16 September 1936, SHAT 2N223/1.

60. Jean Sénac to Prime Minister Sarraut, 28 February 1936, SHAT 2N207/2. Command arrangements were discussed in Chamber Army Committee meetings on 29 January 1936, 3 February 1936, 12 February 1936, 19 February 1936, 4 March

1936, 23 December 1936, 13 January 1937, 10 February 1937, 24 February 1937, and 3 March 1937.

61. "Avis présenté au nom de la Commission de l'Aéronautique sur le projet du loi sur l'organisation de la nation pour le temps de guerre par M. Andraud, Député," *Annales, 16th legislature, session ordinaire, annexe* 6820, 518 (2d sess., 5 March 1936).

62. Gamelin stressed the difference between command and coordination in a letter to Daladier of 1 April 1938, SHAT 2N208.

63. For the CHEDN, see Chapter 2.

64. *PV,* CPDN, 2 October 1936, SHAT 2N21/1.

65. Ibid., 17–18.

66. *PV,* CPDN, 5 December 1936, and supporting documents, SHAT 2N21/1. The *Comité de Guerre* was the wartime version of the CPDN, expanded in size and chaired by the president of the republic.

67. *PV,* Cham. Army Comm., 24 February 1937.

68. "Avis présenté au nom de la Commission de la Marine Militaire sur le projet du loi sur l'organisation de la nation pour le temps de guerre par M. Pinay," *Annales, 16ᵉ legislature, session ordinaire, annexe* 2214, 25 March 1938, 1241.

69. "Avis présenté au nom de la Commission de l'Aéronautique, *Annales, 16ᵉ legislature, session ordinaire, annexe* 3858, 24 March 1938, 466. For a proposal by Senator Rembaud to eliminate the air ministry, see *PV,* Sen. Army Comm., 1 December 1937.

70. *JO, Chambre,* 2d sess., 24 March 1938.

71. The Senate Army Committee had already worked through these issues during debates on Senator Jacquy's bill for the creation of a single Minister of National Defense with authority over under–secretaries of state representing the army, navy, and air force, *PV,* Sen. Army Comm., 24 March 1937, 17.

72. *PV,* Sen. Army Comm., 3 April and 8 June 1938.

73. Ibid., 13 April 1938.

74. Fabry, *JO, Sénat,* 16 June 1938, 653.

75. Bergeron, ibid., 657.

76. *PV,* Cham. Army Comm., 17 June 1938.

77. Tony Albord, "Les rélations de la politique et de la stratégie," in Albord et al., *La défense nationale* (Paris, 1958), 295–298. The suggestion that the law's unclear demarcations of military and civilian power reflected civilian efforts to avoid responsibility for the consequences of possible military failure appears in Bernard Chantebout, *L'organisation générale de la défense nationale en France depuis la fin de la seconde guerre mondiale* (Paris, 1967), 65.

78. Chantebout, *L'organisation générale de la défense,* 74.

79. Ibid., 6–7.

80. Adamthwaite suggests that France needed a prime minister's office as a "central, co-ordinating organ" and foreign and domestic policy advisory body (Anthony Adamthwaite, *France and the Coming of the Second World War* [London, 1977], 358).

81. Paul-Boncour, *Entre deux guerres,* 3:135.

82. Jean-Louis Crémieux-Brilhac, *Les Français de l'an 40,* Vol. 1, *La guerre oui*

ou non? (Paris, 1990), 88–90; For example, Daladier was warned on 30 March 1939 that the decree laws of 20 March 1939 allowing exceptional measures to stimulate arms production would have had no effect unless the armed forces took the initiative to exploit them (Crémieux-Brilhac, *Les Français de l'an 40,* 1:72).

83. Letter SGCSDN to Daladier (undated but in a dossier marked April 1939), SHAT 2N209/1.

84. Minister of National Defense, "Rapport général annuel au sujet de l'état de la préparation de l'organisation du pays pour le temps de guerre," 21 July 1939, 6.

85. The briefing of 22 January 1940 from which this list was taken, "La loi du 11 July 1938/Le CSDN," SHAT 2N223/3, does not mention that the regulation of 28 November 1938 and a subsequent decree of 19 October 1939 dealt with female labor, conscripted in some cases, Hélene Campinchi, "Les femmes et l'effort de guerre en France et dans les pays alliés," *Revue de défense nationale,* new series 3 (1947): 288.

86. Minister of Defense, "Rapport," 11. For example, evacuation plans and major improvements in passive defense against air attack were made after the crisis of September 1938 revealed the urgent need ("Rapport," 25, 28).

87. Ibid., 7, 12.

88. Contrôleur de l'Armée Liebermann, "Note sur la mobilisation industrielle dans l'industrie privée des fabrications de guerre," (n.d. except for control rubber stamp 27 February 1940), SHAT 6N324.

89. The 1936 law is omitted from this account because it was not inspired by the same vision of national security policy as the law of 11 August 1938. Rather, the Popular Front government that assumed power in June 1936 imposed nationalization to control the "merchants of death," to make French industry more efficient, and to improve the lot of French workers (Herrick Chapman, *State Capitalism and Working-Class Radicalism in the French Aircraft Industry* [Berkeley and Los Angeles, 1991], 101–102).

90. Kim Munholland, "Between Popular Front and Vichy: The Decree Laws of the Daladier Ministry, 1938–40" (unpublished essay), 12–14.

91. Crémieux-Brilhac, *Les Français,* 1:436, 439–440.

92. Chapman, *State Capitalism,* 215–216. For an individual example, see Georges Sadoul, *Journal de Guerre, 39–40 (2 septembre 1939–20 juillet 1940)* (Paris, 1977), 17.

93. Jean-Marie d'Hoop, "La politique française du réarmament: d'après les travaux de la commission d'enquête parlementaire," *RHDGM* 4 (1954): 11, 19.

94. André Maurois, *Why France Fell,* trans. Denver Lindley (London, 1941), 51. For more on the muddled French mobilization, see Alexander, *Republic in Danger,* 354–355 and Raoul Dautry, *PV,* Cham. Army Comm., 27 September 1939.

95. Crémieux-Brilhac, *Les Français,* 1:457.

96. Alistair Horne, *To Lose a Battle* (Harmondsworth, Eng., 1969), 128.

97. Tony de Vibraye, *Avec mon groupe de reconnaissance: aout 1939–aout 1940* (Paris, 1943).

98. Jean Vidalenc, "Les divisions de série "B" dans l'armée française pendant la campagne de France 1939–1940," *RHA* 1 (1980): 111.

99. For the hatred and envy that transfers attributed to influence ("*piston*")

could spark within a unit, see Marcel Pétain and Michel Caron, *100 jours, 100 nuits aux avant postes* (Paris, n.d., 80).

100. Campinchi, "Les femmes et l'effort de guerre," 289.

101. *Evénements, Annexes,* 3:811 (Paul-Boncour testimony).

102. J.-M. Bourget, "L'organisation du pays pour le temps de guerre," *Les débats* 12 February 1924, SHAT 2N203/1. Compare Richard, "Rapport."

103. See, for example, Daladier's testimony, *PV,* Cham. Army Comm., 17 December 1936, 12.

Chapter 2. A Staff College for the Nation in Arms

1. Charles de Gaulle, "Création d'une enseignement relative à la conduite de la guerre," 20 April 1931, SHAT 2N277/1. Compare the suggestion for an advanced *army* college in Hubert Camon, "Une lacune à combler: L'Institut des hautes études militaires," *Revue de France* 9 (1929): 52–64. Thiervoz, "Le Collège des Hautes Etudes de Défense Nationale," 20 June 1936, 2, SHAT 2N277/1.

2. Although Daladier's role is nowhere adequately documented, the best discussion is Hervé Coutau-Bégarie, *Castex: le stratège inconnu* (Paris, 1985), 171.

3. Raymond Tourte, "Impérieuse nécessité du commandement unique," *RMG* 1 (1937): 713.

4. Robert J. Young, "The Strategic Dream: French Air Doctrine in the Inter-war Period, 1919–1939," *Journal of Contemporary History* 9 (1974): 57–76.

5. See, for example, Gen. Maginel, "Le commandement unique," *RMG* 1 (1937): 689–707.

6. Philippe Pétain, "Défense nationale et commandement unique," *RDM* (May–June 1936): 15.

7. For Pétain's position, see Chapter 1.

8. Air Ministry, "Organisation d'un Collège des Hautes Etudes de Défense Nationale," 10 July 1936, dossier CPDN meeting 7 July 1936, SHAT 2N20/3.

9. "Note sur le fonctionnement de l'Ecole de Guerre Navale et des Centres d'Etudes dans le cadre de la défense nationale," n.d., 1, dossier CPDN meeting 29 July 1936, SHAT 2N20/3.

10. Minister of the navy to minister of national defense and War, 11 July 1936, SHAT 2N20/3.

11. For a discussion of the controversial idea that the military schools could contribute to the making of doctrine see Chapter 5 and Lt. de Vaisseau Fenard, "Essai historique comparative du haut enseignement dans l'armée et la marine," 1921, Service Historique de la Marine (SHM) 36P54, annexes 7I271.

12. "Note sur le Collège des Hautes Etudes de la Défense Nationale," 21 July 1936, dossier CPDN meeting 29 July 1936, SHAT 2N20/3.

13. *PV,* CPDN, 29 July 1936, 5. Besides having been the director of the Ecole de Guerre Navale and Centre des Hautes Etudes Navales, Castex had recently produced his five-volume *Théories stratégiques* (Paris 1929–1935), published in English as *Strategic Theories,* abridged, trans., and ed. Eugenia C. Kiesling (Annapolis, 1993).

14. *PV,* CPDN, 29 July 1936, 8.

15. Ibid., 9.

16. For Admiral Castex's role, see Coutau-Bégarie, *Castex,* 171–183.

17. Raoul Castex, "Les Hautes Études de Défense Nationale," *RMG* 1 (1937): 45.

18. Georges Durand-Viel, "Le concours des marins," *RMG* 1 (1937): 29–30, 30.

19. For their records, see Eugenia C. Kiesling, "A Staff College for the Nation in Arms," (Ph.D. dissertation, Stanford University, 1988), 232, 242.

20. Castex, "Conference d'inauguration," CHEDN, 15 October 1936, 4, SHAT 2N279, 2.

21. R. Chalmers Hood, *Royal Republicans* (Baton Rouge and London, 1983), 83.

22. Castex, "Conférence d'inauguration," 4.

23. The natural designation, "national strategy," was used by French soldiers to describe a military strategy inspired by a specific country's physical or moral characteristics. The Anglo-American equivalent to Castex's "general strategy" is "grand strategy."

24. Castex, "Conférence d'inauguration," 9.

25. Ibid., 18.

26. Ibid., 19. For the emphasis on uniformity at the Ecole Supérieur de Guerre, see G. V. Y. Waterhouse, "Some Notes on the E.S.G., Paris," *Army Quarterly* 8 (July 1924): 329.

27. A copy of a memorandum in which Marshal Pétain denounced the lecture program as a waste of time (Pétain, "Collège des Hautes Etudes de la Défense Nationale," 2 July 1937, 2–3, SHAT 2N23/2) with the director's vociferous rejoinders is in Box 17 of the latter's papers at SHM.

28. These lectures closely followed the corresponding chapters of Castex, *Théories stratégiques,* vol 3.

29. Castex, "La guerre politique," SHAT 2N287, 36.

30. Castex, "Rapport de fin d'instruction de la 2ème Session (1937–1938)," 5 May 1938, 3, SHAT 2N281 (hereafter Castex, "Report 1937–1938" and other dates). He could have borrowed an orientation lecture for officers assigned to the intelligence bureau of the general staff, 2/EMA, "La situation politique et militaire en europe," 10 February 1936, SHAT 7N2521.

31. Castex, "La guerre politique," 18 November 1937; cf. Castex, *Strategic Theories,* 261.

32. SHAT 2N279.

33. Hereafter Schweisguth, "Données." The lecture's title, "Aspects Militaires d'une Guerre de Coalition," and subtitles, "Intégrité de Frontières" and "L'Assistance," do not do justice to the contents. The 1936, 1937, and 1938 texts are in Schweisguth's papers in the French *Archives Nationales* 351 AP Carton 7.

34. In the 1937 version of the lecture, Schweisguth replaced the section on Soviet assistance to the Petite Entente with a discussion of the possibility of sending a French expeditionary force to the Danube three or four months after the beginning of hostilities (Schweisguth, "Données," 1937, 38–43).

35. Ibid., 1936, 73. This passage was omitted in the later versions of the lecture.

36. There were five such excursions in the first year, eighteen in the second, and twenty-three in the third (Castex, "Report 1938–39," 6, SHAT 2N285).

37. An argument for the superiority of teamwork over unified command appears in Castex, "Conférence d'inauguration," 11.

38. Castex, "Report 1936-37," Annex 2, 2-3, SHAT 2N278/2.

39. Ibid., 3.

40. The directing staff found it difficult to create equally important tasks for all participants, and not much could be found to occupy the man from the Ministry of Pensions.

41. Only the lecture's outline survives, but there is no doubt about Castex's answer to its opening question—"Le programme offensif des Rouges. Que faut-il en penser?"

42. It is instructive to compare the CHEDN in this respect with its postwar successor, the Institut des Hautes Etudes de la Défense Nationale. The institute was also designed to teach how to implement policy but not how to make it (J. Breuillac, "Il faut enseigner la défense nationale," *RDN*, new ser. 5 [1949]: 46), but it was also required to examine questions not yet fully resolved by higher authority. For example, the study committees of the first session examined various structures for organizing a war economy and concluded that, although government direction would be required, the profit motive should be retained as an incentive to production. Such inquiries, which required the evaluation of competing policies, would not have taken place at the CHEDN and have led a careful observer to describe the new institute as "a study and research group rather than a teaching establishment" (Colonel Nemo, "La formation des cadres de défense nationale," *RDN*, new ser. 14 [1958]: 483). The permission, even obligation, to analyze policy alternatives reflects the requirements of a postwar world that did not allow the luxury of static, unexamined doctrines. As Nemo laments, "Today, the truth is so quickly overtaken by time that one hesitates to teach it and sometimes even to state it" (480-481).

43. The postwar institute had about seventy-five participants a year and also offered three month-long regional sessions to increase the national element of what had been a Parisian enterprise.

Chapter 3. Training the Peacetime Army

1. Gerhard L. Weinberg, *A World at Arms: A Global History of World War II* (Cambridge, 1994), 109.

2. For comparisons of French and German doctrine, see Robert A. Doughty, *The Breaking Point* (Hamden, CT, 1990), and Jeffrey A. Gunsberg, "The Battle of the Belgian Plain, 12-14 May 1940: The First Great Tank Battle," *JMH* 56 (1992): 207-244.

3. For the relevant laws, see Chapter 1.

4. The authorized professional strength was 30,000-plus officers and 106,000 other ranks. Conscript classes normally averaged about 250,000 men but were reduced to half that number during the "lean years" of 1935-1939.

5. Debeney argues that adequate training would have been possible under the one-year regime had legislators "respected the law they voted" by improving the instructional camps, recruiting sufficient cadres, and minimizing leave (Marie-Eugène

Debeney, *La guerre et les hommes: Reflexions d'après-guerre* [Paris, 1937], 111–112).

6. Julien Brossé, *Les éléments de notre défense nationale* (Paris, 1936), 17.

7. For example, the two contingents of 1922 contained 149,616 and 110,083 men, Etat-Major de l'Armée (EMA), "Annexe à la circulaire ministérielle No.6812 I/II du 10 July 1922," 10 July 1922, SHAT 7N2331.

8. Gen. Penet, "Instruction de la 1ère fraction de la classe 24," 21 August 1924, SHAT 7N4006/3.

9. The general staff directed that the experiment occur in first incorporation of 1925 within ten specified infantry regiments and various other units (Debeney, "Instruction du contingent avec le service de 18 Mois," 25 April 1925, SHAT 7N4006/2).

10. 3/EMA, "Directives pour l'instruction de contingent sous le régime du service de 18 Mois" [n.d. but refers to directive of 22 August 1922], SHAT 7N4006/1.

11. 1/EMA, "Instruction du contingent avec le service de 18 mois," 17 September 1925, SHAT 7N4006/2.

12. See "Directives générales sur l'instruction," 20 April 1935, EMA, "Circulaire relative à l'instruction générale des cadres et de la troupe (active et réserve)," 5 March 1937, SHAT 7N4006/1, "Directives sur l'instruction," 25 January 1937, "Notes sur l'instruction," 15 December 1937 and 7 November 1938.

13. For training in the German Army, see Richard Louis DiNardo, "Germany's Panzer Arm: Anatomy and Performance" (Ph.D. dissertation, City University of New York, 1988), 66–67.

14. For the use of newly trained radio men as instructors, see E. W. Fales, "Report of Duty with 502nd Combat Tank Regiment, Angoulême, France," 1933 (G-2 19,998-W), USNA RG165 2015-1159/3.

15. Richard G. Tindall, "Period of Duty with the French Army" (War Department date 2 November 1933) (G-2 19,791-W), USNA RG165 2015-1161/1.

16. Gaston Billotte, "Compte-rendu au sujet des effectifs des 5ème et 23ème DI," 29 March 1934, SHAT 7N2294.

17. Ibid.

18. Ibid. The twelve-month law authorized only ten days of leave, as opposed to the three periods of twenty, twenty, and twenty-five days provided under the eighteen-month regime, but special leaves were often granted to agricultural workers in acknowledgement of their political importance (2/EMA, "Extrait du rapport annuel sur l'instruction du 9ème C.A., 12ème C.A., 13ème C.A.," 14 March 1928, SHAT 7N2301/6).

19. Sumner Waite, "Organizational and Unit Training. Visit to a Section of the French Defensive System on the Italian Frontier and the 15th Battalion of Chasseurs Alpins," 21 March 1938 (G-2 24,121-W), USNA RG165 2015-1244/1.

20. Lt. X, "L'armée nouvelle," *La Revue des Vivantes* 4 (July 1930): 904–918. A précis of the piece appears as "Deficiencies of the French Army in Organization and Training," 18 August 1930 (G-2 16,568), USNA RG165 2015-1060.

21. Jean-Paul Sartre, *War Diaries: Notebooks from a Phony War November*

1939–March 1940, trans. Quintin Hoare (London, 1984), 16; Fernand Grenier, *Journal de la drôle de guerre septembre 1939 juillet 1940* (Paris, 1969), 249.

22. Fales, "502nd Combat Tank Regiment," USNA RG165 2015-1159/3, 3.

23. Lt. "X," "L'armée nouvelle," 405–406.

24. Lee A. Bessette, "Report on Tour of Duty with 502nd Tank Regiment at Angoulême, France," 20 October 1933 (G-2 19,846-W), USNA RG165 2015-1165/1.

25. Maxime Weygand, "Rapport sur les Manoeuvres de Lorraine en 1927," 20 December 1927, SHAT 1N93/5.

26. "The Aisne Maneuvers French Army, October 1931," 6 November 1931 (G-2 17,889-W), USNA RG165 2015-1085/7.

27. James A. Lester, "French Maneuvers at Valdehon," 22 September 1934 (G-2 20,794-W), USNA RG165 2015-1173/5. Lester, who praised the appearance of the troops in the final review, described the participating Thirteenth and Fourteenth DI as, respectively, about average and above average compared to other French units.

28. Tindall, "Period of Duty with the French Army," USNA RG165 2015-1161/1.

29. Edwin E. Schwein, "Bitche" (War Department date 14 February 1931), USNA RG165 2015-1064/1 (original emphasis). Observing French units in attack somewhat raised Schwein's morale.

30. Joseph Monteilhet, *Les institutions militaires de la France 1814–1932* (Paris, 1932), 427.

31. William W. Harts, "French Mobilization," 17 October 1929, 32 (G-2 15,569-W), USNA RG165 2015-801/29.

32. Lack of reservists, particularly those filling communications slots, severely hampered exercises by the 42d DI in August 1928 (Louis Maurin, "Rapport sur la Manoeuvre de Mailly 7-13 August 1928," 12–13, SHAT 1N93/5).

33. Harts, "French Mobilization," 34, USNA RG165 2015-801/29.

34. Ménard, "Résumé de la note sur l'instruction en 1939," 28 October 1938, SHAT 2322/6. For the *Ecoles de Perfectionnement,* see Chapter 4.

35. "Synthèse des rapports sur l'instruction en 1937," 1 February 1938, 30 January 1939, SHAT 7N4002/3, quoted in Henry Dutailly, *Les problèmes de l'armée* (Paris, 1980), 255. Active naval units underwent a similar transformation "into training companies, into every variety of school, into depots, and into everything else, losing their organization and readiness for battle in the process" (Raoul Castex, *Strategic Theories,* abridged, trans., and ed. E. C. Kiesling [Annapolis, 1993], 325).

36. Maurice Gamelin, "Instruction dans le Cadre du Service de Deux Ans," 30 August 1935, SHAT 7N4006/4.

37. Great Britain. War Office. General Staff. Monthly Intelligence Summary (hereafter War Office, MIS), March 1936, 230.

38. By late October 1935, de Lattre reckoned that a fifth of the noncommissioned officers of his regiment had borrowed money for essential military items since the promulgation of the June 1935 decree laws (Jean de Lattre de Tassigny, *Ne pas subir: Ecrits 1914–1952* [Paris, 1984], 168). In 1937 Daladier admitted that retired noncommissioned officers were denied "an honorable and decent existence," *PV,* Cham. Army Comm., 1 December 1937.

39. 1/EMA, "Note au sujet de l'Organisation Générale de l'Armée," 6 Novem-

ber 1925, quoted in François-André Paoli, *L'Armée française de 1919 à 1939*, 4 vols. (Paris, 1969–1971), 3:59.

40. As late as October 1929, General Debeney still expected a pre-military education law to be passed in that year, Debeney, "Armée nationale ou armée de métier," *RDM*, 7th series 53 (5 October 1929): 259. Minister of War Daladier advocated compulsory pre-military education in a meeting of the Senate Army Commission on 17 December 1936. In Germany, though the Versailles Treaty barred the government from organizing physical education programs, there were in 1932, 66,542 sports societies with 7,000,000 members, J. Monteilhet, *Les institutions militaires* (Paris, 1932), 425). France in 1937 had 12,000 approved societies devoted to sport, physical training, or preliminary military training. Ten thousand of these societies were "*in some degree*" under military control, but only 4,000 provided pre-military training.

41. A full 120,000 conscripts received the preliminary training brevet in 1935 (F. G. Beaumont-Nesbitt, "The Present Military Situation in France Compared with That in Germany, as Disclosed by the Annual Report on Germany, 1936, (Paragraphs 386–479)," 5 July 1937, 3 FO371 C5048/122/17). Only 2,866 (7 percent) of the 38,355 communes had firing ranges, and much of the instruction had to be provided by the 15,000 members of the *Gardes républicains* (minister of war to president of Chamber d'Agriculture de la Loire-Inférieure, 7 March 1928, SHAT 5N598/3). For the inadequacy of the incentive, see Monteilhet *Institutions militaires*, 425. Cf. James A. Lester, "Organization (General): The French Forces," 21 September 1935 (G-2 21,850-W), USNA RG165 2015-1208/1.

42. Gen. Baratier, "Education nationale et prémilitaire," *Le Temps*, 5 October 1934, 1.

43. Right-wing attitudes are reported in War Office, MIS, April 1937. One exception to the Left's general hostility to preinduction training was "Aviation Populaire," Popular Front Air Minister Pierre Cot's ambitious and expensive effort to introduce the working class youths to flying (John M. Sterling, "Organization and Results of Popular Aviation Training in France," 16 January 1939 [G-2 24,766-W], USNA RG165 2081-1452/10; Horace H. Fuller, "Individual Training: Pre-military Technical Training," 10 December 1937 [G-2 23,905-W], USNA RG165 2081-1452/7).

44. Monteilhet, *Institutions militaires*, 425.

45. Typical was a situation in which 1,300 men from three regiments shared a thirty-five-hectare maneuver area and a fifty-meter range with only four firing positions while some garrisons had no training facilities whatsoever (Dutailly, *Problèmes de l'armée*, 237). Urban garrisons generally lacked training space (Monteilhet, *Institutions*, 428).

46. Dutailly, *Problèmes de l'armée*, 239; EMA, "Circulaire relative à l'instruction générale des cadres et de la troupe (active et réserve)," 5 March 1937, 33, SHAT 7N4006/1; for the inadequacy even of the camps for cavalry exercises, see "Rapport d'inspection du général Massiet," 20 December 1938, 9, quoted in Dutailly, *Problèmes de l'armée*, 256.

47. Stanley Ford, "Exercises of the 19th Division of Infantry," 18 October 1932 (G-2 18,835-W), USNA RG165 2015-1104/4.

48. Stehle, Riom deposition, 24 June 1941, SHAT 1K224/5.

49. The regulation is mentioned in MIS, March 1939, 226.

50. Tindall, "Period of Duty with the French Army," USNA RG165 2015-1161/ 1; Maj. James B. Ord, "Maneuvers at CAMP de MAILLY, July 26–27," 9 August 1929 (G-2 15,332-W), USNA RG165 2015-978/8; War Office, MIS, October 1929, 263; War Office, MIS, October 1931, 180–181; War Office, MIS, December 1931, 60; War Office, MIS, August 1934, 63. The U.S. embassy in Paris reported the skimpy supply of ammunition for reserve training, "Ammunition Allowances for Reservists," 19 April 1933 (G-2 19,281-W), USNA RG165 2265-C-36/7. Much of the ammunition used in the 1920s came from suspect wartime stocks (Pierre Hoff, *Les programmes d'armement de 1919 à 1939* [Vincennes, 1972], 79).

51. Hoff, *Les programmes d'armement*, 422.

52. Ibid., 424–425. One artillery regiment received more ammunition for training reservists—one round per reservist and five per reserve officer—than it did for its own use, Sumner Waite, "Artillery Service Practice," 12 October 1937 (G-2 23,781-W), USNA RG165 2015-1238/30.

53. Gen. Preaud, Riom testimony 17 May 1941, 4–5, SHAT 1K224/5.

54. But a British commentator treated ten rounds as a significant number (War Office, MIS, September 1936, 196). An American visitor to a dragoon battalion describes weekly marksmanship practice in which soldiers fired five rounds at each distance (Sumner Waite, "Organizational and Unit Training: Visit to 3rd Dragons Portés Battalion, Lunéville," 15 October 1938 [G-2 24,603-W], USNA RG165 2015-827/42), and five rounds per firing session was also the number reported for 1933 in Tindall, "Period of Duty with the French Army," USNA RG165 2015-1161/1.

55. For the *cinéma du tir,* see Dutailly, *Problèmes de l'armée,* 236.

56. "A good number [of the reservists] were unfamiliar upon mobilization with the handling of the new equipment" (Georges Blanchard, Riom Deposition, 11 June 1941 SHAT 1K224/5). For the suggestion that doctrine had not yet been devised for employing the new matériel, see Capt. X, "La défense contre avions dans les unités d'infanterie" *RI* 95 (July–September 1939): 478.

57. Jean Marot, *Abbéville 1940: Avec la division cuirassée DE GAULLE* (Paris, n.d.), 44. Unfamiliarity with their equipment was not a uniquely French problem. Because the 157th Brigade of 52d Division of the British Expeditionary Force (BEF) received its equipment only upon its departure from England in June 1940, none of the soldiers who arrived to fight in France had ever fired an antitank rifle or antitank gun or seen a tank (Basil Karslake, *1940 The Last Act: The Story of the British Forces in France After Dunkirk* [Hamden, CT, 1979], 172, 262).

58. Hoff, *Programmes d'armement,* 361.

59. This almost incredible story is from a lecture by Chef de Bataillon Desfemmes as reported in Gen. Gilson, "L'évolution des matériels de transmissions de 1920 à 1939," *RHA* 23 (1967): 68.

60. Jean-Marie d'Hoop, "La politique française du réarmament: d'après les travaux de la commission d'enquête parlementaire," *RHDGM* 4 (1954): 20.

61. Hoff, *Programmes d'armement,* 240; d'Hoop, "Politique française," 16.

62. Hoff, *Programmes d'armement,* 251.

63. Gilson, "L'évolution des matériels," 79.

64. Russell H. Stolfi, "Equipment for Victory in France in 1940," *History* 55 (1970): 2.

65. See Suzannet's account of an inspection trip, *PV,* Cham. Army Comm., 8 December 1937.

66. Hoff, *Programmes d'armement,* 429.

67. Ibid., 428; Lt. Col. Béguier, *Les étapes d'un régiment breton: Le 71ᵉ R.I. et R.I.A. en 1939 et 1940* (Paris, 1953), 88. See Mènard, 3–4, SHAT 2322/6, for the impact of material deficiencies on instruction. General Touchon testified at Riom that the absence of tanks and aircraft prevented exercises in cooperation or instruction in defense against German methods (Touchon, Riom deposition, 1–2). Although only 500 FT tanks remained in service in 1940, that was the only machine most French infantrymen knew (Stolfi, "Equipment for Victory," 2).

68. Jeffrey Clarke, "Military Technology in Republican France: The Evolution of the French Armored Force, 1917–1949" (Ph.D. dissertation, Duke University, 1969), 205.

69. The only diesel tank in the French arsenal, the FCM Model 36 Infantry Tank, proved too expensive for large-scale production.

70. Jean De Lattre de Tassigny, *Ne pas subir: Écrits 1914–1952* (Paris, 1984), 173.

71. Ministry of National Defense (MDN), Direction de l'Infanterie. "Instruction des éclaireurs motocyclistes," 13 January 1937, SHAT, 9N130/6.

72. Guy Chapman, *Why France Fell* (New York, 1968), 62. French pilots faced similar problems for they could hardly make optimal use of the excellent but unfamiliar Marane-Saulnier and Dewoitine fighters that they received in the spring of 1940 (see Williamson Murray, *The Change in the European Balance of Power* [Princeton, 1984], 107).

73. "Synthèse," quoted in Dutailly, *Problèmes de l'armée,* 255, notes that training was impeded in 1938 by lack of munitions, aircraft, communications equipment, and fuel.

74. Lack of gasoline would halt many of the "rare tank exercises" held during the phony war (Alistair Horne, *To Lose a Battle* [Harmondsworth, Eng., 1969], 225).

75. Maurin, "Rapport," 13 SHAT 1N93/5.

76. War Office, MIS, August 1934, 60.

77. War Office, MIS, October 1930, 234, and November 1936; William W. Harts, "French Maneuvers in 1928," 25 September 1928 (G-2 14,144), USNA RG165 2015-978/7; F. C. Harrington, "Report of States with French Infantry and Artillery Regiments," 10 October 1933, USNA RG165 2015-1158/1; Hoff, *Programmes d'armement,* 420; Georges Sadoul, *Journal de guerre (2 septembre 1939–20 juillet 1940)* (Paris, 1977), 118; F. Soulet, *La 36ᵉ Division d'infanterie à l'honneur 1939–1940* (Paris, n.d.), 37.

78. Gilson, "L'évolution des matériels," 80.

79. Sumner Waite, "Spoken Views on National Defence Policy, Preparedness: Notes on a conversation with a General Staff Officer," 11 October 1938 (G-2 24,285-W), USNA RG165 2015-1049/56; Chapman, *Why France Fell,* 62.

80. Robert Felsenhardt, *1939–1940 avec le 18ᵉ Corps d'Armée* (Paris, 1973), 10, 16.

81. Tony de Vibraye, *Avec mon groupe de reconnaissance* (Paris, 1943), 18–19.

82. Chapman, *Why France Fell,* 62.

83. de Vibraye, *Avec mon groupe de reconnaissance,* 19–20. For the "bizarre" vehicles received by the Seventy-first RI, which, if they worked at all, bore little resemblance to those assumed in the regimental mobilization plan, see Béguier, *Les étapes d'un régiment breton,* 6. For the "gypsy camp," see Soulet, *36ᵉ Division,* 14.

84. Martin S. Alexander, *The Republic in Danger* (Cambridge, 1992), 354. In November 1939, the Third Army was 32 percent understrength in trucks, many of which had been returned to the interior for repair (Alexander, *Republic in Danger,* 366).

85. "RAPPORT du Général DUPORT, Membre du CSG au sujet du séjour de la 15ème Division au camp du Valdehon," 22 August 1927, 1-2, SHAT 7N2294. As early as 1929, the army sought funds to provide every soldier with a second pair of shoes (Hoff, *Programmes d'armement,* 78), but the problem remained as late as February 1940 (Sumner Waite, "Visit to the 1st Armored Division [Division Cuirassée]," 6 February 1940 [G-2 25,501-W], USNA RG165 2015-1223/15). In 1934, the French Army had 4,970,000 pairs of shoes (88 percent of requirements), 3,980,000 pairs of trousers (69 percent), 2,950,000 rucksacks (75 percent), and 2,985,000 water bottles (58 percent); see Hoff, *Programmes d'armement,* 122.

86. Ministry of War, Direction de l'Infanterie, 2ème Bureau, Recrutement, "Arrête relatif à la répartition entre les dépots et à l'appel à l'activité de la 3ème fraction de la classe de 1939 et de la 1ère fraction de la Classe de 1940," n.d. (June?) 1940, SHAT 7N2471.

87. Those soldiers who wore their own shoes to war in September 1939 received the promised compensation only in December (Jean-Louis Crémieux–Brilhac, *Les Français,* 2 vols. [Paris, 1990], 2:431). Jean-Paul Sartre's feet were warmer than most, but he looked rather peculiar in Simone de Beauvoir's ski boots.

88. Commandant Vivet, "Inspection of the 42th BCC," 6 December 1939, SHAT 9N161/1.

89. Hoff, *Programmes d'armement,* 216.

90. Harrington, "Reports of Stays," USNA RG165 2015-1158/1.

91. War Office, MIS, "The Tactical Tendencies of the French Army," June 1928, 63; Marc Lami, *Un peu de gloire, un peu d'humeur, beaucoup de sang . . . : Epopée d'une batterie de 75 en 1940* (Paris, 1945), 13.

92. Only three were available for one entire regiment (Harvey H. Smith, "Report of Tour of Duty with 501st Tank Regiment Tours—France," 15 August–15 November 1935 [G-2 22, 161-W] USNA RG 165 2015-1213/1). A report on the French Tank School began with a reference to "the tremendous amount of paper work the company CO has to do personally without a typewriter" (William Harts, "Report of Tour of Duty with the French Tank School, Versailles, France," 29 October 1928 [G-2 14,267-W], USNA RG165 2277-C-136).

93. D. Barlone, *A French Officer's Diary (23 August 1939–1 October 1940),* trans. L. V. Cass (Cambridge, 1942), 29–30. Cf. Marc Bloch, *Strange Defeat,* trans. Gerard Hopkins (New York, 1968), 7.

94. Horne, *To Lose a Battle,* 225.

95. Adolphe Goutard, *The Battle of France 1940,* trans. A. R. P. Burgess (London, 1958), 80.

96. Felsenhardt, *1939–1940,* 93.

97. Lami, *Un peu de gloire,* 13.

98. Tindall, "Period of Duty with the French Army," USNA RG165 2015-1161/1.

99. *Action française,* 9 September 1933, 2; Robert Poulaine, *Le Temps,* 8 September 1935, 6.

100. Robert-Pimenta, *Le Temps,* 4 September 1938, 3.

101. Gamelin, "Note sur l'instruction en 1938," 5 January 1938, Annex, "Enseignements à tirer des manoeuvres de 1937," 2, SHAT 7N4001.

102. Daladier to military governor of Metz, 9 December 1938, SHAT 9N161/5.

103. Robert-Pimenta, *Le Temps,* 14 September 1937, 2.

104. Ibid., 22 September 1937, 1.

105. Ibid., 18 September 1937, 9.

106. Ibid., 29 September 1937, 3. One cynic suggested, however, that Hore-Belisha indulged a dry sense of humor by describing the reservist as of the same (unspecified) caliber as the active soldier and pronouncing the army to be free of "mechanical discipline" ("Vivat," "A propos des grandes manoeuvres 1937," *Action francaise,* 25 September 1937, 5–6).

107. Imperial General Staff (IGS), "Visit to French and German Manoeuvres, 1937," 15 October 1937, PRO FO371 7703/136/18.

108. War Office, MIS, August 1934, 61.

109. Ibid., 62.

110. Horace H. Fuller, "French Maneuvers in the Hautes-Alps," 19 September 1938 (G-2 24,539-W), USNA RG165 2015-1237/7. For umpires' tendency to facilitate attacking operations, see B.-E.-M. Wanty, "Une année de guerre en Espagne," *RI* 90 (January–June, 1937): 932.

111. Quoted in Goutard, *Battle of France,* 80; cf. de Vibraye, *Avec mon groupe de reconnaissance,* 42. Commandant Vivet reported that other work had put the 42d BCC at least a month behind schedule, "Inspection of the 42th BCC," 6 December 1939 SHAT 9N161/1.

112. Sadoul, *Journal de guerre,* 121.

113. Béguier, *Les étapes d'un régiment breton,* 84.

114. Marcel Pétain and Michel Caron, *100 jours, 100 nuits aux avant postes* (Paris, n.d.), 38.

115. Paul Marie de la Gorce, *The French Army: A Military-Political History,* trans. Kenneth Douglas (New York, 1963), 289. Unlike the French, the German Army had a systematic training program for the winter of 1939–1940; see S. J. Lewis, *Forgotten Legions, German Infantry Policy 1918–1941* (New York, 1985), 97.

116. Robert Bourget-Pailleron, "Le soldat de la dernière guerre," *RDM* 8:60 (September–October 1940): 164–165.

117. Barlone, *French Officer's Diary,* 28 (entry for 18 February). Grenier's diary also mentions frequent visits to the cinema as the only respite from boredom, and

Lami reports the tribulations imposed on his operations by a certain battalion commander's keenness for films (Lami, *Un peu de gloire,* 12).

118. Sadoul, *Journal de guerre,* 86, 240–241, n.1.

119. See Grenier, *Journal de la drôle de guerre,* 53–54, 131–135, for rare references to martial exercises.

120. Sadoul, *Journal de guerre,* 216.

121. Leave arrangements were more generous from January 1940 and reached peacetime standard on 7 May 1940 (Horne, *Fall of France,* 236). The most common entry in Private Grenier's diary is "on leave for twenty-four (or forty-eight) hours." Altogether, 250,000 peasants were released from military service (Maurice Gamelin, *Servir,* 3 vols. [Paris, 1954–1959], 1:219, and Ladislas Mysyrowicz, *Anatomie d'une défaite* [Lausanne, 1973], 346).

122. *Evénements, Annexes,* 5:1167 (Bruneau testimony).

123. de Vibraye, *Avec mon groupe de reconnaisance,* 85.

124. Béguier, *Les étapes d'un régiment breton,* 69.

125. Sadoul, *Journal de guerre,* 87; Felsenhardt, *1939–1940,* 61.

126. Quoted in Crémieux-Brilhac, *Les Français,* 2:527.

127. René de Chambrun, *I Saw France Fall* (Rahway, NJ, 1940), 104–105. For the impact of makework tasks on morale, see Sadoul, *Journal de guerre,* 152.

128. Goutard, *Battle of France,* 80.

129. The most famous example is the four-year plan of 7 September 1936, in which the General Staff's request for 9 billion francs was increased by Leon Blum's Popular Front government to 14 billion (see D'Hoop, "Politique française," 9).

130. Ibid., 10.

131. Hoff, *Programmes d'armement,* 233–235; Stolfi, "Equipment for Victory," 19.

132. Currus, "La rénovation de notre armement d'infanterie," *RI* 94 (January–June 1939): 882.

133. Hoff, *Programmes d'armement,* 237–238. Upon mobilization in September 1939, the Fifty-fifth DI (B reserve) had not one of its complement of fifty-two 25mm antitank guns (four for the reconnaissance group, twelve for each of three infantry regiments, and twelve for the divisional antitank company). Only in April 1940 did the division acquire an anti-tank company and were the 75s of divisional anti-tank battery replaced with new 47mm antitank guns (Hoff, *Programmes d'armement,* 241). In December 1939, Third and Fourth Army A divisions had only half of their antitank weapons and the B divisions had none at all (Alexander, *Republic in Danger,* 366).

134. Hoff, *Programmes d'armement,* 428–429.

135. For French armor doctrine, see Chapter 7.

136. Doughty, *Breaking Point,* 288.

137. Pierre Héring, "Rapport d'ensemble sur les manoeuvres de l'ouest en 1937," SHAT 1N97/3.

138. Soulet, *36ᵉ Division,* 9–11.

139. Carl von Clausewitz, *On War,* ed. and trans. Michael Howard and Peter Paret (Princeton, 1976), 102–103.

Chapter 4. The Unready Reserve

1. General von Seeckt, quoted in Gen. Brindel, "La nouvelle organisation militaire," *RDM* (May–June 1929): 501.

2. In active divisions mobilized in September 1939, 26 percent of the officers and noncommissioned officers and 40 percent of the enlisted men were career or active duty troops. The figures fell to 18 percent and 2.5 percent for category A reserve divisions while B reserve divisions had almost no regular troops (Henry Dutailly, *Problèmes de l'armée* [Paris, 1980], 419). Compare Jeffrey A. Gunsberg, *Divided and Conquered* (Westport, CT, 1979), 88; and Guy Chapman, *Why France Fell* (New York, 1968), 339.

3. France mobilized 5,782,000 men, 5,108,000 of them French. Of these, 2,680,000 went into combat and service units, 1,640,000 into the army of interior (depots and territorial security), and 1,460,000, mostly men of the second reserve, were employed in industry and administration (Lt. Col. Lugand, "Les forces en presence au 10 mai 1940," *RHDGM* 3/10–11 [June 1953]: 5–6). In comparison, the German Army of September 1939 totaled 3,706,104 men, including the 2,321,266 of the Field Army, 426,798 construction troops, and a Replacement Army of 958,040 (Matthew Cooper, *The German Army 1933–1945* [London, 1978], 164).

4. Tested, albeit, with mixed results. To wipe out the memory of poor performance by some reserve units, the postwar French army abolished the title *division de réserve* in favor of *division de formation* (War Office, MIS, October 1934, 148). For the French reserve army in the interwar period see Robert A. Doughty, *The Seeds of Disaster* (Hamden, CT, 1985), chap. 2. For earlier background, see Douglas Porch, *The March to the Marne* (New York, 1981), and Gary P. Cox, *The Halt in the Mud: French Strategic Planning from Waterloo to Sedan* (Boulder, San Francisco, Oxford, 1994).

5. Passed in 1927, twelve-month service came into effect in 1930, when the age of incorporation was raised to twenty-one years. Christophe Prochasson, "Les grandes dates de l'histoire de la conscription," *RHA* 9 (1982): 67–69, provides a useful chronology.

6. Marie-Eugène Debeney, "Armée national ou armée de métier," *RDM* 7:53 (September–October 1929): 253.

7. Gen. Brindel, "Nouvelle organisation militaire," *RDM* 7:51 (May–June 1929): 487. The argument appears in Richard D. Challener, *The French Theory of the Nation in Arms, 1866–1939* (New York, 1955), 179–181.

8. Julien Brossé, *Les élements de notre defense nationale* (Paris, 1936), 15.

9. The active army, the *disponibles,* and key reserve officers formed the *couverture,* a million-man force to hold the frontiers while the remainder of the army mobilized (Robert J. Young, "Preparations for Defeat," *JES* [1972]: 164). Semiannual inductions insured that France always had one-half class of men who had finished basic training and were ready to take their places in the *couverture.*

10. The call-up of other reservists required an act of parliament. Two-year service was achieved for the classes of 1935 to 1939, the so-called *années creusés,* by retaining the youngest class of *disponibles* as the "*disponibilité sous les drapeaux en situation d'activité.*"

11. War Office, MIS, October 1934, 148.

12. For the calculation that a three-week training period actually allowed for only fifteen days of training, see EMA "Note établié par l'Etat-Major de l'Armée et résumant les directions données pour l'instruction des reservistes," 19 July 1932, SHAT 6N428/1.

13. For the cost, see Lt. Col. Reboul, "Le malaise de l'armée: le projet de service d'un an," *RDM* 7:26 (March–April 1925): 46. Socialist deputies usually voted against funding exercises while the center-left Radical Socialist party split fairly evenly in 1927 between those who voted for a reserve convocation out of patriotism and those who opposed it in deference to popular sentiment (William W. Harts, "Instruction of Reservists," 13 December 1927 [G-2 13,114-W], USNA RG165 2015-928/2).

14. François-André Paoli, *L'Armée française de 1919 à 1939,* 4 vols. (Paris, 1969–1971), 4:62.

15. 1/EMA, "Note au sujet de l'organisation générale de l'armée," 6 November 1925, quoted in Paoli, *L'Armée française,* 3:59; "Instruction générale pour la convocation des réservistes en 1927," SHAT 7N2333/11; Stanley H. Ford, "Active Duty Training Periods for Reserve Enlisted Men, Noncommissioned Officers, and Officers," 26 November 1930 (G-2 16,893-W), USNA RG165 2015-928/15; James B. Ord, "Training Instruction for Reservists French Army (Effective 1931)" (G-2 17,436-W), USNA RG165 2015-928/19.

16. 1/EMA, "Note au sujet de l'organisation générale de l'armée," 6 November 1925, quoted in Paoli, *L'Armée française,* 3:59.

17. In some densely populated regions, an intermediate echelon—the group of subdivisions—was added between the region and the subdivision. See subsequent discussion of mobilization centers.

18. The home regions of all French units are listed in Paoli, *L'Armée française,* 3:95–110.

19. For some of the implications of regional affiliation, see Jean Vidalenc, "Les divisions de série "B" dans l'armé française pendant la campagne de France 1939–1940," *RHA* 1 (1980): 111. Health was a major concern to the parliamentary committees responsible for military matters.

20. Mobilization centers were spaced so that reservists would not live more than fifty kilometers, two hours by train or bus, from their center (James B. Ord, "French Mobilization," 17 October 1929 [G-2 Report 15,569-W], USNA RG165 2015-801/29).

21. [Jean?] Duval, "L'armée française de 1938," *Revue de Paris* 40 (July–August 1938): 721.

22. Ministry of War, Direction de l'Infanterie, 2ème Bureau, Recrutement, "Arrête relatif à la répartition entre les corps et à l'appel à l'activité de la 3ème fraction de la classe de 1933 et de la 1ère fraction de la classe de 1934," 12 March 1933, SHAT 9N106 (hereafter, "Arrête 1933").

23. For North Africa, see Joseph Monteilhet, *Les institutions militaires de la France 1814–1932* (Paris, 1932), 414–415.

24. This calculation includes only regular, not alpine, regiments and understates

the diversity of recruiting pools by leaving out men from Paris and the nineteenth (North African) region.

25. Ministry of War, Direction de l'Infanterie, 2ème Bureau, Recrutement, "Arrêté relatif à la répartition entre les corps et à l'appel à l'activité de la 2ème fraction de la classe de 1937 et de la 1ère fraction de la classe de 1938," June (?) 1937, SHAT 9N106 (hereafter "Arrête 1937").

26. Only thirteen bureaus (18 percent of the total) in 1935 and fourteen in 1938 (16 percent) fed more than one regiment.

27. Compare "Arrête 1933" and "Arrête 1937," SHAT 9N106.

28. 1EMA, "Repartition des Contingents," (n.d., but probably 1922), SHAT 7N2331, stated explicitly that no more than one-third of any unit's soldiers should come from a single locality.

29. "Extrait du rapport d'instruction du 11th Corps d'Armée (1927–1928)," SHAT 7N4014/1, and "Arrête 1933," SHAT 9N106.

30. Special dispensation for fathers was provided in the recruitment law of 31 March 1928 and overrode unit quotas; various agricultural lobbies were unsuccessful in their pleas that sons of farmers be granted similar privileges.

31. For a lengthy list of specialties see the Law of 25 July 1919 in SHAT 7N2331. Men seeking secretarial jobs had to submit writing and typing samples two months before their call-up.

32. Gaston Billotte, "Compte-rendu au sujet des effectifs des 5ème et 23ème DI," SHAT 7N2294.

33. The list of forbidden units was published by the minister of national defense on 24 November 1937 and 26 May 1939. For barriers to undesirable officer candidates, see Jean Fabry, "Maintien du morale dans l'Armée," 8 October 1935, SHAT 5N601/2.

34. Gen. Carence, "A.S. des renseignements sur les militaires PR," 20 August 1928, SHAT 5N601/3. Georges Sadoul attributed his unexpected reassignment in September 1939 to his being on the PR list and discovered that his service record contained references to severe punishments that he had never received (Georges) Sadoul, *Journal de guerre* (Paris, 1977), 22, 33.

35. Louis Maurin, "A/s enquêtes spéciales sur les candidats E.O.R.," 19 April 1935, SHAT 5N601/3; Edouard Daladier, "A.S. des enquêtes spéciales et du classement sur les listes PR," 29 May 1937, SHAT 5N601/3.

36. Jean-Paul Sartre, *War Diaries,* trans. Quintin Hoare (London, 1984), 8.

37. For an example of what the author calls "strange corporate and regional pride," see ibid., 226.

38. In contrast with the French Army, Wehrmacht units were recruited geographically to the extent that the distribution of the necessary specialties allowed. Every combat unit had an ersatz formation to supply a stream of trained replacements from its home district and to handle the unit's convalescent casualties until their return to combat (U.S. War Department, *Handbook on German Military Forces* [Washington, D.C., 1945], 58). The value of regional homogeneity was such that the inherent difficulties "were deliberately and consciously taken in stride" (Martin van Creveld, *Fighting Power: German and U.S. Army Performance, 1939–1945* [Westport, CT, 1982], 75). Strict regional organization broke down under the strain of re-

placing the losses suffered on the Eastern Front (Omer Bartov, *Hitler's Army: Soldiers, Nazis, and War in the Third Reich* [Oxford, 1991], 36).

39. *JO, Chambre,* 2d sess., 2 December 1927, 3495. The connections between active and "spin-off" regiments lay in personnel, not tactical organization, as the "spin-offs" were part of reserve rather than active divisions.

40. Only 40 percent of reservists served in units derived from their active service units, Monteilhet, *Institutions militaires,* 436. The fortress units, which were expected to be able to mobilize for action in thirty–six hours, were the most strictly regional; only two of the reserve officers of the 162nd *Régiment d'Infanterie de Forteresse* were not from Lorraine (René de Chambrun, *I Saw France Fall* [Rahway, NJ, 1940], 40). Ironically, the Lorrainers who filled many of the units were supposed to do their conscript year elsewhere as part of the army's encouragement of the spread of French.

41. Louis Colson, "Instruction sur la répartition et l'affectation des reservistes dans le Plan "E," 30 July 1937, 9–10, SHAT 7N2334/1. For the difficulty of integrating "floating islands" of tankers, cavalrymen, and sailors into an battalion of chasseurs *alpins,* see Lt. Carrère, "Physionomie d'une période de réservists," *RI* (January–March 1935): 296.

42. Marc Lami, *Un peu de gloire* (Paris, 1945), 19.

43. Gen. Meullé-Desjardins, "Convocation profonde des Cadres de la 45th DI," 3 October 1934, SHAT 7N3017/3.

44. Marcel Pétain and Michel Caron, *100 jours, 100 nuits anx avant postes* (Paris, n.d.), 14–15.

45. Fernand Grenier, *Journal de la drôle de guerre septembre 1939 juillet 1940* (Paris, 1969), 163, 215. The drunkards were presumably "citizens of the world."

46. Mechanized cavalry units came up to war strength with *disponibles* alone, although some cavalry reservists were required for divisional reconnaissance groups (War Office, MIS, November 1934, "Mechanization in the French Cavalry Arm," 13; Jeffrey Clarke, "Military Technology in Republican France" [Ph.D. dissertation, Duke University, 1969], 101; Monteilhet, *Institutions militaires,* 419).

47. Brindel, "Nouvelle organisation," 484; Stanley H. Ford, "New French Tank Regulations," 3 February 1931, 2 (G-2 17,131-W), USNA RG165 2281-C-140. Journalists observing the reserve maneuvers of 1927 reported that men who had done their active service in armored units were unprepared for their reserve service in infantry units (Charles R. Alley, "Training of Reservists," 26 October 1928 [G-2 14,264-W] USNA RG165 2015-928/7). The Wehrmacht handled this problem by giving every tank crewman a thorough basic infantry training (Richard Louis DiNardo, "Germany's Panzer Arm: Anatomy and Performánce" [Ph.D. dissertation, City University of New York, 1988], 66–67).

48. D. Barlone, *A French Officer's Diary,* trans. L. V. Cass (Cambridge, 1942), 5–6.

49. Joseph Dufieux, *Evénements, Annexes,* 4:889 (Dufieux testimony).

50. Robert Felsenhardt, *1939–1940 avec le 18ᵉ Corps d'Armée* (Paris, 1973), 8.

51. For a picture of the United States Army that makes French units appear stable in comparison, see John Sloan Brown, *Draftee Division: The 88th Infantry Division in World War II* (Lexington, KY, 1986), 23–25.

52. Lami, *Un peu de gloire,* 2.

53. Grenier, *Journal de la drôle de guerre,* 41–44, 147, 233; Sadoul, *Journal de guerre,* 80.

54. See Chapter 1 for the pernicious effects of recalling troops from the front.

55. Gunsburg, *Divided and Conquered,* 104; *Evénements, Annexes,* 2:434 (Gamelin testimony).

56. F. Soulet, *La 36ᵉ Division d'infanterie à l'honneur 1939–1940* (Paris, n.d.), 22.

57. Lucien Carron, *Fantassins sur l'Aisne mai–juin 1940* (Grenoble and Paris, 1943), 11–13, 26–27, 64.

58. Lt. Col. Béguier, *Les étapes d'un régiment breton* (Paris, 1953), 91.

59. Tony de Vibraye, *Avec mon groupe de reconnaissance* (Paris, 1943), 15; Lami, *Un peu de gloire,* 2–3.

60. Felsenhardt, *1939–1940,* 93–104, and Marc Bloch, *Strange Defeat,* trans. Gerard Hopkins (New York, 1968), 7.

61. Lami, *Un peu de gloire,* 14–15.

62. Sadoul, *Journal de guerre,* 59.

63. For a list of mobilization centers see Paoli, *L'Armée française,* 3:211–216. The large number of centers allowed such geographical dispersion that "it can almost be said that reservists are mobilized at home" (Ord, "French Mobilization," 30, USNA RG165 2015-801/29).

64. Duplicate personnel files were kept at the mobilization centers and had to be checked periodically for consistency for those of the recruiting bureaus (Ord, "French Mobilization," 3, USNA RG165 2015-801/29).

65. 1/EMA, "Organisation générale," quoted in Paoli, *L'Armée française,* 3:57.

66. EMA, "Instruction relative à l'organisation et au fonctionnement des Centres de Mobilisation," 23 April 1929, SHAT 7N4018/2.

67. For the thoroughness of this preparation, see Peter C. Bullard, "Equipment for Mobilization Training," 8 June 1928, USNA RG165 2279-C-22 and D. Barlone's report upon taking command of a company in August 1939 that everything was "perfectly planned" (Barlone, *French Officer's Diary,* 2). Not everything was sufficiently thought through, however, and the partial mobilization of September 1938 revealed that aging reservists could not wear stockpiled uniforms cut to fit young conscripts (Pierre Hoff, *Programmes d'armament de 1919 à 1939* [Vincennes, 1972], 420; de Vibraye, *Avec mon groupe de reconnaissance,* 16).

68. Gen. Lafont, "Rapport d'ensemble sur les convocations d'unités de formation en 1935," 21 November 1935, SHAT 7N4018. For the cadre convocations, see 3/EMA, "Exercises de cadres d'Armée, Convocations profondes de cadres," 16 December 1936, SHAT 1N68/3.

69. Giraud, "Effectif des centres de mobilisation," 11 July 1928, SHAT 7N2418/1.

70. Report by Gen. Pougin, Second Corps, 1927, SHAT 7N2300/2; Memo of 13 March 1927, SHAT 7N2300/2; "Rapport sur la convocation des cadres de la 10ᵉ Division," 1935, SHAT 7N4018.

71. "The operation of these centers still keeps many soldiers and noncommissioned officers on special duty and the overhead in purely combat personnel is far

above what was anticipated" (Ord, "French Mobilization," 30, USNA RG165 2015-801/29). Another American officer reported that 13,781 of France's 106,000 professional soldiers had noncombatant positions in the metropolitan army (T. Bentley Mott, "Directives générales sur l'instruction," 20 April 1935 [G-2 13,707-W], USNA 2015-766/26). For the poor performance of mobilization center personnel in September 1938, see Sumner Waite, "Spoken Views on National Defence Policy, Preparedness: Notes on a Conversation with a General Staff Officer," 11 October 1938 (G-2 24,285-W), USNA 2015-1049/56, and Horace H. Fuller, "Changes in Articles of the Recruiting Law Dealing with Individual Training," 28 March 1939 (G-2 24,907-W), 2015 901/104.

72. Béguier, *Les étapes d'un régiment breton,* 3.

73. Sumner Waite, "Strength of Light Mechanized Divisions," 2 February 1937 (G-2 23,147-W), 2, USNA RG165 2015-827/38.

74. The 39 percent figure comes from the class of 1940; see "Arrêté relatif à la répartition entre les dépots et à l'appel à l'activité de la 3ème fraction de la classe de 1939 et de la 1ère fraction de la classe de 1940 . . ." June(?) 1940, SHAT 7N2471.

75. Monteilhet, *Institutions militaires,* 435–437. But Montheilet's assertions must be seen in the light of his own argument that reserve training and mobilization would proceed much more smoothly had the peacetime army not existed at all.

76. 1/EMA, "Organisation générale," Paoli, *L'Armée française,* 3:56–61.

77. A cadre exercise in 1936 revealed that 90 percent of the radio operators in the Fourth Infantry Division were unfamiliar with the current apparatus but no mechanism existed to instruct them outside of the slow cycle of convocations by class (Gen. Champon, "Rapport sur la convocation profonde des cadres de cette Division en 1936," 3 November 1936, SHAT 7N4019).

78. School teachers performed their reserve training during school holidays, and employees of the Ministry of Post, Telephone, and Telegraph were not normally expected to serve in July, August, and September (Frank P. Lahm, "Active Duty Training Periods for Reserve Enlisted Men, Noncommissioned Officers and Officers," 15 January 1934 [G-2 20,070-W], USNA RG165 2015-928/15, 11; Ford, Active Duty "Training Periods," USNA RG165 2015-928/15).

79. When the class of 1924 was called up between March 1930 and March 1931, 40,000 of the 230,000 men involved received agricultural exemptions (Paoli, *L'Armée française,* 4:61–62). Concern for the French farmer was obvious even in orders promulgated after the war began (Daladier Note, 8 November 1939, SHAT 7N2333/1, 7–8).

80. "Instruction générale pour la convocation des réservistes en 1927," SHAT 7N2333/11.

81. For example, the reservists who joined the Thirty-second RI for a three-week training period at La Courtine camp in the summer of 1934 were organized into a separate reserve battalion with one active officer per reserve company (Harold M. Rayner, "Duty Preparatory to Commencement of Ecole de Guerre, Paris, France," 27 October 1934 [G-2 20,939-W], USNA RG165 2015-1187).

82. "Compte-Rendu de la visite faite le 13 Mai à Orleans à l'occasion de la convocation des réservistes au 8th Régiment de Chasseurs," (n.d. but apparently 1927), SHAT 7N2333/1.

83. Sumner Waite, "Commissioned Personnel—Mobilization of Personnel: Lack of Regular Officers, French Army," 13 December 1938 (G-2 24,700-W), USNA RG165 2015-1266/1.

84. "ELEMENTS de réponse aux remarques faites par la Commission de l'Armée de la Chambre des Députés au sujet des convocations de réservistes," 22 April 1939, SHAT 7N2333/1.

85. Ord, "Training Instruction," USNA RG165 2015-928/19.

86. Louis J. Fortier, "Training of the French 23rd Division," 20 October 1937 (G-2 23,804-W), USNA RG165 2015-1237/4.

87. This was, in fact, not a true vertical convocation because most of the 8,000 men involved were members of a single class and because the entire division did not participate. Still, it was an unusually large fragment, and training took place in a single camp rather than at separate regimental centers. The Forty-first DI drew its cadres from the Tenth DI.

88. The Forty-first DI had done well in a *convocation profonde* ("Renseignements relatifs à la valeur des unités de formation," SHAT 7N4018; Major Reeve, "Report," 1 December 1934, PRO C8181/85/17).

89. James A. Lester, "Maneuvers of a Division of Reservists at Mourmelon," 4 October 1934 (G-2 20,835-W), USNA RG165 2015-1173/7, 2.

90. Gaston Prételat, "Convocation de la 41e DI," November 1934, SHAT 1N94/7.

91. Gen. Pigeaud, Directeur de l'Arbitrage, "Observations générales," SHAT 1N94/7.

92. Charles de Gaulle, "Evénements survenus dans le secteur de groupe d'arbitrage No.2," 6 October 1934, SHAT 1N94/7.

93. "Extraits des compte-rendus d'arbitrage concernant l'artillerie de la 41 DI," SHAT 7N2294.

94. See Pigeaud and de Gaulle, SHAT 1N94/7. This result would not have surprised anyone familiar with the 1927 call up of the class of 1922, in which "the marches were very fatiguing to men accustomed to a sedentary life."

95. For a similar assessment of French reservists, see Carrère, "Physionomie," 308–316.

96. For the more radical ideas offered by the military correspondent of *Le Temps,* see Gen. Baratier, *Le Temps,* 5 May 1935, translated in Military Attaché, Paris, "Public or Spoken Views [sic] on the National Defense Policy, Preparedness" (G-2 No.21,502-W), 9, USNA RG165 2015-1160/3. Having once been Foch's chief of staff, Baratier was believed by the British "to provide a useful indication of the outlook of the General Staff" (War Office, MIS, October 1937, 146).

97. But he expressed surprise that his unit then spent fifteen days "training like recruits," Pétain and Caron, *100 jours,* 16.

98. de Vibraye, *Avec mon groupe de reconnaissance,* 42–43.

99. *PV,* Cham. Army Comm., 20 March 1935; *PV,* Sen. Army Comm., 21 November 1934; U.S. Military Attaché, 23 October 1934 (G-2 20,884-W), USNA RG165 2015-1173-8.

100. Baratier, "L'expérience de Mourmelon," *Le Temps,* 13 October 1934, 1.

101. Louis Colson, "Convocation en 1935 d'unités constituées," 30 December 1934, SHAT 7N2333/2.

102. Parliament did authorize the minister of war to summon for this exercise reservists from the Fifty-second DI who had already completed a period of reserve training. The year 1935 also saw a vertical convocation of the Sixtieth Infantry Brigade (Colson, "Convocation en 1935," SHAT 7N2333/2).

103. The units called up in 1936 were drawn from seven divisions, three fortified regions, and two fortified sectors (1/EMA, "NOTE au sujet des convocations d'unités constituées prévues pour l'année 1936," 17 December 1935, SHAT 7N2333/2).

104. "Renseignements numeriques sur les convocations de réservists depuis l'époque de leur rétablissement," 25 January 1939, SHAT 6N428/1; Colson, "Convocation en 1939 d'unités constituées," 22 December 1938, SHAT 7N2333/2.

105. Maurice Gamelin, "Convocation des Cadres des divisions et unités de formation," 13 January 1933, SHAT 7N4008/4. For the schedule of a representative convocation, see Champon, "Rapport," 3 November 1936, SHAT 7N4019.

106. Soulet, *36ᵉ Division,* 13.

107. Lafont, "Rapport d'ensemble sur les convocations d'unités de formation en 1935," 21 November 1935, SHAT 7N4018.

108. "Rapport sur la convocation profonde de la 67ème Division," SHAT 7N4018. For more positive reports on cadre convocations see Moyrant, "Convocation profonde de certaines unités de la 15th Région," 19 December 1935, SHAT 7N4018, and Champon, "Rapport," 3 November 1936, SHAT 7N4019.

109. Champon, "Rapport," SHAT 7N4019.

110. For example, the Fourth DI performed its 1936 cadre exercise without twenty-six of its twenty-seven allotted antitank guns (Champon, "Rapport," SHAT 7N4019). The Twenty-second Division completely lacked 25mm cannons, 60mm mortars, chenillettes, and ER17 and ER22 radios ("Convocation profonde de la 22 DI [20–26 September 1936]," SHAT 7N4019/1).

111. Gen. Oficquendan, "Convocations profonds en 1939," 3 March 1939, SHAT 7N4020/1.

112. Pétain claimed on 23 July 1927 that the army needed 24,000 active and 95,000 reserve officers (War Office, MIS, July 1927, 95). Another source indicates that reservists would make up 70 percent of the infantry officers, 60 percent of the cavalry, 80 percent of artillery and train, 72 percent of engineer officers, and 60 percent of those in the Air Corps (Henri Mayerhoeffer, *RI,* 1 September 1928, quoted in "Recruiting and Training of Infantry Reserve Officers" [G-2 14,150-W], USNA RG165 2015-928/6). Baratier claimed that even active formations would go to war with 80 percent reserve officers, a percentage found in World War I only in reserve divisions (Baratier, *Le Temps,* 24 August 1934, 1).

113. Regular officers came from four sources. The most prestigious route was the two-year course at St. Cyr and L'Ecole Polytechnique (see A. Tanant, "Nos grands écoles II: Saint Cyr," *RDM* 7:32 [March–April 1926]: 39–58, and Maurice d'Ocagne, "Nos grands écoles IV: L'école polytechnique," *RDM* 7: 33 [May–June 1926]: 515–533). The second route, eighteen months at *l'école militaire de l'infanterie et des chars de combat de Saint-Maixent,* trained noncommissioned and reserve officers

for regular commissions (L. Borie, "Nos grandes écoles XIV: Saint-Maixent," *RDM* 7: 43 [January–February 1928]: 549–568). Mechanical specialists came from a one-year *cours d'éléves officiers mécaniciens de l'école des chars de combat de Versailles,* whose admissions requirements paralleled those of Saint-Maixent. Finally, some experienced noncommissioned officers were commissioned to fill the army's need for instructors, administrators, and supervisors of technicians (see J. P[erré] and R. S., "Les cadres de l'infanterie et des chars de combat: Leur recrutement et leur instruction," *RI* 94 [June–September 1939]: 1114–1140).

114. Baratier disparages this source of officers in *Le Temps,* 24 August 1934, 1–2.

115. The top 5 percent of those who earned the *brevet de preparation militaire supérieure* followed the same route as the men from the *grandes écoles* (Gen. Thoumin, "Les écoles d'Infanterie de 1919 à 1939," *RHA* 10 [1954]: 95).

116. In 1933, 14,000 men achieved the *brevet de préparation militaire supérieure* (Baratier, *Le Temps,* 5 October 1934, 1). Because the number of men with the brevet exceeded requirements, the army could afford to be selective (Mayerhoeffer [G-2 1,150-W], USNA RG165 2015-928/6; see also Thoumin, "Les écoles," 95, and Perré, "Cadres").

117. Felsenhardt, *1939–1940,* 26–27.

118. In comparison, German reserve officer candidates, even under wartime conditions, spent about eighteen months in training (U.S. War Department, *Handbook on German Military Forces,* 76.1).

119. Robert Bourget-Pailleron, "Le soldat de la dernière guerre," *RDM* 8:60 (September–October): 160.

120. Ibid., 161.

121. Mayerhoeffer (G-2 1,150-W), USNA RG165 2015-928/6; War Office, MIS, September 1936, 192. Strife also existed between graduates of St.Cyr and Saint-Maixent, and a ruckus between officer candidates from the two institutions in 1931 ended the practice of joint summer field exercises (Thoumin, "Les écoles," 93).

122. Commandant Altairac, "Role de l'officier de réserve appelé à accomplir une périod dans un bataillon de réservists," *RI* 91 (1932): 75.

123. Sartre, *War Diaries,* 203.

124. Ibid., 206.

125. Emilie Carles, *A Life of Her Own: The Transformation of a Country-woman in Twentieth-Century France,* trans. Avriel H. Goldberger (Harmondsworth, Eng., 1992), 199–201.

126. Sadoul, *Journal de guerre,* 116.

127. But Horne exaggerates in referring to the "more democratic Wehrmacht," (Alistair Horne, *To Lose a Battle* [Harmondsworth, Eng., 1969], 136). Communist Grenier describes most of the junior officers as "understanding" (*Journal de la drôle de guerre,* 71). French privates resented the fact that reserve officers enjoyed a standard of living beyond their peacetime means (Sadoul, *Journal de guerre,* 90).

128. "Individual Training Periods to be undergone by Reserve Officers, 3 May 1937" (G-2 23,396-W), USNA RG165 2015-735/27.

129. Promotion requirements as set out in the law of 8 January 1925 were not always scrupulously observed: "political influence may be brought to bear and may

sometimes result in upsetting the correct application of the system" ("Promotion of Reserve Officers," 2 June 1927 [G-2 12,327-W], USNA RG165 2015-735-11).

130. Baratier, *Le Temps,* 24 August 1934.

131. The figures are from the War Office, MIS, November 1933, December 1934.

132. *Le Temps,* 29 September 1936, 3. See also the report of British observers of Thirty-sixth DI exercises at Souge camp, War Office, MIS, August 1934, 64. General Thoumin describes the plight of the hypothetical company commander who receives ten reserve officers requiring training in command but can scrape up only a section or two from his skeleton company. On the rare occasions when formations were brought up to full strength for maneuvers, commanders had little desire to turn the precious training opportunity over to unknown reservists (Thoumin, "Les écoles," 102).

133. *Le Temps,* 30 May 1937, 4.

134. Monteilhet, *Institutions militaries,* 430, argues that professional officers had commands only one year in four.

135. War Office, MIS, January 1928, 74. Only the most competent reserve officers and noncommissioned officers were to be placed in charge of reservists (EMA, "Circulaire," 5 March 1937, SHAT 7N4006/1). See reports on exercises of the Nineteenth DI (War Office, MIS, August 1934, 65) and Fifteenth DIM (War Office, MIS, November 1934, 30).

136. War Office, MIS, February 1933, 146; P. Jouffrault, *Les spahis au feu: La 1re Brigade de Spahis pendant la campagne 1939–1940* (Paris, 1948), 24; Chambrun, *I Saw France Fall,* 29.

137. Altairac, "Role de l'officier de Réserve," 76–82.

138. Thoumin, "Les écoles," 102–103.

139. Sample lectures and issues of *L'Officier de Reserve* can be found in SHAT 7N4006. There were 1,108 reserve officer schools in 1929–1930 (Paoli, *L'Armée française,* 3: 149).

140. Henri Albert Niessel, "Les écoles d'Officiers de Réserve," *RDM* 7:61 (January–February 1931): 407 (SHAT 7N4008/3).

141. Participation rates also varied widely among branches of services, with the following enrollment percentages reports for the thirteenth region in 1930: infantry/tanks, 28 percent; colonial infantry, 26 percent; cavalry, 67 percent; supply, 65 percent; artillery, 68 percent; colonial artillery, 20 percent; engineers, 75 percent; air force, 81 percent; and gendarmerie, 0 percent (Gen. Duchêne, "Rapport concernant l'activité des E.P.O.R. pendant le semestre d'été," 5 September 1930, SHAT 7N4011).

142. Gen. Tanant, 30 July 1930, SHAT 7N4014/1.

143. Gen. Vaulgrenaut, "Réponse au questionnaire concernant les écoles de Perf. des O.R. pendant la periode d'été 1930," 4 October 1930, SHAT 7N4011/1.

144. Bloch, *Strange Defeat,* 5.

145. Baratier, *Le Temps,* 24 August 1934, 1.

146. Reserve Captain Mura, "Les cours de perfectionnement pour les officiers de réserve," *Le Temps,* 5 October 1934.

147. R.-J. Rousseau, "Les officiers de réserves," *Le Temps,* 26 August 1934, 4.

148. Colson, "Period d'instruction des jeunes officiers de réserve," 1 December 1933, SHAT 7N4008/3.

149. 1/EMA Note 25 September 1935, SHAT 7N2322/6.

150. "Projet de loi no. 5043 (Deputé Daladier), presenté 17 January 1939," 27 May 1938, SHAT 7N2322.

151. Horace H. Fuller, "Changes in Articles of the Recruiting Law Dealing with Individual Training," 28 March 1939 (G-2 24,907-W), USNA RG165 2015-901/104.

152. Published as J. Perré, "Le char moderne: Ses possibilités et ses servitudes: Son emploi dans l'attaque," *RI* 92 (January–June 1938): 620–639.

153. Ibid., 634.

154. Reservists filled 90 percent of the noncommissioned officer slots in most units (Mott, "Instruction," [G-2 13,707-W], USNA RG165 2015-766/26).

155. See, for example, Béguier, *Les étapes,* 92. Even the active cadres contained many relatively inexperienced noncommissioned officers. Of the 106,000 noncommissioned officers (sergeants, sergeants-chefs, adjudants, adjudant-chefs) required under the 1927–1928 organization, only 50,000 were careerists, who served an average of fourteen years. Of the remainder, 36,000 were conscript corporals and corporaux-chefs who had volunteered for an additional period of service ranging from six months to five years, and 20,000 were noncommissioned officers with less than five years service ("Note sur les cours pour les sous-officiers de carrière," n.d. [apparently 1928], SHAT 7N2301). On the impact of the twelve-month service law, see Maurice Gamelin, *Servir,* 3 vols. (Paris, 1954–1959), 2:9.

156. An invention of 1920s, the rank of corporal-chef identified members of the active contingent suitable for promotion to reserve sergeant after their first reserve exercise.

157. The weakness of the reserve section leaders is stressed in "Report of Manoeuvres carried out by the 15th Division from 20th to 22nd August 1934," War Office, MIS, November 1934, 37. Reserve noncommissioned officers in one battery knew nothing of the operation of its 75mm guns (Lami, *Un peu de gloire,* 5).

158. War Office, MIS, November 1931, 19; H. H. Fuller, "Non-Commissioned Officers in Metropolitan Infantry (Tanks excepted)," 12 July 1937 (G-2 23,567-W), RG165 2015-901/93.

159. James A. Lester, 15 November 1935 (G-2 22,003-W), USNA RG165 2015-901/87.

160. EMA, Direction de l'infanterie," "Effectifs en sous-officiers des corps de troupe d'infanterie," 18 May 1936, SHAT 9N119/5.

161. See "RAPPORT du Général Sutterlin, Commandant l'A.D./41 de formation, consécutif à la convocation de la 41st DI à Mourmelon du 14 au 30 Septembre 1934," SHAT 7N2294.

162. *L'Echo,* quoted in James A. Lester, "Maneuvers of a Division of Reservists at Mourmelon," 4 October 1934 (G-2 20,835-W), USNA 2015-1173/7.

163. Carrère, "Physionomie," 301.

164. Pétain and Caron, *100 jours,* 19.

165. de Vibraye, *Avec mon groupe de reconnaissance,* 27, 89.

166. Sartre, *War Diaries,* 170–171.

167. See, for example, Lafont, "Rapport," SHAT 7N4018; Georges Blanchard,

"Convocation verticale du 113th Batallion du Génie," 6 December 1937, SHAT 7N4014/1; Gen. Mussel, "Rapport d'ensemble du General Commandant la 1ère Région, relatif à la convocation, en 1934, des Cadres des 1ère Division, 2ème et 51ème Divisions de formation," 7 September 1934, SHAT 7N4017; War Office, MIS, November 1934, 37.

168. 3/EMA, "Note au sujet de l'extension aux Sous-Officiers des Convocations profondes de cadres," 25 November 1936, SHAT 7N4020/1; Perré, "Cadres," 1138.

169. Maximé Gamelin, "Ecoles de Perfectionnment des s/offs de Réserve," 14 February 1931, SHAT 7N4008/3.

170. Felsenhardt had the unusual qualification of being able to offer a first-hand description of the effectiveness of dive bombers in Spain, but his assessment was rejected by the officer who ran the course (Felsenhardt, *1939–1940*, 28).

171. Henri Albert Niessel, "Les écoles de sous-officiers de réserve," *RDM* 8:9 (March–April 1932): 411–425. The figure 100,000 constituted about one-third of the reserve noncommissioned officers.

172. Prételat, "41th DI," SHAT 1N94/7; Horace H. Fuller, "Changes in Articles of the Recruiting Law Dealing with Individual Training," 28 March 1939 (G-2 24,907-W), USNA RG165 2015-901/104.

173. The letter called for the replacement of inferior noncommissioned officers with suitable younger men (Gamelin, "Note au sujet de l'encadrement en sous-officiers," 12 December 1939, quoted in *Servir,* 3:248).

174. Grenier, *Journal de la drôle de guerre,* 265.

175. Paoli, *L'armée française,* 3:58.

Chapter 5. The Sources of French Military Doctrine

1. "Doctrine comes from the Latin word *docere,* which means 'to teach.' A doctrine is then what one teaches, it includes the essential ideas which govern the instruction and employment of the army" (Marie-Eugène Debeney, *La guerre et les hommes: Reflexions d'après-guerre* [Paris, 1937], 264).

2. Robert A. Doughty, *The Seeds of Disaster: The Development of French Army Doctrine 1919–1939* (Hamden, CT, 1985), and Ladislas Mysyrowicz, *Anatomie d'une défaite: Origines de l'effondrement militaire française de 1940* (Lausanne, 1973).

3. For "viable," see Doughty, *Seeds of Disaster,* 5, 12.

4. Ibid., 178–183.

5. Ibid., 181, 182, 187.

6. Ibid., 181.

7. Ibid., 179.

8. Ibid., 187.

9. Ibid., 91.

10. For the argument that the conservatism of the French Army reflected unwillingness to disturb the relationship among its branches, see Faris Russell Kirkland, "The French Officer Corps and the Fall of France" (Ph.D. dissertation, University of Pennsylvania, 1982), 274. On French caution, see R. K. Sutherland,

"Report on the Course at the ESG 1928-9 and 1929-30," 30 June 1930 (G-2 16,437-W), USNA RG165 2277-C-151, 6; Fuller, "Aix" USNA RG165 2015-1223/3, 2-3; "Life and Training in a French Infantry Regiment," War Office, MIS, September 1936, 198; "Tactical Tendencies," War Office, MIS, June 1928, 72; "Annual Report," War Office, MIS, January 1933, 90; "Report of Manoeuvres carried out by the 15th Division from 20th to 22nd August 1934, War Office, MIS, November 1934, 37; "Note on Tactics and Military Policy," War Office, MIS, October 1935, 230.

11. For the practical problems of disseminating doctrine, see Chapter 4.

12. Marshal Franchet d'Esperey, "Indépendance et imagination," *Revue Militaire Générale* 1 (1937): 12.

13. France, Ministry of Defense, *Centenaire de l'Ecole Supérieure de Guerre 1876–1976*, 38. See also Eugène Debeney, "Nos grandes écoles VIII: L'École Supérieure de Guerre," *RDM* January 1927): 85.

14. Furthermore, Churchill saw it as entirely "natural, therefore, that we should place ourselves under their command, and that their judgment should be accepted" (Winston Churchill, *Their Finest Hour* [Boston, 1949], 35–36).

15. The official expositions of French doctrine are the War Ministry's *Instruction provisoire sur l'emploi tactique des grandes unités* (Paris, 1921) and (Paris, 1936), hereafter *IGU* 1921 and *IGU* 1936. For Debeney's role, see Doughty, *Seeds of Disaster*, 6.

16. Doughty, *Seeds of Disaster*, 5.

17. Michael Geyer argues for a similar division in the contemporary German Army between "idealists" or "professional strategists" who derived their principles from history, and technocrats and ideologues who seized the opportunities of the moment (Michael Geyer, "German Strategy in the Age of Machine Warfare, 1914–1945," in Peter Paret, ed. *Makers of Modern Strategy* [Princeton, 1986], 527–597).

18. A mobile warrior's recommendation of the material method is exemplified in Captain Charles de Gaulle, "Doctrine à priori ou doctrine des circonstances," *RMF* 15 (January–March 1923): 306–307. For the contrary view that "technology serves tactics, but it does not shape them. It does not overturn the general principles but can only modify their application, modes of applying them," see X, "L'Artillerie dans le combat des chars," *RA* 113 (January–June, 1934): 58.

19. Jean Delmas, "Aperçu des méthodes," *Bulletin Trimestriel of the Association des Amis de l'Ecole Supérieure de Guerre* 57 (1st trimester 1973): 36.

20. Mahan insisted on the superiority of the historical method for the study of strategy: "The movements which precede and prepare for great battles which, by their skill and energetic combination, attain great ends without actual contact of arms, depend upon factors more permanent than the weapons of the age and therefore furnish principles of more enduring value" (Ronald Spector, *Professors of War: The Naval War College and the Development of the Naval Profession* [Newport, RI, 1977], 45).

21. Raoul Castex, *Théories stratégiques*, 5 vols. (Paris, 1929–1935), 1:51–52.

22. De Gaulle, "Doctrine à priori." Compare the argument that "principles remain fixed and methods change with every war," in XXX, "La guerre future et l'aviation: Avions et cuirassés: les expériences américaines," *RDM* (November–December 1921): 814.

23. X, "L'artillerie dans le combat des chars," *Revue d'artillerie* 114 (January–June 1934): 58

24. See also Lt. Col. Druène, "Deux siècles d'histoire de l'artillerie française," *RHA* 11 (1955): 149–166, where Generals Buat and Jean Colin are treated as representatives of two different types of historical education (162).

25. At this time the naval staff also acquired a historical section and began publishing the *Revue Maritime*.

26. Mysyrowicz, *Anatomie d'une défaite,* 35; for history as a substitute for experience, see 21–22.

27. Doughty, *Seeds of Disaster,* 90.

28. See ibid., 75, for evidence that the historical articles published in the *Revue d'infanterie* from 1928 to 1938 focused almost exclusively on World War I or on colonial campaigns and therefore offered no alternative model for modern doctrine.

29. France, Ministry of Defense, *Centenaire de l'Ecole Supérieure de Guerre 1876–1976,* 22 (hereafter *Centenaire*).

30. Marc Bloch, *Strange Defeat,* trans. Gerard Hopkins (New York, 1968), 117.

31. Ibid. (original emphasis).

32. Gen. Camon, "L'Institute des hautes études militaires," *La Revue de France* (1929): 54, 58–59. For representative programs of instruction at the CHEM, where historical lectures were used solely to illustrate positive arguments, see SHAT 2N264/2.

33. Camon, "L'Institute des hautes études," 58–59.

34. Marius Daille, *La Bataille de Montdidier* (Paris, 1922); for the importance of Montdidier in the War College curriculum, see Doughty, *Seeds of Disaster,* 81–83.

35. Paul Azan, "But et programme de la Revue Militaire Générale," *RMG* 1 (1937): 7.

36. Debeney, *La guerre et les hommes,* 265.

37. Jean Delmas, "Aperçu des méthodes," *Bulletin Trimestriel* 57 (January–April 1973): 39.

38. Ibid.

39. For the argument that in the 1890s the French Army created a false historical pedigree for offensive ideas that could not be defended in material terms, see de Gaulle, "Doctrine à priori," 314.

40. Narcisse Chauvineau, *Une invasion, est-elle encore possible?* 2d ed. (Paris, 1940), xxi.

41. Gen. Vauthier, *La défense nationale* (Paris, 1938–1939), 30–31.

42. A. Krebs, "Considérations sur l'offensive," *RMG* 1 (September 1937): 361.

43. Mysyrowicz, *Anatomie d'une défaite,* 21–22. The same message appears in *IGU* 1936, 15.

44. Gen. Brindel, "Nouvelle organisation militaire," *RDM* 7:51 (May–June 1929): 483.

45. The order appeared in Gamelin, "Directive sur l'instruction," 25 January 1937, 52, quoted in Henry Dutailly, *Les problèmes de l'armée de terre française* (Paris, 1980), 232. References to it appear in Edouard Jean Requin, *D'une guerre à l'autre* (Paris, 1949), 214, and *PV,* Cham. Army Comm., 1 December 1937, 2.

46. "Note au sujet de la Division Cuirassée à expérimenter en 1937," 28 November 1936, SHAT 1N36/4.

47. André Beaufre, *Memoires 1920–1940–1945* (Paris, 1965), 47.

48. Jeffrey A. Gunsberg, *Divided and Conquered* (Westport, CT, 1979), 106.

49. Richard G. Tindall, "Period of Duty with the French Army," 12 October 1933, 24 (G-2 19,791-W), USNA RG165 2015-1161/1; Gilman C. Mudgett, "Tour of Duty with the 11e Escadron d'Auto-Mitrailleuses de Cavalerie at Orleans, Loiret, France," 31 August 1932, USNA RG165 2015-1128/1.

50. Stefan T. Possony, "Organized Intelligence: The Problem of the French General Staff," *Social Research* 8 (1941): 231.

51. See Chapter 2.

52. See Alphonse Georges, "Avis du Général Georges," 13 September 1937, SHAT 1N46/3; Gamelin, "Emploi des chars moderns," 30 September 1937, SHAT 7N4026/3.

53. Possony, "Organized Intelligence," 232. Beaufre's desire to establish his postwar credentials as a strategist gave him an interest in distancing himself from the interwar high command.

54. Kirkland, "French Officer Corps," 283. The "astonishing" article was Henri Mainié, "Motorisation et mécanisation," *RI* (July–December 1937): 1359–1365.

55. See Kirkland, "French Officer Corps," 187; Mysyrowicz, *Anatomie d'une défaite,* 27.

56. The American attaché reported the new regulations to be aimed specially at Generals Niessel and Dufieux (Horace H. Fuller, "Amendment of Regulations Governing the Liberty of Army Officers to Publish Articles on Certain Subjects," 15 June 1939 [G-2 25,049-W], USNA RG165 2015-1270/1, 2–3).

57. Colson, 3/EMA No.6585, 11 October 1935, SHAT 7N4013/1.

58. 3/EMA, "Note pour le Général Chef de l'E.M.A. au sujet de la crise de la literature militaire et des moyens d'y remédier," 5 December 1935, SHAT 7N4013.

59. Kirkland, "French Officer Corps," 164, 250, argues that the *Revue militaire française* published articles too unorthodox for the *Revue d'infanterie* and was "suppressed" in 1936 but ignores the new *Revue militaire générale*.

60. Louis Franchet d'Esperey, "Indépendance et imagination," *RMG* 1 (1937): 11. The "complete independence" promised to the journal's contributors was modified not only by the requirements of military secrecy but the need to avoid any "excès de fantasie capable de troubler les esprits" (Azan, "But et programme," 7). Authors serving in the armed forces were forbidden to mention their military functions, all works on certain subjects had to be cleared with the Ministry of War, and political or religious subjects were banned (Gamelin, 3/EMA No.7282, 17 November 1936, SHAT 7N4013).

61. Amédée Bernard, "Théorèmes de défense nationale," *RMG* 2 (1938): 24.

62. The interwar ESG is described in "The 'Ecole Supérieure de Guerre,' Paris," *Journal of the Royal United Service Institution* 70 (1925): 1–7.

63. For ESG's debt to Von Moltke, see G. V. Y. Waterhouse, "Some Notes on the E.S.G., Paris," *Army Quarterly* 8 (July 1924): 329. German criticism of French inflexibility appears in *Militärwissenschaftliche Rundschau* of October 1942, trans-

lated into French as "L'état-major français est-il responsable de la défaite de 1940?" in SHAT, Fonds Picard, 1K121/5.

64. Henri Bonnal, "Conférence sur les méthodes utilisées en France et en Allemagne pour acquérir l'unité de doctrine" (1901), 25, quoted in Delmas, "Aperçu des méthodes," 41.

65. France, Ministry of Defense, *Centenaire*, 21.

66. Delmas, "Aperçu des méthodes," 45. The Centre des Hautes Etudes Militaires, the next tier in French military education, did have an official solution for every problem. A student could choose to defend his own answer—"after *discussion and reflection*" (original emphasis)—but was still required to apply the school solution to any further stages in the exercise (Gen. Bineau, "Conference d'introduction," Centre des Hautes Etudes Militaires, December 1936, 19, SHAT, Fonds Picard, 1K121/5).

67. Ralph K. Smith, "Report on Methods of Instruction at the ESG, Paris," 13 July 1937 (G-2 23,635-W) USNA RG165 2277-C-193/1. Also a product of the Sorbonne and of the U.S. Army War College, Smith would go on to command the Twenty-seventh Infantry Division in an attack on the Gilbert Islands.

68. Waterhouse, "Some Notes on the E.S.G.," 329. Only hospital interns were said to work harder than ESG students (France, Ministry of Defense, *Centenaire*, 24).

69. R. K. Sutherland, "Report on the Course at the ESG 1928–9 and 1929–30," 30 June 1930, 4 (G-216,437-W), USNA RG165 2277-C-151.

70. War Office, MIS, November 1931, 15.

71. Ibid., 7. Remember that one of the arguments adduced against establishing a national defense college was that it would question national policy.

72. For ESG professor Colonel Louis de Grandmaison's championship of *l'offensive à l'outrance* before World War I, see Michael Howard, "Men against Fire: The Doctrine of the Offensive in 1914," in Peter Paret, ed., *Makers of Modern Strategy* (Princeton, 1986), 520–521. Debeney denied that the ESG had supported Grandmaison's ideas (Possony, "Organized Intelligence," 226 n.16).

73. This assessment, from Gen. Trentinian (*L'état-Major en 1914* [Paris, 1927], 50), is as valid for the interwar as for the prewar period.

74. Lt. de Vaisseau Fenard, "Essai historique comparative du haut enseignement dans l'armée et la marine," 1921, Service Historique de la Marine 36P54, annexes 7I271.

75. Doughty, *Seeds of Disaster*, 5.

76. Quoted in ibid., 57.

77. For a comprehensive discussion of the entire debate, see Doughty's chapter "Defense of the Frontiers."

78. Gamelin, "La question du système fortifié à créer sur notre frontière de Belgique," (n.d.), 3–4, SHAT, Fonds Gamelin, 1K224/7 (original emphasis).

79. Ibid. (original emphasis). Gamelin's wording here and in "every maneuver idea excludes a uniform distribution of forces" ("Direction générale sur l'instruction [D.G.I.]," 30 April 1935, quoted in Dutailly, *Problèmes de l'armée*, 229) echoes Raoul Castex, *Strategic Theories*, abridged, trans., and ed. E. C. Kiesling (Annapolis, 1993), 102–109.

80. Louis Maurin, "Rapport sur la Manoeuvre de Mailly 7–13 August 1928," 141, SHAT 1N9315.

81. Weygand, "Note to Minister of War," 16 January 1933, quoted in François-André Paoli, *L'Armée française de 1919 à 1939,* 4 vols. (Paris, 1969–1971), 4:29–31.

82. *IGU* 1936, 16.

83. James A. Lester, Military Attache's Report, 9 January 1936 (G-2 22,121) USNA RG165 2015-1212/1.

84. Winston S.Churchill, *The World Crisis,* vol. 2 (New York: 1972), 5.

85. See, for example, V. Ye. Savkin, *The Basic Principles of Operational Art and Tactics* (Moscow, 1972; trans. U.S. Air Force, published by GPO), 168–169, in which "maneuverability" and "mobility" are used synonymously, and U.S. Marine Corps Field Manual 1 "Warfighting" (Washington, D.C., 1989), 58–60, which defines maneuver as movement to gain advantages in space and time and contrasts maneuver with the employment of firepower.

86. *IGU* 1936, 16.

87. For "maneuver by fire," see ibid., 58–59.

88. Original emphasis.

89. Castex, *Strategic Theories,* 102, 119.

90. Col. Ailleret, *L'art de la guerre et la technique,* quoted in Druène, "Deux siècles d'histoire de l'artillerie français," 165.

91. Gamelin, "Notice sommaire concernant la défensive sur un grand front," 28 October 1931, 10, SHAT 7N4025/1.

92. Pierre Héring, "Projet d'Instruction Provisoire sur l'Emploi Tactique des Grandes Unités: Observation du Général Héring," 25 July 1936, 6, SHAT 7N4001. The artillery course taught that "movement is essentially of fire" (Mysyrowicz, *Anatomie d'une défaite,* 21).

93. See Jean Perré, "La guerre des chars," *RI* 87 (July–December 1935): 951–1014.

94. Robert A. Doughty, "The French Armed Forces, 1918–40," in Allan R. Millett and Williamson Murray, *Military Effectiveness,* vol. 2 (London, Sydney, Wellington, 1988), 55.

95. 3/EMA, "Resumé des idées exposées par le Général Gamelin les 23 et 24 mars 1937 au CHEM," 1, SHAT 7N421.

96. Dutailly, *Problèmes de l'armée,* 230.

97. Gamelin, "Direction générale sur l'instruction (D.G.I.)," 30 April 1935, quoted in Dutailly, *Problèmes de l'armée,"* 228.

98. Ibid., 229 (original emphasis).

99. Ibid., 231 (original emphasis).

100. Sumner Waite, "Combat Arms, Modern Infantry." Appendix: "Evolution of Infantry Since the World War. Present Status and Future Trends," 9 May 1939 (G-2 24,983-W), USNA RG165 2015-1267/1.

101. James H. Cunningham, "Organization and Use of French Infantry Division as Taught at the Ecole Supérieure de Guerre," 20 June 1927 (G-2 12,394-W), USNA RG165 2015-721/34.

102. Robert A. Touchon, Riom Testimony 24 March 1942, SHAT 1K224/Carton 2/Dossier 3.

Chapter 6. A Very Careful Doctrine

1. Some of the material in this chapter has been published as Eugenia C. Kiesling, "If It Ain't Broke, Don't Fix It: French Military Doctrine Between the Wars," *War in History* 3 (1996).
2. They are contained in *IGU* 1921 and *IGU* 1936, discussed in Chapter 5. For the most comprehensive discussion of French doctrine, see Robert A. Doughty, *Seeds of Disaster* (Hamden, CT, 1985).
3. "La puissance du feu s'est affirmée écrasante" and "Le feu est le facteur prépondérant du combat: L'attaque est le feu qui avance, la défense est le feu qui arrête" (IGU 1921, 10, 62).
4. "Le mode d'action par excellence."
5. "Les effets du feu sont d'ordre à la fois matériel et moral. Ils créent des zones de mort oùles troupes subissent des pertes massives et foudroyantes qui les frappent d'impuissance et les clouant au sol. Oule material est détruit, oules organisations sont bouleversées" (*IGU* 1936, 53–54, SHAT 7N4003/1; in boldface in original).
6. In charge of bringing the 1921 regulations up-to-date was a commission of sixteen officers chaired by General Georges and including Pujo, Meulle-Desjardins, Duffour, Boucherie, Hubert, Loizeau, Touchon, Montagne, Sisteron, Sivot, Mendras, Pugens, Kergoat, Tarrade, and Navereau.
7. "Certaines leçons que celle-ci a laissées si vivantes dans les coeurs et l'esprit" (*IGU* 1936, preface).
8. War Office, MIS, August 1934, 63.
9. Louis Maurin, "Rapport sur la Manoeuvre de Mailly 7–13 August 1928," SHAT 1N93/5.
10. EMA, "Circulaire," 5 March 1937, SHAT 7N4006/1.
11. Stanley H. Ford, "Divisional Exercises of the 23rd Division of Infantry," 10 October 1932 (G-2 18,819-W), USNA RG165 2015-1104/3.
12. Ladislas Mysyrowicz, *Anatomie d'une défaite* (Lausanne, 1973), 74.
13. Documents in SHAT 1N79/12.
14. Adolphe Goutard, *Battle of France, 1940,* trans. A. R. P. Burgess (London, 1985), 116.
15. "Personne ne l'a jamais pensé," Alphonse Georges, Riom testimony, 10 July 1941, SHAT, Fonds Georges, 1K95.
16. Each of the company's twelve squads had one light automatic weapon, "Post-war Tactical and Technical Tendencies," War Office, MIS, September 1934, 9, 196.
17. James B. Ord, "Mailly," USNA RG165 2015-978/8.
18. Louis J. Fortier, "The French Infantry Battalion," 26 January 1938 (G-2 23,992-W), USNA RG165 2015-721/41.
19. War Office, MIS, October 1930, 236.
20. James B. Ord, "Lorraine Maneuvers, September 1930," 10 October 1930 (G-2 16,747-W), USNA RG165 2015-1060/10.
21. Stanley H. Ford, "Maneuvers at La Courtine," 4 September 1931 (G-2 17,709-W), USNA RG165 2015-1085/3; War Office, MIS, December 1931, 60. See Chapter 6 for the French Army's lack of emphasis on fire by the individual infantry-

man. See Ord, "Mailly," USNA RG165 2015-978/8,5, and "Lorraine Maneuvers," USNA RG165 2015-1060/10.

22. "Report of manoeuvres of 1 DC 11–14 September 1935," War Office, MIS, January 1936, 114.

23. Maurice Gamelin, *Servir*, 3 vols. (Paris, 1954–1959), 3:455.

24. "Life and Training in a French Infantry Regiment," War Office, MIS, September 1936, 197.

25. "The South Eastern Manoeuvres," War Office, MIS, November 1936, 21.

26. Terrain features determined the size of each bound, but 600–1,000m was deemed ideal (Lt. Col. Sumner Waite, 25 October 1937 [G-2 23,808-W], USNA RG165 2015-1223). Translation of Julien Brossé, "The Support of Infantry by Fast Tanks and Artillery," from *Revue militaire générale*.

27. James H. Cunningham, "Organization and Use of French Infantry Division as Taught at the Ecole Supérieure de Guerre," 20 June 1927 (G-2 12,394-W), USNA RG165 2015-721/34. A 1938 document gives 5,500m as the range beyond which 75mm guns could not support infantry for fear of short rounds falling on friendly troops (Sumner Waite, "The Tactical Employment of Divisional Artillery in Support of Tank Action," 13 May 1938 [G-2 24,266-W], 4, USNA RG165 2015-1245/2).

28. This description comes from an American translation of the "Provisional Memorandum Concerning the Employment of D Tanks in Liaison with Infantry," 13 July 1934, USNA RG165 2015-1223/7 (hereafter D Tank Memorandum), 3 note.

29. See Fuller, "Aix," USNA RG165 2015-1223/3; Horace H. Fuller, "French Maneuvers in Normandie, 24 September 1937, USNA RG165 2015-1237/1; for the 1913 regulations, see Jean Delmas, "Aperçu des méthodes," *Bulletin trimestriel de l'association des amis de l'École Supérieure de Guerre* 57 (January–April 1973): 44.

30. Sumner Waite, "Armament and Equipment—Organization. Tanks," 23 September 1936 (G-2 22,804-W), USNA RG165 2015-1223/1.

31. 3/EMA, "Note au sujet des observations faites à la suite de l'exercise de cadres de la division cuirassée," 1 July 1937, SHAT 7N3421.

32. Julian F. R. Martin, "Étude comparative des engins blindés de combat en service dans les armées française et allemande le 2 septembre 1939, 10 June 1941, Riom deposition, SHAT 1K224/5. For the comparative simplicity and reliability of German radio sets, see U.S. War Department, *Handbook on German Military Forces* (Washington, D.C., 1945), 434–435. For communications in a representative French exercise, see Charles Delestraint, "Execution de l'attaque dans la zone du regiment du centre: Exposé des faits et enseignements généraux," 4, SHAT 9N157/3. For a history of French radio communications, see Gen. Gilson, "L'évolution des matériels," *RHA* (1967).

33. The Sixteenth Chasseur Battalion of the Third DCR, for example, had no radios to links its tanks, artillery, and infantry (Pierre Hoff, *Programmes d'armament de 1919 à 1939* [Vincennes, 1972], 430). The sets provided to the Seventeenth RA worked so badly that its commander depended on mounted messengers to maintain contact with the unit 13km away (François Valentin, "Souvenirs des années 38–39–40 dans les Ardennes," in Maurice Vaisse, ed., *Ardennes 1940* [Paris, 1991], 95). Only one-fifth of the R-35 light tanks had radios (Paul Huard, *Colonel de Gaulle et ses blindés: Laon [15–20 mai 1940]* [Paris, 1980], 37).

34. "The tactical tendencies of the French Army" (extracts of Edmund Ironside's report and notes by three other British officers who attended Cycle d'information pour Généraux et Colonels at Versailles November–December 1927), War Office, MIS, June 1928, 72.

35. Gilman C. Mudgett, "Tour of Duty with the 11e Escadron d'Auto-Mitrailleuses de Cavalerie at Orleans, Loiret, France," 31 August 1932 USNA 2015-1128/1.

36. Richard G. Tindall, "Period of Duty with the French Army," 12 October 1933, 24 (G-2 19, 791-W), USNA RG165 2015-1161/1, 24.

37. For the proscription of *batailles de rencontre* see *IGU* 1936, 75.

38. Mudgett, "11e Escadron," USNA RG165 2015-1128/1, 29.

39. War Office, MIS, June 1928, 73; War Office, MIS, November 1934, "Report of Manoeuvres Carried Out by the 15th Division from 20th to 22nd August 1934," 36.

40. The true balance was first revealed by Adolphe Goutard, *1940: La guerre des occasions perdues* (Paris, 1956), and receives detailed analysis in R. H. S. Stolfi, "Reality and Myth: French and German Preparations for War, 1933–1940" (Ph.D. dissertation, Stanford University, 1966), whose key findings are published in Stolfi, "Equipment for Victory in France in 1940," *History* 55 (1970): 1–20. Stolfi reports that France produced 61,645 tons of tanks prior to 10 May 1940 against a German and Czech total of 36,650 tons and that the French had a numerical advantage in every class of tank (Stolfi, "Equipment for Victory," 9).

41. For a discussion of financial considerations, see Robert Frankenstein, *Le Prix du réarmament français, 1935–39* (Paris, 1982).

42. For a list of writings on the subject, see François-André Paoli, *'Armée française*, 4 vols. (Paris: 1969–1971), 3:188.

43. Documents in SHAT 1N93/1.

44. Maxime Weygand, "Maneouvres de Lorraine," SHAT 7N4023/9; documents in SHAT 1K161/7 and 1N93/5. The U.S. military attaché reported that the organizers of the Lorraine maneuvers limited the quantity of fuel available to the participants in order to create realistic problems for the supply officers (Robert L. Walsh, "Air Maneuvers in Lorraine," 13 September 1930 [G-2 16,639-W], USNA RG165 2015-1060/7).

45. Documents in SHAT 9N162/1. Eventually light tanks were organized in five-tank and heavy tanks in three-tank sections.

46. Pol-Maurice Velpry, "Infanterie et chars de combat," *RMF* 25 (1927): 305–328. As Inspector General of Tanks in 1936, General Velpry would fight for armored divisions formed largely of medium tanks, Henry Dutailly, *Problèmes de l'armée* (Paris, 1980), 153. For an example of his analysis, see Velpry, "Les Grandes Unités mécaniques," September 1936, SHAT 7N3421.

47. Debeney, "Instruction générale sur la manoeuvre de Mailly," SHAT 7N4023/11; Maurin, "Rapport sur la Manoeuvre de Mailly," SHAT 1N93/5.

48. Maurin, "Rapport," 155–157.

49. Paoli, *L'Armée française*, 3:189.

50. Ibid., 3:191–192.

51. War Office, MIS, October 1928, 257. If reservists proved to be poor drivers, the previous year's Lorraine maneuvers had shown the conscripts to be even worse

while "the little Annamites hardly seemed capable of controlling lorries on steep hill roads" (263).

52. T. Bentley Mott, "Cavalry Training," 4 June 1929 (G-2 15,112-W), USNA RG165 2015-827/17.

53. Harold R. Winton, *To Change an Army* (Lawrence, KS, 1988), 33.

54. A phrase attributed by the French to General von Seeckt, EMA note 21 January 1928, SHAT 1N30/1.

55. Ord, "Lorraine Maneuvers," USNA RG165 2015-1060/10. In a 1935 map exercise, General Robert Altmeyer's motorized formations had to yield the field to mounted elements able to operate without gasoline (draft letter, Altmeyer to minister of war, 22 June 1935," SHAT, Fonds Altmayer, 1K161, carton 5).

56. Paoli, *L'Armée française,* 3:192. In 1935 Weygand advised the War Ministry to limit the extent of motorization in order to reduce dependence on imported fuel and to protect France's equine stocks (Weygand to minister of war, No.151/S, 11 January 1935, SHAT 1N35/1).

57. Financial constraints stretched the relatively small-scale cavalry mechanization ordered in 1930 over four years, while the cost of a completely motorized army was estimated at the end of 1931 to be 1,126 million francs (Paoli, *L'Armée française,* 4:78–79).

58. Not everyone saw disadvantages in mixing various kinds of units. General Brécard proposed that cavalry units ought to contain mounted and mechanized units whose strengths would complement one another and emphasized France's lack of petrol as an argument against complete mechanization (see "The Motorization of Cavalry," 29 June 1933 [G-2 19,477-W], 23, USNA RG165 2015-827).

59. See Chapter 4.

60. Chauvineau, *Une invasion,* quoted in Donald J. Harvey, "French Concepts of Military Strategy (1919–1939)" (Ph.D. dissertation, Columbia University, 1953), 166.

61. These concerns are skeptically reported in Paoli, *L'Armée française,* 4:78.

62. "Lettre du Général Billotte au CEMGA et étude jointe," 12 June 1938, in Dutailly, *Problèmes de l'armée,* 144.

63. The figure appears in Marie-Eugène Debeney, *La guerre et les hommes: Reflexions d'après-guerre* (Paris, 1937), 71.

64. "Remarques du Général Gamelin sur l'emploi des divisions d'infanterie motorisée," Dossier CSG study session October 1936, 3, SHAT 1N36/4.

65. The staff proposed instead the motorization of the Tenth DI, held back to maintain order in Paris, and that of the Thirteenth DI at Besançon ("Note au sujet de la motorisation de trois divisions nouvelles," 10 February 1937, SHAT 7N3421).

66. See, for example, Gamelin to Carence, 24 April 1933, SHAT 1N65/11; Gamelin to Duffieux, 24 April 1933, SHAT 1N65/8; "Notice provisoire sur l'emploi des chars D en liaison avec l'infanterie," 13 July 1934, USNA RG165 2015-1223/7; R. Martin, "Conférence du Général Martin au Centre des Hautes Etudes Militaires le 17 Janvier 1936 sur l'emploi des chars," SHAT 9N157/2.

67. By a decree of 4 July 1930 (Paoli, *L'Armée française,* 4:78).

68. The early confusion of nomenclature is demonstrated by a general staff study entitled, "Note pour le Général Chef d'Etat-Major Général de l'Armée relative

à l'organisation d'une division légère *motorisée,"* 26 October 1933, whose opening section deals with "L'organisation d'une division légère *mécanisée"* (Paoli, *L'Armée française* 4:80; author's emphasis). A decree of 30 May 1933 described one brigade of the Fourth Cavalry (the future First Light Mechanized) Division as "mechanized" and the other as "motorized." The "mechanized" brigade contained wheeled AMDs and motorcycles as well as a regiment of tracked AMCs and AMRs while the "motorized" brigade of AMRs and dragoons was wholly tracked. Thus the distinction was not between roadbound and all-terrain vehicles but between a unit whose combat power rested in its armored fighting vehicles and a mechanized infantry unit. As late as 1937, Debeney still complained of the confusion between the two terms (*La guerre et les hommes,* 73).

    69. The Citroen-Kergresse AMC hardly qualified as a armored vehicle, but the 14.5-ton Renault AMC 1935 was a light tank.

    70. Weygand, "Note," in Paoli, *L'Armée française,* 4:83.

    71. The Division Morocain ought to have been the Division Infanterie Morocain, but the Division Infanterie Motorisé got there first (Gamelin, *Servir,* 2:261; Jeffrey J. Clarke, "Military Technology in Republican France" [Ph.D. dissertation, Duke University, 1969], 117). "Légèrté," wrote General Debeney, was an important asset of the DLM and was to be assured by minimizing both the number of vehicle models assigned to the unit and size of its infantry component (*La guerre et les hommes,* 75).

    72. See, for example, Alistair Horne, *The French Army and Politics, 1870–1970* (London, 1984), 56. For the Panzer divisions, see Richard L. DiNardo, "Germany's Panzer Arm: Anatomy and performance" (Ph.D. dissertation, City University of New York, 1988), 110–114. Dutailly exaggerates the German numerical advantage, giving the DLM 132 tanks and 132 AMRs against the Panzer division's 448 tanks and 44 armored cars (Dutailly, *Problèmes de larmée,* 318–319). Horne says that each Panzer division had either 218 or 276 tanks against the DLM's 174 (Alaistair Horne, *To Lose a Battle* [Harmondsworth, Eng., 1969], 12–15). Stolfi puts the DLM's complement of tanks and AMRs at 240 and argues for the overall superiority of the French machines (Stolfi, "Equipment for Victory"). Harvey ("French Concepts of Military Strategy," 157) claims that the DLM had no tanks at all, but, by his definition, neither did the first Panzer divisions.

    73. The AMC 35 (Renault ACGI Light Tank) weighed 14.5 tons, carried a 47mm (25mm in one version) gun and a 7.5mm coaxial machine gun, had 25mm of armor, and traveled at a top speed of 40 kilometers per hour. Weygand admitted that the AMC was obsolete even at the moment of production (Hoff, *Programmes d'armament,* 277), and a French expert deemed it inadequate in speed, protection, and armament (James A. Lester, "Maneuvers, Field Exercises, Reviews, and Inspections: French Maneuvers at Mailley-le-Camp," 28 October 1935 [G-2 21,950-2], USNA RG165 2015-1195/4).

    74. With 13mm of armor and a machine gun or 25mm gun, the 6.5 ton 1933 and 1935 Renault AMRs were very light tanks masquerading as armored cars. In 1940, 316 AMRs and 98 AMCs were in service (Martin, "Etude comparative," SHAT 1K224/5).

    75. Even in 1936 a lecturer at the ESG admitted that the DLM was a vulnerable

formation and might not be able to protect itself (War Office, MIS, July 1936, 109–110).

76. "Le canon et le char," *Action Française*, 25 July 1934, 2, written in reply to André Pironneau, *Echo de Paris*, 7 July 1934. For a more optimistic description of armored warfare by an *Action Française* journalist, see H. de Trezne, "Canon, char, et cavalrie: Le canon, trait de lumière," in which tanks are praised as the weapons of bold risk takers rather than as calculating "tacticians à lorgnons et à comptes-goutees."

77. For the DLM's partnership with the motorized infantry see Weygand, "Note pour le Général Chef d'Etat-Major Général de l'Armée relative à l'organisation d'une division légère motorisée," 26 October 1933, quoted in Paoli, *L'Armée française*, 4:80–83, and War Office, MIS, July 1936, 109–110.

78. Maxime Weygand, *Mémoires*, 3 vols. (Paris, 1957), 2:352.

79. See Perré, "La refont de la réglementation relative aux chars de combat," *RI* 75 (November 1929): 666, for the adequacy of the FT.

80. With a maximum *road* speed of 4.8 miles per hour and a range of twenty-five to thirty miles, the FT was useful only for infantry support (Doughty, *Seeds of Disaster*, 117. The father of the French tank, General Estienne, thought so little of the FT that he recommended that they be reequipped with 25mm or 30mm cannons and distributed among infantry divisions for employment as stationary anti-tank weapons (Hoff, *Programmes d'armament*, 138–139).

81. See Clarke, "Military Technology," 28; Heinz Guderian, *Die Panzertruppen*, 2d ed. (Berlin, 1938), 14; *Evénements, Annexes*, 1:249 (Weygand testimony); Debeney, "Les exigences da la guerre de matériel," *RDM* 8:12 (March–April 1933): 276; War Office, MIS, August 1934, 67; Gen. T. Delelain, "Etude sur l'emploi des chars moderns," 20 November 1931," SHAT 9N157/2; Hoff, *Programmes d'armament*, 318–319.

82. Eric Morris et al., *Weapons and Warfare of the 20th Century* (London, 1980), 130–131; Clarke, "Military Technology," 22–22. Estienne served as Inspector of Tanks from the establishment of the Inspectorate in 1921 until his retirement in November 1927, after which he remained a member of the infantry department's tank technical section (Steven Ross, "French Net Assessment," in Williamson Murray and Allen R. Millet, eds., *Calculations* [New York, 1992], 151).

83. Clarke, "Military Technology," 29. Gen. Guderian took the 2-C to be characteristic of interwar French thinking (Guderian, *Panzertruppen*, 14), but the 2-C, slow, thinly armored, and mechanically unreliable, was moribund long before its June 1934 cancellation.

84. In a 1920 speech Estienne predicted a breakthrough force of rupture tanks weighing 50 or 100 tons, supported by armored infantry and artillery, followed up by exploitation tanks (Clarke, "Military Technology," 57).

85. Jean-Baptiste Estienne, "Résumé de mes convictions sur la politique des chars de combat exposée hier au Générale Corap," 20 October 1933, SHAT 9N157/2.

86. For the official program, see Paoli, *L'Armée française*, 3:163; for Estienne's activities, see Clarke, "Military Technology," 77–79.

87. The thirty-two ton B1bis, the first four of which appeared in May 1937, car-

ried a crew of four protected by 60mm of armor plate and was armed with a hull-mounted 75mm gun and, in the turret, a 47mm antitank gun and a 7.5mm coaxial machine gun. Advanced design features included self-sealing petrol tanks, a good lubrication system, fireproof bulkheads, a gyroscopic compass, an electric compass, and an escape hatch for empty shell cases (Peter Chamberlain and Chris Ellis, *Pictorial History of Tanks of the World 1915–45* [Harrisburg, PA, 1972]). A German officer called the tank "the best in the world just as the original French 75mm surpassed all others of its type" (F. G. Beaumont-Nesbitt, "The Present Military Situation," 5 July 1937, PRO FO371 C5048/122/17, 13). Wartime praise for the B1bis appears in Horace H. Fuller, "Armaments and Equipment—Organizational—Standard. French tanks—47mm long anti-tank gun," 5 June 1940 (G-2 25,747-W), USNA RG165 2281-C-156/6, and Gervais W. Trichel, "Armament and Equipment—Organizational, Standard. Assembly of B1-bis and S.O.M.U.A. Tanks," 6 June 1940 (G-2 25,755-W), USNA RG165 2281-C-162/2.

88. Clarke, "Military Technology," 99. Originally part of the artillery, tanks were placed under the control of the Direction de l'Infanterie on 28 March 1928 and a Section des Chars de Combat was created within the infantry branch on 9 August 1929 (Paoli, *L'Armée française,* 3:164).

89. Minutes of meeting of 19 March 1926, quoted in Paoli, *L'Armée française,* 3:163; Doughty, *Seeds of Disaster,* 141.

90. Paoli, *L'Armée française,* 3:164.

91. Cost was probably the biggest deterrent to a heavy tank program, but also to be considered was the possibility that disarmament talks might limit tank tonnage.

92. For Pétain's response to Doumergue, see Doughty, *Seeds of Disaster,* 141. Journalists in the late 1930s believed that France had a heavy tank that no one had seen because it was too massive to be permitted on the Paris streets for the Bastille Day parade (Alexander Werth, *The Twilight of France, 1933–1940* [London, 1942], 201, quoted in Clarke, "Military Technology," 81).

93. Tank production was shifted from the artillery to a new Direction des fabrications d'armement by a decree of 29 April 1933 (Gamelin, *Servir,* 2:113).

94. For radios, see Gilson, "L'évolution des matériels," 61; "D Tank Memorandum," 21.

95. Hoff, *Programmes d'armament,* 326.

96. Velpry, memo to Gen. Dufieux, of 14 May 1936, quoted in *Evénements, Annexes,* 4:887 (Dufieux testimony).

97. Doughty, *Seeds of Disaster,* 143.

98. Delelain, SHAT 9N157/2. The army took delivery of the first 10 D1s in 1931, 70 more in 1932, 30 in 1933, and 50 in 1934 (Hoff, *Programmes d'armament,* 329).

99. Weygand, *Memoires,* 2:407.

100. *Evénements, Annexes* 4:1056–1058 (Dufieux testimony).

101. Gamelin, *Servir,* 1:269, 2:82–83. Pétain offered a more charitable assessment of the D1 in a note of 25 July 1934, quoted in Hoff, *Programmes d'armament,* 277.

102. Charles Delestraint, "Propriétés techniques et tactique elementaire du chars D1," 24 April 1933, SHAT 9N157.

103. The infantry's quiescence up to this date can be deduced from Renault's manifest surprise (described in Clark, "Military Technology," 147) at the news that the D tank program was to be abandoned in favor of the development of a light tank. The CSG adopted the D2 on 24 March 1934.

104. Created for the new DLMs, cavalry tanks, like naval cruisers, were meant to outfight whatever they could not outrun and to outrun whatever they could not outfight. Doughty calls the SOMUA, a 20–ton machine armed with a 47mm gun and a machine gun and capable of 45 kilometers per hour, the best tank on the battlefield in 1940 (Doughty, *Seeds of Disaster,* 170).

105. *PV,* CSG, 23 May 1934, SHAT 1N34/1; Martin S. Alexander, *The Republic in Danger* (Cambridge, 1992), 123.

106. Gamelin, *Servir,* 2:290–291.

107. Harvey, "French Concepts of Military Strategy," 154.

108. Instruction sur l'emploi des chars de combat, 1929, 12, quoted in Doughty, *Seeds of Disaster,* 142.

109. "Cycle d'information pour Généraux et Colonels at Versailles November–December 1927," War Office, MIS, June 1928, 68.

110. Keeping even World War I tanks at infantry pace was a problem (Clarke, "Military Technology," 25).

111. For the importance of harnessing the tank to the methodical battles, see R. Martin (détachement d'expériences d'emploi d'engins blindés), "Rapport du Colonel commandant le détachement, camp de Coëtquiden," 23 July 1922, 31, 33, 37, SHAT 9N164; Doughty, *Seeds of Disaster,* 145–146 and 211 n.28; D Tank Memorandum, 4. For the number of guns required, see Faris Russell Kirkland, "French Officer Corps and the Fall of France" (Ph.D. dissertation, University of Pennsylvania, 1982), 177. Although tanks did not reduce the number of artillery tubes required, they might economize on shells by providing accurate close fire support and increasing the overall tempo of the battle (Sumner Waite, "The Tactical Employment of Divisional Artillery in Support of Tank action," 13 May 1938 [G-2 24,266-W] 2, USNA RG165 2015-1245/2).

112. John Sloan Brown, *Draftee Division: The 88th Infantry Division in World War II* (Lexington, KY, 1986), 99–100. For an American soldier's skepticism about the value of machines that drew artillery fire and were hard to communicate with, see David Kenyon Webster, *Parachute Infantry* (Baton Rouge and London, 1994), 68.

113. Delestraint, SHAT 9N157/3; See also Dutailly, *Problèmes de l'armée,* 412–413.

114. See Gen. Cabotte, "Note," 28 April 1933, SHAT 9N157/3, and D Tank Memorandum, 10.

115. For "manoeuvres plus or moins abracadabrantes," see Pierre [?], *Evénements, Annexes,* 5:1184 (Bruneau testimony). The tank's role in the methodical battle is set out in *IGU* 1936, 83.

116. Adolphe Goutard, "La bataille pour les divisions cuirassées," *Revue de Paris* 66 (1959): 29.

117. The light infantry tanks that began to replace the FT in 1935 relied on flags for communication with one another and with the infantry, Martin, "Etude comparative," SHAT 1K224/5. A set designed for service within light tank battalions, the

ER 54, was not ready in 1940 (Dutailly, *Problèmes de l'armée,* 413). For some of the problems with the light tank radio program, see Gilson, "L'évolution des matériels," 70.

118. See Martin's testimony at Riom, 31 March 1942, SHAT 1K224/2, 1441. The British manual *Mechanised and Armoured Formations* took the same position in insisting that "direct frontal assault on prepared positions will be costly unless supported by adequate covering fire" (Winton, *To Change an Army,* 113).

119. For Mailly, see War Office, MIS, September 1929, 210; the "umpire's pencil" in Captains Pierre Chazal-Martin and Suire, "Etude mathématique de la puissance des armes anti-chars," *RI* (July–September 1939): 255.

120. War Office, MIS, October 1928, 262.

121. Surely it was not a cavalryman's assumption that tanks shared horses' aversion to stepping on living bodies.

122. Frank P. Lahm, "Artillery Support of an Infantry Attack with Tanks," 25 October 1933 (G-2 19,820-W), USNA RG165 2015-1164/1; Estienne, "Convictions," SHAT 9N157/2.

123. See Sumner Waite, "Tank Warfare," 25 May 1937 (G-2 23,440), USNA RG165 2281-C-156/3. Ralph K. Smith confirms growing French confidence in the effectiveness of antitank defense, "especially in the light of reports from the Spanish combats" ("French Tactical Doctrine, Organization, and Material," [G-2 23,691-W], USNA RG165 2277-C-193/2). According to F. O. Miksche, *Blitzkrieg* (London, 1941), 37, European general staffs saw the battle of Guadalajara as a cautionary example of the vulnerability of motorized forces.

124. Perré, "Autre réflexions sur la défense contre les chars," *RI* (January–June 1934): 284.

125. Julien F. R. Martin, "Conférence," SHAT 9N157/2.

126. Henry Martin, "Réflexions sur la défense contre les chars," *RI* 84 (January–June 1934): 275.

127. Martin's lecture noted that current German production tank weighed a mere seven tons ("Conference," 22). The Puteaux could penetrate 15mm of armor plate, the thickness of the PzKpfw II's plate, at 400m, and the prototype PzKpfw III, whose armor was 30mm thick, was tested only in 1937 (Stolfi, "Equipment for Victory," 15).

128. War Office, MIS, August 1934, 67–68.

129. See René R. Studler, "Armament and Equipment—Organizational Standard," 18 September 1938 (G-2 24,525-W), USNA RG165 2100-106/4; Stolfi, "Equipment for Victory," 17; Sumner Waite, "Anti-Tank Defense," USNA RG165 2015-1126/2. The penetrating power of the French 47mm gun was demonstrated against a SOMUA tank in a costly friendly fire incident (Trichel, "Armament and Equipment," USNA RG165 2281-C-162/2). The 47mm 1937 *biflèche,* of which 1,280 had been delivered by June 1940, was superseded in 1939 by the more complicated 47mm 1939 *triflèche.* The existence of effective antitank artillery was of little use to those units, especially the B reserve divisions, stuck with insufficient numbers or obsolete models. The Tenth Corps Fifty-fifth and Seventy-first DIs had 9 25mm antitank guns instead of 104 and 75mm's rather than the regulation 47mm's (Jeffrey A. Gunsberg, *Divided and Conquered* [Westport, CT, 1979], 100).

130. Harvey H. Smith, "Report of Tour of Duty with 501st Tank Regiment Tours—France," 15 August–15 November (G-2 22,161-W) USNA RG165 2015-1213/1.

131. Gamelin, *PV,* CSG 23 May 1934, 10, SHAT 1N34/1; Sumner Waite, "Organizational and Unit Training," 15 March 1937 (G-2 23,273-W), USNA RG165 2015-1179/4, 3.

132. Horace H. Fuller, "Armament and Equipment—Organization. Tanks," 1 June 1937 (G-2 23,451-W), USNA RG165 2281-C-156/4.

133. Albert Seaton, *The Russo-German War 1941–1945* (Novato, CA, 1990), 86.

134. Frank P. Lahm, "Reflexions on the Combat of Modern Tanks," 22 November 1933 (G-2 19,913-W), USNA RG165 2015-1164/2, 5.

135. Sumner Waite, "Service Firing with the Hotchkiss 25mm Anti-tank Gun and with a 75mm Anti-tank Battery," 13 October 1937 (G-2 23,786-W), 3, USNA RG165 2015-1239/1.

136. Geoffrey Perret, *There's a War to be Won: The United States Army in World War II* (New York, 1991), 101.

137. S. J. Lewis, *Forgotten Legions: German Infantry Policy 1918–1941* (New York, 1985), 53.

138. For the reaction to de Gaulle, see B. H. Liddell Hart, *The German Generals Talk* (New York, 1948), 91; on German doctrine, see Matthew Cooper, *The German Army 1933–1945* (London, 1978), 150–154, and Raymond Sereau, "L'évolution de l'arme blindée en allemagne de 1935 à 1945 vue par un ancien officer de la Wehrmacht," *RHA* 6 (1950): 67–76.

139. See Fuller, "French Maneuvers in Normandie," USNA RG165 2015-1237/1.

140. See Billotte's report in SHAT 1N68/8 and a conversation between Billotte and British military attaché Colonel F. Beaumont-Nesbitt, quoted in Williamson Murray, *The Change in the European Balance of Power 1938–1939* (Princeton, 1984), 100. Billotte seems less concerned about the fact that, as of 1 August 1938, only 20,000 of the 210,000, antitank mines ordered had reached the army (Hoff, *Programmes d'armament,* 425).

141. Captain Soury, "Le Combat contre les engins cuirassés par le major von Schell de l'Etat-Major général de la Wehrmacht," *RI* 46 (July 1937): 98–99.

142. Ibid., 102.

143. Ibid., 118. But not all Frenchman believed that their highly visible and relatively immobile 75s would be an asset in antitank warfare (Capt. Brouillard, "Cas concrets de défense contre les chars," *RI* 90 [January–June 1937]: 883.

144. French doctrine considered 60–80 tanks per kilometer to be a large-scale attack (Ralph K. Smith, "French Tactical Doctrine," USNA RG165 2277-C-193/2).

145. Soury, "Combat contre les engins cuirassés," 136.

146. Brouillard, "Cas concrets," 884. Brouillard appears to assume a twelve-kilometer-per-hour advance. A French study that is somewhat less favorable to the antitank gun postulated a rate of fire of twelve rounds per minute for 37mm antitank gun and six rounds per minute for the 75mm used in an antitank role (Chazal-Martin and Suire, "Etude mathématique," 269).

147. Brouillard, "Cas concrets," 882.

148. Touchon, Riom Deposition, 27 Mai 1941, SHAT 1K224/5.

149. Sumner Waite, "Organizational and Unit Training," USNA RG165 2015-1179/4, 2.

150. Of the German tanks in September 1939, 90 percent were PzKpfw Is and IIs (Cooper, *German Army,* 155).

151. *PV,* CSG study session, 14 October 1936, 13, SHAT 1N36. See also "Le problème Militaire Français," 1 June 1936, SHAT 7N3697, quoted in Dutailly, *Problèmes d'armament,* 326; C/EMA note no. 366 of 8 October 1936, quoted in 2/EMA "Avis du 3e Bureau sur 'L'étude de la division cuirassée,'" 4 February 1937, SHAT 7N3421; "Note relative aux possibilités de création de 2 D.CR.," 23 July 1936, SHAT 7N2293/3, quoted in Dutailly, *Problèmes de l'armée,* 155.

152. Dutailly, *Problèmes de l'armée,* 328. The proposed division had no organic infantry but would be assigned, depending on whether the mission was *couverture* or battle, either one or two light infantry brigades (Dutailly, *Problèmes de l'armée,* 333–334).

153. Ibid., 336.

154. Héring was the sort of man picked to command the Blue (German) forces in double-action wargames, and it has been suggested that he was responsible for Blue's aggressive attack in CSG's 1937–1938 exercise (Jean Delmas, "Les exercises du Conseil Superieure de la Guerre 1936–1937 et 1937–1938," *RHA* 4 [1979]: 29–56). Gamelin's consistent ability to produce unanimous votes in the council meant that "the Council's decisions concerning military doctrine and Army organization reflected the average view of the oldest generals" (Paul Marie de la Gorce, *The French Army,* trans. Kenneth Douglas [New York, 1963], 294.

155. de la Gorce, *French Army,* 294.

156. For the retarding effect on French armor development of Charles de Gaulle's insistence that an armored force required professional troops, see Brian Bond and Martin Alexander, "Liddell Hart and de Gaulle: The Doctrines of Limited Liability and Mobile Defense," in Peter Paret, ed., *Makers of Modern Strategy from Machiavelli to the Nuclear Age* (Princeton, 1986), 615–617.

157. The remark to the CSG is from Doughty, *Seeds of Disaster,* 163, and the 1939 comment is from Goutard, "La bataille pour les divisions cuirassées," 30–31.

158. Gamelin opposed including such ancillary units as a reconnaissance group in the armored division (*PV,* CSG study session, 14 October 1936, SHAT 1N36).

159. Six different opinions on the use of armor appear in EMA, "Note au sujet des divisions nouvelles," November 1936, SHAT 1N36/4.

160. Dutailly, *Problèmes de l'armée,* 402.

161. 3/EMA, "Note au sujet des observations faites à la suite de l'exercise de cadres de la division cuirassée," 1 July 1937, SHAT 7N3421.

162. Dutailly, *Problèmes de l'armée,* 156.

163. Gamelin, *Servir,* 2:290. The proposed experiments would have involved the armored division's cooperation with an infantry division and with a DLM ("Note au sujet de la Division Cuirassée à expérimenter en 1937," 28 November 1936, SHAT 1N36/4). Gamelin pursued cadre map and terrain exercises with notional armored divisions (Charles Delestraint, "Programme des exercices de chars modernes à Sissione 1–30 April 1937," SHAT 7N4014/3).

164. Figures from Hoff, *Programmes d'armament,* 329.

165. Arguing for the impossibility of creating a medium tank from scratch in 1938, Doughty, however, treats the B tank as an unfortunate diversion rather than a happy accident (*Seeds of Disaster,* 163).

166. The "Notice provisoire sur l'emploi des chars modernes," 15 December 1937, SHAT 9N157/1.

167. After the introduction of the versatile D and B tanks, the official distinction between accompaniment and maneuver tanks was one of mission rather than technical characteristics (Gamelin, "Resumé," SHAT 7N421).

168. "Rapport de présentation au CSG de la question de la constitution de G.U.'s cuirassées," dossier for CSG meeting 15 December 1937, SHAT 1N37 (original emphasis).

169. de la Gorce, *French Army,* 273. "Note provisoire sur la grande unité cuirassée," 4 June 1938, SHAT 9N3455/3, stressed the integration of the future armored division with other units.

170. Doughty, *Seeds of Disaster,* 165; Dutailly, *Problèmes de l'armée,* 156–157. Bruneau eventually got his armored command, that of the First Armored Division, in 1940.

171. Dutailly, *Problèmes de l'armée,* 158, Gamelin, *Servir,* 2:289. The new organization reduced the 198 tanks required to equip a six-battalion armored division by two-thirds to 66.

172. Dutailly, *Problèmes de l'armée,* 158; EMA, "Divisions nouvelles," SHAT 1N36/4. In his testimony at Riom on 19 March 1942, Héring complained bitterly that his arguments for independent armored divisions convinced "only one disciple and that was General von Brauchitsch" (Pierre Cot, *Le procès de la République,* 2 vols. [New York, 1944], 2:74). Blum's testimony that only Héring had pushed for armored divisions earned a "?" in the margin from Gamelin, who clearly wished to share the status of unheeded prophet. Doughty praises Héring as one "who at least partially understood the value of tanks" (*Seeds of Disaster,* 181).

173. Gamelin's "Secret Note No.4617 on the Employment of Large Armored Units" is described in two reports by U.S. assistant military attaché Sumner Waite: "Tactical Doctrine—Theories of Mechanization and Motorization: Organization, Characteristics, and Employment of Large Armored Units," 20 December 1939 (G-2 25,406-W), USNA RG165 2015-1223/14, and "Tactical Doctrines—Theories of Mechanization and Motorization: French and German Armored Units," 8 August 1939 (G-2 25,173-W), USNA RG165 2015-1223/12.

174. For the delays produced for the Third DCR by the lack of engineering troops to clear roads during the critical fighting south of Sedan, see Doughty, *Breaking Point,* 287.

175. The CSG authorized a second DLM on 29 April 1936, but the SOMUA tanks were available only in 1938. The Third DLM was formed in 1939, and the three remaining cavalry divisions were transformed into five new light cavalry divisions (DLC), each with one horse-mounted brigade, one mechanized brigade, one artillery regiment, one divisional antitank battery, and ancillary troops. Each mechanized brigade contained an armored regiment (15 AMDs, 22 AMRs, and 14 H-35s) and a mo-

torized infantry regiment (Gunsberg, *Divided and Conquered,* 103; Robert A. Doughty, *The Breaking Point* [Hamden, CT, 1990], 80–81).

176. Doughty, *Seeds of Disaster,* 174. Of the year 1937 as a whole, Gamelin announced that he doubted that "the army had ever known such a period of activity" (Gamelin, *Servir,* 2:291).

177. The first two armored divisions were created in January 1940, a third in March 1940, and Charles de Gaulle's Fourth DCR in May 1940. The Fourth DCR was an improvised collection of two untrained battalions of B tanks, two battalions of R-35 infantry tanks, a chasseur battalion, and, in lieu of the 105mm howitzers in the normal establishment, two untrained 75mm artillery groups (U.S. Military Attaché, London, "Operations of French armored Divisions," 3 February 1941 [G-2 42284], USNA RG165 2015-1271/27).

178. Waite, "Employment of Large Armored Units," USNA RG165 2015-1223/ 14.

179. Many, however, paid no attention whatsoever; not one of the copies of a French translation of Guderian's *Achtung Panzer* distributed to French garrison libraries had had its pages cut as of the winter of 1937–1938 (Anthony Adamthwaite, *France and the Coming of the Second World War, 1936–1939* [London, 1977], 166).

180. Daladier admitted that massed tanks might be used—on the flat plains of eastern Europe (Daladier, *PV,* Sen. Army Comm., 17 December 1936).

181. Waite, "French and German Armored Units," USNA RG165 2015-1223/12, 3; for French emphasis on speed, power, and mass, see note no.4617, "Employment of Large Armored Units," 18 December 1938. Similarities between two French and German doctrines are also emphasized in Major Gervaise, "Tactique des engins blindés," *RI* 91 (July–December 1937): 1024–1051.

182. The organic reconnaissance element in Charles de Gaulle's notional armored division made it closer to Guderian's model, see U.S. military attaché, London, "Operations," USNA RG165 2015-1271/27.

183. Waite, "French and German Armored Units," 5.

184. Ibid., 1.

185. Ibid.

186. Hoff, *Programmes d'armament,* 303.

187. "Renseignements des manoeuvres allemandes en 1935 (Extracts from 2/ EMA Note No.184/A1 25 July 1936)," 3 (annex to Héring, "Note: Projet d'instruction provisoire sur l'emploi tactique des grandes unités: observation du Général Héring," 25 July 1936), SHAT 7N4001.

188. René Cailloux, "Les enseignements de la guerre d'Espagne," *RI* 92 (January–June 1938): 684.

189. Col. Fraser, telegram 17 September 1938, PRO FO371 C10082/36/17.

190. Doughty, *Seeds of Disaster,* 160.

191. See Alexander, *Republic in Danger,* 346–347. *Le Temps,* 12 November 1939, reported that General Reinhardt's tanks were forced to withdraw before the barricades established by the capital's defenders (Sumner Waite, "Limitations of the Armored Division," 22 November 1939 [G-2 25,350-W], USNA RG165 2015-1223/ 13).

192. Julien Dufieux, *Candide* (4 October 1939), quoted in Goutard, "La bataille pour les divisions cuirassées," 34.

193. Robert Felsenhardt, *1939–1940 avec le 18ᵉ Corps d'Armée* (Paris, 1973), 53.

194. Waite, "Employment of Large Armored Units," USNA RG165 2015-1223/14.

195. Jeffrey A. Gunsberg, "The Battle of the Belgian Plain, 12–14 May 1940: The First Great Tank Battle," *Journal of Military History* 56 (1992): 207–244. Gunsberg reckons that Prioux lost between 75 and 98 Hotchkiss tanks and 30 out of 87 SOMUAs while the Germans, who could recover crippled and broken-down machines, suffered 49 tanks destroyed and about 110 temporarily out of action (241–242).

196. Ibid., 243.

197. Perret, *There's a War to be Won,* 43.

198. Smith, "French Tactical Doctrine," (G-2 23,691-W), USNA RG165 2277-C-193/2. Cf. Ralph K. Smith, "Report on Methods of Instruction at the ESG, Paris," 13 July 1937 (G-2 23,635-W), USNA RG165 2277-C-193/1.

199. Beaumont-Nesbitt, "Present Military Situation" PRO FO371 C5048/122/17.

200. For the less charitable notion that the French officers who sought reassurance from their doctrine were necessarily "frightened, rejected, insecure, resentful," see Kirkland, "French Officer Corps," 235.

Conclusion

1. For Gamelin's change of strategy, see Donald W. Alexander, "Repercussions of the Breda Variant," *FHS* 8 (1974): 459–488, and Robert A. Doughty, *The Breaking Point* (Hamden, CT, 1990), 12–18.

2. The figures are in Jeffrey A. Gunsburg, *Divided and Conquered* (Westport, CT, 1979), 275. German causalities were 27,074 killed, 111,034 wounded, and 18,384 missing (Alistair Horne, *To Lose a Battle* [Harmondsworth, Eng., 1969], 649).

3. The war plan in effect at the outbreak of the war was Plan E, itself a modification of Plan Dbis (3/EMA, "Note sur les bases du plan E," 25 August 1937, in Henry Dutailly, *Problèmes de l'armée* [Paris, 1980], 353). For Plan D, see François-André Paoli, *L'armée française,* 4 vols. (Paris, 1969–1971), 4:48–49.

4. Doughty (*Breaking Point,* 325–332) emphasizes doctrinal differences, while Jeffrey A. Gunsberg ("The Battle of the Belgian Plain, 12–14 May 1940," *JMH* 56 [1992]: 240–244) treats the two armies as more evenly matched.

5. See Marc Bloch, *Strange Defeat,* trans. Gerard Hopkins (New York, 1968), 150.

6. *Evénements, Annexes,* 5:1271 (Véron testimony).

7. Philip C. F. Bankwitz, *Maximé Weygand* (Cambridge, MA, 1967), 264.

8. For French mobilization as a plot against the French working class, see Fernand Grenier, *Journal de la drôle de guerre* (Paris, 1969), passim.

9. For the French tendency to read their excellent intelligence reports for evi-

dence of German weaknesses while ignoring signs of German strength, see Eugène Carrias, *La pensée militaire française* (Sceaux, 1960), 210–211.

10. Robert Felsenhardt, *1939–1940 avec le 18ᵉ Corps d'Armée* (Paris, 1973), 53.

11. Adolphe Goutard, "La bataille pour les divisions cuirassées," *RP* 66 (1959): 27.

12. "Tactical Tendencies," War Office, MIS, June 1928, 66. The French Army had acknowledged the importance of air-artillery cooperation during World War I but proved slow to develop the necessary liaison between ground and air force (John H. Morrow, *The Great War in the Air: Military Aviation from 1909 to 1921* [Washington and London, 1993], 284).

13. R. Martin, "Conférence du Général Martin au Hautes Etudes Militaires le 17 Janvier 1936 sur l'emploi des chars," 50, SHAT 9N157/2. An instruction on the subject dated 24 January 1929 remained in force in 1934, D Tank Memorandum, 15.

14. Col. Argueyrolles, "Gouvernons vers le large," *Revue de cavalerie* 14 (1934): 487–489.

15. D Tank Memorandum, 4. An appendix refers to experiments with a radio set capable of receiving transmissions from aircraft, 21.

16. Douglas Colyer, "Report on maneuvers in the West 13–18 September 1937," PRO FO371 C6808.

17. *IGU* 1936, 83.

18. Gen. Gilson, "L'évolution des matériels," *Revue historique de l'armées* 23 (1967): 72; Faris Russell Kirkland, "The French Air Force and the Fall of France" (Ph.D. dissertation, University of Pennsylvania, 1982), 105; For the need for air-ground cooperation exercises, see Henri Laporte, "Une 'aviation d'infanterie' est-elle désirable?" *RI* (July–September, 1939): 83.

19. Sumner Waite, "Visit to the 1st Armored Division (Division Cuirassée)," 6 February 1940 (G-2 25,501-W) USNA RG165 2015-1223/15.

20. See Horace H. Fuller, "Field Exercise. Employment of Tanks in An Attack," 3 January 1939 (G-2 24,728-W), USNA RG165 2015-1223/10; Waite, "Visit to the 1st Armored Division," USNA RG165 2015-1223/15. For the seriousness with which the French Army took the training of air observers, see Ralph K. Smith, "Report on Methods of Instruction at the ESG, Paris," 13 July 1937 (G-2 23,635-W), USNA RG165 2277-C-193/1, 2.

21. PRO, FO371 6821/122/17. The statement can also be found in British Cabinet documents, see Williamson Murray, *The Change in the European Balance of Power 1938–39* (Princeton, 1984), 108 n.50.

22. Captain X, "La défense contre avions dans les unités d'infanterie," *RI* 95 (July–September 1939): 485.

23. Ibid., 506.

24. *PV,* Sen. Army Comm., 7 March 1934.

25. General Gransard's Tenth Corps, which planned to fortify the Sedan sector with 60,000 mines, was able to place only 1,200 (Gunsburg, *Divided and Conquered,* 100, 102).

26. Gordon W. Prange, *At Dawn We Slept: The Untold Story of Pearl Harbor* (Harmondsworth, Eng., 1981), 122.

27. Gaston Prételat, "Rapport sur l'exercice de Cadres d'Armée exécuté par le IIᵉ

Armée du 30 Mai au 3 Juin 1938 dans la région de SEDAN-MONTMEDY," 23 June 1938, SHAT 1N67/3. In May 1940, Von Rundstedt's Army Group A had 44 divisions, 7 of them armored and 3 motorized (Doughty, *Breaking Point,* 33). The German spearhead, Guderian's Nineteenth Panzer Corps, reached the Meuse three hours earlier than Prételat had estimated.

28. Alphonse Georges, "Exercice de Cadres de la 2ème Armée Exécuté du 30 Mai au 3 Juin 1938," 3 August 1938, SHAT 1N69/3.

29. Maxime Weygand to Chief of Staff Gamelin, 29 December 1934, SHAT 1N57/6. Reconnaissances did take place by tiny groups of officers traveling as tourists in private cars (see Pétin note, 1? February 1933, SHAT 1N65/10). In April 1933, for example, Altmeyer requested permission to take six officers with him into Belgium but, because so many military "tourists" were making the trip that year, was limited to three (SHAT 1N65/13).

30. Altmeyer, SHAT 1K161.

31. Martin S. Alexander, *Republic in Danger* (Cambridge, 1992), 233.

32. Ibid., 306.

33. 2/EMA "Obligations d'assistance mutuelle pouvant incomber à la France," 9 July 1936, 8, Daladier archives 1DA6 dossier 4/subdossier d.

34. Robert J. Young, *In Command of France* (Cambridge, MA, and London, 1978), 232.

35. Bonnet was behind the French failure to sign the political agreement upon which the military convention hinged (Alexander, *Republic in Danger,* 309). On his personal copy of Bonnet's deposition (SHAT 1K224 carton 4 dossier 1), Gamelin underlined the words from "offensive by" to "German occupation" and placed an angry exclamation mark in the margin.

36. Alexander, *Republic in Danger,* 311.

37. *PV,* CSG, 28 May 1932, 10.

38. Gamelin, *PV,* CSG 4 June 1936, 9.

39. For the reminder that the Marne was a French victory over the Germans, see Gen. Trentinian, *L'état-major en 1914* (Paris, 1927), 11.

40. Currus, "La rénovation de notre armement d'infanterie," *RI* (January–June 1939): 882.

41. Matthew Cooper, *The German Army 1933-1945* (London, 1978), 138-149.

42. André Maurois, *Why France Fell* (London, 1941), 50.

43. Weygand, "Note," 16 January 1933, quoted in Paoli, *L'Armée française,* 4:29-31.

44. Alexander, *Republic in Danger,* 95.

45. Paul Marie de la Gorce, *The French Army,* trans. Kenneth Douglas (New York, 1963), 288-289. Chief of the Imperial General Staff Field Marshal Sir Edmund Ironside noted in his diary of 24 March 1940 that "[the French] are all confident of success. . . . They say clearly that the Germans will only be beaten if their army is knocked out" (Roderick Macleod, *The Ironside Diaries* [London, 1962], 233).

46. de la Gorce, *French Army,* 293.

47. Composed of the 1st DLM, 9th and 25th DIM, 4th, 60th, 21th DI, and 68th

DI, and two independent tank battalions, 7th Army would have been a powerful reserve. See Alexander, "Repercussions of the Breda Variant," 459–488.

48. Doughty, *Breaking Point,* 16.

49. Ibid., 326.

50. Lowell M. Riley, "Major Military Operations. Visit to the French Front," 6 October 1939 (G-2 25,257-W), USNA RG165 2015-1271/4, 6.

51. Sumner Waite, "Visit to the 1st Armored Division," 6 February 1940, 7 (G-2 25,501-W), USNA RG165 2015-1223/15.

52. Sumner Waite, "Principal Foreign Policies. French Reaction Toward Czechoslovakian Question and Nazi Movement in Luxembourg—German Motorization," 14 May 1938 (G-2 24,268-W) USNA RG165 2657-C-304/2.

53. Richard G. Tindall, "Period of Duty with the French Army," 12 October 1933, 24 (G-2 19,791-W), USNA RG165 2015-1161/1.

54. Macleod, *Ironside Diaries,* 232.

55. War Office, MIS, January 1936, 111.

56. Beaumont-Nesbitt, "Report," 17 September 1936, 7, FO371 C6616/172/17.

57. War Office, MIS, April 1937, "General Survey of the French Army and French Military Policy during 1936," 232.

58. F. Beaumont-Nesbitt, "Present Military Situation," 20 December 1937, PRO FO371 C5048/122/17.

59. Ibid., PRO FO371 C8758/122/17.

60. Ibid.

61. See Chapter 3.

62. Hore-Belisha to Cabinet, 29 September 1937, PRO FO371 6821/122/17. For the suggestion that Hore-Belisha's evaluation may have been shaped by his relationship to Liddell Hart, who opposed the creation of a British armored force for offensive operations on the Continent, see Alexander, *Republic in Danger,* 273. For increasingly dismal British assessments of the French Air Force, see reports by Air Attaché Group Captain Douglas Colyer from September 1936: PRO FO371 C6774/172/17, FO371 C6436/122/17; FO371 C6808; William Strang's report on a conversation with Colyer, PRO FO371 C6790/122/17; Wing Commander Goddard, "The French Air Force: Efficiency and Readiness for War (in Comparison with the German Air Force)," 19 September 1938, PRO FO371 C10163/36/17.

63. Imperial General Staff (IGS), "Visit to French and German Manoeuvres, 1937," 15 October 1937, PRO FO371 7703/136/18. The minute is by Mr. Mallet.

64. Douglas Colyer, "Report on the French Air Force," 6 September 1937, FO371 C6436/122/17.

65. B. H. Liddell Hart, *History of the Second World War,* vol. 1 (New York, 1972), 17.

66. Telegram from Sir Eric Phipps describing a conversation with Vittorio Cerruti, 1 November 1937, PRO FO371 R7304/2143/22. But Donald C. Watt describes Cerrutti as "violently anti-Nazi and Francophile" (*How War Came* [London, 1989], 204).

67. Telegram from Sir Reginald Hoare (Bucharest), 3 December 1937, PRO FO371 R8169/2143/22.

68. Clausewitz, *On War,* 118.

69. Ibid., 120.

70. Ibid., 102.

71. For a description of a "republican synthesis" that achieved social, economic, and political stability at the price of immobility, see Stanley Hoffmann, "Paradoxes of the French Political Community," in Hoffman et al., *In Search of France* (New York, 1963), 1-21.

72. Bankwitz, *Maximé Weygand,* 223-239.

73. Ardant du Picq, quoted in ibid., 231.

74. Maurice Gamelin, *Servir,* 3 vols. (Paris, 1954-1959), 1:27-35.

75. Raised most notoriously by Paul Reynaud in the Chamber of Deputies on 15 March 1935, the distinction had been the subject of a general debate as early as 25 February 1920.

Selected Bibliography

Archival Collections

Paris

Archives National:
  Archives Edouard Daladier
  Papiers Henri Schweisguth, series 351 AP
  Commission de l'Armée de la Chambre des Députes:
    Minutes 13th Legislature, 1924–1928; 14th Legislature, 1928–1929; 15th Legislature, 1932–1936; 16th Legislature, 1936–1940.
  Commission de l'Armée du Sénat:
    Minutes 15th Legislature, 1932–1936; 16th Legislature, 1936–1940.

Vincennes

Service historique de l'Armée de terre
  Archives: Cabinet du Ministère de la Guerre, Comité Permanent de la Défense Nationale, Conseil Supérieur de la Défense Nationale, Conseil Supérieur de la Guerre, Etat-Major de l'Armée
  Personal Papers: Fonds Altmeyer, Colson, Gamelin, Georges, Picard
Service historique de la Marine
  Castex Papers

London

Public Record Office
  Foreign Office papers, series FO371

Washington, D.C.

National Archives (USNA)
  Record Group 165 (Military Intelligence Division)

Documents and Memoirs

Barlone, D. *A French Officer's Diary (23 August 1939–1 October 1940)*. Trans. L. V. Cass. Cambridge, 1942.

Beaufre, André. *Mémoires 1920–1940–1945*. Paris, 1965.

Béguier, Lt. Col. *Les étapes d'un régiment breton: Le 71ᵉR.I. et R.I.A. en 1939 et 1940*. Paris, 1953.

Bloch, Marc. *Strange Defeat: A Statement of Evidence Written in 1940*. Trans. Gerard Hopkins. New York, 1968.

Bourget-Pailleron, Robert. "Le soldat de la dernière guerre." *Revue des deux mondes* 8:60 (September–October 1940): 161–169.

Conquet, Alfred G. *L'enigme de notre manque de divisions blindées 1932–1940): Avec une réfutation de certaines résponsabilitiés imputées au Maréchal Pétain*. Paris, 1956.

Cot, Pierre. *Le procès de la république*. 2 vols. New York, 1944.

Daladier, Edouard. *The Defence of France*. London. 1939.

Debeney, Marie-Eugène. *La guerre et les hommes: Reflexions d'après-guerre*. Paris, 1937.

Delater, G. *Avec la 3ᵉ D.L.M. et le Corps de Cavalerie*. Grenoble and Paris, 1946.

Felsenhardt, Robert. *1939–1940 avec le 18ᵉ Corps d'Armée*. Paris, 1973.

France. Assemblée Nationale. *Journal officiel de la république française 1870–1940*. *Chambre des députés. Débats parlementaires et documents parlementaires*.

——. *Journal officiel de la république française 1870–1940. Sénat. Débats parlementaires et documents parlementaires*.

——. Session de 1947. No. 2344. *Rapport fait au nom de la commission chargée d'enquêter sur les événements survenus en France de 1933 à 1945 par M. Charles Serre*. 2 vols. Paris, 1951.

——. Session de 1947. No. 2344. *Rapport fait au nom de la commission chargée d'enquêter sur les événements survenus en France de 1933 à 1945. Annexes. Témoignages et documents recueillis par la commission d'enquête parlementaire*. 9 vols. Paris, 1951.

France. Minister of War. EMA. *Instruction provisoire du 6 octobre 1921 sur l'emploi tactique des grandes unités*. Paris, 1925.

——. *Instruction sur l'emploi tactique des grandes unités*. Paris, 1940.

Gamelin, Maurice. *Servir*. 3 vols. Paris, 1954–1959.

Gauché, George L. *Le deuxième bureau au travail, 1935–1940*. Paris, 1953.

Gaulle, Charles de. *The Complete War Memoirs of Charles de Gaulle*. New York, 1972.

Great Britain. War Office. General Staff. *Monthly Intelligence Summary*.

Grenier, Fernand. *Journal de la drôle de guerre septembre 1939 juillet 1940*. Paris, 1969.

Huard, Paul. *Le Colonel de Gaulle et ses blindés: Laon (15–20 mai 1940)*. Paris, 1980.

Jouffrault, Gen. *Les spahis au feu. La 1ʳᵉ Brigade de Spahis pendant la campagne 1939–1940*. Paris, 1948.

Karslake, Basil. *1940 The Last Act: The Story of the British Forces in France After Dunkirk.* Hamden, CT, 1979.

Keller, Pierre. *La division de Metz (42ᵉ D.I.) pendant la bataille de France.* Paris, 1947.

Lami, Marc. *Un peu de gloire, un peu d'humour, beaucoup de sang . . . : Epopée d'une batterie de 75 en 1940.* Paris, 1945.

Lattre de Tassigny, Jean de. *Ne pas subir: Ecrits 1914-1952.* Paris, 1984.

Loustaunau-Lacau, Georges. *Mémoires d'un français rebelle, 1914-1948.* Paris, 1948.

Macleod, Roderick, and Denis Kelly, eds. *The Ironside Diaries 1937-1940.* London, 1962.

Marot, Jean. *Abbeville 1940. Avec la division cuirasée DE GAULLE.* Paris, n.d.

Maurois, André. *Why France Fell.* Trans. Denver Lindley. London, 1941.

Paul-Boncour, Joseph. *Entre deux guerres. Souvenirs sur la IIIᵉ République.* 3 vols. Paris, 1946.

Pétain, Marcel, and Michel Caron. *100 jours, 100 nuits aux avant postes.* Paris, n.d.

Prételat, Gaston. *Le destin tragique de la ligne Maginot.* Paris, 1950.

Requin, Edouard Jean. *Combats pour l'honneur (1923-1940).* Paris, 1946.

————. *D'une guerre à l'autre.* Paris, 1949.

Reynaud, Paul. *In the Thick of the Fight, 1930-1945.* Trans. James D. Lambert. New York, 1955.

Sadoul, Georges. *Journal de guerre (2 septembre 1939-20 juillet 1940).* Paris, 1977.

Sartre, Jean-Paul. *War Diaries: Notebooks from a Phony War November 1939-March 1940.* Trans. Quintin Hoare. London, 1984.

Serrigny, Bernard. *Trente ans avec Pétain.* Paris, 1959.

Soulet, F. *La 36ᵉ Division d'infanterie à l'honneur 1939-1940.* Paris, n.d.

Spears, Edward. *Assignment to Catastrophe.* 2 vols. New York, 1954-1955.

Valentin, François. "Souvenirs des années 38-39-40 dans les Ardennes." In Maurice Vaisse, ed., *Ardennes 1940,* 94-96. Paris, 1991.

Vibraye, Tony de. *Avec mon groupe de reconnaissance: août 1939-août 1940.* Paris, 1943.

Weygand, Maxime. *Mémoires.* 3 vols. Paris, 1957.

Other Works

Adamthwaite, Anthony. *France and the Coming of the Second World War, 1936-1939.* London, 1977.

————. "War Origins Again." *Journal of Modern History (JMH)* 56 (1983): 100-115.

Albord, Tony. *Pourquoi cela est arrivé, ou les résponsabilités d'une génération militaire.* Nantes, 1947.

————. "Les rélations de la politique et de la stratégie." In Tony Albord et al., *La défense nationale,* 275-304. Paris, 1958.

Alexander, Donald W. "Repercussions of the Breda Variant." *French Historical Studies* 8 (1974): 459-488.

Alexander, Martin S. "Les réactions à la menace stratégique allemande en Europe occidentale: la Grande Bretagne, la Belgique et le 'Cas Holland' (décembre 1938–février 1939)." *Cahiers d'histoire de la seconde guerre mondiale* 7 (1982): 5–38.

———. *The Republic in Danger: General Maurice Gamelin and the Politics of French Defence, 1933–1940.* Cambridge, 1992.

Altairac, Commandant. "Role de l'officier de réserve appelé à accomplir une période dans un bataillon de réservists." *Revue d'infanterie (RI)* 81 (July–December 1932): 73–87.

Argueyrolles. "Gouvernons vers le large." *Revue de cavalerie* 14 (1934): 45–64, 168–193, 243–266, 367–386.

Armengaud, Paul. "L'atmosphère du champs de bataille." *RI* 94 (January–June 1939): 994–1034.

Azan, Paul. "But et programme de la *Revue militaire générale.*" *Revue militaire générale (RMG)* 1 (1937): 2–8.

———. "Organisation de la Défense Nationale." *RMG* 2 (1938): 253–258.

Bankwitz, Philip C. F. *Maximé Weygand and Civil-Military Relations in Modern France.* Cambridge, MA, 1967.

———. "Maxime Weygand and the Army-Nation Concept in the Modern French Army." In John Cairns, ed., *Contemporary France: Illusion, Conflict, and Regeneration,* 168–199. New York, 1978.

Barge, Walter Shepard. "The Generals of the Republic: The Corporate Personality of High Military Rank in France, 1889–1914." Ph.D. dissertation, University of North Carolina at Chapel Hill, 1982.

Beaufre, André. *1940: The Fall of France.* Trans. D. Flower. New York, 1968.

Bernard, Amédée. "Théorèmes de defense nationale." *RMG* 2 (1938): 5–37.

Bond, Brian, and Martin Alexander. "Liddell Hart and De Gaulle: The Doctrines of Limited Liability and Mobile Defense." In Peter Paret, ed., *Makers of Modern Strategy: From Machiavelli to the Nuclear Age,* 598–623. Princeton, 1986.

Borie, L. "Nos grandes écoles XIV: Saint-Maxent." *Revue des deux mondes (RDM)* 7:43 (January–February 1928): 549–568.

Breuillac, J. "Il faut enseigner la défense nationale." *Revue de défense national (RDN)*, new ser. 5 (January 1949): 36–48.

Brindel, Gen. "La nouvelle organisation militaire." *RDM* 7:51 (May–June 1929): 481–502.

Brossé, Julien. *Les éléments de notre défense nationale.* Paris, 1936.

Brouillard, Capt. "Cas concrets de défense contre les chars." *RI* 90 (January–June 1937): 879–907.

Buffotot, Patrice. "The French High Command and the Franco-Soviet Alliance 1933–1939." *Journal of Strategic Studies (JSS)* 5 (1982): 546–556.

———. "La perception du réarmement allemand par les organismes de renseignement français de 1936 à 1939." *Revue historique des armées (RHA)* 6 (1979): 173–184.

Cailloux, René. "Les enseignements de la guerre d'Espagne." *RI* 92 (January–June 1938): 670–691.

Cairns, John. "Along the Road Back to France, 1940." *American Historical Review (AHR)* 6 (1959): 583–603.

_____. "Great Britain and the Fall of France: A Study in Allied Disunity." *JM* 27 (1955): 369–409.

_____. "March 7, 1936. Again: The View from Paris." In H. W. Gatzke, ed., *European Diplomacy Between Two Wars, 1919–1939,* 172–192. Chicago, 1972.

_____. "Some Recent Historians and the 'Strange Defeat' of 1940." *JMH* 46 (1974): 50–84.

Camon, Hubert. "Une lacune à combler: L'Institut des Hautes Etudes Militaires." *Revue de France* 9 (1929): 52–64.

Campinchi, Hélene. "Les femmes et l'effort de guerre en France et dans les pays alliés." *RDN,* new ser. 3 (1947): 287–301.

Carrère, Lt. "Physionomie d'une période de réservists." *RI* 86 (January–March 1935): 294–318.

Carrias, Eugène. *La pensée militaire française.* Sceaux, 1960.

Carron, Lucien. *Fantassins sur l'Aisne mai–juin 1940.* Grenoble and Paris, 1943.

Castellan, Georges. *Le réarmement clandestin de Reich 1930–1935: Vu par le 2e bureau de l'état-major français.* Paris, 1954.

Castex, Raoul. "Les 'Arrières.'" *RDN,* new ser. 4 (1948): 3–20.

_____. "Les Hautes Études de Défense Nationale." *RMG* 1 (1937): 37–49.

_____. "Les servitudes de la stratégie." *RMG* 1 (1937): 208–224.

_____. *Strategic Theories.* Abridged, trans., and ed. E. C. Kiesling. Annapolis, 1993.

Chabert, Henry. "A Possible Historical Mistake: The Causes of the Allied Military Collapse in May, 1940." *Proceedings of the Western Society for French Historical Studies* 1 (1974): 379–390.

Challener, Richard D. "The French Army and the Generals: The Gravediggers Revisited." In Harry Coles, ed., *Total War and Cold War: Problems in Civilian Control of the Military,* 91–107. Columbus, 1962.

_____. *The French Theory of the Nation in Arms, 1866–1939.* New York, 1955.

Chambrun, René de. *I Saw France Fall.* Rahway, NJ, 1940.

Chantebout, Bernard. *L'organisation générale de la défense nationale en France depuis la fin de la seconde guerre mondiale.* Paris, 1967.

Chapman, Guy. "The French Army and Politics." In Michael E. Howard, ed., *Soldiers and Governments: Nine Studies in Civil-Military Relations,* 51–72. London, 1957.

_____. *Why France Fell.* New York, 1968.

Chapman, Herrick E. *State Capitalism and Working-Class Radicalism in the French Aircraft Industry.* Berkeley and Los Angeles, 1991.

Chauvineau, Narcisse. *Une invasion, est-elle encore possible?* 2d ed. Paris, 1940.

Chazal-Martin, Pierre, and Capt. Suire. "Etude mathématique de la puissance des armes anti-chars." *RI* 95 (July–September 1939): 255–299.

Clarke, Jeffrey J. "Military Technology in Republican France: The Evolution of the French Armored Force, 1917–1949." Ph.D. dissertation, Duke University, 1969.

Cointet, Jean-Paul. "Gouvernement et haut-commandement en France entre les deux guerres." *Défense nationale* 33 (1977): 83–100.

Cooper, Matthew. *The German Army 1933–1945: Its Political and Military Failure.* London, 1978.

Coutau-Bégarie, Hervé. *Castex: le stratège inconnu.* Paris, 1985.

Crémieux-Brilhac, Jean-Louis. *Les Français de l'an 40.* 2 vols. Paris, 1990.

Cugnac, Gen. de. "La Tour de Babel." *RMG* 1 (1937): 679–688.

Currus. "La rénovation de notre armement d'infanterie." *RI* 94 (January–June 1939): 861–882.

Daille, Marius. *La Bataille de Montdidier.* Paris, 1922.

Debeney, Marie-Eugène. "Armée national ou armée de métier." *RDM* 7:53 (September–October 1929): 241–276.

––––––. "L'Ecole Supérieure de Guerre." *RDN* 37 (1927): 84–103.

––––––. "Encore l'armée de métier." *RDM* 8:29 (July–August 1935): 279–295.

––––––. "Les exigences da la guerre de matériel." *RDM* 8:12 (March–April 1933): 259–286.

––––––. "La motorisation des armées modernes." *RDM* 8:33 (March–April 1936): 279–295.

––––––. "Nos grandes écoles VIII: L'Ecole Supérieure de Guerre." *RDM* 7:37 (January–February 1927): 84–103.

de la Gorce, Paul Marie. *The French Army: A Military-Political History.* Trans. Kenneth Douglas. New York, 1963.

Delmas, Jean. "Aperçu des méthodes." *Bulletin trimestriel de l'association des amis de l'Ecole Supérieure de Guerre* 57 (January–April 1973): 35–47.

––––––. "Les exercises du Conseil Supérieure de la Guerre, 1936–1937 et 1937–1938." *RHA* 6 (1979): 29–56.

Dhers, P. "Le Comité de Guerre de 25 mai 1940." *Revue d'histoire de la Deuxième Guerre Mondiale (RHDGM)* 3 (1953): 165–183.

DiNardo, Richard Louis. "Germany's Panzer Arm: Anatomy and Performance." Ph.D. dissertation, City University of New York, 1988.

Doughty, Robert A. *The Breaking Point: Sedan and the Fall of France, 1940.* Hamden, CT, 1990.

––––––. "The French Armed Forces, 1918–40." In Allan R. Millett and Williamson Murray, eds., *Military Effectiveness,* vol. 2, *The Interwar Period,* 39–69. London, Sydney, Wellington, 1988.

––––––. *The Seeds of Disaster: The Development of French Army Doctrine 1919–1939.* Hamden, CT, 1985.

Dreifort, John E. "France, Britain, and Munich: An Interim Assessment." *Proceedings of the Western Society for French Historical Studies* 1 (1974): 356–375.

Druène, Lt. Col. "Deux siècles d'histoire de l'artillerie française." *RHA* 11 (1955): 149–166.

Duchêne, Gen. "Avons-nous un Ministre de la défense nationale?" *RDM* 8:44 (January–February 1938): 40–50.

Durand-Veil, Admiral Georges. "Le concours des marins," *RMG* 1 (1937): 29–30.

Duroselle, Jean-Baptiste. *La décadence: 1932–1939.* Paris, 1979.

Dutailly, Henry. *Les problèmes de l'armée de terre française (1935–1939).* Paris, 1980.

––––––. "La puissance militaire de la France en 1938, vue par le Géneral Gamelin, l'état-major de l'armée et le secrétariat générale de la défense nationale." *RHM* 10 (1983): 4–9.

Duval, Gen. [Jean?]. "L'armée française de 1938." *Revue de Paris (RP)* 45 (1938): 721–747.

"The E.S.G., Paris." *Journal of the Royal United Services Institute (JRUSI)* 70 (1925).

France. Ministry of Defense. *Centenaire de l'Ecole Supérieure de Guerre 1876–1976.*

Franchet d'Esperey, Marshal. "Indépendance et imagination." *RMG* 1 (1937): 11–12.

Frankenstein, Robert. *Le prix du réarmament français.* Paris, 1982.

Gaddis, John Lewis. *Strategies of Containment.* Oxford, 1982.

Gamelin, Maurice. "Hier et Demain." *RMG* 1 (1937): 25–28.

Gaulle, Charles de. "Doctrine à priori ou doctrine des circonstances?" *Revue militaire français (RMF)* 15 (January–March 1925): 306–328.

————. *Vers l'armée de métier.* Paris, 1934.

Geyer, Michael. "German Strategy in the Age of Machine Warfare, 1914–1945." In Peter Paret, ed., *Makers of Modern Strategy: From Machiavelli to the Nuclear Age,* 527–597. Princeton, 1986.

Gibson, Irving M. [pseud. of Arpad V. Kovacs]. "Maginot and Liddell Hart: The Doctrine of Defense." In Edward Mead Earle, ed., *Makers of Modern Strategy,* 365–387. 2d ed. Princeton, 1971.

Gilson, Gen. "L'évolution des matériels de transmissions 1920 à 1939." *RHA* 23 (1967): 57–78.

Girardet, Raoul. *La Société militaire dans la France contemporaine, 1815–1939.* Paris, 1953.

Goubard, P. *Bulletin trimestriel de l'association des amis de l'Ecole Supérieure de Guerre* 57 (1st trimester 1973): 13–29.

Goutard, Adolphe. "La bataille pour les divisions cuirassées." *RP* 66 (1959): 22–39.

————. *1940: La guerre des occasions perdues.* Paris, 1956. Trans. by A. R. P. Burgess as *The Battle of France, 1940.* London, 1958.

————. "Un an à l'Institut des Hautes Etudes de Défense Nationale." *RDN,* new ser. 6 (July 1950): 74–84.

Grimaux, H. "Essai sommaire sur les corps cuirassés." *RMG* 2 (1938): 531–547.

Guderian, Heinz. *Die Panzertruppen.* 2d ed. Berlin, 1938.

Gunsberg, Jeffrey A. "The Battle of the Belgian Plain, 12–14 May 1940: The First Great Tank Battle." *JMH* 56 (1992): 207–244.

————. "Coupable ou non? Gamelin et la défaite de 1940." *RHA* 4 (1977): 145–163.

————. *Divided and Conquered: The French High Command and the Defeat of the West, 1940.* Westport, CT, 1979.

Harvey, Donald J. "French Concepts of Military Strategy (1919–1939)." Ph.D. dissertation, Columbia University, 1953.

Heywood, T. G. G. "General Gamelin: Chief of the French General Staff of National Defence." *JRUSI* 83 (1938): 607–613.

Hoff, Pierre. *Les programmes d'armement de 1919 à 1939.* Vincennes, 1972.

Hoffman, Stanley. "Paradoxes of the French Political Community." In Stanley Hoffmann et al., *In Search of France,* 1–117. New York, 1963.

Hood, R. Chalmers. *Royal Republicans: The French Naval Dynasties Between the World Wars.* Baton Rouge and London, 1983.

Hoop, Jean-Marie, d'. "La politique française du réarmament: d'après les travaux de la commission d'enquête parlementaire." *RHDGM* 4 (1954): 1-26.

Horne, Alistair. *The French Army and Politics, 1870-1970.* London, 1984.

————. *To Lose a Battle: France 1940.* Harmondsworth, Eng., 1969.

Howard, Michael. "Men Against Fire: The Doctrine of the Offensive in 1914." In Peter Paret, ed., *Makers of Modern Strategy: From Machiavelli to the Nuclear Age,* 510-526. Princeton, 1986.

Hughes, Judith. *To the Maginot Line.* Cambridge, MA, 1971.

Jackson, Robert. *The Fall of France May-June 1940.* London, 1975.

Kemp, Anthony. *The Maginot Line—Myth and Reality.* London, 1981.

Kiesling, Eugenia C. "A Staff College for the Nation in Arms: The Collège des Hautes Etudes de la Défense Nationale." Ph.D. dissertation, Stanford University, 1988.

Kirkland, Faris Russell. "The French Air Force in 1940: Was It Defeated by the Luftwaffe or by Politics?" *Air University Review* 36 (1985): 101-117.

————. "The French Officer Corps and the Fall of France—1920-1940." Ph.D. dissertation, University of Pennsylvania, 1982.

Kovacs, Arpad. "French Military Legislation in the Third Republic." *Military Affairs (MA)* 12 (1949): 1-13.

Krebs, A. "Considérations sur l'offensive." *RMG* 1 (1937).

Kuisel, Richard F. "Technocrats and Public Economic Policy: From the Third to the Fourth Republic." In John C. Cairns, ed., *Contemporary France: Illusion, Conflict, and Regeneration,* 228-253. New York, 1978.

Laffargue, André. *Justice pour ceux de 1940.* Paris, 1952.

Laporte, Henri. "Une 'aviation d'infanterie' est-elle désirable?" *RI* 95 (July-September 1939): 61-88.

————. "La défense antichars." *RI* 93 (July-December 1938): 1140-1187.

Laure, Auguste. *Pétain.* Paris, 1941.

Le Goyet, P. "Evolution de la doctrine d'emploi de l'aviation française entre 1919 et 1939." *RHDGM* (1969).

Lestien, Gen. "La commission d'enquête parlementaire et les événements militaires du 10 mai au 11 juin 1940." *RHDGM* 3 (1953): 184-191.

Lewis, S. J. *Forgotten Legions: German Infantry Policy 1918-1941.* New York, 1985.

Lugand, Lt. Col. "Les forces en présence au 10 mai 1940." *RHDGM* 3 (1953): 5-48.

Luttwak, Edward N. *The Grand Strategy of the Roman Empire from the First Century A.D. to the Third.* Baltimore and London, 1976.

Maginel, Gen. "Le commandement unique." *RMG* 1 (1937): 689-707.

————. "L'intervention de l'aviation dans la lutte terrestre." *RMG* 2 (1938): 675-684, 505-529.

Mainé, Henri. "Motorisation et mécanisation," *RI* 91 (July-December 1937): 1359-1365.

Martin, Henry. "Réflexions sur la défense contre les chars." *RI* 84 (January-June 1934): 268-276.

Maurin, Louis. "Gouvernement et commandement (mai–juin 1940)." *RHDGM* 2 (1952): 1–28; 3 (1953): 1–14.

Michel, Henri. *La défaite de la France.* Paris, 1980.

———. "L'oeuvre de la commission parlementaire chargée d'enquêter sur les événements survenus en France de 1933 à 1945." *RHDGM* 1 (1951): 94–96.

Millett, Allan R., and Williamson Murray. *Military Effectiveness.* 3 vols. London, Sydney, Wellington, 1988.

Monteilhet, Joseph. *Les institutions militaires de la France 1814–1932.* Paris, 1932.

Morris, Eric, et al. *Weapons and Warfare of the 20th Century.* London, 1980.

Morrow, John H. *The Great War in the Air: Military Aviation from 1909 to 1921.* Washington, D.C., and London, 1993.

Mott, T. Bentley. "The Machinery of Promotion in the French Army." *Army and Navy Journal* 76 (1939): 1195.

Murray, Williamson. *The Change in the European Balance of Power 1938–39: The Path to Ruin.* Princeton, 1984.

Mysyrowicz, Ladislas. *Anatomie d'une défaite: origines de l'effondrement militaire française de 1940.* Lausanne, 1973.

Nemo, Col. "La formation des cadres de défense nationale." *RDN,* new ser. 14 (1958): 471–486.

Niessel, Henri Albert. "Les écoles de sous-officiers de réserve." *RDM* 8:9 (March–April 1932): 411–425.

Ocagne, Maurice, d'. "Nos grands écoles IV: L'école polytechnique." *RDM* 7:33 (May–June 1926): 515–533.

Pacquier, Col., et al. "Combien d'avions allemands contre combien d'avions français le 10 Mai 1940?" *RDN,* new ser. 4 (1948): 741–759.

Paoli, François-André. *L'Armée française de 1919 à 1939.* 4 vols. Paris, 1969–1971.

Perré, Jean. "Autre réflexions sur la défense contre les chars." *RI* 84 (January–June 1934): 277–288.

———. "Le char modern. Ses possibilités et ses servitudes. Son emploi dans l'attaque." *RI* 92 (January–June, 1938): 620–639.

———. "La guerre des chars." *RI* 87 (July–December 1935): 951–1014.

———. "La refont de la réglementation relative aux chars de combat." *RI* 75 (September–December 1929): 664–686.

[Perré, Jean], and R. S. "Les cadres de l'infanterie et des chars de combat: Leur recrutement et leur instruction," *RI* 94 (June–September 1939): 1114–1140.

Perret, Geoffrey. *There's a War to be Won: The United States Army in World War II.* New York, 1991.

Pétain, Philippe. "Défense nationale et commandement unique." *RDM* 8:34 (May–June 1936): 5–17.

———. "La sécurité de la France au cours des années creuses." *RDM* 8:28 (March–April 1935): i–xx.

Pichon, J. "Guerre d'hier et de demain, defensive et motorisation." *RMF* 58 (October 1935): 5–30; 59 (January 1936): 5–43; 60 (April 1936): 5–31.

Porch, Douglas. "Arms and Alliances: French Grand Strategy and Policy in 1914 and 1940." In Paul Kennedy, ed., *Grand Strategies in War and Peace,* 125–144. New Haven and London, 1991.

_____. *The March to the Marne*. Cambridge and New York, 1981.

Posen, Barry A. *The Sources of Military Doctrine: France, Britain, and Germany Between the World Wars*. Ithaca, NY, 1984.

Possony, Stefan T. "Organized Intelligence: The Problem of the French General Staff." *Social Research* 8 (1941): 213–237.

Prochasson, Christophe. "Les grandes dates de l'histoire de la conscription." *RHA* 9 (1982): 67–69.

Reboul, Col. "Le Malaise de l'Armée: Le projet de service d'un an." *RDM* 7:26 (March–April 1925): 32–49.

Reussner, André. "La réorganisation du haut-commandement au mois de mai 1940." *RHDGM* 3 (1953): 49–59.

Ross, Steven T. "French Net Assessment." In Williamson Murray and Allan R. Millet, eds., *Calculations: Net Assessment and the Coming of World War II*. New York, 1992.

Roy, Jules. "Le mission aérienne d'accompagnement de l'infanterie au combat: Faut-il la supprimer ou l'adapter." *RI* 92 (January–June 1938): 640–653.

_____. "Le problème de l'accompagnement aérien de l'infanterie." *RI* 94 (January–June 1939): 513–520.

Salisbury-Jones, Guy. *So Full a Glory: A Biography of Marshal Jean de Lattre de Tassigny*. London, 1954.

Sereau, Raymond. "L'évolution de l'arme blindée en allemagne de 1935 à 1945 vue par un ancien officier de la Wehrmacht." *RHA* 6 (1950): 67–76.

Serrigny, Bernard. "L'Organisation de notre défense nationale." *RDM* 7:59 (September–October 1930): 30–37.

Shirer, William L. *The Collapse of the Third Republic*. New York, 1969.

Soury, Capt. "Le combat contre les engins cuirassés par le major von Schell de l'état-major général de la Wehrmacht." *RI* 46 (July 1937): 73–137.

Stolfi, Russell H. "Equipment for Victory in France in 1940." *History* 55 (1970): 1–20.

_____. "Reality and Myth: French and German Preparations for War, 1933–1940." Ph.D. dissertation, Stanford University, 1966.

Tanant, A. "Nos grandes écoles II: Saint Cyr." *RDM* 7:32 (March–April 1926): 39–58.

Thoumin, Gen. "Les écoles d'infanterie de 1919 à 1939." *RHA* 10 (1954): 85–103.

Tissier, Pierre. *Le procès de Riom*. London, 1942.

Tournoux, Jean-Raymond. *Pétain and de Gaulle*. Trans. O. Coburn 1964.

Tournoux, Paul Emile. *Haut Commandement: Gouvernement et défense des frontières du nord et de l'est, 1919–1939*. Paris, 1960.

Tourte, Raymond. "Impérieuse nécessité du commandment unique." *RMG* 1 (1937): 708–715.

Trentinian, Gen. *L'état-major en 1914 et la 7e Division du 4e Corps 10 août au 22 septembre 1914*. Paris, 1927.

Vaisse, Maurice. *Securité d'abord: La politique française en matière de désarmement, 9 december 1930–14 avril 1934*. Paris, 1981.

Vauthier, Gen. *La défense nationale*. Paris, 1938–1939.

Velpry, Pol-Maurice. "Infanterie et chars de combat." *RMF* 25 (1927): 305–328.

Vial, Jean. "La défense nationale: son organisation entre les deux guerres." *RHDGM* 5 (1955): 11–32.

Vidalenc, Jean. "Les divisions de série "B" dans l'armée française pandant la campagne de France 1939–1940." *RHA* 1 (1980): 106–126.

Wanty, B.-E.-M. "Une année de guerre en Espagne." *RI* 90 (January–June 1937): 917–955.

Waterhouse, G. V. Y. "Some Notes on the E.S.G., Paris." *Army Quarterly* 8 (1924): 325–333.

Watt, Donald C. *Too Serious a Business: European Armed Forces and the Approach of the Second World War.* Berkeley and Los Angeles, 1975.

Weinberg, Gerhard L. *A World at Arms: A Global History of World War II.* Cambridge, 1994.

Weygand, Maxime. "L'état militaire de la France." *RDM* 8:36 (September–October 1936): 721–736.

————. *Histoire de l'armée française.* Paris, 1961.

————. "How France Is Defended." Address at Chatham House, 16 May 1939. *International Affairs* 18 (1939): 459–477.

————. *Ist Frankreich stark genug?* Translation of *La France, est-elle defendue?* Berlin, 1983.

————. "L'unité de l'armée." *RMG* 1 (1937): 15–19.

Wieland, Volker. *Zur Problematik der franzosischen Militarpolitik und Militardoktrin in der Zeit zwischen den Weltkriegen.* Boppard am Rhein, 1973.

X. "L'artillerie dans le combat des chars." *Revue d'artillerie* 113 (January–June 1934): 42–58.

X, Capt. "La défense contre avions dans les unités d'infanterie." *RI* 95 (July–September 1939): 477–506.

X, Lt. "L'armée nouvelle." *La Revue des Vivantes* 4 (July 1930): 904–918.

XXX. "La guerre future et l'aviation: Avions et cuirassés: les expériences américaines." *RDM* 6:66 (November–December 1921): 815–825.

Young, Robert J. "L'Attaque Brusquée and Its Use as a Myth in Interwar France." *Historical Reflections* 81 (1981): 93–113.

————. "French Military Intelligence and Nazi Germany, 1939-1939." In Ernst May, ed., *Knowing One's Enemies: Intelligence Assessment Before the Two World Wars,* 271–309. Princeton, 1984.

————. "French Military Policy and the Munich Crisis of 1938: A Reappraisal." *Historical Papers* (1970): 186–206.

————. "La Guerre de Longue Durée: Some Reflections on French Strategy and Diplomacy in the 1930's." In Adrian Preston, ed., *General Staffs and Diplomacy Before the Second World War.* London, 1978.

————. *In Command of France: French Foreign Policy and Military Planning, 1933-1940.* Cambridge, MA, and London, 1978.

————. "Preparations for Defeat: French War Doctrine in the Interwar Period." *Journal of European Studies* 2 (1972): 155–172.

————. "The Strategic Dream: French Air Doctrine in the Inter-War Period, 1919–1939." *Journal of Contemporary History* 9 (1974): 57–76.

Index

Adamthwaite, Anthony, 3
Aircraft
  against tanks, 160
  in ground support role, 176–77
Air Force
  attitude toward ground support, 43, 177
  British assessment of, 176, 185
  and CHEDN, 43, 46, 51
  and commander-in-chief, 31–34
  doctrine, 43
  receives new planes in 1940, 204n.72
Alexander, Martin S., 5, 9–10
Allies, eastern
  assistance to, 58–59, 140, 162
  French relations with, 53–54
  obligations to, 54–55, 180
Altmeyer, General Robert, 179
AMC (Automitrailleuse de Combat), 147–48, 229n.73
Antiaircraft defense, 176–77
Antitank doctrine
  foreign, 158
  foreign assessments of French, 158–60
  perceived efficacy of, 156–71, 237n.191
Antitank guns, 156–60, 233nn.127,129
  German divisional allotment, 161
  lack of, 159
  place of in French doctrine, 157
  unavailability of for training, 207n.133
Antitank mines
  lack of, 178, 234n.140, 239n.25
Ardennes sector, 173, 177–79
Armor doctrine, 144, 151, 161, 163–67
  compared with German, 169–71, 181, 184
  compared with U.S., 155, 171
Armored cavalry. See DLM; Mechanization
Armored division. See DCR; DLM
Armor exercises, cancellations of, 163, 165

Arms and equipment, unfamiliarity with, 67, 73–75, 80, 82, 93, 106, 211n.47, 213n.77
  in British army, 203n.57
Army, French
  administrative burdens in, 77–78, 83, 109–10
  and CHEDN, 44
  communist soldiers in, 184–85
  foreign assessments of, 68–70, 79, 101, 107, 183–87
  material deficiencies of, 73–77
  mission of, 96
  regional organization of, 87–94
  structure of, 63
Army organization laws (1927–1928), 26, 63, 70, 85–87, 91–92, 96

Bankwitz, Philip, 175
Barlone, Captain D., 77, 80, 94
Barrard, General (41st DI), 101–3
Beaufre, Captain André, on French doctrine, 125–26
Belgium
  in French strategy, 62, 173, 178–80, 183
  mentioned at CHEDN, 53, 57
  and motorization, 147, 173
  reconnoitered by army "tourists," 240n.29
  uncertain policy of, 181
Billotte, General Gaston
  impresses British attaché, 184–85
  inspects troops in 1934, 66–68, 90
  in 1940 campaign, 171
  on pre-military training, 72
  tests Maginot Line, 159, 185
Bineau, General Henri, nominated to direct CHEDN (Collège des Hautes Etudes de la Défense Nationale), 45, 50